'The fight for indigenous rights will not stop, nor will the quest for an enduring and just settlement with the first Australians. I am confident that there are enough people who care and who are prepared to take up the fight for justice and work towards that settlement. Above all else, people of good will, both indigenous and non-indigenous, must take a stand to ensure there is no turning back.'

ROBERT TICKNER is a country boy who grew up in Forster on the NSW central coast and came to Sydney on a scholarship to get a law degree. After some years as an academic he became an Aboriginal Legal Service lawyer and an Alderman of the Sydney City Council. In 1984 he won the federal seat of Hughes and in 1990 became the federal Minister for Aboriginal and Torres Strait Islander Affairs. Until his tenure in the post, the average period of Ministers in this position had been less than two years. Robert Tickner served for six years, overcoming the justifiable scepticism of the indigenous community and gaining their support for building a reform program.

Prime Minister Paul Keating, Pat Dodson, the founding Chair of the Council for Aboriginal Reconciliation, and myself, on the occasion of the Prime Minister's first meeting with the Council, 1992.

This project has been assisted by the Commonwealth Government through the Australia Council, its arts funding and advisory body.

First published in 2001

Allen & Unwin
83 Alexander Street
Crows Nest NSW 2065
Australia
Phone: (61 2) 8425 0100
Fax: (61 2) 9906 2218
Email: frontdesk@allen-unwin.com.au
Web: http://www.allenandunwin.com

National Library of Australia
Cataloguing-in-Publication entry:

Tickner, Robert.
   Taking a stand.

   Bibliography.
   Includes index.
   ISBN 1 86508 051 9.

   1. Aborigines, Australian – Government policy. 2.
   Aborigines, Australian – Legal status, laws, etc. I. Title.

323.119915

Set in 10/12 pt New Baskerville by DOCUPRO, Canberra
Printed by Australian Print Group, Maryborough, Vic.

10 9 8 7 6 5 4 3 2 1

CONTENTS

Preface		ix
Acknowledgements		xi
Abbreviations		xii
Time line of events		xiii
1	The historical context: From massacres to Mabo	1
2	The reconciliation process	27
3	ATSIC: A radical shift towards self-determination	48
4	Aboriginal deaths in custody	66
5	Mabo: A peaceful beginning	83
6	The battle begins and the lines are drawn	106
7	Wik ignites	130
8	A strategic win and a bitter defeat	144
9	The Commonwealth draws the fire	165
10	Getting the Native Title Act over the line	191
11	Land for the dispossessed	221
12	The Torres Strait Islanders: Australia's forgotten indigenous people	237
13	Heritage, culture and Hindmarsh Island	255
14	Aboriginal health: A fixable problem	287
15	The world is watching: International action to protect indigenous rights	302
16	Does reconciliation stand a chance?	313
Primary written sources		327
Index		338

To Diane Hudson
*without whose professionalism
and dedication this book would
not have been possible*

PREFACE

This story belongs to those Aboriginal and Torres Strait Islander people who are real heroes—Lowitja (Lois) O'Donoghue, Patrick Dodson, Mick Dodson, David Ross, Noel Pearson, Marcia Langton, Eddie Mabo, Getano Lui Jnr and many others. They are indigenous Australians who through their political courage, intelligence and stand for justice have made their indelible mark on modern Australia. This book is written as a tribute to them and to the many indigenous Australians with whom I worked during my term of office. Sadly, since the completion of the book, one of those people, Charles Perkins, has passed away.

This book is an insider's account of momentous initiatives in Australian indigenous affairs between 1990 and 1996: the start of the process of reconciliation; the national response to the Royal Commission into Aboriginal Deaths in Custody (RCIADIC); the evolution of the Aboriginal and Torres Strait Islander Commission (ATSIC); the establishment of the position of the Aboriginal and Torres Strait Islander Social Justice Commissioner; the fight for the Native Title Act and the National Land Fund; the enhancement of international human rights protection for indigenous people; and the launch of the Human Rights and Equal Opportunity Commission (HREOC) Inquiry into the stolen generations. It is my hope that telling this story will contribute to the unfolding agenda of Aboriginal and Torres Strait Islander affairs.

Indigenous affairs government policy in 1990–96 did not happen in a vacuum. There has been a backdrop of 202 years of often unhappy relations between governments and indigenous people. Chapter 1 gives an overview of that history.

The principles of the reconciliation process were conceived as a framework and a strategy to be unanimously endorsed by the Australian parliament to ensure that indigenous aspirations were a central focus of our national agenda in the decade leading to the centenary of

Federation. Whether or not the process of reconciliation achieves the objectives set out in the Commonwealth's *Council for Aboriginal Reconciliation Act 1991* remains to be seen. An ongoing genuine and active national commitment to that process by all political parties represented in parliament was always seen to be crucial to the achievement of a genuine reconciliation in this country.

Regrettably, since the election of the Howard government, the Coalition commitment to the process of reconciliation, measured by its policies and attitudes towards Australia's indigenous people, has suffered severe setbacks.

The Council for Aboriginal Reconciliation ceased to exist on 1 January 2001. During 2001 Australia celebrates the centenary of Federation. At this time, and in the years following, Australia will be subject to increasing international scrutiny concerning the position of indigenous Australians and the nation's progress towards reconciliation. Recent events, including the active stand taken by hundreds of thousands of Australians in support of reconciliation on the Sydney Harbour Bridge, in Melbourne, Brisbane and other parts of the country, have shown that politicians cannot turn their backs on the reconciliation process.

Finally, this book is written as a contribution to that process in the profound hope that the lessons of recent history will convince more people of goodwill from all sections of the community that justice for and reconciliation with Aboriginal and Torres Strait Islander Australians is something worth believing in and fighting for.

ROBERT TICKNER
Sydney, 2001

ACKNOWLEDGEMENTS

I wish to extend my appreciation to my publisher, John Iremonger of Allen & Unwin, Rebecca Kaiser, Venetia Somerset for her editorial work, Tom Uren for his unwavering determination that this book be published, to the readers, David Horton, Andrew Marcus, and Colin Tatz, and to Kath Taperell and Roger Millis for their constructive comments. Garth Nettheim as an inspiration and a scholar provided ongoing advice and counsel. But as always I accept full responsibility for the final outcome.

Special thanks and appreciation as well to my long-serving electorate staff, Anne Nicholls and Margaret Dwyer, and to the team of loyal ministerial and other support staff who I had the privilege to work with over those six years, including Mario Bartolic, Noel Baxendell, Simeon Beckett, Sue Briton-Jones, Murray Chapman, Amanda Conroy, Greg Crough, Destiny Devow, Howard Glenn, Ribna Green, Jill Guthrie, Trish Hardy, Del Hickie, Gary Highland, Diane Hudson, Toni Janke, Sue Kee, Kevin Keeffe, Helen Kennedy, Fred Leftwich, Sean McLaughlin, Kathryn Matthews, Stanley Ngangara, Kirstie Parker, Peter Schnierer, Noreen Solomon, Kath Taperell, Julie Tongs and Paul Willoughby.

Without the support of rank-and-file ALP members, my campaign director Ken McDonell and the electors of Hughes, I would not have had the privilege of serving in the federal parliament and I thank them for that.

Finally to the indigenous heroes whose courage and determination to fight for the human rights of their people and who inspired this book, my most heartfelt thanks for the privilege of serving as your minister.

All profits from the sale of this book will go direct to the Indigenous Law Centre at the University of New South Wales to contribute towards legal strategies, both domestic and international, to advance indigenous rights.

ABBREVIATIONS

ACTU	Australian Council of Trade Unions
ALP	Australian Labor Party
AMIC	Australian Mining Industry Council
APG	Aboriginal Provisional Government
ATSIC	Aboriginal and Torres Strait Islander Commission
CDEP	Community Development Employment Project
CERD	International Convention for the Elimination of All Forms of Racial Discrimination
CLC	Central Land Council
COAG	Council of Australian Governments
DEET	Department of Employment, Education and Training
ERC	Expenditure Review Committee
HREOC	Human Rights and Equal Opportunity Commission
ICC	Island Coordinating Council
ICCPR	International Covenant on Civil and Political Rights
ILC	Indigenous Land Corporation
NAC	National Aboriginal Conference
NAHS	National Strategy on Aboriginal and Torres Strait Islander Health
NFF	National Farmers' Federation
NGO	non-government organisation
NLC	Northern Land Council
OEA	Office of Evaluation and Audit
PM&C	Department of the Prime Minister and Cabinet
PNG	Papua New Guinea
RCIADIC	Royal Commission Into Aboriginal Deaths In Custody
TSIAB	Torres Strait Island Advisory Board
TSRA	Torres Strait Regional Authority
WGIP	Working Group on Indigenous Populations

TIME LINE OF EVENTS

1788 Arrival of the First Fleet and establishment of convict settlement at Sydney Cove.

1820 First Christian Aboriginal mission established.

1837 House of Commons Parliamentary Select Committee Report sanctions 'protection policies'.

1860s–1970s Legislation and policies of governments sanction removal of Aboriginal children.

1879 Torres Strait Islands become part of the colony of Queensland.

1920s Massacres of Aboriginal people continue at Forrest River in Western Australia, Yuendumu in the Northern Territory and elsewhere.

1924 Australian Aborigines Progressive Association formed as the first Aboriginal political organisation.

1935 Petition to King George V seeking Commonwealth leadership in Aboriginal affairs.

1937 Aborigines Progressive Association formed.
Governments from across Australia unite to agree on the implementation of assimilationist policies.

1938 'Day of Mourning' organised to protest for Aboriginal rights on the occasion of the 150th anniversary of the First Fleet.
Aboriginal walk-off at Cunmeragunja in NSW in protest against living conditions.

1944	First attempt by Curtin Labor government to secure support for a referendum to give the Commonwealth an Aboriginal affairs power.
1949	The Convention on Genocide ratified by Australia.
1950s	Atomic tests carried out on Aboriginal lands in South Australia.
1958	Establishment of the Federal Council for the Advancement of Aborigines and Torres Strait Islanders (FCAATSI).
1963	Bark petition from Yirrkala in the Northern Territory to the Commonwealth parliament in opposition to mining and in support of Aboriginal rights.
1964	Australian Institute of Aboriginal Studies created.
1960s	Lobbying and political campaigning increases by FCAATSI and Aboriginal Advancement organisations in support of a referendum to give the Commonwealth constitutional power.
1965	Freedom rides in northern NSW challenging racial discrimination; Charles Perkins plays a prominent role. Menzies government passes a Bill which if put to a referendum would have allowed Aboriginal people to be counted in the Census.
1966	Vincent Lingiari leads the Gurindji walk-off in protest against wages and conditions and in support of land rights.
27 May 1967	The Australian people vote by a 90.77 per cent majority at a referendum to give the Commonwealth power to pass laws about Aboriginal people and to allow them to be counted in the Census.
1967	Advisory Council for Aboriginal Affairs established, chaired by Dr H.C. (Nugget) Coombes.
1968	Equal pay decision for Aboriginal stockmen. Bill Wentworth appointed as the first minister to have sole responsibility for Aboriginal affairs.
1970	First initiatives to purchase land for Aboriginal communities initiated by the McMahon government.

1971	*Milirrpum and Others v Nabalco Pty Ltd* (Gove land rights case) finds against existence of native title rights.
	The first Aboriginal Australian, Neville Bonner, appointed to the Senate representing Queensland.
	Peter Howson appointed Minister for Environment, Aborigines and the Arts.
26 Jan. 1972	Tent Embassy established in front of Parliament House.
1972	Eddie Mabo's father dies and Eddie Mabo refused permission to return home for the funeral.
	Aboriginal flag, designed by Harold Thomas, flown at Tent Embassy.
	Policy statement by the McMahon government that recognises the need for Aboriginal people to 'increasingly manage their own affairs'.
2 Dec. 1972	Election of the Whitlam government and Gough Whitlam becomes Minister for Aboriginal Affairs for the first weeks of the new government.
19 Dec. 1972	Gordon Bryant appointed as Minister for Aboriginal Affairs.
1973	First Woodward report recommending establishment of the Northern and Central Land Councils in the Northern Territory.
	Aboriginal Hostels established.
	House of Representatives Standing Committee on Aboriginal Affairs established.
	National Aboriginal Consultative Committee established.
9 Oct. 1973	Senator Jim Cavanagh appointed Minister for Aboriginal Affairs.
1974	Second Woodward report recommending Land Rights Act for the Northern Territory.
	Aboriginal Loans Commission established.
1975	Aboriginal Land Fund Commission established.
	Racial Discrimination Act passed.
6 June 1975	Les Johnson appointed Aboriginal Affairs Minister.

11 Nov. 1975	Dismissal of Whitlam government by Sir John Kerr followed by election of Fraser government in December 1975. Senator Tom Drake-Brockman appointed Minister for Aboriginal Affairs for six weeks following dismissal of Whitlam government.
22 Dec. 1975	Ian Viner appointed Minister for Aboriginal Affairs.
1976	Passage of the Aboriginal Land Rights (Northern Territory) Act by Fraser government. Passage of Aboriginal Councils and Associations Act.
1977	Community Development Employment Projects established.
1978	Conflict between the Bjelke-Petersen government and the federal government concerning Mornington Island and Aurukun.
5 Dec. 1978	Senator Fred Chaney appointed Minister for Aboriginal Affairs.
1979	Noonkanbah sacred site and mining conflict comes to a head in Western Australia.
1980	Creation of the Aboriginal Development Commission.
3 Nov. 1980	Senator Peter Baume appointed Minister for Aboriginal Affairs.
1981	Passage of Pitjantjatjara Land Rights Act in South Australia by the Tonkin Liberal government.
1982	Eddie Mabo commences proceedings in the High Court.
7 May 1982	Ian Wilson appointed Minister for Aboriginal Affairs.
1983	Election of the Hawke Labor government.
11 March 1983	Clyde Holding appointed Minister for Aboriginal Affairs.
1983	NSW Aboriginal Land Rights Act passed by the Wran Labor government.
1984	Charles Perkins appointed Secretary, Commonwealth Department of Aboriginal Affairs. Committee to Defend Black Rights established.

Island Coordinating Council (ICC) created in the Torres Strait.

Passage of interim Commonwealth Aboriginal and Torres Strait Islander Heritage Protection Act.

1985 Announcement of the Commonwealth's preferred model for national Aboriginal land rights legislation and subsequent abandonment of the proposals.

Return of Uluru to Aboriginal ownership.

Bjelke-Petersen government passes Queensland Coastal Islands Declaratory Act attempting to thwart Mabo claim.

1987 Bob Hawke announces proposals to establish the Aboriginal and Torres Strait Islander Commission (ATSIC).

24 July 1987 Gerry Hand appointed Minister for Aboriginal Affairs.

1987 Deaths in Custody Watch Committee established.

16 Oct. 1987 Royal Commission into Aboriginal Deaths in Custody established.

1988 Bicentenary celebrations and national Aboriginal protest on the streets of Sydney.

24 April 1988 Gerry Hand introduces ATSIC legislation into the House of Representatives.

1988 Prime Minister Hawke commits his government to a treaty at the Barunga festival in the Northern Territory.

Torres Strait Islanders call for sovereign independence.

High Court, by 4 to 3, in Mabo (No. 1) invalidates Queensland Coastal Islands Declaratory Act.

March 1990 ATSIC comes into existence with Lois O'Donoghue appointed chairperson.

4 April 1990 Robert Tickner appointed Minister for Aboriginal Affairs (later Aboriginal and Torres Strait Islander Affairs).

10 June 1990 National Aboriginal Health Strategy (NAHS) endorsed by Commonwealth and all state and territory governments.

July 1990	Aboriginal flag flown from Parliament House and Commonwealth government buildings to celebrate NAIDOC Week.
Oct. 1990	Prime Minister Hawke endorses proposals by Minister for Aboriginal Affairs for a formal process of reconciliation to be overseen by a Council for Aboriginal Reconciliation.
13 Dec. 1990	Minister for Aboriginal and Torres Strait Islander Affairs issues a Discussion Paper on proposals for a process of reconciliation.
9 May 1991	Report of the Royal Commission into Aboriginal Deaths in Custody tabled.
31 May 1991	Council for Aboriginal Reconciliation Bill introduced into the House of Representatives.
18 June 1991	Coronation Hill decision.
31 July 1991	Australian government announces decision to become a party to the Optional Protocol of the International Covenant on Civil and Political Rights.
16 Aug. 1991	Passage of Council for Aboriginal Reconciliation Act through Senate confirming unanimous parliamentary vote.
28 Aug. 1991	25th anniversary of Gurindji walk-off.
2 Sep. 1991	Council for Aboriginal Reconciliation Act proclaimed by the Governor-General.
19 Dec. 1991	Portfolio name change to Minister for Aboriginal and Torres Strait Islander Affairs.
20 Dec. 1991	Bob Hawke resigns as Prime Minister after hanging the Barunga statement at Parliament House. Paul Keating becomes Prime Minister.
27 March 1992	National response to the Royal Commission into Aboriginal Deaths in Custody tabled in parliament.
17 May 1992	Alice Springs dam heritage decision.

27 May 1992	25th anniversary of 1967 referendum recognised by unanimous resolutions of both houses of parliament reaffirming commitment to reconciliation process and to the national response to the Royal Commission into Aboriginal Deaths in Custody.
3 June 1992	High Court delivers Mabo judgment.
24 June 1992	Second stage Commonwealth response to the Royal Commission into Aboriginal Deaths in Custody tabled in parliament.
July 1992	Australian government announces decision to allow Australians to make individual complaints alleging breach of Convention on the Elimination of All Forms of Racial Discrimination and the Torture Convention.
5 July 1992	*Rebutting the Myths* produced.
12 Oct. 1992	Western Mining's Hugh Morgan calls for repeal or substantial amendment to Racial Discrimination Act.
28 Oct. 1992	The Prime Minister, Attorney-General and Minister for Aboriginal and Torres Strait Islander Affairs present options to Cabinet for government Mabo response.
5 Dec. 1992	Institute of Public Affairs attacks Mabo decision as having features of Russian Communist land holding.
10 Dec. 1992	Paul Keating launch of UN International Year of the World's Indigenous Peoples and Lois O'Donoghue addresses UN General Assembly.
22 Dec. 1992	AMIC applies pressure on the government concerning alleged invalidity of existing titles.
29 Dec. 1992	Media begins to report land claim on central business district of Brisbane.
Jan. 1993	Swan Brewery heritage application declined.
12 Jan. 1993	Tim Fischer, Leader of the National Party, attacks the 'guilt industry'.
26 Jan. 1993	Eddie Mabo posthumously named as Australian of the Year.

1 Feb. 1993	Mabo Ministerial Committee refuses to adopt recommendation to announce amendment to Racial Discrimination Act.
9 Feb. 1993	John Hewson, Opposition leader, during the federal election campaign maintains cross-party cooperation on Mabo and endorses government's timetable for consultation.
13 March 1993	Keating Labor government re-elected.
March 1993	McArthur River mine issue begins to surface in public debate.
21 March 1993	Joint Australian business community statement in support of the protection of existing titles.
22 March 1993	Lois O'Donoghue, ATSIC Chairperson, writes to Prime Minister in opposition to any suspension of Racial Discrimination Act.
24 March 1993	Office of Indigenous Affairs established in Department of the Prime Minister and Cabinet.
6 April 1993	Mabo Ministerial Committee receives report on progress of consultations.
18 April 1993	WA pastoralist warns of civil war over Mabo.
27 April 1993	Mabo Ministerial Committee meets Aboriginal representatives and receives Peace Plan.
28 April 1993	Mabo Ministerial Committee meets industry representatives and Prime Minister later addresses Evatt Foundation dinner.
11 May 1993	John Hewson announces Coalition Mabo Subcommittee.
14 May 1993	Ian McLachlan addresses H.R. Nicholls Society and warns of dire consequences of Mabo.
16 May 1993	Shadow Minister for Aboriginal and Torres Strait Islander Affairs, Peter Nugent, speaks in support of a just outcome from Mabo.
17 May 1993	Frontbench Coalition MP Peter McGauran says Mabo risks being hijacked by the people who would give us a treaty and reverse Apartheid.

18 May 1993 Further Mabo Ministerial Committee meeting with Aboriginal representatives.

27 May 1993 Commonwealth government letters offering to amend the Racial Discrimination Act to protect McArthur River mine become public.

June 1993 ALP state and territory conferences across Australia pass strong resolutions on Mabo.

3 June 1993 Commonwealth government releases officials' Mabo Discussion Paper and ministers endorse 33 principles for Mabo response.

4 June 1993 Wiradjuri ambit claim over one-third of NSW.

9 June 1993 COAG meeting.

20 June 1993 *Rebutting Mabo Myths* launched.

27 June 1993 Eight major industry groups launch campaign for validation of titles.

28 June 1993 John Hewson releases the Coalition Mabo issues paper.

2 July 1993 Chief Justice of High Court, Sir Anthony Mason, reported as publicly defending the Mabo decision against attacks.

3 July 1993 Wik claim gains major publicity.

4 July 1993 John Howard alleges the Mabo debate has introduced cultural McCarthyism.

8 July 1993 Joint statement by Deaths in Custody Royal Commissioners and leaders of Australian church and faith groups.

15 July 1993 Industry groups attack Wik claim and call for validation of titles.

26 July 1993 Key indigenous organisations express concern that Prime Minister's words are not reflected in drafting instructions.

27 July 1993 Marathon Mabo Ministerial Committee meeting agrees to right of negotiation for Aboriginal people in relation to mining and other proposals affecting native title land.

Late July 1993	Premier Goss intensifies pressure on the Commonwealth to intervene to protect CRA interests against Wik claim.
Early Aug. 1993	Saulwick Poll released showing 88 per cent of people understand the basic principles of Mabo decision.
3 Aug. 1993	Eva Valley meeting.
6 Aug. 1993	CRA's John Ralph writes to Prime Minister and Mabo Ministerial Committee in support of Premier Goss's call for special Commonwealth legislation on Wik.
16 Aug. 1993	Cabinet overrides the Prime Minister's views and gives support to CRA and Premier Goss's views.
2 Sep. 1993	Prime Minister releases outline of proposed Mabo legislation.
20 Sep. 1993	Deputy Prime Minister Brian Howe supports regional autonomy in the Torres Strait.
26 Sep. 1993	Follow-up to Eva Valley meeting in Canberra.
30 Sep. 1993	Breakthrough meeting between Democrats, Greens and ATSIC.
4 Oct. 1993	Melbourne speech by Minister for Aboriginal and Torres Strait Islander Affairs rejecting any weakening of Commonwealth Mabo principles in an attempt to get Coalition or state government support.
6–7 Oct. 1993	Crucial Cabinet meetings where decisions taken to favour state and NT government interests ahead of Aboriginal rights.
8 Oct. 1993	Black Friday press conference.
11 Oct. 1993	Head-to-head negotiations between Prime Minister and Aboriginal representatives.
19 Oct. 1993	Government and Aboriginal negotiators announce agreement on principles of Mabo legislation.
16 Nov. 1993	Prime Minister introduces Native Title Bill into House of Representatives.
25 Nov. 1993	Native Title Bill passes House of Representatives.
2 Dec. 1993	WA government passes law attempting to override Mabo decision.

4 Dec. 1993	Second round of ATSIC Regional Council elections.
9 Dec. 1993	Senate Legal and Constitutional Affairs Committee divides on party lines on Mabo Bill.
14 Dec. 1993	Debate begins in Senate on Native Title Bill.
18 Dec. 1993	Historic Saturday sitting of parliament and near fisticuffs between Coalition Senators over Mabo response.
21 Dec. 1993	Senate passes Native Title Bill.
Dec. 1993	Release of *Rhetoric or Reality?*, House of Representatives Standing Committee on Aboriginal and Torres Strait Islander Affairs report.
1 Jan. 1994	Native Title Act comes into force and Native Title Tribunal created.
20 Jan. 1994	High-profile Aboriginal health visit to the Northern Territory by Health Minister, Graham Richardson.
23 Feb. 1994	Tambo returns home to Palm Island.
6 April 1994	Broome Crocodile Farm heritage decision.
11 & 18 April 1994	Meetings between ministers and indigenous negotiators on proposed Indigenous Land Fund.
12 May 1994	Emergency declaration on Hindmarsh Island.
10 June 1994	Hindmarsh Island emergency declaration extended.
20 June 1994	Indigenous Land Fund Bill introduced into the House of Representatives.
1 July 1994	Torres Strait Regional Authority comes into existence.
9 July 1994	Permanent declaration on Hindmarsh Island bridge.
1 Sep. 1994	Senate refers Indigenous Land Fund Bill to Standing Committee on Finance and Public Administration.
4 Oct. 1994	Going Home conference in Darwin.
23 Dec. 1994	Review of NAHS released.
9 Feb. 1995	Second Senate Committee on Land Fund Bill reports.

10 Feb. 1995	Deputy Prime Minister, ATSIC chairperson and Minister for Aboriginal and Torres Strait Islander Affairs jointly release reports on infrastructure needs in remote communities.
14 Feb. 1995	Justice O'Loughlin invalidates Hindmarsh Island declaration.
28 Feb. 1995	Amended Indigenous Land Fund Bill introduced into the House of Representatives.
29 Feb. 1995	Paul Keating visits Hopevale and speaks out in support of infrastructure and health needs in remote communities.
6 March 1995	Ian McLachlan and Christine Gallus ask misleading questions in the House of Representatives. Ian McLachlan then confesses to sanctioning the secret copying of Minister for Aboriginal and Torres Strait Islander Affairs' mail.
10 March 1995	Ian McLachlan resigns from the Coalition front-bench.
21 March 1995	Indigenous Land Fund Bill passed by the parliament.
29 April 1995	Cabinet ERC rejects pleas for National Centenary of Federation Infrastructure Project for remote communities.
May 1995	Stolen Generations Inquiry to be conducted by HREOC announced.
3 June 1995	Eddie Mabo tombstone unveiled.
4 June 1995	Eddie Mabo tombstone desecrated.
6 June 1995	Fabrication alleged concerning Hindmarsh Island beliefs.
June 1995	Justice Mathews agrees to prepare second Hindmarsh Island heritage report. SA government announces Hindmarsh Island Royal Commission.
2 Aug. 1995	PM&C and ATSIC officers in Social Justice Task-force visit Torres Strait and hear claims for self-government.

12 Sep. 1995	Prime Minister Keating rejects self-government agenda.
19 Dec. 1995	Jervis Bay National Park returns to Aboriginal ownership.
Dec. 1995	Release of Hindmarsh Island Royal Commission report.
3 March 1996	Keating government defeated at general election and John Howard becomes Prime Minister.
11 March 1996	Senator John Herron appointed Minister for Aboriginal and Torres Strait Islander Affairs.
May 1997	Stolen Generations report made public.
27 May 1997	National Reconciliation Convention, Melbourne.
16 Dec. 1997	Howard government responds to Stolen Generations report.
27 May 2000	Corroboree 2000.
28 May 2000	Walk for reconciliation across Sydney Harbour Bridge.
1 Jan. 2001	Council for Aboriginal Reconciliation and formal process of reconciliation ceases to exist unless extended by Commonwealth law.

1

THE HISTORICAL CONTEXT: FROM MASSACRES TO MABO

When I set out to write this limited political memoir focusing on six years in the indigenous affairs portfolio I was, of course, deeply conscious that the public policy achievements of those years did not occur in a vacuum. There had been a preceding 200 years of resistance and struggle by indigenous Australians to have their rights recognised by colonial and, from 1901, state and federal governments of all political persuasions.

Most of us were never taught the true history of our own country, especially the history of the first Australians. It is in this history that we find our own local and immediate chronicles of dispossession and oppression, which have epitomised the relations between the indigenous people of these lands and the governments that have over the last 200 years asserted legal sovereignty under English law.

There are some wonderful writers, commentators and historians who have interpreted this essential history of Australia, and I commend their works to all readers. They include indigenous writers such as Marcia Langton, Henry Reynolds from the non-indigenous community, and many more from both communities. A particularly useful reference (and no home should be without one) is the Encyclopaedia of Aboriginal Australia *edited by David Horton, which has been an invaluable source for this introduction.*

It is nevertheless useful to outline briefly some of the pertinent and significant historical events and political movements that have impacted, sometimes positively and sometimes negatively, on what I regard as the unstoppable march towards the just recognition and respect for indigenous rights in this nation. The developments at national government level in the six years between 1990 and 1996 should be understood in the context of this history.

In 1788 my great, great, great, great-grandfather, John Cross, arrived as a convict in the First Fleet on the ship *Alexandra*. After the European invasion, with the relentless spread of the colonies, the

Aboriginal people, who had lived on this land for the previous 50 000 years, effectively lost control of their lives and would remain subject to the laws and the heavy hand of the European bureaucracy. That iron-fisted control continued into the 1960s. It involved at various times massacres and other genocidal practices such as the deliberate removal of Aboriginal children of mixed heritage, prohibitions on the practice of Aboriginal culture, spirituality and the speaking of languages, and systemic discrimination in the provision of basic services and living conditions that continues in hundreds of Aboriginal communities to this day.

The theft of the land was given legal justification through the doctrine of *terra nullius* or land belonging to no one. This doctrine supported the view that the land to become known as Australia was not subject to the sovereign rights of any people and title could thus be gained by 'peaceful settlement' beginning with the assertion of British sovereignty over the east coast of Australia in April 1770 by Captain James Cook. The legal fiction that Australia was uninhabited swept aside all in its path and remained the recognised law in Australia until the High Court's Mabo decision in 1992.

In reality, though not always, the conquest of the indigenous people was savage, involving massacres and brutality. While much of the genocide is not recorded, there are numerous detailed accounts of such events as massacres, which no Australian intent on discovering the truth of our history can ignore. These massacres were, however, not confined to the first years of the colony, or even to the nineteenth century, but documented cases continued into the late 1920s. One example, in the west of the country, was the Forrest River massacres which were the subject of a Royal Commission. The chain of events began with a station proprietor whipping an elderly Aboriginal man, Lumbia, with a stockwhip. Lumbia retaliated by spearing and killing his attacker. The police hunted him down and ultimately captured him. They obviously did some other hunting as well, because reports soon emerged of wounded Aboriginal people returning to the Anglican mission at Forrest River for medical aid. Charred human remains were also found in the vicinity of the mission. The Royal Commission into these events found that eleven Aboriginal people had been shot in police custody and their bodies burnt. No police were ever convicted for these killings despite the fact that estimates of the death toll were much higher.

In 1928, at Yuendumu in the Northern Territory, police set out on a retaliatory expedition after the murder of a prospector and killed seventeen Aboriginal people in what has become known as the Coniston massacre. The police were exonerated in a subsequent inquiry despite the fact that, as history now recounts, the killings were far more numerous and continued for approximately a year.

If such killings could occur with apparent impunity in the late 1920s it is no wonder that estimates of Aboriginal deaths through massacres have been put as high as 10 000 people in the northern part of Australia alone. There were, of course, acts of resistance to the taking of lands and the increasing presence of the settlers. Many of the leaders of the resistance are well known to Aboriginal people but little known in the wider community. One strong Aboriginal fighter for his people in the early days of the Sydney colony was Pemulwuy, who carried out a guerrilla campaign from 1790 until he was killed in 1802. For his courageous defence of his people and his lands, his head was subsequently placed in the museum of the Royal College of Surgeons in London.

But it was not only the massacres that decimated the Aboriginal population and left them outnumbered and outgunned by the settlers. Their ranks were also savagely depleted by the settlers' diseases. Influenza, pneumonia, typhoid, tuberculosis, smallpox and measles caused a serious and continuing loss of life in Aboriginal communities. Those who survived the massacres and the diseases increasingly found themselves rounded up and moved from their traditional lands to more manageable locations where they could be more effectively controlled by the authorities of the new colonies. This practice was often assisted by native police, who were young Aboriginal men recruited from other parts of the country and therefore with no local allegiance. There were of course different impacts of colonisation and contact in different regions of the country, for example between the south-eastern and northern regions of Australia.

There have been over 200 Christian missions established among indigenous Australians, with the first established by the Anglican Church in 1820; many continue to the present day. The form of the missions ranged from churches with administrative power over communities to those merely conducting local activities such as running schools or hospitals on government-controlled reserves.

There are as many views about the effects of these Christian missions as there are about Christianity itself. While their impact on local communities varied, there is no doubt that it was often considerable. At times the missions functioned as an impediment to the worst excesses of other authorities; others were seen to exercise their own authoritarian control and to be complicit in the policies of removing lighter skinned Aboriginal children from their families. There is also no doubt that the communities they established were not managed by Aboriginal people and were established on a welfare model, leaving the indigenous people with very little effective control over their lives and lands. Often people from divergent tribal groups ended up in the one mission or government reserve land as a result of decisions over which they had no say. It was, however, the powers of the colonial government authorities that were the chief source of the social control exercised over the lives of Aboriginal people. Often this control was implemented under the guise of 'protection' policies formally set out in recommendations of a Parliamentary Select Committee Report on Aborigines made to the House of Commons in 1837.

Protection regimes began with Queensland legislation and were well established in the Australian colonies in the 1830s, and usually associated with the creation of an official Protector of Aborigines. This role had the semblance of preventing some of the worst abuses by non-indigenous people, the gradual introduction of education for Aboriginal children, and the implementation of special laws deemed necessary for Aboriginal well-being. But their well-being was determined entirely by the European lawmakers, and basically 'protection' was about shaping Aboriginal people into a submissive population better suited to 'white' purposes than an independent and resilient people with their own destiny. Even with differences in emphasis and policy among the colonies, the common theme was the introduction of control over Aboriginal people. It permeated every aspect of their lives, from the food they ate and the religion they practised to their freedom of movement and association, even, ultimately, their right to rear their own children. In one form or another these controls continued into the 1950s and 1960s. The degree of control was most rigid in the state of Queensland.

The evolution of the ongoing Aboriginal resistance and opposition to the policies of the protectionist era is not understood by many Australians. When I was at school these practices were endorsed by the education system. It must have taken great courage for Aboriginal people to stand up for their rights where the prevailing attitude was that they were an inferior race and therefore unworthy of being accorded basic human rights and freedoms in their own land. Those indigenous people involved in the developing political movement were to become heroes in the eyes of their people and to this day are justly recognised and lauded for their work.

It should be noted that because of the geographic location and differing colonial experience, Australia's other indigenous people, the Torres Strait Islanders, while experiencing oppressive government policies, were not forced out *en masse* from their traditional lands. They are dealt with separately in Chapter 12.

While there were some acts of organised Aboriginal resistance to government policies, it was not until the 1920s that modern political organisations began. The fledgling organisations of this time were the first steps in what was to become a movement of determined and public struggle for Aboriginal rights. The Australian Aborigines Progressive Association, for example, operated in Sydney from 1924 to 1927, after which police harassment stopped it carrying out its work. The Australian Aborigines League was set up in Victoria by William Cooper and Ebenezer Lovett in 1932. In 1935, in a highly significant move, it attempted to send a petition to King George V proposing that special electorates be established for Aboriginal people and that the Commonwealth create a Native Affairs Department. Thus from soon after Federation, Aboriginal people had lost faith in the capacity of state governments to respect their rights and looked to the Commonwealth for justice. Much of the rest of this book is the most recent story of this struggle.

Organisations in which non-Aboriginal people joined with their Aboriginal brothers and sisters in the fight for Aboriginal rights began to emerge in the 1930s and were usually given the name Aboriginal Advancement Leagues; of these the Victorian League was perhaps the most prominent. For much of the time the non-Aboriginal people were in leadership positions in a movement that sought both to carry on the Aboriginal political struggle and to provide opportunities for the two races to meet socially. It was in some ways a practical initiative in reconciliation long before the term came into vogue. But there were also some political lessons to be learned by the non-Aboriginal members about the importance of Aboriginal people having control of these organisations, something that did not really happen until the late 1960s.

The Aborigines Progressive Association was formed in Dubbo in 1937 with well-known Aboriginal leaders William Ferguson as secretary and Jack Patten as president (Mr Patten's son, Cec, was someone I worked with at the Aboriginal Legal Service in the 1970s). Its objectives were to improve living conditions on reserves controlled by the Aboriginal Protection Board (APB), the granting of full citizenship rights, the reconstruction of the board so that Aboriginal people made up half its members, and the repeal of discriminatory legislation. The association deliberately set out to campaign for change and on 26 January 1938, the 150th anniversary of Governor Phillip's landing at Sydney Cove, together with the Australian Aborigines League, organised a Day of Mourning to counter the official sesquicentenary celebrations. It went on to organise a deputation to Prime Minister Joe Lyons putting forward as its central objective what was to become a recurring theme— the federal government taking over responsibility for Aboriginal affairs.

The actions of the courageous Aboriginal people in all these organisations, standing up against the overwhelming public opinion of the time, deserve our admiration. They were truly leaders ahead of their time. While many of their demands would not find favour with Aboriginal people today, the call for the Commonwealth to take control was an early salvo in what was to become the 1967 referendum campaign.

By 1937 the senior bureaucrats responsible for Aboriginal affairs across Australia met and agreed on a national approach to the treatment of Aboriginal people. So-called 'full bloods' were to be kept on reserves and 'half-castes', lighter skinned Aboriginal people of mixed race, were to be absorbed into the general community. This policy of 'assimilation' became adopted across Australia and was one of the philosophical underpinnings for the policy of separating lighter skinned Aboriginal children from their families for the next 30 years, as well as for the Aboriginal affairs policies of governments more generally.

There were many other important stands taken by Aboriginal people themselves during those years that reflected a growing political movement as well as changing attitudes in the wider community. The role of the Aboriginal protection boards and like bodies in the various states were increasingly viewed with contempt and hostility by Aboriginal people. Not only were the environmental health and living conditions disgraceful on most reserves controlled by the boards, but equally objectionable were the authoritarian powers exercised over the residents by the managers of the reserves—or missions as they were often called.

Across Australia, Aboriginal people were encouraged to behave like Europeans. If they behaved 'appropriately' they could be issued with certificates exempting them from laws applying to other Aboriginal people, such as restrictions on being able to vote and drink alcohol. The Aboriginal artist Albert Namatjira was accorded such status in 1957 in the Northern Territory, only to be arrested a year later for passing liquor to his relatives. Many Aboriginal people referred to such special status as a 'dog licence' or 'dog tag'.

Often people were treated with as little respect as livestock. Children were removed from families, and even the reserve land itself could be taken away and given to non-indigenous people at the whim of some faceless bureaucrat. Resentment came to a head from time to time, as in 1938 at Cummeragunja on the Murray River, where the Aboriginal community walked off the reserve to demonstrate their grievances.

Even when the reserves were being degazetted for use by government or some pastoral or commercial interest, governments often could not get it right. In New South Wales, some 170 Aboriginal reserves were degazetted under the wrong legislation and it took the retrospective legislation of the Wran Labor government in 1983 to fix the blunder. All this land, over the entire history of Aboriginal reserves, was taken without consent or compensation.

Many Australians have forgotten that the first attempt to confer constitutional power on the Commonwealth to legislate for Aboriginal people occurred in 1944 when the Curtin government proposed giving the Commonwealth an Aboriginal affairs power; as the proposal was linked with thirteen other shifts of power to the Commonwealth, it was overwhelmingly defeated at the ensuing referendum. After World War II, pressure increased for intervention by the national government to address Aboriginal rights. This, of course, ultimately required a successful referendum to amend the Constitution. It is an indication of how far change has progressed that in 1951, the year of my birth, when Paul Hasluck became Minister for Territories and thus responsible for Aboriginal policy in the Northern Territory, he 'could not find any senior officer in Canberra who was personally interested or officially concerned about Aborigines'.

Pressure for Commonwealth involvement to overcome the failure of the states in Aboriginal policy came from the Victorian-based Australian Aborigines League and the NSW Aboriginal Progressive Association, as we have seen. Appeals for Commonwealth action on Aboriginal rights also came in the form of the bark petition now proudly on display in Parliament House, Canberra. At the time of its presentation in 1963 this was a plea for a parliamentary inquiry into a controversial government-supported mining project at Yirrkala in the Northern Territory.

In 1964 the Menzies government at least gave some support to research concerning Aboriginal people with the creation of the Australian Institute of Aboriginal Studies as a research body that began collecting a vast repository of Aboriginal heritage and cultural material. This body became the Australian Institute of Aboriginal and Torres Strait Islander Studies (AIATSIS) in 1989.

The momentum for change gathered strength through the work of the Aboriginal advancement organisations in the various states, and it also gained the support of a small number of sympathetic non-Aboriginal parliamentarians in Canberra, on both sides of politics. A vital role was played by a new generation of Aboriginal activists who used the media and political protest to advance their cause. Innovative tactics were employed by Aboriginal people and their supporters. In 1965 about 30 students from Sydney University, including Charles Perkins, went on the famous 'freedom ride', touring towns in northern New South Wales to highlight discrimination. Highly public visits occurred at the Moree baths, where Aboriginal children had not been permitted to swim but where the protesters ultimately forced the local authorities to allow the children access.

Inside federal parliament, the Australian Labor Party (ALP) strongly supported conferring legislative power on the Commonwealth through a referendum. Labor members such as Gordon Bryant had advocated this change since 1957, and he was strongly supported in this goal by Kim Beazley Sr and Gough Whitlam, who continued their advocacy in the coming years. There was, however, at this time no cross-party support for this change. In 1965 the Menzies government passed a bill through the House of Representatives that would, if presented to a successful referendum, have led to the repeal of section 127 of the Constitution, which prevented Aboriginal people from being counted in the Census. The government refused to support ALP proposals to have section 51 (xxvi) amended to allow parliament to pass laws directed towards Commonwealth action to improve the conditions of Aboriginal people.

Billy Wentworth, on the Coalition side, supported constitutional change in this area and actually proposed a constitutional amendment prohibiting racial discrimination, and for this he received ALP support. Despite the limited proposal for deletion of section 127 proposed by the Menzies government bill and passed by the parliament, the government did nothing to take the proposal to a referendum.

In another part of Australia, Aboriginal people were themselves acting to assert their rights. On 23 August 1966 Vincent Lingiari, a Gurindji elder, led his people off the cattle station operated by the giant Vesteys pastoral organisation in protest against their wages and conditions. Their calls for Commonwealth involvement also strongly argued the case for land to establish their own cattle station. They subsequently sent a petition to the Governor-General, with no immediate result. Their stand against injustice, however, attracted national publicity for Aboriginal land rights grievances. The strike developed into a seven-year campaign by the Gurindji for the return of their traditional lands and became a *cause célèbre* across Australia. The campaign was strongly supported by the trade union movement and sparked a campaign for human rights, including land rights, by many Aboriginal people. It was a cry for Commonwealth leadership that would not be acted on until the election of the Whitlam government.

The driving political force for change and the achievement of a national referendum to give the Commonwealth legislative power over Aboriginal affairs came from the Federal Council for the Advancement of Aborigines and Torres Strait Islanders (FCAATSI). The Federal Council for Aboriginal Affairs (FCAA) was established with predominantly non-Aboriginal membership arising from a meeting back in 1958 of mainly Aboriginal advancement organisation representatives and their non-indigenous supporters from the churches and trade unions; it was re-named FCAATSI in 1964. By 1965 about 56 organisations had joined, with an increasing number of Aboriginal people taking leading roles. FCAATSI took on a number of indigenous causes, but its organisational support for the 1967 referendum was crucial. After the referendum the organisation tended to be more volatile, with Aboriginal people justifiably asserting their right to be heard and to control their own affairs.

Convincing the Holt Coalition government to proceed with the referendum, and the resounding 'Yes' vote, was quite an achievement. The Coalition side of politics, with notable exceptions such as Bill Wentworth, had previously opposed change, but by the time of the referendum on 27 May 1967, parliamentary support was unanimous. It was a magnificent coalition of forces that brought about the massive 90.77 per cent 'Yes' vote. No other constitutional referendum proposal has ever received such support from the Australian people. It became a template for what I later hoped to achieve with the Council for Aboriginal Reconciliation Act.

One speech in the parliamentary debate on the referendum proposal stands out. Kim Beazley Sr, later to become Education Minister in the Whitlam government, delivered a speech years ahead of its time in which he recognised that 'the way in which a minority people is treated is the touchstone of national character. The true test of our respect for a minority race is whether we want them to be a distinctive people making a distinctive contribution'. He rightly concluded that 'the whole nation is judged on any Aboriginal policy, anywhere in any state'.

There were divergent views within the parliament and outside it about what the referendum meant. The Coalition Minister for Social Security, Ian Sinclair, said that 'the government had nothing specific in mind and its policies would be worked out during the budget discussions'. Gough Whitlam, Leader of the Opposition, said: 'The Commonwealth can at last bring the resources of the whole nation to bear in favour of the Aboriginals where they live'. Regrettably, to this day this objective has not been achieved.

It should also be remembered that the Commonwealth's own role in Aboriginal affairs policy at that time, responsible as it was for the Northern Territory, had been far from perfect. Even during the latter years of the Menzies government, the Commonwealth had been revoking Aboriginal reserves at a whim and by the stroke of a pen and always without consent or compensation. There was, however, a general expectation in the community that the Commonwealth would take action to improve things.

The Holt government moved to establish a Council for Aboriginal Affairs to provide policy advice to the government. This council was chaired by Dr H.C. (Nugget) Coombs and included two other non-indigenous people, Barrie Dexter, director of the Office of Aboriginal Affairs, and noted anthropologist W.E.H. Stanner. W.C. Wentworth was appointed as the first minister and an Office of Aboriginal Affairs was established within the Prime Minister's Department. Bill Wentworth, once denigrated and even despised by the Left of politics for his strident anti-communist stand, has had an intergenerational interest in and support for Aboriginal people that he retained long after his retirement from politics. In 1984 he was, as I recall, the only person associated with the non-Labor side of politics to attend the return of Uluru to Aboriginal ownership by the Governor-General in the face of an organised boycott of the event by Northern Territory and federal representatives of the Coalition.

One of the council's key recommendations was that properties be purchased for Aboriginal communities, and moves in this direction were eventually made in the dying days of the McMahon government. Commonwealth involvement in matters Aboriginal was, however, limited to a token coordinating role, and the states still had the primary responsibility for Aboriginal affairs.

From 1968 a fair and equitable social change in the form of equal pay for Aboriginal people on cattle stations had the adverse consequence that many Aboriginal people and their families were forced off stations in the Top End, which had for generations relied on a cheap Aboriginal workforce. This further dispossession was to worsen their dependency on welfare and force them to live in alternative, equally squalid accommodation on the outskirts of towns or in church missions. This is not to suggest that the movement to equal pay was other than inevitable and just; its consequences, however, show up the challenges of Aboriginal public policy.

The late 1960s and early 1970s were the years of the Gorton and then briefly the McMahon governments, with Prime Minister McMahon appointing Peter Howson Minister for Environment, Aborigines and the Arts in 1971. So far as the subject matter of this book is concerned these were even more the years of Gough Whitlam who, as Leader of the Opposition, took an active interest in Aboriginal policy issues. The increasing impatience and frustration of Aboriginal people with the Coalition government led to a number of important political and legal developments.

In 1970 Sir Richard Blackburn, sitting as a member of the NT Supreme Court, heard a challenge by leading members of the Yirrkala community in the Northern Territory that sought to have the court recognise the existence of communal native title to land. The community that had been responsible for sending the bark petition to parliament in 1963 remained concerned about the impact of mining on their land. In the decision of Justice Blackburn in the case of *Milirrpum and Others vs Nabalco Pty Ltd and the Commonwealth of Australia,* His Honour relied on a Canadian lower court decision in the case of Calder and found against the Aboriginal people, both on issues of facts and law. It would be another 22 years before the High Court of Australia would overturn his decision with its 1992 Mabo judgment.

Aboriginal people were also taking to the streets to assert their rights. On Australia Day 1972, they established a tent embassy on the lawns in front of Parliament House to bring their grievances to the McMahon government and, perhaps even more importantly, to national attention in an election year. While the immediate catalyst for the protest was an announcement by the government that a new form of general-purpose lease was to be established that was to 'exclude all mineral rights', the dramatically symbolic tent embassy served as a lightning rod for extensive Aboriginal grievances.

The government reacted with indignation and outrage. The embassy was three times torn down by police and each time re-erected. In one celebrated clash, a large contingent of police was outnumbered by a demonstration of 1500 Aboriginal people and their supporters who physically prevented the embassy from being removed. The erection of the tent embassy showed the determination and increasingly militant tactics that the new generation of Aboriginal people were prepared to undertake to assert their rights.

The Liberal Party did, however, make one very important contribution to Aboriginal affairs and to the rights of Aboriginal people during this period. In 1971 an Aboriginal man, Neville Bonner, was appointed to the Senate by the Queensland parliament following the nomination of the Liberal Party to fill a casual vacancy. Neville Bonner came from a humble background and despite his great achievements remained an honourable, modest and gracious human being. He remained conservative on most issues but took a stand against his party and against conservative governments on particular issues. There can be no denying the wonderful achievement of the Liberal Party in supporting him as a senator from 1971 until 1983. He remained the only Aboriginal person ever elected to the national parliament until the Australian Democrats and the people of New South Wales supported the election of Senator Aden Ridgeway in 1998. The ALP, until 2000, had never preselected a single Aboriginal candidate in a winnable seat for either the Senate or House of Representatives, even though statistically it is likely that 90 per cent of Aboriginal people vote Labor throughout Australia, and in the Northern Territory no federal candidate would be elected without the Aboriginal vote.

Another icon in the struggle for Aboriginal rights emerged in 1972 on the lawns in front of Parliament House in the form of the Aboriginal flag. The flag was created the previous year by a Luritja man from central Australia, Harold Thomas. As I see it, the tent embassy and the Aboriginal flag epitomise the unity of Aboriginal people in the fight for their rights. I believe there has always been strong solidarity between rural and urban Aboriginal people across Australia in their collective struggle. One of the reasons for this is that despite differences in the historical evolution of communities, there have been more common experiences than differences. In bearing the brunt of discrimination, theft of land, poor health, high unemployment and consignment to the fringes of society, they all know what it feels like to be treated as 'Aboriginal' in Australia; discrimination has united them. The fact that the Aboriginal flag quickly became such a universally acclaimed rallying symbol shows the extent to which this solidarity exists, and indeed the flag reinforces community cohesion. Even the catalyst for the tent embassy—a new government policy directed towards Aboriginal people in the Northern Territory—aroused the ire of the urban-based Aboriginal activists of Sydney and Melbourne.

When I eventually gained first-hand experience of Canadian and American indigenous policy during my time as minister, I understood a further reason why such Australia-wide solidarity existed. Both Canadian and American governments have deliberately set about legislatively entrenching divisions between different groups of indigenous people. In America, the Bureau of Indian Affairs distinguishes between those American Indians who are members of a recognised tribe and possess the requisite degree of Indian ancestry; in Canada, the government makes a distinction between those Indians who are registered under the Indian Act and those who are not. The consequence has been that in both these countries there is nothing like the common bonds of solidarity in the struggle for rights that exist among Aboriginal people in Australia.

I mean no cheap political point-scoring when I emphasise that, despite the best efforts of Bill Wentworth, the later years of the Coalition government under Gorton and McMahon were dismal ones in Aboriginal affairs. There was, however, at least one important manifestation of a change by the Coalition which showed a shift in the rhetoric if not the reality of policy. This was a policy statement in the last days of the McMahon government that recognised the need for Aboriginal people to 'increasingly manage their own affairs—as individuals, as groups and as communities at the local level'. At least in that general way this articulation of policy was a notable shift from former policies of assimilation.

In the run-up to the 1972 election, right across the policy spectrum of government, there were interest groups and disaffected constituencies who were seeking a change of government, and they achieved their objective on 2 December 1972. Gough Whitlam was Leader of the Opposition, supported by a shadow ministry who were impatient for reform after 23 years in Opposition. A generation of Australians had been born and had passed well into voting age without ever having experienced Labor in government.

To say that the newly elected government had hit the ground running was an understatement. The new Prime Minister decided that until his new ministry was elected by the ALP Caucus, he and his deputy, Lance Barnard, should be sworn in as ministers and share responsibility for all portfolios. Whitlam appointed himself Minister for Aboriginal Affairs and initiated a number of important reforms in less than a month. These included the creation of the Department of Aboriginal Affairs, with Barrie Dexter as permanent head. The creation of a bureaucracy in this area has been criticised, but the fact remains that without some such administrative mechanism the Commonwealth government could not have implemented any of the policies flowing from the 1967 referendum.

Gough Whitlam had the charges dropped against people arrested at the tent embassy the year before. Then, in an action of great significance, he set up a commission to inquire into the granting of land rights in the Northern Territory. This decision was ultimately to result in what remains as the strongest Aboriginal land rights policy in the country. The inquiry was formalised by the appointment of A.E. (Ted) Woodward, a judge of the ACT and NT Supreme Courts. Mr Woodward was no stranger to Aboriginal causes, having appeared for the Aboriginal side in the Gove land rights case. The commission's terms of reference were expanded in 1973 to inquire into Aboriginal land rights in adjacent Aboriginal reserves in Western Australia and South Australia.

Commissioner Woodward presented two reports to the government. The first, in July 1973, resulted in setting up the Northern and Central Land Councils and the second, in 1974, recommended a claims mechanism by which Aboriginal people could put their Northern Territory land claims before an independent Aboriginal land commissioner. The legislation to give effect to this proposal had only just been introduced into the parliament when the Whitlam government was dismissed on 11 November 1975. It was left to the Fraser government to pass a watered-down—though still landmark—version of the legislation in the form of the *Aboriginal Land Rights (Northern Territory) Act 1976* (NT Land Rights Act).

The Whitlam government was responsible for some major initiatives. The first Minister for Aboriginal Affairs, after Whitlam's brief time in the position, was Gordon Bryant, whose active involvement in the Aboriginal cause had gone back decades. He had also been ALP spokesperson on Aboriginal Affairs in Opposition. His appointment was very well regarded by Aboriginal people. The Whitlam government's involvement in Aboriginal affairs is often portrayed by its critics as accident-prone and tempestuous. Then, as now, the media highlighted every program that went wrong and every division in Aboriginal opinion that manifested itself as some kind of national issue. The reality was that Commonwealth government involvement in Aboriginal affairs was unprecedented.

There was no experience of progressive administration to draw on; the state models were hardly examples to be emulated. It was also inevitable that there would be organisations and projects that would fail, sometimes spectacularly. Such failures gave rise to harsh judgments and much political point-scoring against Gordon Bryant, and he was replaced in September 1973 with Senator Jim Cavanagh. In addition to being responsible for building the Department of Aboriginal Affairs, Gordon Bryant had established the first representative Aboriginal body to advise the national government, the National Aboriginal Consultative Committee.

Senator Cavanagh was responsible for an array of Labor initiatives, many of which were the pioneering reforms on which subsequent government policies have been built. Aboriginal Hostels, established in 1973 and still operating successfully, not only provides accommodation for Aboriginal students and others but has also given important administrative experience and training to a generation of Aboriginal people.

The Aboriginal Loans Commission was established in November 1974 to provide loans for Aboriginal people, for housing and for other personal purposes as well as for business ventures. Aboriginal people were, and remain, severely underrepresented among the ranks of business people and home-owners. The dream of greater Aboriginal self-reliance is nothing new. It has been a part of government policy since the early 1970s, though the Howard government and those who republish its rhetoric without serious analysis would have us believe otherwise. The Loans Commission was ultimately responsible for only 1242 housing loans and 437 business loans during the six years of its existence. Statistics are not available on the failure rate of such small business ventures, but as with all small business, especially those carried on by people with no previous experience, the numbers would be high.

The first statutory authority set up to acquire land for dispossessed Aboriginal people was the Aboriginal Land Fund Commission, established in May 1975. The commission had a majority of Aboriginal commissioners, with the anthropologist Charles Rowley in the chair. One difficulty for the commission was that it had no secure funding base from which to plan its activities and was subject to the whims of the budget process. Its activities were also attacked by conservative state governments such as the reactionary Bjelke-Petersen government of Queensland, which refused to transfer pastoral leases to Aboriginal ownership in a blatant act of racial discrimination. It was no wonder that, with such anti-Aboriginal propaganda being pumped out by its opponents, the Land Fund Commission was the subject of controversy and public disputation. It was, however, again a landmark initiative that was to be an important lesson for the Keating Labor government on the need to provide a secure funding base for land acquisition programs.

Other programs funded by the Whitlam government, such as the funding of the Aboriginal medical and legal services, supported Aboriginal people in building community-based organisations that could empower them to deliver services and programs to their own people.

Senator Cavanagh also found himself in public conflict with a senior officer of his department, Charles Perkins, who had begun his public service career in Canberra in 1969 with the then Office of Aboriginal Affairs. Charles Perkins had burst into public prominence in 1965 as a spokesperson for the freedom rides, and he continued to speak out publicly on Aboriginal issues. There was a bitter falling out between Mr Perkins and his minister, and public service disciplinary charges were brought against him, only to be dropped finally at the insistence of Prime Minister Whitlam.

The last Aboriginal Affairs Minister in the Whitlam government was my predecessor in the seat of Hughes, Les Johnson, who was appointed in June 1975 and remained in that position until the dismissal of the Whitlam government. That dismissal robbed him of the honour of guiding the NT Land Rights Act through parliament. He would, I know, have cherished that honour, given his own longstanding commitment to the Aboriginal cause.

There were two other initiatives during the Whitlam government that particularly warrant comment. One was the creation in 1973 of the House of Representatives Standing Committee on Aboriginal Affairs, which still exists but which was renamed the Standing Committee on Aboriginal and Torres Strait Islander Affairs following the comparable change of the portfolio name by the Hawke government.

The work of this committee has been important, not only for the content of the reports it has produced but because it has contributed to a genuine increase in the understanding of indigenous issues by members of parliament and to cross-party cooperation on particular issues. Other committees have been established from time to time by the House of Representatives, including select committees set up to consider specific issues.

The Senate has also set up select committees to consider and inquire into specific issues, and other Senate standing committees have considered particular indigenous issues that come within their terms of reference. A welcome development has been the establishment of parliamentary joint committees, comprising both senators and members of the House, to deal with particular issues such as native title. This offers the possibility of a high-profile parliamentary inquiry process to address policy initiatives such as the outstanding social justice package I refer to throughout this book.

A further initiative of the Whitlam government was to provide a non-negotiable foundation of human rights protection, which Aboriginal people were able to build on in the years ahead. In 1975 the government secured the passage through the parliament of the Racial Discrimination Act (RDA). This Act was passed to give effect to Australia's obligations under the International Convention on the Elimination of All Forms of Racial Discrimination (CERD). The effect of this law was to prohibit racial discrimination in Australia in the terms set out in the Act, which in turn was framed in line with Australia's international obligations. To put it bluntly, without the RDA there would never have been a Mabo decision by the High Court because the RDA blocked attempts by the Bjelke-Petersen government to obliterate the native title rights of the Mabo plaintiffs by special law of the Queensland parliament. Without the RDA there is also no doubt that the Aboriginal native title rights in the aftermath of Mabo would have been eroded or obliterated by state governments. This crucial reform should thus be given the recognition it deserves.

People who were not around in 1975 cannot be expected to understand the passions and anger that the dismissal of the Whitlam government aroused. I was one of many Australians who were so angered by the dismissal of an elected government that I was oblivious to the fact that a landmark shift in social policy had occurred in Aboriginal affairs, not only because of the Whitlam government's policies but also because of broader changes in society.

By 1975 Australians had a deeper understanding than ever before of the imperative for Australia as a nation to address indigenous aspirations. This is not to suggest that discrimination was not still rampant or indigenous disadvantage entrenched, or that indigenous aspirations were not still a low priority of most Australians. But an irreversible shift had occurred. For this change Australia owes a great debt not just to Gough Whitlam but to all those men and women who had worked so hard, both inside and outside the parliament, to change public opinion and to bring about change for the better. It was all worthwhile and it did make a difference.

No more dramatic and incontrovertible confirmation of this shift can there be than the speeches of key Fraser government senators on the occasion of the introduction of the Aboriginal Land Rights (Northern Territory) Bill into federal parliament in 1976. In particular, the speeches of the Minister for Aboriginal Affairs, Ian Viner, and future ministers Fred Chaney and Peter Baume are worthy of note. Although the legislation was a watered-down version of the original Bill introduced by the Whitlam government, it remains to this day the strongest land rights legislation in the country, guaranteeing what is in practice a power for Aboriginal people to prevent mining on their land, a strong role for Aboriginal organisations such as the land councils and, most importantly of all, a strong assertion of Commonwealth law-making power in Aboriginal affairs which the protests of successive Northern Territory governments and sections of the mining industry have failed to dilute.

For those of us who become involved in politics because of our faith in people and our desire to build a better world, the speeches that leading Coalition senators made in support of the Bill were beautiful words. In some ways they were saying things that Gordon Bryant, Kim Beazley Sr, Gough Whitlam, Les Johnson and many others had been saying for years. But these were the representatives of conservative Australia speaking. They were statements of idealism and a reaffirmation of the capacity of our country to achieve progressive reform and grow. Where are the Fred Chaneys, Peter Baumes and Ian Viners of today's Liberal Party? I sometimes wonder whether a new generation of such voices will ever emerge and take a stand.

As a 22-year-old I did not understand that although Malcolm Fraser was the opponent of the ALP, he was nevertheless 'of the old school', and was at least prepared to take a stand in support of the most dispossessed and impoverished Australians—as he did against Apartheid in South Africa. Australia had come a long way from 1972, when the McMahon government was barely prepared to recognise Aboriginal rights of any kind, to three years later when the Coalition passed legislation giving an effective veto over mining on Aboriginal lands in the Northern Territory.

Ian Viner, a Perth Queen's Counsel and Fraser's first Minister for Aboriginal Affairs, presided over a change in the status of the Aboriginal advisory body to the federal government in 1977, abolishing the National Aboriginal Consultative Committee and later in the year creating its replacement, the National Aboriginal Conference (NAC), which met for the first time in February 1978. The NAC had a more restrictive charter than its predecessor, only having a role in advising the government on those issues referred to it by the minister. It was a nationally elected body with state branches and a ten-member national executive. The first chairperson was Lois O'Donoghue who had even then, twenty years ago, already devoted much of her life to the cause of her people. Sadly, as an advisory body the opinions of the NAC were not listened to on most significant issues, and its views frequently aroused the ire of the government.

An important initiative of the Fraser government was begun in 1977 with the introduction of the Community Development Employment Project (CDEP) in twelve remote communities. This program, which can be described as a work-for-the-dole scheme, has been the only viable employment option for hundreds of remote communities, and it was hugely expanded by the subsequent Hawke and Keating governments. It was, however, a very creative policy response by the Fraser government that brought the scheme into existence in the first place.

Another progressive reform during Ian Viner's period of office was the passage of the *Aboriginal Councils and Associations Act 1976*. This legislation established a simple and effective incorporation mechanism for Aboriginal organisations that was more responsive to Aboriginal needs and aspirations than the comparable state government legislation of the time.

Evidence of the shift in thinking on the conservative side of politics concerning the rights of Aboriginal people can also be seen in the preparedness of the Fraser government in 1978 to stand up for the rights of the Aboriginal people at Aurukun and Mornington Island against the wishes of the Bjelke-Petersen National Party government. The Fraser government enacted overriding federal legislation directed towards achieving self-management in those communities. The Queensland government, however, circumvented this by degazetting these Aboriginal communities as reserves. After subsequent negotiation the communities had local government authorities recognised under Queensland law.

The second Fraser government Minister for Aboriginal Affairs was Senator Fred Chaney, who took over the portfolio in 1978 only to find himself embroiled in a controversy with the government of Western

Australia, his home state, involving the then Premier, Sir Charles Court, the father of the current Premier.

Queensland was not the only government busily assaulting the rights of Aboriginal people. The WA government had been deeply involved in promoting the rights of mining companies exploring for diamonds and later oil on an Aboriginal-owned pastoral property at Noonkanbah in the far north-west of the state, which had been bought by the Aboriginal Land Fund Commission. Aboriginal people opposed mining and exploration that would interfere with their sacred sites. The issue had been building in intensity since 1977 and resulted in a full-on confrontation between miners and the Yangngara people in mid-1979, culminating in the WA government using police to enforce entry by the oil-drilling company CRA onto Aboriginal land, thus threatening Aboriginal sacred sites.

The Commonwealth government did not intervene and the whole sorry saga resulted in a trampling on Aboriginal rights and finally exposing the woeful inadequacy of WA Aboriginal heritage laws. No oil was found. Bob Hawke, as leader of the Australian Council of Trade Unions (ACTU), was a strong supporter of Aboriginal rights, with his son Stephen being personally involved in the affected local communities. The incident clearly contributed to the decision of the future Hawke government to implement interim Commonwealth Aboriginal heritage legislation.

The main reform of the Chaney years, 1978–80, was the establishment of the Aboriginal Development Commission (ADC) as a replacement for the Aboriginal Land Fund Commission and the Aboriginal Loans Commission. The ADC had ten part-time appointed commissioners, with Charles Perkins as chair and principal officer. By all accounts Mr Perkins formed a close working relationship with Minister Chaney. He remained in the position until March 1984 when he was appointed by Clyde Holding as Secretary of the Department of Aboriginal Affairs. The ADC became involved in its own share of controversies, but with hindsight it made an important bridge between the first tentative Commonwealth involvement in Aboriginal affairs by the Whitlam government and the landmark shift towards indigenous empowerment that ATSIC represents.

There were two important High Court decisions in this era that showed the determination of Aboriginal people to use the Australian legal system in an attempt to have their rights recognised and that ultimately culminated in Mabo.

The head of the NSW Aboriginal Legal Service, Paul Coe, initiated an action that sought not only to challenge the doctrine of *terra nullius* but to go much further to challenge the very basis of sovereignty itself. Whatever the merits of the political tactics of launching such a claim, the case, *Coe v. the Commonwealth*, was thrown out at an early stage, with only Justice Lionel Murphy providing some encouragement to the plaintiff. It was, however, a clear signal that Aboriginal people were not prepared to allow the 1971 decision of Justice Blackburn to stand.

The other case was pivotal to the Mabo decision itself. The matter in question was brought to the High Court by an indigenous man from Cape York, John Koowarta, in a case that bears his name. In 1982 the High Court, by a majority, upheld the validity of the RDA. In this decision Sir Ronald Wilson, then a High Court judge, was in the minority, as he was to be in the first Mabo case. Sir Ronald, as a brilliant lawyer, found himself in good conscience, true to his oath of office, finding against Aboriginal interests in both cases. This outcome is somewhat ironic in view of the courageous moral leadership he was to provide later in the reconciliation process and the stolen generations inquiry.

The Koowarta case was an extraordinary saga involving attempts to purchase a property by Aboriginal interests, the refusal by the Bjelke-Petersen government to transfer the property to Aboriginal people, the successful challenge to this refusal in the High Court, and finally the circumvention of the High Court decision invalidating the Queensland government action, by gazetting the area as a national park and therefore making it no longer available to purchase by Aboriginal people. The actions of the Queensland government, which was as rabidly anti-environmental as they were anti-Aboriginal, showed that they hated the 'blacks' even more than they hated the 'greens'.

An interesting and important development in the late 1970s was the formation of the Aboriginal Treaty Committee (a group of non-indigenous Australians) in which poet Judith Wright and Nugget Coombs were prominent participants. The committee supported proposals by the NAC for a treaty between indigenous Australians and the Australian government. A name suggested for the agreement was 'Makarrata'. The group was successful in bringing about a Senate Legal and Constitutional Affairs Committee inquiry (1981–83) into the feasibility of such an agreement.

In 1980, Liberal Senator Peter Baume was appointed Minister for Aboriginal Affairs. He had already demonstrated a strong interest in the portfolio through his involvement with AIATSIS. A small 'l' Liberal and a medical practitioner, he sought to build on the structures put in place by his predecessors. Peter Baume is a person I greatly respect for his commitment to genuine liberal principles.

The last Minister for Aboriginal Affairs in the Fraser government was South Australian MP Ian Wilson, who was appointed in 1982 and served until the election of the Hawke government in March of 1983.

Ian Wilson was involved in a series of major disputes with Charles Perkins.

The election of the Hawke Labor government in 1983 saw the appointment of Clyde Holding as minister. Formerly Leader of the Opposition in the Victorian parliament, Clyde came to Canberra a seasoned political veteran and a close political ally and supporter of Prime Minister Hawke. He has a fierce and uncompromising opposition to racism of any kind. While minister he formed deep and ongoing friendships with many Aboriginal people.

Bob Hawke was also someone deeply committed to trying to advance the human rights of Aboriginal people. It is popular in some sections of the Labor Party and the community to disparage that commitment, in my view without justification. I do not pretend that there was not a dashing of Aboriginal expectations on national land rights legislation during his government, but I have no doubt that Bob Hawke held the cause of Aboriginal rights as the nation's greatest priority and had intense personal commitment to this cause.

Labor had been elected to office with a policy of implementing a system of national land rights to override state governments by Commonwealth legislation if necessary. While the detail of the policy was not set out in the ALP manifesto, clearly stated were both a policy of Aboriginal rights to veto mining on their land and a commitment to provide for the commercial acquisition of land for dispossessed Aboriginal people. Labor's policy commitment for a uniform national system of land rights evolved because, almost without exception, state governments, including Labor governments, had failed to legislate effectively in this area.

When the Hawke government was elected in 1983, only South Australia could be said to have substantial land rights legislation in addition to the Northern Territory, where Commonwealth legislation applied. In South Australia, a similar scenario to what had occurred at the Commonwealth level in 1976 was played out. Proposals had been developed by the Dunstan and Corcoran governments to pass land rights legislation, and the Pitjantjatjara Land Rights Act was ultimately passed by the newly elected Tonkin Liberal government in 1981. The Act transferred 103 000 square kilometres of inalienable freehold title to Aboriginal ownership.

In New South Wales, land rights legislation had been passed by the Wran Labor government in 1983, but its provisions fell short of the expectations of the parliamentary committee report that preceded it. Importantly, however, the legislation did create a fund for the acquisition of land, with the funding base enshrined in legislation. Ownership of reserves was transferred to local land councils and limited opportunities were provided for claims to be made on vacant crown land.

In Victoria, two former Aboriginal reserves had been transferred to Aboriginal ownership, and in Tasmania no land rights legislation existed. Policy in both Queensland and Western Australia reflected a previous era in Aboriginal affairs administration. In Queensland, the Bjelke-Petersen government was in power and Aboriginal people had no rights whatsoever to make any claim over land. All they could hope for was a tenuous hold over their former reserve lands in the form of a paternalistic 'Deed of Grant in Trust'.

In Western Australia, the Burke Labor government had recently won office and soon after the 1983 federal election appointed a respected barrister, Paul Seaman QC, to produce a report on Aboriginal land rights in Western Australia. The ALP and the trade union movement had sided with Aboriginal people in the Noonkanbah dispute and there was considerable support within the party to act to improve the appalling level of Aboriginal land ownership in Western Australia. In that year, and indeed to this day, there existed a category of land known as Aboriginal reserves. In 1983, however, there were great expectations that change would occur fairly quickly. Mr Seaman's report recommended sweeping reforms in line with the ALP national policy of supporting an Aboriginal right to control mining on their lands. The mining industry, supported by other industry groups, particularly pastoralists, embarked on a vigorous public campaign of opposition. The Burke government, later recognised for its cosy relationship with big business, willingly capitulated and rejected the key recommendations of the Seaman report.

This was the land rights landscape across Australia as Minister Holding developed his proposals for a uniform national land rights scheme in 1984. In early 1985 the government announced a preferred model for national land rights which I believed, even at that time as a new backbench MP, was doomed to fail.

Clyde Holding appointed Charles Perkins to the long-coveted position of Secretary of the Department of Aboriginal Affairs, and together they did their best to defend the government's proposal in the ALP Caucus and in the public domain. As a national model it sought to put in place what was considered a balanced and achievable package that would attempt to minimise the attacks of the mining industry by conferring no right of veto over mining on Aboriginal land. The problem was that the mining industry was insatiable in its demands and was not the least bit appeased by this initiative, which sought to water down ALP policy. They began to orchestrate a media onslaught against the ALP across Australia with an inflammatory and dishonest advertising campaign, as they would later do in an attempt to subvert the Keating government's Mabo response.

The problem for the minister and the government was that there were no significant Aboriginal organisations supporting the government's proposals. The powerful Aboriginal land councils in the Northern Territory embarked on their own national campaign in opposition to the proposed erosion of Aboriginal right of veto in the NT Land Rights Act, which was a part of the government's proposals for the national model. In New South Wales, Tasmania, Victoria and large parts of Queensland, where Aboriginal people had been dispossessed absolutely, their limited ability to make claims over vacant crown land by asserting traditional title meant that there was very little in the proposal for them. The failure to advance a land acquisition fund compounded their alienation from the proposals. No doubt the economic rationalist proponents in the government's leadership at that time would have thwarted such a proposal.

But worst of all, for the government, the WA Labor Premier, Brian Burke, joined in a disgraceful states' rights campaign against the Commonwealth proposals. The ultimate outcome was that the Commonwealth abandoned its proposals on the understanding that the WA government would introduce its own watered-down land rights proposals. Subsequently even these were rejected by the conservatively dominated upper house in Western Australia. Until the Mabo decision and the subsequent native title legislation, the best Aboriginal people in Western Australia could hope for was a 99-year lease of the Aboriginal reserve to the local community, which gave them less security of title than a Perth suburban home-owner. This was a bitter irony because many of the reserves were in the traditional country of Aboriginal people where their descendants had lived for generations.

I think it would be wrong for history to judge Clyde Holding harshly for his role in this period. Ultimately, he was like all Aboriginal Affairs ministers thus far, a non-Cabinet minister as a result of the decision of the Prime Minister of the day, invited into the inner sanctum of Cabinet only for Aboriginal affairs issues where he would have been hopelessly outnumbered by economic rationalists who had very little empathy with Aboriginal aspirations. The whole episode, however, was immensely damaging to the government as a whole and regrettably it was largely a self-inflicted injury.

On a more positive note, Clyde Holding was a reformist minister and was responsible for the first Commonwealth heritage protection legislation, initially enacted as an interim measure in 1984 and confirmed in 1986. Commonwealth legislation was also passed to override the failure of the Victorian upper house to allow Aboriginal ownership of two former Aboriginal reserves, and Commonwealth legislation was

The handover of Jervis Bay National Park
In 1994 the Commonwealth began negotiations with Aboriginal people in the Wreck Bay community adjacent to the Commonwealth-controlled Jervis Bay National Park—now Booderee National Park—to address their long-held aspirations for ownership of the park. The proposal won wide support in the Jervis Bay region, from national environmental organisations and even from conservative local newspapers.

On 14 December 1995, at Green Patch, a very special spot in the Jervis Bay Park, and in a natural grass amphitheatre swollen with hundreds of indigenous people and their many supporters, the park was returned to Aboriginal ownership. At the suggestion of John-Paul Janke, an Aboriginal colleague, I had earlier wandered down to the beach and put huge handfuls of sand in my suit pocket. At the end of my speech, and with the sparkling backdrop of the Jervis Bay waters, I told the crowd that I had a surprise for them. In the manner of Gough Whitlam returning the Gurindji land to Vincent Lingiari, I reached into my pocket and put a handful of sand into the hand of community representative, Phillip McLeod. The symbolism of the event was not lost on the people present.

passed to transfer the Wreck Bay Aboriginal community lands to local ownership adjacent to the Jervis Bay National Park.

Without doubt, the most memorable event during Clyde Holding's term as minister was the return of Uluru (Ayers Rock) and Kata Tjuta (Olgas) to Aboriginal ownership. Both of these magnificent land forms were formerly part of an Aboriginal reserve but were excised from the reserve in 1958, without compensation, let alone consultation, with Aboriginal people, and declared a national park. In 1985, by Commonwealth legislation, the land was transferred to Aboriginal ownership with lease-back and joint management arrangements for the continuing enjoyment of the national park by all Australians. The Coalition campaign in opposition to this highly symbolic and uplifting return was disgraceful. They were supported by the NT government, which waged a national advertising campaign in opposition. The final handback of the title deeds by the Governor-General, Sir Ninian Stephen, was an event that will live in my memory forever. The magnificence of Uluru was silhouetted by the late afternoon sun as we stood in the red earth of central Australia, surrounded by hundreds of Aboriginal and non-Aboriginal Australians united in our celebration of justice done. The model of joint management at Uluru has since won international acclaim and visitors have the opportunity to learn the stories of the Pitjantjatjara and Yankuntjatjara people.

Gerry Hand assumed responsibility for Aboriginal affairs in 1987. Gerry is a gifted negotiator and political strategist, skills well honed from a lifetime of involvement in the Victorian Labor movement. As the key factional organiser and negotiator for the Left in Canberra, he was a very popular choice for the portfolio. He had been a close ally of the NT land councils in their opposition to the uniform national land rights proposals, and he enjoyed the trust of key sections of Aboriginal leadership. It was, of course, during their lobbying and demonstrations against the government's proposals that Aboriginal negotiating skills were refined and would later be invaluably deployed in the aftermath of Mabo.

The most significant reform during Gerry Hand's time as minister was the creation of ATSIC, which I deal with in Chapter 3. The magnitude of this achievement should not be underestimated. As with Clyde Holding, Gerry had to endure unbelievable pressure and vicious personal attacks by the Coalition on himself and his staff. For my part, a most lamentable occurrence during his time as minister was his falling out with Charles Perkins. This occurred during the political bloodbath that enveloped the government during the formation of ATSIC when the Coalition raised a series of alleged accountability issues which then became the subject of inquiries, none of which resulted in any substantial finding against Mr Perkins. In the midst of these accusations, however, tensions developed over Gerry's need to be accountable to the parliament and to have the necessary relationship with the head of his department. The result was that Charles Perkins resigned from the position in 1988.

This was also the bicentennial year when most of the nation celebrated the 200 years of European colonisation. On Australia Day, 26 January, Aboriginal people and their supporters from around the nation held their own protest in Hyde Park in support of Aboriginal rights as their brothers and sisters had done 50 years before. It was also in June 1988 that Prime Minister Hawke visited the Barunga festival and was presented with the historic Barunga Statement.

It was at this festival that Bob Hawke advanced the idea of some kind of treaty. However, at this time there was no government strategy of any kind in place that could conceivably have led to a treaty or for that matter an agreement of any kind. Furthermore, the proposal was met with outrage by the Coalition, who whipped themselves into frenetic point-scoring, asserting that a treaty with indigenous people was inconceivable and that it would divide Australians. All this was despite the ready and comfortable use of the word 'treaty' by political leaders of all political persuasions in Canada, the United States and New Zealand.

But reasoned debate was impossible, and because the necessary groundwork had not been done before Bob's statement at Barunga, the proposal for a treaty was soon put into the too hard basket by the government until this and the associated issues were addressed through the strategic advancement of the reconciliation process.

In 1988 Gerry Hand was also deeply involved in responding to threats by Torres Strait Islander leadership to proclaim their own sovereignty. He visited Torres Strait and the outcome was an inter-departmental committee that sought to address the grievances of the Islanders. Gerry was a very popular minister with Aboriginal people and deservedly so. A hallmark of his work was the respect he showed to the Aboriginal people he dealt with.

In writing this necessarily brief overview of government policies and interaction with the indigenous people of this land, I have passed over many aspects of these relationships because of space. I encourage people who want to understand more to read the increasing number of Aboriginal historians who can educate us all about the true history of our country.

For my part, I hope that this overview contributes to an under-standing of the background to my own time as minister and how the subsequent policies of the Hawke and Keating Labor governments were the result of lessons of history and were built on the achievements of previous national governments. We must always remember that Austra-lian governments only began to address indigenous injustice little more than 30 short years ago. Above all, I believe that it is from Aboriginal people themselves that the driving force for change has emerged. Their voices have been speaking out for 211 years, but it is only in the last 30 that the rest of us have begun to listen.

2

THE RECONCILIATION PROCESS

The process of reconciliation set in motion by the Hawke government has been under sustained attack. But its principles, unanimously adopted by the Australian parliament and enshrined in law in 1991, intentionally laid the foundations for a social movement which I believe cannot be stopped. The resulting groundswell of public opinion and action is a beacon of hope for the achievement of social justice for Australia's indigenous people.

The reconciliation process also provides a tangible framework for a change in relations between indigenous and non-indigenous Australians. That formal process of reconciliation was put in place not only because of the work of people of goodwill in parliament but especially because the wider community rallied behind a concept whose time had come. How that coalition of progressive forces was put together is a story in itself and one which gives some confidence that a genuine and lasting negotiated settlement may one day be reached between the indigenous people of this country and the Australian government.

The Aboriginal affairs portfolio had been a battle zone in Australian public life in the years immediately before I inherited it in April 1990. Gerry Hand had played a principled role in persisting with the establishment of ATSIC, which became a reality on 5 March 1990. The Coalition had turned what should have been a reasoned public debate about the establishment of the Commission into a political bloodbath, Coalition members scoring false points against the government at every opportunity.

The proposal for a treaty or negotiated agreement between indigenous people and the government had been raised by the NAC and the Aboriginal Treaty Committee in the late 1970s. It was raised again by Bob Hawke at Barunga in 1988 but had not progressed because of the implacable opposition of the Coalition. Both Andrew Peacock and John Howard, as leaders of the Liberal Party, had campaigned against the very concept of a treaty.

From day one in the job, my central goal as minister was to set up a political agenda and framework for change that would elevate the aspirations of indigenous people to a central place in the national consciousness and debate in the lead-up to the centenary of Australian nationhood in 2001. The challenges were formidable. The concept of a reconciliation process had no substantial base of support within the Coalition and, indeed, among Aboriginal and Torres Strait Islander people. Even in the Labor Party there was virtually no support, though the concept of a national reconciliation (in general terms with no specific reference to Aboriginal affairs) had been a central part of Bob Hawke's 1983 election platform. Within the ALP, political discussion still focused narrowly on some kind of treaty but with no political strategy developed to achieve the outcome.

Charles Rowley's inspiring book *Recovery: The Politics of Aboriginal Reform*, a copy of which was given to me by a local schoolteacher soon after I became minister, traces the development of the aspirations of indigenous people for social justice, including a history of the political demand for some kind of treaty or formal document and the struggle for social justice. It concludes:

> There must be, among our political leaders, people with the capacity to
> undertake this major national task. Australians may yet be fortunate to
> find again, as in other crises, leaders with guts and an interest in
> justice, prepared to meet propagandist fire with fire and fight for an
> Aboriginal recovery. This is not a job for saints, but for politicians with
> both vision and guile. It requires also a real sense of responsibility for
> consequences, so that (to quote Weber again) the person with 'the
> calling for politics . . . somewhere reaches the point where he says
> "Here I stand: I can do no other".'

I had no illusions of self-importance or personal grandeur, but after reading this passage I felt an unstoppable conviction that I had a responsibility to take up that challenge. The task would involve more than just carrying the hearts and minds of my own party. Cross-party support for the reconciliation process would be crucial in achieving the necessary shift in Australian public opinion. The 1967 referendum voted for a change in the Constitution to confer on the Commonwealth a law-making power in Aboriginal affairs. It was a turning point in Australian history. It had been achieved with a record-breaking majority for two reasons: it was a just cause, and it had unanimous support in parliament, underpinned by a community-based campaign for reform.

But such cross-party support was not to be sought at the expense of principle. It had to be achieved on indigenous terms. There were three key aspirations which had to be safeguarded at all costs and which became for me the non-negotiable foundation of the reconciliation process.

First, the lingering deep prejudice against Aboriginal and Torres Strait Islander people was still deeply ingrained in too many sections of the Australian community. I had seen it in my own upbringing in country New South Wales. It was clear that a key part of the reconciliation process had to be an effective national program to combat racism. Not only did much more have to be done in schools but significant resources needed to be directed towards the wider community. I had no doubt that such an initiative would, over time, contribute to a climate of understanding and respect for the original inhabitants of this country. Such a campaign had also been a longstanding demand of indigenous people.

The first objective of the reconciliation process would therefore be to educate non-indigenous Australians about Aboriginal and Torres Strait Islander history and culture, the extent of the disadvantages these people still experienced, and the need to address indigenous human rights as a central objective of the reconciliation process. Above all, the educational and public awareness strategy would contribute to building a community-based movement for reconciliation and indigenous social justice.

A second objective was to put on the nation's public policy agenda the issue of some formal document or agreement as one of the outcomes of the reconciliation process. On the indigenous side, though there had been repeated calls for a treaty, no serious discussion had taken place about what the terms of such a document might be or, an even tougher question, who would negotiate an agreement. The focus of the debate had to be shifted from a preoccupation with the word 'treaty' as the title of the agreement to its form and content. The strategy also had to include a consultation and reporting process on the desirability of some formal document of reconciliation (by whatever name), the possible terms of such a document, and how it might come about.

Third, the reconciliation process was intended to be the driving force for the nation to address indigenous aspirations, human rights and social justice. A political movement in support of these aspirations had to be built. The lack of such effective and organised support had been a crucial factor in the success of the Australian mining industry and the WA Labor government in killing off the proposed national land rights legislation in the mid-1980s. From the beginning it was stressed that there can be no reconciliation without justice, a sentiment that the present Governor-General, Sir William Deane, articulates with conviction.

I knew that if we got the unanimous support of parliament for the initiative, that in itself would send a powerful message to the nation of the importance of reconciliation. When politicians are involved in mindless point-scoring about Aboriginal and Torres Strait Islander affairs the people who lose out are indigenous people themselves—people who in their daily lives still endure prejudice and lack of respect for their rights. The results and aftermath of the 1996 election confirmed the indisputable truth of this view.

In May 1990, a month after my appointment, our portfolio's contribution to the Governor-General's speech for the opening of parliament said:

> The Government is committed to playing an educative and leadership role in bringing about a deeper understanding on the part of non-Aboriginal Australians of the culture, past dispossession and continuing disadvantage suffered by Aboriginal and Torres Strait Islander people.
>
> The Government also remains committed to a genuine reconciliation with Australia's indigenous people. In particular, it will be seeking wide community support and bipartisan political endorsement of an instrument of reconciliation, variously referred to as a treaty or compact, between Aboriginal and Torres Strait Islander Australians and the wider community.

The speech also said that the 'form and content of such a document . . . cannot be finalised until extensive consultation is initiated with Aboriginal and Torres Strait Islander people and with other Australians'.

To prepare the Coalition for this approach, Bob Hawke wrote to Dr John Hewson, the new Opposition Leader, of the government's wish for a more bipartisan approach in indigenous affairs and put forward the idea of an instrument of reconciliation. He made it clear that the government was not necessarily wedded to the word 'treaty': 'What I believe is important is that there be a process of reconciliation. In my view the consultation process will be as important as the eventual outcome. But there is little hope of a worthwhile outcome, even to consultations, without the support of the majority of Australians'. He expressed his hope 'that the Coalition in any response will leave open the possibility of a bipartisan approach'. The letter was sent to the Australian Democrats and to premiers, leaders of the Opposition and of other parties in all states and territories. Nick Greiner, then NSW Liberal Premier, was one of the first to respond positively.

Further pressure was put on the Coalition to adopt a more bipartisan approach to indigenous affairs. John Hewson was urged to adopt the same approach as Premier Greiner. We publicly assured Dr Hewson of our sincerity on the issue and reminded people that it was Labor support for the Coalition government that had contributed to the overwhelming result in the 1967 referendum.

Strong letters of support for this approach were written by the leaders of most Australian churches during this period. The editorial writers of major newspapers welcomed the new approach and the Melbourne *Age* concluded that 'there is also a practical political case for bipartisanship; neither party will gain if the Aboriginal issue is allowed to become an increasing cause of internal division and external embarrassment'. David Gill, general secretary of the Australian Council of Churches, wrote to me: 'One disappointment of the churches has been the breakdown in the federal parliament of the past bipartisan support for Aboriginal issues. I wish to commend you for your initiative in seeking bipartisan support for an instrument of reconciliation'. This response was typical of the solidarity received from church leaders and from so many other community leaders. The success of the new approach was quite remarkable.

Letters of support for the reconciliation concept came from the most surprising sources. The Queensland National Party Leader of the Opposition, Russell Cooper, wrote: 'There is much to learn from our indigenous people, in particular, their oneness with the land, its plants and animals—a firmly balanced ecosystem to which our latter day inhabitants cannot aspire . . . I can assure you of the Queensland National Party's cooperation with the undertaking and await your further advice'. I almost fell out of my chair upon reading this letter.

John Hewson's reply was eagerly awaited. When it came, it bore the marks of Michael Wooldridge's guiding hand. Michael had been appointed the Shadow Minister for Aboriginal Affairs after the 1990 election and was to play a very constructive role in the coming year. The tenor of the reply, indicating a willingness to put some of the unproductive divisions aside, was very encouraging. The Opposition did not rule out eventual support for some kind of formal document or instrument of reconciliation but it 'remained to be convinced' on the issue. The fact that they had not slammed the door on it was a dramatic shift from the hostile and aggressive approach of much of the previous parliament.

This shift in Coalition policy, however, was only the first step on what was to be a very long road towards the unanimous passage of the legislation through parliament, necessary to establish the reconciliation process on a secure basis. At this point, having been in office for only a few months, I had no idea how to craft the detail of the initiative and picked the brains of a great many people, indigenous and non-indigenous alike. The challenge was to devise a process that would enjoy the support of both indigenous and non-indigenous opinion leaders and would keep faith absolutely with indigenous aspirations. There were some treasured moments during the remainder of 1990 and the early parts of 1991, in the spontaneous expressions of support for the concepts we were developing. It was truly a process whose time had come.

Many events and many people shaped my thinking during that period. On 1 June 1990 I attended the handback of Meripah Station, the first pastoral property in Queensland to be openly transferred to Aboriginal interests. Meripah Station was adjacent to Archer Bend National Park, a former pastoral property whose transfer to Aboriginal ownership had been blocked by the Bjelke-Petersen government.

The Meripah handback was a simple affair. Attending were the chairperson of ATSIC, Lois O'Donoghue, the Queensland Minister for Family Services and Aboriginal and Islander Affairs, Anne Warner, the media and a small crowd of very proud Aboriginal people, among them John Koowarta. A wiry, battle-scarred Aboriginal man called Woompi Keppell, stepped up to receive the title to Meripah Station on behalf of his people. He made a speech that would have made Nelson Mandela proud:

> I welcome to everyone that here today.
>
> I'm going to tell you something what's been happening on this land here. This is the footprint from my old people, that they been living this land. You see, all these houses here, been nothing here; all Aborigine camp right along here. Just down here, about quarter of a mile down here, full Aborigine camp, that's main camp . . .
>
> . . . You know, I would say this is the land what we been asking Government, or we asking some department, can we get our land back. What for? What we worry, what we got in our mind, what we got in our heart. We think from our grandfathers, we think from our father and from our mother, still in my heart. When I come here, I made this place from my father and mother, even from my uncle and cousin. Lot been get sent away from here—police caught them—to Palm Island. They all died, finished.
>
> Now I think there's a great world to us today. I much appreciate that we all here from all directions. I do understand to the white people and I do understand to my own people. I am talking with the low hearted, with everyone. I recognise police and I recognise everybody, even my own people. You know, you gotta think how we going to cooperate on this country or whatsoever. Are we going to cooperate on the world or on the country? How we going to come to a relationship?

Woompi's speech captured and reinforced so much of what I believed and hoped to achieve through the reconciliation process. The essential question the nation had to face was the one he asked: how are we going to cooperate and how are we going to come to a relationship?

In outlining the development of the reconciliation process, I acknowledge the extensive work already done on these issues by many indigenous and non-indigenous Australians. The churches have been longstanding proponents of a reconciliation concept, and there have been those who put forward invaluable models of how a process might work. Fr Frank Brennan in particular made a useful contribution, though I disagreed with him on several fundamental issues. Together with Professor James Crawford, he proposed the establishment of an Aboriginal Recognition Commission with a focus on dealing with grievances put forward by Aboriginal people.

I was also particularly committed to the view that the government should not at this time in the nation's history close off options on the parameters or contents of some document of reconciliation or on the process itself. There had to be open and genuine consultation and negotiation.

First, it was important to use the decade leading to the 2001 centenary for all it was worth to advance the struggle for indigenous rights. The 1988 Bicentenary 'protests' had been essentially just that, a response to the non-indigenous agenda. There had been very little emphasis in the lead-up to 1988 on the need to address indigenous aspirations as a precondition to celebrating the bicentenary. Our strategy was to contribute to the political momentum of the struggle for indigenous rights by setting up a process that would finish on 1 January 2001 and that would put considerable national and international pressure on the nation to address the human rights of indigenous people as a precondition of any proper celebration of Australian nationhood in 2001. Second, the process had to be more than some grievance procedure. We had to mount a campaign in the wider community in support of indigenous rights and to build bridges of understanding about indigenous issues and people.

It became clear that any reconciliation process should have its key objectives and processes enshrined in legislation that would survive a change in government. During the early period of the Hawke government, Lionel Bowen, the respected Deputy Prime Minister and Attorney-General, had attempted a process of constitutional change through the establishment of the Constitutional Commission. This group of experts, drawn from a wide spectrum of the community, carried out extensive public consultation on proposals for constitutional change and ultimately advocated sweeping reforms. But the attempt failed because the non-government political parties were not locked into the process and because the commission was set up by administrative decision, not enshrined in legislation, which meant that its work never achieved the necessary cross-party support.

In the non-indigenous community among the many people I talked with were former ministers responsible for Aboriginal affairs—Fred Chaney, Peter Baume, Clyde Holding, Gerry Hand and Billy Wentworth. A chance meeting and conversation with Stephen Hawke helped clarify one particular issue. A council of indigenous people to guide the reconciliation process nationally was being explored, but Stephen supported the idea of a national council of both indigenous and non-indigenous people who would work together to advance reconciliation, and this conversation confirmed my developing view.

But it was in the indigenous community that the political challenge was greatest. Aboriginal and Torres Strait Islander people, having been sold down the river so often, were naturally suspicious of what was being advocated. It was a tough job to persuade them of our determination to keep faith with their aspirations. A potential turning point was a meeting of the Federation of Land Councils held at Ja Ja in the Northern Territory, which is adjacent to the site of the proposed Jabiluka Uranium Mine (approved by the Howard government in 1999). At that meeting in July 1990 was the most extraordinarily diverse group of indigenous opinion leaders from around Australia, ranging from Galarrwuy Yunupingu, chair of the Northern Land Council (NLC), to Michael Mansell from Tasmania. In a shaded, open-air meeting space, surrounded by the Kakadu landscape, I was on my feet for two hours talking nonstop and answering questions about the proposals.

When I was called back the next day, Geoff Clarke, from Framlingham, Victoria, speaking on behalf of the meeting, said it 'liked' what was said but wanted to reserve its judgment. I had gone into the lion's den and emerged relatively unscathed and, indeed, fortified.

In October 1990 Bob Hawke endorsed, virtually without amendment, the specific proposals put to him. But the proposal for the establishment of a Council for Aboriginal Reconciliation 'and Justice' was apparently seen by his advisers as over the top. The title was changed to the Council for Aboriginal Reconciliation. After this I always mentioned justice when I spoke on 'reconciliation', and the concept was later enshrined in the legislation establishing the Council. The two principles were, and remain, inseparable, as Sir William Deane keeps pointing out. Indeed, the success or otherwise of the reconciliation process will be substantially judged on whether or not the national government delivers on the social justice objective of the process. The jury is still out on this question, and ever more regrettably so since the election of the Howard government.

In November 1990 Bob Hawke wrote to the Leader of the Opposition, building on the basis of already developing cross-party support and saying that the government welcomed the fact that the Coalition had not ruled out some formal instrument of reconciliation.

A Cabinet submission was prepared embodying the essential elements of the proposal. In December Cabinet endorsed without dissent and with little debate the submission proposing the establishment, by legislation, of a Council for Aboriginal Reconciliation with a preamble that included a social justice and human rights objective in the reconciliation process. Cabinet also endorsed the proposal for an extensive process of public consultation with both Aboriginal and Torres Strait Islander people and the wider community.

Bob Hawke and I jointly issued a statement announcing the government's in-principle support for the process of reconciliation. A discussion paper was prepared and distributed the length and breadth of the country. With the most limited exceptions, it was to be endorsed by both indigenous and non-indigenous people as the basis for the reconciliation process. The paper again stressed the three elements of the process essential for keeping faith with indigenous aspirations: the public awareness campaign, and the commitments to social justice and to setting up a process for reaching some formal document as a formal basis for reconciliation. It was proposed that legislation lock in the process until 1 January 2001 and establish a 25-person Council for Aboriginal Reconciliation chaired by an Aboriginal person and representing both indigenous and non-indigenous Australians. Members would include the ATSIC chair and deputy chair and church, business, trade union, ethnic and other community leaders. The Council would bring together Australians publicly committed to advancing the interests of Aboriginal and Torres Strait Islander people and capable of delivering support for the reconciliation process from significant sections of the community. It was also proposed that the leaders of the Opposition and the Australian Democrats be consulted on the appointment of the members of the council, as would indigenous people.

Again we had strong support from the churches. Even before the end of December 1990, Rev. Gregor Henderson, general secretary of the Uniting Church, had expressed support for the process and urged each of the seven state and territory church synods to come out publicly urging the Coalition to support the process. John Hewson issued a cautiously worded statement—the Opposition was prepared to discuss the government's proposals. We were still a very long way from the unanimous passage of the legislation through parliament.

In May 1991 the two very senior Anglican church leaders in Australia publicly declared their support for the detail of the reconciliation process and called on the federal Opposition to give the process their support. In a joint statement, Keith Rayner and Donald Robinson, Archbishops of Melbourne and Sydney, said that real progress in granting land rights and setting and meeting goals for improvements in Aboriginal health, education, housing and employment was central to the integrity of the reconciliation process.

And so it went on. Letter after letter of support was forthcoming for the detail of the proposed process of reconciliation set out in the discussion paper. Even the Girl Guides' Association of Australia came out in support, as did a number of Australia's major corporations. Martin Ferguson, then president of the ACTU, helped greatly by building support for the process within the trade union movement.

A particular coup was the letter of support, in principle, for the process signed by the president of the National Farmers' Federation (NFF), John Allright; and there was a further letter of support from the Confederation of Australian Industry. I travelled the length and breadth of the country with my media adviser, Paul Willoughby, not only speaking to every available media outlet but also going behind the scenes to talk to editorial executives in every major newspaper in the country, with the exception of the *Courier Mail* and the *Financial Review* and then only because we ran out of time. The result was an active interest in the process and, virtually without exception, editorials in support of it calling for cross-party support.

It was fundamental to the success of the reconciliation process that it enjoy the overwhelming support of indigenous people as manifested through their elected representatives. I did everything in my power to canvass the widest range of indigenous opinion. As in any political campaign, there are make-or-break moments. One such moment was when the proposals were taken to a full meeting of the Central Land Council (CLC), held on a day when federal parliament was also meeting. The stakes were very high. If this highly respected and representative Aboriginal organisation were to give the thumbs down to the proposal, it would have been the end of all we were trying to achieve.

The day's events were thus of great political significance. I got leave from parliament and flew to Alice Springs and Hermannsburg and then went by four-wheel drive to a remote place further east where the full CLC was meeting. It was a world away from Canberra. The meeting was chaired by the CLC's chair, David Long, a man whose confidence I had already gained through my work with him on NT land rights issues. The meeting was attended by over 100 representatives from Aboriginal communities throughout central Australia and my words were translated into three Aboriginal languages. People sat around on the ground in groups under a vast tarpaulin. Coincidentally, there was an ABC *Four Corners* TV crew at the meeting making what turned out to be an unremarkable program on Aboriginal health, but no amount of persuasion on my part could convince them to film those magnificent moments in Australian history.

I spoke in great detail about what would be involved in the reconciliation process. In hindsight I think the turning point came when I spoke about the need for a public awareness campaign on indigenous issues. Indigenous people are crying out for non-indigenous people to be educated about their history and culture. All of them have felt the discrimination that results from the crushing ignorance of generations of non-indigenous Australians, who have been told nothing in their school years about indigenous history, culture and aspirations.

I explained that a few weeks before at Captain Cook's Cottage in Melbourne with my daughter Jade I had seen a picture of Captain Cook 'discovering' Australia, as if Australia had never existed before and no one had been there when Cook arrived. There were pictures of rock wallabies but none of Aboriginal people. I said that these continuing false portrayals of Australian history needed to be addressed as an essential part of the reconciliation process. People appeared genuinely moved by this story.

After hours of explanation and questioning, Gus Williams, a well-known Aboriginal country singer from Hermannsburg, moved support from the CLC for the proposals, which were then unanimously adopted.

I had mentioned to David Long and to the CLC director, David Ross, that by 9.30 that night I would be back in Canberra to attend a Cabinet meeting at which a further submission to advance the reconciliation process would be put forward. They gave me a handful of red earth to take with me as a sign of solidarity. During the Cabinet meeting that night, I quietly and privately put some of it beside my papers on the Cabinet table as a gesture of acknowledgement of the responsibility I felt.

The meetings continued over the succeeding months, high-pressured and with high stakes, but the result was that by the time the reconciliation legislation reached parliament there was no significant indigenous opposition to what was being proposed. In fact there was very wide support.

The Coalition had been put into the position where they had little political option but to support the process. To have done otherwise would have left them isolated. This is not to diminish Michael Wooldridge's efforts to get Coalition support for the reconciliation process. To use his own words, later spoken in the debate on the Native Title Act,

> I personally travelled the country and visited every Liberal Party and National Party state and territory leader in Australia. I discussed our position with them. I asked for their views, I argued, I cajoled and I begged. I took a submission back to shadow cabinet. We discussed it again in the party room. All the time, the Minister for Aboriginal Affairs and I would talk, discuss our differences, see where there was common ground and see where there were problems. I drank his whisky; he drank my red wine.

I found Michael to be a person of integrity who, while protecting the interests of his party, was prepared to negotiate in good faith on the implementation of shared objectives.

Before the legislation went to parliament, however, its precise terms had to be negotiated with the ATSIC Board of Commissioners. They made it clear that it was crucial to them that the word 'treaty' was not excluded from the possible agenda of indigenous aspirations. I told them that while the Coalition did not support the use of that word, it was in everyday current use in Canada by conservative politicians and was certainly not excluded by the terms of the reconciliation legislation. I stressed, however, that it was important that the debate move on from a narrow focus on the name of the document to more substantive issues like what might be in the document and who might negotiate it. On that basis the board gave their support to take the proposal forward to parliament. Again, had they not done this it would have been impossible to proceed. A hallmark of the relationship between Aboriginal people and the government at this time was one of seeking negotiations in a climate of mutual respect.

The Council for Aboriginal Reconciliation Bill 1991 was introduced into the House of Representatives on 31 May 1991 and debated on 5 June. When it was passed in the early hours of the morning with unanimous support, Michael Wooldridge extended his hand and we shook hands across the table. Sadly, virtually no media reported the event in any substance at the time. It was, however, a real achievement for parliament and confirms my long-term faith in people. The Bill passed through the Senate on 16 April 1991, and came into force on Monday, 2 September 1991.

The appointment of each member of the Council for Aboriginal Reconciliation was particularly challenging because, as the legislation required, they had to win widespread Aboriginal and Torres Strait Islander support as well as support from Labor, the Coalition, and the Democrats. It was necessary to ensure the appointment of exceptionally talented people who had the greatest collective capacity to build support for the reconciliation process in the Australian community.

The first appointments were Patrick Dodson (chair), Sir Ronald Wilson (deputy chair), Archie Barton AM, Sol Bellear, Essie Coffey OAM, Robert Champion de Crespigny, Ted Egan AM, Rick Farley, Jennie George, Mary Graham, Bill Hollingsworth, Senator Cheryl Kernot, Bill Lowah, Ray Martin, Allan Mosby, Rose Murray, Peter Nugent MP, Lois O'Donoghue CBE AM, Senator Margaret Reynolds, Wenten Rubuntja, Esmeralda Saunders, Helen Sham-Ho MLC, Ian Spicer, Alma Stackhouse OAM, and Galarrwuy Yunupingu AM.

The most crucial appointment was that of chairperson. The person proposed, Patrick Dodson, was the most difficult to persuade. Patrick was a highly respected Aboriginal person, a former Catholic priest, director of the CLC, and subsequently Aboriginal Deaths in Custody Royal Commissioner and director of the Kimberley Land Council. Anybody who knew Patrick's record and the agenda of the reconciliation process knew that he was the person to take the position. My best efforts at persuasion left his agreement unresolved and, much to my despair, he went fishing. The Prime Minister's personal phone call finally secured his agreement.

The excitement of appointing the Council was marred by a painful incident at the press conference at which the appointments were to be announced. I was walking towards the venue, the Western Australian Museum, with Patrick Dodson, Sir Ronald Wilson and Michael Wooldridge. We were met by Robert Bropho, an Aboriginal man whose protests against the redevelopment of the Swan Brewery had made him a very public figure in Western Australia. As we entered the building, with the others looking on, Robert Bropho barred my progress and stood about one foot from my face in front of every TV network in the country screaming abuse at me in an attempt to get publicity for his cause.

It was one of the most devastating political experiences of my life. There was nothing I could do but remain calm and attempt to start a dialogue, knowing that the evening TV news would not focus on the strength of cross-party and indigenous commitment to the reconciliation process but on the confrontation during the day's events. Eventually, after some peacemaking negotiation during which I undertook to go to Mr Bropho's base at the Lockridge Camp Site on the outskirts of Perth, we successfully completed the launch of the Council. I kept my promise and the next day spent about three hours with Mr Bropho and his community. I don't think I satisfied his concerns, but it was a very productive meeting and confirmed the importance of patient negotiations between government representatives and indigenous people.

The Barunga Statement

We the indigenous owners and occupiers of Australia call on the Australian Government and people to recognise our rights:

- to self-determination and self-management including the freedom to pursue our own economic, social, religious and cultural development;
- to permanent control and enjoyment of our ancestral lands;
- to compensation for the loss of use of lands, there having been no extinction of original title;
- to protection and control of access to our sacred sites, sacred objects, artefacts, designs, knowledge and works of art;
- to the return of the remains of our ancestors for burial in accordance with our traditions;
- to respect for and promotion of our Aboriginal identity, including the cultural, linguistic, religious and historical aspects, including the right to be educated in our own languages, and in our own culture and history;
- in accordance with the Universal Declaration of Human Rights, the International Covenant on Economic, Social and Cultural Rights, the International Covenant on Civil and Political Rights, and the International Convention on the Elimination of All Forms of Racial Discrimination, including rights to life, liberty, security of person, food, clothing, housing, medical care, education and employment opportunities, necessary social services and other basic human rights.

We call on the Commonwealth Parliament to pass laws providing:

- a national elected Aboriginal and Islander organisation to oversee Aboriginal and Islander affairs;
- a national system of land rights;
- a police and justice system which recognises our customary laws and frees us from discrimination and any activity which may threaten our identity or security, interfere with our freedom of expression or association, or otherwise prevent our full enjoyment and exercise of universally recognised human rights and fundamental freedoms.

We call on the Australian Government to support Aborigines in the development of an International Declaration of Principles for Indigenous Rights, leading to an International Covenant.

And we call on the Commonwealth Parliament to negotiate with us a Treaty or Compact recognising our prior ownership, continued occupation and sovereignty and affirming our human rights and freedoms.

Another event in Australian politics and public life affecting the reconciliation process occurred on Friday, 20 December 1991, on the last day and at the last event in the prime ministership of Bob Hawke. The previous day Paul Keating had successfully challenged his leadership and Bob was to go out to Yarralumla to resign as Prime Minister, with Paul to be sworn in later that day. The night before, after the Caucus vote, there was a party, or rather a wake, in the Cabinet rooms hosted by Bob, which was crowded with hundreds of people from the media, parliament and Labor staffers. It was a very sad affair for many, but Paul Willoughby and I realised there was still one job to be done before Bob finally terminated his commission.

Back on 12 June 1988, a very famous painting by Aboriginal people from the Northern Territory had been presented to Bob Hawke at the Barunga Sports and Cultural Festival. Attached to the painting were a series of Aboriginal demands that have become known as the Barunga Statement, a document of great political significance to Aboriginal people across Australia. The statement was presented to the Prime Minister by the chairpersons of the Central and Northern Land Councils, Wenten Rubuntja and Galarrwuy Yunupingu, and among its demands was a call for a treaty. The paintings surrounding the statement are a reminder of where the words originate—they are stories of the land. The work calls on Aboriginal people to come together to celebrate their culture.

When he received the Barunga Statement on 12 June 1988, Bob Hawke promised to display it in Parliament House in Canberra, saying it would then be there 'for whoever is the Prime Minister of this country, not only to see but to understand and also to honour'.

While the treaty debate became a subject of deep political division in 1988, the Barunga Statement retained its great significance to Aboriginal people, but it had never been hung in Parliament House as promised because of a dispute between senior Aboriginal people in the Northern Territory over the cultural appropriateness of displaying one of its panels. When this was resolved by repainting the panel (in the backyard of Kevin Keeffe, one of my advisers), the work was available for hanging at Parliament House, awaiting a suitable occasion.

Now not only the opportunity but the necessity to hang the painting arose as Bob Hawke lived out his last hours as Prime Minister of Australia. He agreed to perform the deed and we put out a promotional news release that night for the event the next day.

The hanging of the Barunga painting can be dismissed by cynics as staged and inconsequential, but for those of us who shared a commitment to Labor and to the Aboriginal cause, it was an event of great substance. I thought of it then, and I do now, as Bob passing the baton to Paul Keating, who was to be sworn in as Prime Minister later that morning. I think my chief motive for being involved in the event was to lay it on the line that the party and Aboriginal people expected that leadership from Paul Keating.

That day Bob Hawke, in front of a very large crowd, reminded people what he had said about displaying the statement at Parliament House:

> It is indeed very fitting indeed that my last official act as Prime Minister is to hang the Statement in Parliament House. This is no ordinary ceremony because what we're about is symbolising the commitment of my Government . . . to the indigenous people of Australia and its presence here calls on those . . . who follow me. It demands of them that they continue efforts to find solutions to the . . . abundant problems which still face the Aboriginal people of this country. . .
>
> What we've got to understand is that if you are really serious in this country as you come to the end of this century, the first century of our existence as a nation, and you want proudly to take Australia into the 21st century there is no chance that you are going to be able to do that unless you do have a reconciliation. Personally I would like to see that embodied in a document. I think it is infinitely more preferable that we have the courage to do that but it is also true that the document itself in one sense is not the important thing. The important thing is what is in our minds and in our hearts. . .

With the change of leadership of the ALP and the beginning of Paul Keating's prime ministership, the cross-party cooperation in indigenous affairs continued. This was reflected in a motion the government moved in the House of Representatives on 27 May 1992, on the 25th anniversary of the 1967 referendum. The motion was also moved in the Senate and passed unanimously. It expressed support for the reconciliation process and the government's response to the Royal Commission into Aboriginal Deaths in Custody and included a central tenet of support for the principle of self-determination. May 27 is an important date, the significance of which will increasingly be understood in Australian history. This significance was further deepened by the 1997 Reconciliation Convention in Melbourne held on the 30th anniversary of the referendum.

Debate on the motion acknowledged the history of the 1967 referendum proposal and the contribution of people from both sides of politics and from the community to its passage through parliament and then to the successful referendum. The passage of that referendum is the foundation of Commonwealth action in Aboriginal affairs. Without that change to the Constitution there would have been no legal or constitutional capacity for the national parliament to make any laws directed towards Aboriginal people.

There are some essential lessons to be drawn from that successful campaign for Aboriginal rights:

- The combined activity of MPs and community organisations concerned with Aboriginal people profoundly shaped and influenced the then government's position and that of the Opposition.
- Issues of justice for indigenous Australians ought to transcend party-political point-scoring.
- Nothing less than our identity as a nation and place in the world are at stake.
- Federal parliament has a consequent moral and political responsibility to act to redress Aboriginal disadvantage and to seek to meet Aboriginal aspirations.

If parliamentarians would only listen to the voices of indigenous Australians and put aside differences and speak with one voice, then that true leadership would of itself send a powerful message to the wider community. These lessons are of enormous contemporary importance.

The *Council for Aboriginal Reconciliation Act 1991* required the Council to be reappointed every three years. Sir Ronald Wilson had indicated that he did not wish to serve a further term and I was instinctively drawn to Ian Viner, former Liberal Minister for Aboriginal Affairs, as an alternative appointment. I had met him only twice before, once when I had spoken to him briefly at a meeting of retired parliamentary members at Parliament House, and once at a meeting during the Mabo debate in the Perth Town Hall in 1993. It was at that meeting that he had spoken so strongly in support of 'human rights, not states' rights', in his open advocacy of the recognition of indigenous rights in the aftermath of the Mabo decision. He accepted the appointment as the Council's deputy chair and has continued to speak out on issues of principle to further the reconciliation process.

Members of the second Council for Aboriginal Reconciliation were Patrick Dodson (chair), Ian Viner QC (deputy chair), Archie Barton AM,

The Reconciliation and Schooling Strategy

From 1990 to 1993 Aboriginal and Torres Strait Islander education came under my portfolio. An important initiative promoted during that time—and driven relentlessly by Howard Glenn from my office—was the Reconciliation and Schooling Strategy, which provided a focus for the reconciliation initiatives in the education system. Several initiatives in that strategy have not been adequately followed up:

- national collaborative curriculum schemes to improve the quality of in-service training of teachers of Aboriginal studies;
- the pre-service training of teachers;
- the Sister Schools scheme, which encourages contact between students of predominantly non-Aboriginal schools and Aboriginal schools;
- projects to help Aboriginal school communities research and prepare local histories for use in the Aboriginal studies curriculum; and
- initiatives to encourage Aboriginal community leaders to visit schools and talk to students.

The Prime Minister ought to be leading the campaign at heads of government level to overcome indigenous disadvantage in education.

Julie Brockman, Linda Burney, Robert Champion de Crespigny, Rick Farley, Jennie George, Ian Gray, Jackie Huggins, Senator Cheryl Kernot, Marcia Langton AM, Bill Lowah, Ray Martin, Peter Nugent MP, Lois O'Donoghue CBE AM, Charles Perkins AO, Senator Margaret Reynolds, Helen Sham-Ho MLC, Ian Spicer, Alma Stackhouse OAM, Pedro Stephen, Marjorie Thorpe, Gus Williams, and Galarrwuy Yunupingu AM. Gus Williams was subsequently replaced by Wenten Rubuntja, who had been a member of the first Council.

The new members reflected the government's determination to take the Council and the reconciliation process to a new level in the aftermath of Mabo and to accelerate the pace of the process.

When the Council's second term came to an end, John Howard's government exercised its prerogative to change the membership, as is their right. Tragically, however, Patrick Dodson was not reappointed as chair and was replaced by Evelyn Scott. While in no way critical of Evelyn Scott, many believe that the continuing appointment of Pat Dodson would have provided the necessary continuity and given the

wider community confidence that the government remained committed to the process.

Buck-passing between state and federal governments is a pitiful
excuse for the failure of government to act on the reconciliation
process's social justice agenda. Unless action is taken with Commonwealth leadership to address, or at least legislatively lock in commitment
to address, indigenous human rights and disadvantage on a wide range
of issues—education, health, infrastructure, heritage protection, law
and justice—there will be no proper national celebration of the centenary of Australian federation. Even before the 1996 election, I was
pessimistic about Labor's commitment to deliver on the social justice
agenda. In 1995 I had been through the political fight of the 1995/96
Budget and had unsuccessfully sought to convince Cabinet to take
significant initiatives to address indigenous health and living conditions
through a Centenary of Federation Infrastructure Project. But at least
the Keating government was committed to implementing the unfinished
Mabo response in the form of a third-stage social justice package.

In the aftermath of the 1996 election of a Coalition government
prepared to use indigenous people as a political football, the prospects
for reconciliation became abysmal. It gives me no joy to record this
fact. Nothing would give me more pride in my country and boost my
faith in humanity than a Howard government which was prepared to
show both a genuine respect and a commitment to negotiate honestly
and openly with Australia's indigenous people.

Australians cannot say they have not been warned. At the beginning of National Aboriginal and Torres Strait Islander week in July
1996, Sir William Deane reminded the nation that disadvantages in
Aboriginal communities must be more effectively addressed in the
'four and a half years leading to the centenary of our nation than they
have been in the ninety five and a half years that have passed since
Federation. Unless it is more effectively addressed true reconciliation
with Aboriginal peoples will be unlikely and Australia will remain a
diminished nation as it enters its second century'.

Federal parliament must be continually reminded by concerned
Australians that in 1991 it voted unanimously to pass the legislation
starting the reconciliation process. That legislation provides that,

> as a part of the reconciliation process, the Commonwealth will seek an
> ongoing national commitment from governments at all levels to
> cooperate and coordinate with the Aboriginal and Torres Strait Islander
> Commission as appropriate to address progressively Aboriginal
> disadvantage and aspirations in relation to land, housing, law and
> justice, cultural heritage, education, employment, health, infrastructure,

economic development and any other relevant matters in the decade leading to the centenary of federation, 2001.

Significant steps to implement this agenda were taken by the Keating government through its first- and second-stage response to Mabo: the Native Title Act and the establishment of the National Land Fund. The Howard government, however, has abandoned the social justice package that Labor proposed as its third-stage response. If the Coalition fails to act it becomes ever more imperative that the federal Opposition commit themselves to the unfinished business of the social justice package. Kim Beazley is an honourable and sensitive person who has the capacity to be a great Australian prime minister, but an important part of Labor's constituency wants to know whether Kim and an alternative Labor government are prepared to honour this ALP commitment. Without such a commitment to fundamental reforms to achieve an equitable distribution of resources, many Aboriginal people will continue to be condemned to third world conditions.

In the last days of May 1997 in Melbourne, about 2000 delegates, indigenous and non-indigenous, gathered for the Australian Reconciliation Convention. The convention was not only addressed by both Prime Minister Howard and Opposition Leader Kim Beazley but perhaps more significantly, by Aboriginal and Torres Strait Islander leaders from across Australia. It dominated media reports for days and was widely recognised as a turning of the tide of public debate against the attacks on indigenous rights by the Howard government and others.

At the end of the convention participants from all walks of life issued a united call to the nation, affirming that 'reconciliation between Australia's indigenous peoples and other Australians is central to the renewal of this nation as a harmonious and just society which lives out its ethos as a fair go for all; and until we achieve such a reconciliation the nation will remain diminished'. The statement declared that reconciliation and renewal of the nation can only be achieved through a 'peoples movement to make reconciliation a reality'.

There has been a small glimmer of hope of a more enlightened approach on the part of the Howard government. John Howard at least admitted, before the last federal election, that the angry and provocative tone of his speech to the Reconciliation Convention in Melbourne in May 1997 was a mistake. Despite reappointing Senator Herron as Minister for Aboriginal and Torres Strait Islander Affairs after the 1998 election, he did take the first tentative step towards potential dialogue with indigenous people by appointing Phillip Ruddock as minister responsible for reconciliation. Mr Ruddock is a former chairperson of the House of Representatives Standing Committee on Aboriginal

Affairs and has had an ongoing interest in indigenous issues. Any initiatives he takes will be in vain, however, without a renewed commitment to the social justice agenda by the government. John Howard's empty rhetoric professing commitment to indigenous health, education and employment (reported without any serious analysis by the media) is in stark contrast to the lack of effective government programs in these areas.

Unless the social justice agenda is addressed through Commonwealth and prime ministerial leadership, using the power of the 1967 referendum as necessary, it is possible that the future will be marred by angry demonstrations and political protests by indigenous people and their supporters, both within Australia and throughout the world. It is my profound hope this scenario does not come to pass.

And it need not. These are basic human rights issues able to be tackled through national leadership by one of the most affluent nations on earth. Indigenous human rights and aspirations must be addressed as a non-negotiable part of the reconciliation process, not because of international pressure but to give effect to Australia's ethos of a fair go. But it will take leadership from the prime minister. No indigenous affairs minister alone has sufficient political clout and influence to bring about the change.

If issues such as the reform of gun laws can be driven by prime ministerial leadership and the processes of the Council of Australian Governments (COAG) meetings, then surely the human rights of indigenous people should be accorded no lesser respect and priority by our prime ministers, premiers and chief ministers. No lesser authority than the Governor-General has put this message on the line. We cannot say we were not warned. There can be no reconciliation without justice.

3

ATSIC: A RADICAL SHIFT TOWARDS SELF-DETERMINATION

Before the creation of ATSIC, the indigenous individuals and communities to whom government programs were directed had no say in determining what the programs would be and how they would be implemented.

The minister sat in faraway Canberra, able to take major decisions affecting indigenous communities across Australia.

The advent of ATSIC changed all that. By law the minister was stripped of almost all powers over the detail and direction of indigenous programs. Those powers were placed in the hands of an elected national board of commissioners and a network of indigenous regional councils around Australia whose members were elected to represent their communities.

The philosophy behind the creation of the new body was 'self-determination'. The creation of ATSIC reflected a commitment of the government to this principle, which was later accepted by all state and territory governments and unanimously by both houses of federal parliament. Indigenous people were thus able to take greater control over the shape and future direction of their communities and development. Although a radical new vehicle for the administration of government programs, ATSIC, contrary to the view of its critics, was also a pacesetter in public accountability.

As the legislation envisages, ATSIC was intended to be the first step towards self-determination, later leading to greater involvement in the planning and delivery of other programs at all levels of government.

Future governments should build on the threshold shift to indigenous empowerment which ATSIC represents by exploring further ways to enhance self-determination and decentralised democratic decision-making and indigenous control of government programs affecting their communities.

―――――

It was one of ATSIC's first appointed commissioners, Gus Williams from Hermannsburg, who in the early months of ATSIC's existence described it as a 'new baby'. He was making the point in his own way that it was a new creation and something unique and special. He recognised that it would take time for its early problems to be worked through. He impressed on us all in those early days the need for patience and the need to support ATSIC to allow it to develop.

ATSIC was legislated into existence on 5 March 1990 during the federal election campaign, its creation a radical step along the road to self-determination for indigenous people in this country. Before its creation, the Commonwealth Minister for Aboriginal Affairs was responsible for a government department, the Department of Aboriginal Affairs, which administered a range of Commonwealth government programs directed to improving the economic and social conditions of indigenous people. The most advanced democratic position Aboriginal people had been able to achieve was that of an advisory council and the limited consultation role described in Chapter 1.

The creation of ATSIC represents a radical shift in decision-making powers from remote governments in Canberra to the elected local representatives of indigenous people. It is important that the huge political significance of this shift be understood. ATSIC is a unique vehicle to empower elected Aboriginal and Torres Strait Islander people to make the executive budgetary and policy decisions about expenditure in the indigenous affairs budget. Rather than serving merely as an advisory council, like its predecessors, it has real decision-making powers. Decisions are taken by a national Board of Commissioners and by regional councils established across Australia.

Other countries, such as Canada and New Zealand, may lead Australia in their recognition of indigenous rights by treaty arrangements, but in the public administration of indigenous affairs no other government has been prepared to legislate to transfer executive control of an annual budget of over $1 billion to the elected representatives of indigenous people. During the time of the Labor government at international conferences and with delegations visiting Australia, ATSIC aroused considerable interest as a model that might be adopted by other governments to meet the aspirations of indigenous people.

It is pointless to pretend that ATSIC is without fault. It is a democratically elected body originally comprising some 700 regional councillors and, as with all elected bodies, invariably throws up a wide spectrum of humanity with all their collective strengths and weaknesses. When the various parliaments, or local government, throw up the occasional crook, sex offender, travel rorter or political embarrassment, society does not reject the institution of democracy or the parliament. If we did then the federal parliament should be abolished forthwith. But how easy it is for the opponents of Aboriginal people to condemn the very existence of ATSIC because of the failings of a few individuals among the hundreds of ATSIC elected representatives.

So many times I have seen breaches of public accountability standards in indigenous affairs which, had they occurred in the non-Aboriginal community, would barely have attracted a mention, while comparable Aboriginal breaches have attracted front-page publicity in national newspapers.

One of dozens of examples was an alleged lack of accountability in a Tennant Creek Aboriginal health service reported on the front page of the *Australian*. I am confident that if there was a major fraudulent misappropriation in the Tennant Creek hospital it would not even be reported in a national newspaper, let alone on the front page.

Even Aboriginal people who criticise ATSIC and call for its abolition do not want to return to the bad old days when the minister in Canberra held all the power. Almost without exception, they want more self-determination, and more indigenous control, not less.

I continue to defend the concept of ATSIC and its capacity to evolve further to advance self-determination, as it has done through the creation of the Torres Strait Regional Authority (TSRA). It is a proud Labor reform, and during those early years of its existence I was able to see from the inside the way in which the organisation developed and Aboriginal and Torres Strait Islander people, both within the commission and outside it, began to gain a deeper understanding of the important shift to self-determination that had occurred.

I was with ATSIC from the very beginning, and it was my job to work with the new body in what Lois O'Donoghue called a partnership between commissioners as the elected arm, the administration of ATSIC, and myself as minister. It was at times a roller-coaster ride. Dealing with the new ATSIC presented a huge challenge in public administration unprecedented in the history of the Commonwealth. Not since Federation had a minister been accountable to parliament for the actions and decisions of an elected body with executive decision-making powers outside his or her control.

The proposals for ATSIC were first raised while Clyde Holding was Minister for Aboriginal Affairs. On 14 July 1987, Prime Minister Hawke held a press conference at which he announced that the Department of Aboriginal Affairs would be abolished and in its place a new Aboriginal and Torres Strait Islander Commission would be established with Charles Perkins as administrative head.

The following week Gerry Hand took over from Clyde Holding and on 10 December made a major statement on indigenous affairs policy called *Foundations for the Future*, in which he announced further details of the proposal to establish a commission. The new commission was to encompass all Aboriginal affairs portfolio functions, replacing four existing bodies: the Department of Aboriginal Affairs, the Aboriginal Development Commission, Aboriginal Hostels, and the Australian Institute of Aboriginal Studies. The last two organisations were later removed from the purview of the *Aboriginal and Torres Strait Islander Commission Act 1989* (ATSIC Act). The foreshadowed legislation would establish what was then called the Aboriginal Economic Development Corporation (later the Aboriginal and Torres Strait Islander Commercial Development Corporation). Gerry Hand announced that the new commission would start operation on 1 July 1988, but as events unfolded it was to be almost two tumultuous years before that happened.

In introducing the Aboriginal and Torres Strait Islander Bill on 24 April 1988, Gerry Hand claimed that the legislation 'is the product of a great deal of consultation with Aboriginal and Torres Strait Islander communities'. More than 21 000 copies of *Foundations for the Future* and 1000 copies of a video were distributed to 1000 separate indigenous communities and organisations. Gerry reported to parliament that 537 preliminary meetings had been held involving about 14 500 people to discuss the proposals before his extensive meetings with communities and organisations. Even his critics acknowledged the extent of the consultation. Charles Perkins has said that the consultation process on the ATSIC proposals was among the most exhaustive and protracted series of negotiations he had ever undertaken.

The fight for the establishment of ATSIC saw an obstructive Senate Committee inquiry into the proposed legislation, a Senate Privileges inquiry into the conduct of aspects of the portfolio, allegations by the Coalition of a 'black mafia' within the Department of Aboriginal Affairs, the sacking of the Board of the Aboriginal Development Commission, allegations against Charles Perkins as secretary of the Aboriginal Affairs Department and head of the Aboriginal Development Commission, censure motions against Gerry Hand, relentless daily questions in parliament making allegations of impropriety against officials, most of which are to this day not proven, a campaign of industrial action by the trade union covering departmental employees in favour of the status quo, a special inquiry by the Auditor-General, a further inquiry by a special investigator, and the removal of Charles Perkins as secretary of the department. This cynical campaign smeared the Aboriginal Affairs portfolio, the minister and his staff. But above all it caused great hurt to Aboriginal people. It was a practice run for the campaign the Coalition was to wage against the native title legislation in 1993.

ATSIC officially existed from March 1990. At this time, in the period before regional councils were established, it was the government-appointed board of five commissioners that had the decision-making power over the distribution of the ATSIC budget. As soon as I became minister in April, I began to establish my relationship with those commissioners: Lois O'Donoghue, chair; Sol Bellear, deputy chair; Sue Gordon, a Western Australian magistrate; Gus Williams, a community leader; and Terry O'Shane, a streetwise and determined maritime worker from far north Queensland and brother of magistrate Pat O'Shane. Right from the beginning the board made the tough decisions about priorities in such things as health, housing, infrastructure and land acquisition. It also controlled many programs for which ATSIC was responsible but which made only a small contribution to redressing the ongoing shortcomings in the exercise of their responsibilities by main-stream government departments and agencies.

It is a simple fact, which the media and most politicians seem incapable of understanding, that ATSIC funding is supplementary funding which has never been adequate to make up for the failure of mainstream government departments at all levels to do their jobs and seriously address Aboriginal disadvantage in areas of health, housing, employment and education. For example, Aboriginal people, per head of population, have less spent on them than non-indigenous Australians by state and Commonwealth health departments.

As minister, I had no power under the ATSIC Act to issue specific directions to the new commissioners. The only power vested in the minister is a power of general direction, which does not confer a power over individual board decisions. The minister does have a right to information, however, and one early difference I had with the board was over the question of access to its business papers prior to its meetings. It was my policy to refuse to lobby individual members of the ATSIC Board on forthcoming business, despite the requests of MPs (including Labor MPs) and others. It was, however, important that ATSIC's books be totally open to the minister, and the board ultimately accepted my assertion that the Act conferred on the minister an unrestricted right of access to information on the commission.

I have a good nose for political trouble and an obsessive commit-ment to public accountability. There is no one in ATSIC, in Aboriginal organisations or in government who dealt with me who could not have known that my commitment to public accountability was non-negotiable. I no doubt annoyed public servants with this preoccupation and offended some Aboriginal leaders. My concern was not based on any lack of inherent accountability in the new commission—it is in my view a highly accountable body by virtue of the strong provisions in the Act—but I knew that the political opponents of Aboriginal people would use any lapse in public accountability to smear all indigenous organisations and to attack and erode Aboriginal rights.

This is precisely what happened in the first months of the Howard government. By all accounts it was the Treasurer, Peter Costello, who, with others in the Cabinet, was the driving force in attacking ATSIC and in the spurious appointment of the special auditor, which the courts ultimately found to be illegal. The minister, Senator John Herron, publicly attacked ATSIC, but it was subsequently revealed that he was not even aware of the existence and valuable work of the Office of Evaluation and Audit (OEA)—described later in this chapter—established under the ATSIC Act. The new minister seemed to think that flying visits to Aboriginal communities were a substitute for policy.

If there were serious allegations of improper conduct I would have them investigated at the highest level, usually by the OEA. If there were allegations of criminal behaviour that warranted investigation I had no hesitation in referring them to the police. When there were serious allegations about the administration of the NLC, a body incorporated under Commonwealth legislation and one of the most politically powerful Aboriginal organisations in the country, I called in the Auditor-General to make a special investigation. The NLC implemented the Auditor-General's recommendations comprehensively and promptly. Rarely has a minister in any government of his or her own volition, without prompting or pressure, called in the Auditor-General in such a matter.

There was not one occasion when I failed to initiate a prompt investigation of alleged wrongdoing within ATSIC. Despite my referrals of alleged wrongful conduct to all relevant authorities, rarely was there evidence of criminal behaviour; often complaints were made by disgruntled applicants for funding or for some political purpose.

One of my first discoveries on public accountability was that the level of unacquitted grants in mid-1990, soon after the establishment of ATSIC, stood at approximately $250 million as a result of failures in the former Department of Aboriginal Affairs. This issue gave rise to one of my earliest direct head-to-head negotiations with the ATSIC Board. The result was that the board took a tougher stand on unacquitted grants than any minister had been prepared to take in the past and denied future funding, except in the most exceptional circumstances, to any indigenous organisation that had not acquitted previous grants.

The first ATSIC election for regional councillors was due to be held on 3 November 1990, and at the time nominations closed I happened to be in Alice Springs at an ATSIC-organised event attended by Lois O'Donoghue and ATSIC's CEO, Bill Gray (later Commonwealth electoral commissioner). It was a very tense time. The success or failure of ATSIC rode on whether there was enough indigenous interest in the election. I was distraught when the chairperson of the

NLC, Galarrwuy Yunupingu, called for a boycott of the elections the day before nominations closed in a statement which I think, in hindsight, he may well regret. There were, however, a large number of nominations on closing day.

There was a hitch just before the election. The ATSIC election rules had been tabled in the House of Representatives but not in the Senate, creating a *prima facie* failure to comply with the ATSIC Act. This placed the elections at risk and could have resulted in great inconvenience to Aboriginal and Torres Strait Islander people and such political embarrassment that my job would have been on the line. As it turned out, the Attorney-General's Department found a way through the problem. In fact everything had been done by ATSIC officers to get the proper tabling of the rules, but unknown to me, and contrary to two assurances provided to me in writing, there was a mix-up by officials that resulted in the documents not being properly tabled. From the legal opinion provided by the Attorney-General's Department, I was confident that the election could proceed properly. The election process was subsequently challenged in the Federal Court of Australia but the challenge was dismissed.

A critical point in the ATSIC evolution occurred during the formulation of the government's response to the Royal Commission Into Aboriginal Deaths In Custody (RCIADIC). ATSIC officials and commissioners took a leading role in achieving a whole-of-government response to the Royal Commission's recommendations. One memorable moment occurred immediately before Cabinet considered the government's response in March 1991. For the first time in the 91-year history of Australian government, indigenous people attended a Cabinet meeting. Lois O'Donoghue had written to Bob Hawke seeking to address the Cabinet, and he had readily agreed. Lois, in the company of Commissioners Alf Bamblett and Steve Gordon, was magnificent.

On an earlier occasion, in May 1990, when I was having one of my first meetings with her, the conversation turned to the children who had been taken from their families. Lois had just said quietly, 'I was one of those children'. Now, in the Cabinet room, she told her personal history. She was not grandstanding or dwelling on the past. She was simply telling Cabinet about the true history of this country and the terrible toll inflicted on Aboriginal families by those forced separations, so graphically illustrated by the report *Bringing Them Home*. This was Australian history in the making, Aboriginal people telling the Cabinet what they needed to be reminded of. You could have heard a pin drop. The only other occasion I have seen Cabinet ministers so affected was in the presence of Nelson Mandela.

The Stolen Generations

The Royal Commission into Aboriginal Deaths in Custody provided a stark illustration of the pervasive nature of the practice: 43 of the 99 people whose deaths were investigated had experienced childhood separation from their natural families through intervention by government authorities, missions or other institutions. In the government's response to RCIADIC, funding was boosted to establish and extend link-up services to help reunify families, but I knew much more needed to be done.

There had been occasional calls for some form of inquiry into the effects of this past policy, principally from the Secretariat of the National Aboriginal and Islander Child Care (SNAICC) and from a small number of similar organisations. There had been, however, no pressure of any kind on the government for such an inquiry from the wider Aboriginal community. In October 1994, I was invited to deliver the opening speech at a Darwin conference convened by Aboriginal people who had been affected by these past policies, entitled 'Going Home'. In that speech I took a calculated and planned public stand in support of some form of study or inquiry into that practice.

I promised to discuss the proposal with the Attorney-General, Michael Lavarch, ATSIC and the Aboriginal and Torres Strait Islander Social Justice Commissioner. Prior to that speech I had not discussed the proposal with any ministerial colleagues, and had not even told Lois O'Donoghue of my intended action even though I knew she would be at the conference and would be very pleased to hear my words.

That speech was the source of what was ultimately to be the HREOC Inquiry into the Children Who Were Taken Away. The opportunity to give effect to the proposal arose in the government's 1995 Justice Statement and in May 1995, with full and active support of Attorney-General Michael Lavarch, I announced that HREOC's President, Sir Ronald Wilson, would head a national inquiry into the former practice. He was supported by the Aboriginal and Torres Strait Islander Social Justice Commissioner, Mick Dodson.

The landmark report *Bringing Them Home* was released in May 1997, when the Australian Reconciliation Convention was being held in Melbourne, and over a year after Labor lost office. It had been in the hands of the government for seven weeks. The report shocked most non-indigenous Australians and led to an ongoing

national debate on the past practice and what should be the
appropriate response of government and the community.

The report emphasises that the past actions of governments
and organisations had been evaluated not on the basis of contemporary values but in the light of the legal values and principles
which applied at the time. One of the most controversial conclusions was not only that the forcible removal of children was a
gross violation of their human rights, a discriminatory act contrary to Australia's expressed views at the UN at that time, but
that it was also an act of genocide in violation of the Genocide
Convention ratified by Australia in 1949. The Convention on
Genocide not only prohibits the killing of a race of people but
also includes 'forcibly transferring children . . . to another group
. . . with intent to destroy, in whole or in a part a national,
ethnical, racial or religious group'. However, as Australia's most
distinguished genocide scholar, Professor Colin Tatz, has highlighted, the removing of Aboriginal children from their families
is only one of many arguable acts of genocide within the meaning
of the Convention which has occurred since 1788.

The Howard government's formal response to the recommendations was released on 16 December 1997. In a public statement,
HREOC welcomed the government's positive initiatives but
expressed regret about the lack of the government's understanding of a core recommendation, namely the need for a public
apology. There were, of course, other disagreements with the
government's response and, in particular, the commission stressed
that the recommendation concerning the need for monetary
compensation for people affected by the removal was an 'essential
component of reparation for past wrongs'.

At first, Mr Howard and his government defended the refusal
to make a formal government apology on the grounds that it
would be an admission of liability that would require compensation to be paid, contrary to their announced policy. It then
emerged that the government's chief general counsel had advised
that an apology could be framed to avoid legal liability. The
government then began to justify the refusal to apologise purportedly on the basis that there were many Australian citizens not
born here who would not embrace such a statement. This argument, however, lost any credibility it might have when the
Chairman of the Federation of the Ethnic Communities' Council
of Australia (FECCA) reminded the government that the council
had itself already made such an apology along with 53 other

community groups. The integrity of the government's position was further undermined when the *Sydney Morning Herald* published a Herald-AG McNair poll which found that 65 per cent of respondents agreed that there should be an official acknowledgement and an apology for the suffering caused by the policy of forced removal.

The government's failure to apologise confirms yet again how important it is that it shows respect to the concerns of indigenous people and is prepared to really listen to their grievances. There is no substitute for the display of *bona fides* and the establishment of a proper basis of relationship between indigenous people and governments. A formal government apology would hardly be an aberration in national or international affairs. As Professor Colin Tatz has pointed out, the Germans said sorry to the Jews minutes before reunification.

Across the Tasman, the government of New Zealand has, pursuant to the Treaty of Waitangi, both issued formal apologies and paid compensation. Specifically in relation to apologies related to past injustices to other indigenous people, the US government has apologised for its overthrow of the Kingdom of Hawaii, the Canadian government has apologised for its role in relation to special residential schools, and the Norwegian King has apologised for past government treatment of the Sami. In the words of Mr Howard's conservative predecessor in office, Malcolm Fraser, 'True reconciliation does not involve only material things—it also involves matters of the spirit. This is where the question of an apology does not say "I am guilty". It is recognition that our society perpetuated a wrong and that we are sorry it happened.'

An important event in the portfolio was the recruitment in December 1990 by Michael Codd, head of the Department of the Prime Minister and Cabinet (PM&C), of Dr Peter Shergold to the ATSIC administration as acting deputy CEO. Dr Shergold, a public servant of exceptional capacity, complemented the long experience of Bill Gray, who had had an important part in formulating the ATSIC legislation. Peter Shergold was a former economist from the University of New South Wales and during his time with the commission managed to blend loyalty to the Board of Commissioners with a genuine abiding professional partnership with me as the minister. Together with Lois O'Donoghue, we formed a great team, with a relationship of trust and shared commitment. Dr Shergold was appointed ATSIC's CEO in December 1991. When his term of office ended, I was able to gain Cabinet support and the agreement of the ATSIC Board for the appointment of Pat Turner, an Aboriginal woman and experienced public servant, who performed her role with strength and integrity. All my appointments in the portfolio were based on merit and I am pleased to record that 50 per cent of them were women.

Later it was to be as the result of the leadership provided by Lois, as ATSIC chair, during the Mabo debate that for the first time in the history of the nation indigenous people were involved in face-to-face negotiations with the Prime Minister. ATSIC played a crucial coordinating role among indigenous community organisations and land councils, which helped to cement alliances and develop and deepen understanding of ATSIC the institution. They were truly momentous times and undoubtedly led to an enhanced recognition within the Australian community that ATSIC had the potential to be an important political voice for indigenous Australians.

Some important institutional aspects of ATSIC's operation, put in place by its legislation, make a significant contribution to public accountability. I sought to build on this contribution and developed the concept of an annual report, *Social Justice for Indigenous Australians*, which detailed all Commonwealth expenditure on Aboriginal and Torres Strait Islander programs. This publication was first released at the time of the budget, but later at other times of the year. It showed, clearly and publicly for the first time, where every dollar of Commonwealth funding goes in indigenous affairs, not just funding channelled through ATSIC but also through other government departments in an endeavour to make them more accountable. State and territory governments were encouraged to emulate this initiative.

One of the myths in Aboriginal and Torres Strait Islander affairs is that the funding is swallowed up by some vast bureaucracy. The facts show how false this is. At the time of the 1996 federal election, only 14 per cent of ATSIC's total budget was spent on administration, including the total cost of operating its elected arm and democratic processes. In my view, ATSIC staff are doing a very competent job in one of the hardest areas of public administration. About half of them are Aboriginal and Torres Strait Islander people, and indigenous people occupy half of senior executive positions. Another important achievement is that in 1996 more than a quarter of ATSIC's elected representatives were women, which is a better record than most state and territory parliaments.

A unique feature of the ATSIC Act is the creation of the Office of Evaluation and Audit. This is an independent statutory office which reports directly to the Board of Commissioners and to the minister. Mainstream government departments have their own internal audit processes, but the internal auditors report to the departmental secretary or to others in the bureaucracy and not directly to the minister. To the best of my knowledge there is no comparable body to this office in the public sector in the Commonwealth or at state or territory level. In my opinion every government minister, state and Commonwealth, should be able to call on such independent scrutiny of his or her department as a matter of course.

In dealing with the board, it was always open to the minister to issue a 'general direction' under the Act because it was the only legal authority he or she had over the board's day-to-day decisions. The power to issue a general direction by the minister had already been judicially considered in an earlier case involving Gerry Hand's dealing with the Aboriginal Development Commission, which confirmed that the minister's powers in this regard were limited. I was determined to use this ministerial power only as a last resort. To do otherwise could have opened a Pandora's box of future directions by ministers who did not share my commitment to self-determination and who wanted to sit behind their Canberra desks and tell indigenous people what was good for them by dictating policy in key areas. I wanted to get through my term negotiating with ATSIC to overcome issues of concern rather than using the heavy hand of the law and ministerial direction and I was able to achieve this with no loss of public accountability.

Two examples show the way this was done. On one occasion an ATSIC regional council adjacent to Canberra was planning to time its meeting in Canberra to coincide with an Aboriginal protest during the native title debate. It was obvious that if that happened it could be alleged that the individual councillors were being paid to protest. The problem was overcome, after some direct negotiation with the entire ATSIC Board, when ATSIC's chairperson and the board used their powers to constrain regional councillors from meeting outside their areas except with the prior permission of the chairperson.

On another occasion, in 1995, the Board of Commissioners by majority vote sought to waive the income test levels for housing loans to provide an entitlement to Aboriginal and Torres Strait Islander people who had a temporary high income. This would, of course, have provided a direct benefit to board members. While I understood that they had a valid point about their limited tenure of office and lack of financial security, I thought the decision was politically damaging for ATSIC. I expressed my concerns at a board meeting and it decided to exclude commissioners from benefiting.

It was also important to defend and promote the concept of ATSIC in the public domain, and I often had to do so in the face of misinformation about it, courtesy of some of the worst elements of talkback radio. I had one celebrated radio encounter with Alan Jones in his 2UE studio which was filmed by ABC television. The summary of the encounter by the government's media service read something like, 'Jones had Tickner in the studio for 45 minutes, news and commercial free, and the radio melted'. It was like that, and I relished the opportunity to respond vigorously to Alan Jones' continued outrageous allegations in face-to-face debate when he could not cut off my response, which he had done in telephone interviews. Not surprisingly, this was the last time he invited me into the studio. (In his November 1996 *Media Watch* newsletter, Gerard Henderson reported on Alan Jones' 'intense personal crusades' against me and Frank Walker. Mr Jones admitted on air that he had spent 'a lot of time' in my electorate supporting my Liberal opponent during the 1996 election campaign.)

To combat the misinformation put out by such people, in 1992 a booklet, *Rebutting the Myths*, was published which set out to destroy the damaging mythology about the portfolio on issues of accountability, sacred sites, alcohol abuse and free cars for Aboriginal people. The booklet was put together with help from ATSIC staff and enlivened by some clever Bruce Petty cartoons.

The first elections for the 60 ATSIC regional councils took place on 3 November 1990. On 1 March 1991 the new commissioners took office: George Mye (Torres Strait), Shireen Malamoo (Qld North), Gerhardt Pearson (Qld Far North), Kerry Blackman (Qld South), Ian Delaney (Qld Metropolitan), Gerry Moore (NSW East), Sol Bellear (NSW Metropolitan), Steve Gordon (NSW West), Ted Stevenson (Tasmania), Alf Bamblett (Victoria), Charles Jackson (South Australia), Robert Tipungwuti (NT North West), Yikaki Maymuru (NT North East), Geoff Shaw (Central Australia), Leah Bell (WA South), Neil Phillips (WA Metropolitan) and Reg Birch (WA North). In a remarkable turn of events Sol Bellear was again elected ATSIC's deputy chair, Lois O'Donoghue remained the government appointed chair, and David Ross and June Oscar were the other appointed commissioners required by the ATSIC Act at that time. By and large I got on well with the board and we had some challenging times together.

After the 1993 election, Prime Minister Keating moved to establish an Office of Indigenous Affairs within PM&C as an alternative source of policy advice to ATSIC. The establishment of such an office was Coalition policy before the election, and something I strenuously opposed. This body was to frustrate indigenous aspirations on key issues in the coming three years. From time to time PM&C failed miserably to work at advancing the human rights of Aboriginal and

Torres Strait Islander people. I had numerous run-ins with the department, including its very senior officers, because of their failure even to consult ATSIC about such fundamental questions as changes in Commonwealth–state relations that directly affected indigenous people.

An important reform process took place in the ATSIC legislation in August 1993 following a committee of review set up by the commission itself. The number of regional councils was reduced from 60 to 35, with a separate regional authority to be created for the Torres Strait. The fact that the reform went so smoothly was a credit to all involved. Its package made the positions of commissioners full-time, and Cabinet supported my proposal to make the ATSIC Board a totally elected body. The Democrats and the Coalition at first combined in the Senate to reject these amendments but ultimately the Democrats voted with the government to allow them to pass. In 1996 the Howard government amended the ATSIC Act to postpone the implementation of a totally elected ATSIC Board and chairperson until after the 1999 regional council elections.

The election for the second round of ATSIC regional councillors took place on 4 December 1993, with TSRA members to be elected in March 1994. The voter turnout was over 30 per cent, as it had been in the previous election. This compares to a turnout in South Australian and Western Australian local government elections during the same period, where voting was not compulsory, of 20 and 15 per cent respectively. The ATSIC turnout is also comparable to average voting levels in non-compulsory trade union elections. It is also certainly dramatically better than the participation of shareholders in most corporate annual general meetings and elections. I believe that ATSIC cannot legitimately be attacked as being unrepresentative of indigenous people, especially when its electorate includes people who have the poorest standards of education of any group in the Australian population.

The new commissioners were Joseph Elu (Torres Strait), Gerhardt Pearson (Qld Far North West), Ian Delaney (Qld Metropolitan), Stephen Walsh (Qld North) replaced by Terry O'Shane, Ray Robinson (Qld South), Des Williams (NSW East), Chris Williams (NSW Metropolitan), Steve Gordon (NSW West), Alf Bamblett (Victoria), Lucas Maynard (Tasmania), Yami Lester (South Australia), John Paterson (NT North), Charles Perkins (NT Central), Spencer Riley (WA South West), Guy Parker (WA Central), Teddy Biljabu (WA South East), and Glynis Sibasado (WA North). Lois O'Donoghue and David Ross were reappointed as commissioners.

Charles Perkins was elected deputy chair, a considerable achievement for him. He had gone full circle from his controversial departure as the head of the Department of Aboriginal Affairs to the most senior elected position in ATSIC. Charles and I had a long association, and his book, *A Bastard Like Me*, had had a great impact on me in my early twenties because of the tremendous courage and leadership he had displayed in the 'freedom rides'. During his period of exile he launched some damaging attacks on ATSIC, which was perhaps understandable given what he had been through. Ironically, he was to become one of ATSIC's strongest defenders.

It is no disrespect to him to say that as minister I was kept busy just keeping up with Charles Perkins' political game plan, as were others in both the indigenous and non-indigenous community. When Paul Keating first became Prime Minister, without any consultation with me, he met with Charles, presumably to take counsel from him. Within one hour Charles was leading an occupation of the old Parliament House in support of international legal action for indigenous rights. It fell to me to negotiate with the protesters in the full glare of television lights. I did so and the occupation ended. Later on Charles was to be a member of the 'Kitchen Cabinet' of the then Opposition Leader, John Hewson, in the lead-up to the 1993 election, which contributed to the hostility of some Labor people towards him. Both of us knew from the time of his 1993 election to the ATSIC Board that peace had to be made in the interests of ATSIC and the broader interests of the indigenous cause. To do otherwise would have caused intolerable and unproductive tensions within the board. We did this and I have to say that, despite his critics, I found him a most engaging person; he certainly gave every impression of wanting to work closely with me, as I did with him for the benefit of ATSIC and indigenous people.

Lois O'Donoghue maintained her role as the appointed chairperson with my strong support. There was no doubt that some members of the board would have liked at various times to challenge her appointment, but she was a tough and respected person who earned her right to chair the board many times over by her magnificent contribution during the native title debate.

A sad time during the term of the second ATSIC Board was the resignation of Commissioner Alf Bamblett. Allegations had been made against him by some Aboriginal people in Victoria and had been extensively publicised in the *Age*. Believing that issues of public accountability were non-negotiable, I acted on the allegations immediately and appointed an independent person, Ian Viner, to conduct an investigation. His report found serious issues concerning a conflict of interest and other matters touching on Commissioner Bamblett's responsibilities as a commissioner. The police confirmed that no crime had been committed, but he had arguably breached acceptable standards of public behaviour and he resigned. He had made a valuable contribution to the government's RCIADIC response, and in my dealings with him I found him to observe a higher standard of ethics than some of his detractors, both inside and outside parliament.

In October 1995, after consultations with ATSIC, the government announced that it would be initiating further reforms to boost ATSIC's accountability. These included requiring regional council meetings to be open to the public except in certain circumstances similar to those in which local government meetings can be closed. This would entitle the public to inspect documents such as codes of conduct, written procedures for meetings, management plans, and other key ATSIC documents.

After the election of the Howard government, the ATSIC legislation was amended to allow the government of the day to continue to appoint the ATSIC chairperson and one other commissioner. This government, not surprisingly, did not reappoint Lois O'Donoghue and replaced her with Gatjil Djerrkura, a quietly spoken and very moderate Aboriginal leader from the Northern Territory. It is a measure of the failure of the Howard government's policies that within a year or so Gatjil was at loggerheads with both the minister and the government.

A major question confronting indigenous people, parliament and the wider community is where to now for ATSIC and self-determination. It is clear to me, as I have already emphasised, that what indigenous people want is more self-determination, not less. It is also indisputable from all the available evidence that policies of assimilation have had catastrophic social consequences. The fact that the Howard government, including John Herron, has flirted with such ideas has taken indigenous affairs policy back to the 1950s. Most lamentable has been the parroted, empty rhetoric against welfare and dependency while the new government has at the same time savaged policies and programs specifically aimed at greater indigenous self-reliance and independence. Land forms perhaps the most crucial foundation of increased self-reliance and diminished dependency, but Aboriginal land aspirations have been, almost without exception, opposed by the Coalition.

The establishment of the TSRA and the push for the establishment of a similar authority for the Kimberley is a clear manifestation of the direction in which Aboriginal and Torres Strait Islander people themselves wish to move. It is neither possible nor desirable for the national government to attempt to push the self-determination genie back into the bottle. A major challenge will be the extent to which future national governments are prepared to give effect to the original intention of the ATSIC Act, namely that ATSIC should play a significant role in influencing the administration of the programs of other Commonwealth departments and those of other levels of government.

Steps towards greater self-determination will inevitably be made in local communities and in regions. At the 1995 UN Global Diversity Conference in Sydney, Lois O'Donoghue made an important speech recognising that there was likely to be a move to establish a series of regional authorities across Australia with devolved power and decision-making. Indeed, the ATSIC Board adopted a policy of increasingly devolving its decision-making power to its regional councils. It seems to me that indigenous people in this country will drive the agenda further in this direction. This shift fits well into the continuing emphasis on regional agreements by Aboriginal people to resolve issues of native title disputation. But whatever specific approach is chosen, there is no doubt that the trend will be towards greater empowerment and self-determination. This is in line with the developing international law of indigenous human rights.

In conclusion, something needs to be said in response to the emerging ideological and Coalition-driven propaganda which suggests that Labor was somehow committed to a 'welfare' model of Aboriginal policy. The historical record shows otherwise. Labor's creation of ATSIC, support for self-determination principles, the passage of the Native Title Act, the creation of the Indigenous Land Fund and evolving policies for directly funding communities and regions were all directed towards the empowerment of Aboriginal people. They were intended to create an economic base and place decision-making and responsibility in the hands of the people themselves. Virtually every one of Labor's reforms in this direction were opposed by the Coalition, who now chant the mantra of self-sufficiency, not welfare.

Two examples regularly trotted out to demonstrate this new-found self-sufficiency are in fact perfect examples of the success and importance to Aboriginal people of self-determination and land rights. One is the forestry project of the Tiwi Land Council and another is YBE, a successful longstanding Aboriginal-owned business enterprise in which Gatjil Djerrkura has played the leading role and whose success has flowed from Aboriginal land ownership in the region.

There are of course no quick-fix solutions to the daunting problems faced by Aboriginal and Torres Strait Islander people in remote communities. My fear is, however, that the recycled Coalition 'anti-welfare' rhetoric will be used to justify the national government's failure to fulfil its responsibilities to expand public expenditure in social justice programs. The demands of people in the remote communities for proper schools for their children, a decent water supply, sewerage systems and access roads to their communities are not a call for welfare but for their rights to an equitable share of government resources. Most non-indigenous Australians already enjoy these rights and they are not called 'welfare'.

Labor in office never suggested that government policies on their own can solve all the problems in remote or other communities. Clearly, much must be done by indigenous leaders and by the people themselves in those communities. There are dozens of examples where these locally driven changes are occurring, ranging from community decisions to exclude alcohol and developing industries in arts and craft and tourism to the creative use of the CDEP scheme to build and maintain community infrastructure. I am confident that these community-driven initiatives will swell in numbers, but I am far less confident that our current government leaders have any commitment to ensuring an equitable share of resources to those communities. The new rhetoric compounds my fear. As Professor Garth Nettheim said in a major paper delivered in September 1998: 'Despite strident suggestions to the contrary, it is the absence or inadequacy of special programs to overcome such disadvantages, rather than the existence of such programs, that affronts ideals of equality in Australia.'

4

ABORIGINAL DEATHS IN CUSTODY

The chilling life stories told in the 99 individual reports of the Royal Commission Into Aboriginal Deaths in Custody provide an insight for non-indigenous Australians into the tragedy and misery experienced by successive generations of Aboriginal people. In large measure the suffering was a direct result of the actions and policies of Australian governments of all political persuasions. These policies were, and remain, the cause of the vast overrepresentation of Aboriginal people in prison and the consequent continuing high number of Aboriginal deaths in custody.

RCIADIC's final report, together with its 339 recommendations, accepted almost in entirety by all governments and all political parties in 1992, provide a detailed and practical blueprint for government policy reform to address this injustice. An extensive public accountability regime, far beyond what RCIADIC itself recommended, was set up by the Commonwealth to keep all governments to their promises.

State and territory governments were given the direct responsibility for implementing recommendations relating to police, prisons and reform of the criminal justice system. These amounted to two-thirds of the total number of recommendations and were focused on reducing the number of Aboriginal people in custody.

Towards the end of 1999, eight years since the tabling of the report that recommended prison as a last resort, the gaols of the nation have a vastly disproportionate number of Aboriginal prisoners. While there have been examples of positive reform initiatives by state and territory governments and some welcome statistical trends on deaths in police custody, the overall outcome is bleak.

Regrettably, there has been a high-profile and regressive auction by political parties to outbid each other in 'law and order' election campaigns and the implementation of mandatory and harsh sentencing policies. The effect of these policies will be to create more broken lives. There is a better way and RCIADIC showed us that way.

———

There is no doubt that the Royal Commission would not have been established without the political campaign and lobbying efforts of Aboriginal people themselves. The fact that Aboriginal people have been overrepresented and disadvantaged at all stages of the criminal justice system was established beyond doubt in the 1960s and 1970s as a result of research by such people as the late Elizabeth Eggleston and Professor Colin Tatz. The latest available figures show that in 1998, while indigenous people represent less than 2 per cent of the Australian adult population, they comprise 19 per cent of the total prison population.

Not long after the Royal Commission's report was tabled, Garrie Gibson, chair of the Caucus Social Justice Committee and a close comrade of mine, made a telling point:

> According to figures . . . obtained from the June 1991 National Prison Census, there were more than 2,000 Aboriginal people in prison. If there were only the same proportion of Aboriginal people in prison as the proportion of Aboriginal people in the Australian population, there would be about 1,600 less Aboriginal prisoners. At an average cost of $50,000 per annum to keep a prisoner, the over representation is costing the Australian community $80 million a year. That is $80 million that would be better spent on addressing the massive disadvantage faced by Aboriginal people which the Royal Commission so clearly identified.

It would be surprising if Aboriginal people themselves ever doubted that this was the case. Concern about this overrepresentation and disadvantage prompted the establishment of Aboriginal legal services, controlled by Aboriginal people and first funded by governments in the early 1970s. The services expanded from humble beginnings in Redfern, Sydney, to a spread of community-controlled services across Australia.

But still the disadvantaged position of Aboriginal people continued, and concern began to build within the Aboriginal community about the large number of Aboriginal people dying in police and prison custody. The Committee to Defend Black Rights was established in 1984, following the acquittal of police charged over the death of John Pat after his arrest in Roeburne, Western Australia. The spokesperson for the organisation was an Aboriginal woman, Helen Corbett, and thus began the campaign for a royal commission. The campaign was assisted in 1986 by Minister Clyde Holding, who allocated $10 000 to enable the families of 22 people believed to have died in custody, to prepare a case for the conduct of an inquiry.

In 1987 a new organisation, the Deaths in Custody Watch Committee, also campaigned on the issue with the backing of sections of the wider community. Pressure for a royal commission increased in that year with fifteen deaths in custody compared with eight in 1986, a rate already higher than the immediately preceding years.

The case for a royal commission became increasingly unanswerable with each high-profile death in custody such as that of Lloyd Boney in Brewarrina, New South Wales, on 6 August 1987. There had been a wave of publicity and public concern about the number of these deaths and the inadequate public explanations about the circumstances, where the possibility of foul play could not be discounted. Prime Minister Hawke obtained the support of state and territory governments and a royal commission was formally established on 16 October 1987. It was never solely a Commonwealth royal commission but a national one formally supported by all state and territory governments.

Originally 44 deaths were referred to RCIADIC, but this was ultimately expanded to include an inquiry into the 99 Aboriginal deaths in custody occurring in police prison or youth detention centres between 1980 and 1989. RCIADIC was given wide terms of reference to examine the life history of the deceased and all action taken by the authorities before and after the deaths. Significantly, the federal Opposition joined with the state and territory governments in supporting the establishment of RCIADIC, and there was a large measure of cross-party support for its work.

A Federal Court judge, Mr Justice Muirhead, was appointed Commissioner and produced an interim report at the end of 1988. The immensity of the task, however, was by then understood; the number of commissioners was increased to five and RCIADIC's role extended to cover the social, cultural and legal factors that might have contributed to the deaths. Justice Muirhead was appointed administrator of the Northern Territory and Elliott Johnston AO QC became the national Commissioner in April 1989. The other commissioners were Lew Wyvill QC, D.J. O'Dea, Hal Wootten AC QC, and Patrick Dodson, who was to report on the underlying issues giving rise to the disproportionate numbers of Aboriginal people in custody.

RCIADIC established an Aboriginal Issues Unit in each state and in the Northern Territory which kept in close contact with communities, provided input to the inquiry, and undertook the most rigorous examination of the lives and circumstances of the deaths of the 99 people. Public hearings were held, families represented by legal counsel, evidence taken from all relevant witnesses wherever possible and all aspects of custodial cases and legal process examined. The reports on individual deaths were released progressively from January 1989.

Although a relatively small number of RCIADIC's reports into the individual deaths recommended further action against a small number of police and prison officers, it did not find that any of the deaths were the result of deliberate and unlawful violence or brutality by police or prison officers. Understandably, many of the still grieving families of those who died in custody found it very difficult to accept that their loved one had died of natural causes or by their own hand. For most of them the pain remains to this day.

Significantly, however, RCIADIC's individual reports provide a graphic insight into the appalling living conditions and tragic lives of the human beings who might otherwise remain an anonymous statistical death in custody. Just one such story is that of Malcolm Charles Smith, whose death was one of the 99 investigated. The circumstances of his life and death, as chronicled by Commissioner Hal Wootten, should be read and their meaning understood by us all. The words speak for themselves.

Malcolm Charles Smith: An Aboriginal death in custody

At 1.25 p.m. on 29 December 1982 Malcolm Charles Smith, an Aboriginal prisoner in the Malabar Assessment Unit (MAU) of the Metropolitan Reception Prison (MRP) at Long Bay, Sydney, went into a toilet cubicle and locked the door behind him. About half a minute afterwards a piercing scream came from the cubicle. Prison officers rushed to the door and, when there was no response to their inquiries, knocked it off its hinges and found that the handle of an artist's paintbrush had been driven through Malcolm Smith's left eye, so that only the metal sheath and hairs were protruding. He was quickly attended to by nursing staff and a doctor and transferred to Prince Henry Hospital, as an emergency case. Despite all possible care, he died at 11.41 a.m. on 5 January 1983.

No one at the MAU that day was at fault. Each officer was doing his or her duty in the normal way and had no reason to expect what would happen. When Malcolm inflicted the fatal injury on himself, the officers responded promptly and sensibly and can only be commended for the way they handled a most distressing incident. Equally, the medical attention which he subsequently received was beyond criticism.

Malcolm Charles Smith: An Aboriginal life in custody

So much for how Malcolm died. Why did he die? Why was he in prison, seeking to pluck out his eye? The answer begins (depending on how long a perspective one takes), somewhere between 26 January 1788 and 5 May 1965. On the former day there commenced the European settlement that, in Rowley's phrase, was to mean 'the progress of the Aboriginal from tribesman to inmate'. It was to spread across the continent overwhelming people like the Paakantji, who occupied the rich hunter-gatherer habitat on the banks of the Darling, and the Ngiyampaa, their neighbours to the north-east. By the operation of massacre, individual killing, introduced diseases, destruction of food supplies, sexual exploitation, introduction of alcohol and dispossession from the land with which their whole life was entwined, these peoples were reduced to small remnants and many of them herded without regard to tribal affiliations into what were in effect concentration camps, although known as stations or 'missions', where they were denied civil rights in the name of protection and forced into a state of dependency in which many are still enmeshed. Whoever made the policies they enforced, it was usually the police that Aboriginals saw as the immediate agents of oppression.

Some bold spirits managed to maintain a precarious independence. Malcolm's parents, Gladys of Paakantji descent, who lost an arm in a shooting accident at sixteen, and her husband Joseph of Ngiyampaa descent, lived a roving fugitive life along the Darling between Ivanhoe, Menindee and Wentworth, travelling in horse drawn vehicles and sleeping under tarpaulins, and supporting themselves by casual work on stations and fruit blocks, and by hunting and fishing, as their family grew to thirteen children. Always on the move, their constant concern was to escape the attentions of 'the welfare', and its agents the police, lest they suffer the fate of so many Aboriginal families and be forced to live on a reserve or have their children snatched away, often never to be seen again. Gradually they came to settle with related families at Dareton, near Wentworth, where irrigation farmers valued the easily accessible pool of casual labour. They lived in humpies built from discarded materials, where Gladys cared for her large family while Joe built a reputation as a reliable worker. Here disaster struck. Gladys died and despite the efforts of Joe and his elder daughters, 'the welfare' caught up with the younger children.

Immediately prior to 5 May 1965, the other date from which Malcolm's story may be commenced, he was a happy, healthy and free eleven-year-old, albeit grubby, living in a humpy, and truant from a school made unattractive by racial prejudice and irrelevance to his life. He was taken away from his family by police, cut off from his family, whom he did not see again until he was nineteen, and sent to Kempsey, over 1500 kilometres away on the coast, beyond the boundaries of their accessible world. When he finally rediscovered them at the age of nineteen, it was too late for him to start a normal life. The intervening eight years, mainly in despotic institutions of various kinds, had left him illiterate and innumerate, unskilled, and without experience of normal society. He had been taught a model of human life based not on mutual respect, cooperation, responsibility, initiative, self-expression and love, but on dominance and subservience, rigid discipline and conformity, repression and dependence, humiliation and fear, with escape or defiance as the only room for initiative. He had experienced the law as a system which gave him no rights, no representation, and no consideration, ignored the existence of his family, and treated him as having no place outside an institution.

Instead of being socialised into the family and kin network so important to Aboriginals, he had been 'socialised' to survive in institutional communities. He was to spend nine years of the remaining nine years eight months of his life in gaols, where he found greater opportunities for freedom and privacy than he had known for the previous eight years in juvenile homes. In gaol he was respected by staff and prisoners alike for his strong character, leadership, sporting prowess and artistic talent, and there he built his friendships and social relations. His five intervals of liberty, totalling only eight months, offered an environment with which he was ill-equipped to cope, and little opportunity for employment or constructive activity. The first two occasions lasted two or three months, the rest only a few weeks. All but the last ended as a result of petty theft or illegal use of a motor car. The society which had deprived him of the opportunity to grow up in a family and learn to live in a free community offered him no assistance whatever in adjustment or rehabilitation, but visited his every lapse with penal sentences. In many cases the sentences were extremely harsh.

Yet the bonds to his family formed in early childhood remained strong, and it was in a misguided attempt to assume the role of its protector that he committed his one serious crime, killing a man whom he believed to be ill-treating his sister. In gaol he had assumed the role of protector of weaker prisoners, but in his inexperience of life outside gaol, he so misjudged the situation that his distraught sister disowned him as a brother, and other members of his family gave evidence against him. Returned to gaol, he was seen by his prisoner friends as a changed man, obsessed with religion he little understood and carrying a Bible he could not read. Burdened by guilt, he became psychotic and embarked on a series of self-mutilatory acts, culminating in his fatal third attempt to put out his eye in obedience to the Biblical text: 'If thy eye offend thee, pluck it out'.

His death is part of the abiding legacy of the appalling treatment of Aboriginals that went on well into the second half of this century in the name of protection or welfare. It is history, but history of critical importance today. It is history that few Australians know, and which our historians are only now piecing together.

Without a knowledge of it we cannot hope to understand Aboriginal/White relations today, for they are deeply moulded by that history. We will not understand the ill-suppressed hatred which many Aboriginals feel towards police, and their deep distrust of officialdom generally. We will fail to appreciate how many Aboriginal men and women there are now in the community carrying deep scars from that history, scars that prejudice not only their own lives but those of their children. We will run the risk that, as has happened so often, we will repeat the mistakes of the past.

RCIADIC's final report, delivered to the government in March 1991, confirmed the picture of the 99 people who had died in custody. The average age at death was 32. Forty-three had experienced childhood separation from their natural families through intervention by state authorities, missions or other institutions; 83 were unemployed at the date of their last detention; 43 had been charged with an offence at or before the age of fifteen—just kids; only two of the 99 had completed secondary schooling; 43 were taken into custody in the period immediately before their deaths on matters directly related to the over-use of alcohol, and in the remaining cases RCIADIC concluded that alcohol was a contributing factor in their being taken into custody for the last time. The standard of health of the 99 varied from poor to very bad. The average age of those dying from natural causes was a little over 30.

The circumstances of the deaths of those who died by their own hand were deeply disturbing. Thirty of the deaths resulted from hanging, by means of objects such as strips of sheeting and blankets, football socks, a length of electric flex, a belt, the sleeve of a cardigan, a bandage and a pair of jeans. Other deaths occurred as the result of shocking mutilation such as a razor to the throat and a paintbrush driven into an eye, as in the case of Malcolm Smith.

A central finding of RCIADIC was that Aboriginal people had not died in custody at a rate disproportionate to their numbers in the police cell and prison population. The crucial factor was the extent to which they were overrepresented in custody. My office did a calculation to determine the comparable number of non-indigenous people who would have died in custody during the time of the 99 deaths, assuming a comparable level of overrepresentation in custody, and the number was 8500. Just image the public outcry if 8500 non-indigenous Australians were to die in custody over a period of less than ten years. This gives some indication of the extent of the impact on the Aboriginal community of the overrepresentation of its people in custody. RCIADIC calculated the rate at that time as nationally 29 times that of the general community.

Two-thirds of the recommendations dealt with issues associated with police, prisons, coronial inquests and the criminal justice system, particularly focusing on recommendations directed at reducing the number of Aboriginal people in custody. A pivotal finding was the following:

> The single significant contributing factor to incarceration is the disadvantaged and unequal position of Aboriginal people in Australian society in every way, whether socially, economically or culturally. Much of the national report and the associated regional reports is devoted to demonstrating the existence of that inequality and disadvantage. The report documents, in a way never before achieved, the impact of European settlement upon Australia's indigenous peoples, their dispossession and subordination within a dominant and often hostile society frequently motivated by self-interest, the development of racist attitudes both overt and hidden and the way in which these attitudes became institutionalised in the very practices of legal, educational, welfare and Aboriginal assistance authorities.

RCIADIC emphasised the principle of self-determination as central to the process of addressing the underlying issues giving rise to the disproportionate rate of imprisonment. Even Elliott Johnston, a senior and experienced lawyer with considerable knowledge of Aboriginal issues, stressed that he had no real idea of the degree of 'pin pricking domination, abuse of personal power, utter paternalism, open contempt and total indifference which confronted Aboriginal people in their everyday lives'. He saw the creation of conditions that eliminate the systematic and entrenched disadvantage that permeated every aspect of Aboriginal lives as a prerequisite for self-determination.

RCIADIC made 339 comprehensive recommendations directed to governments at all levels to address that disadvantage.

When the report was tabled in parliament on 9 May 1991, I committed the Commonwealth to supporting a national whole-of-government response since the recommendations affected numerous portfolios and concerned governments at all levels. The strategic intention was that the report would not be marginalised as solely the responsibility of an Aboriginal affairs portfolio at either the Commonwealth or state level. It was imperative that police and corrective services institutions were committed to implementing the responses. I had the task of coordinating the Commonwealth response across all portfolios, supported by PM&C, and also the responsibility of bringing together a national response, including those of state and territory governments. This was an unprecedented opportunity to work towards a comprehensive response that would lock governments into a long-term agenda of reform in indigenous affairs.

In December 1991, at the initiative of PM&C, the Cabinet resolved on a package of measures with interim funding of $7–9 million for three main areas: improvements in police and custodial systems; family counselling; and additional support for Aboriginal legal services. The Commonwealth boosted the funding of Aboriginal legal services by $2 million. The remainder was to be allocated to state and territory governments for issues within their jurisdiction.

The Commonwealth's strategy was to provide a small financial sweetener to the states and territories to draw them into the national response process. To that extent it was a well-intentioned bureaucratic initiative, but I was uneasy at the time with funding state and territory governments. The announcement created understandable resentment in the minds of some Aboriginal people that governments, not organisations controlled by the Aboriginal community, would benefit from this funding. The consequence of this hostility was that the great bulk of future funding was channelled through Aboriginal-controlled organisations.

An interdepartmental group of officials prepared the first draft of the Commonwealth response. It was a deeply disappointing document. Of the 339 recommendations, almost half had not been agreed to by government departments and agencies. This was of very great concern as I believed that the Commonwealth should set the pace. My office therefore committed ourselves to drive the process. I determined that I would chair a series of working groups of officials around key areas of the recommendations—law and justice, health and substance abuse, employment, education and youth policy.

The task meant taking each of the recommendations and getting agreement from the relevant government department and minister who would need to take responsibility for implementing it. This was a daunting job of writing, lobbying and negotiation in which a key group of ATSIC officers, together with my own staff, played a magnificent role. Often my senior adviser, Kathleen Taperell, was still lobbying and organising in other ministerial offices in the early hours of the morning. The result was that the Commonwealth supported all but one recommendation. The overwhelming majority were also supported by state and territory governments, who followed the Commonwealth's lead after the Commonwealth pressured them by, for example, sending letters to premiers and chief ministers personally signed by Prime Minister Hawke.

The one recommendation the Commonwealth did not support was that which was rejected expressly at the request of the ATSIC Board, namely that ATSIC be taken outside the ambit of the *Public Service Act 1922*. The board's reasons were twofold: by being part of the Commonwealth administrative family, ATSIC would be in a better position to influence the policy direction of other Commonwealth departments and agencies; and by being subject to the Public Service Act, ATSIC employees would continue to have mobility throughout the Australian Public Service.

ATSIC commissioners and staff together with my office set about developing a package of funding measures to take to Cabinet to boost Commonwealth resources to tackle the underlying issues of health, substance abuse, housing, employment, education and other areas which RCIADIC found to be the root cause of the disproportionate rate of Aboriginal imprisonment. Again, the proposed package not only had to be negotiated with the ATSIC Board but had to be agreed with all relevant government departments, agencies and ministerial offices.

I have already referred to the Cabinet meeting addressed by Lois O'Donoghue, Alf Bamblett and Steve Gordon where the Commonwealth response to RCIADIC was to be determined. After the three ATSIC commissioners left, Cabinet discussion began. I recall Gerry Hand as my only real vocal supporter. Between us, speaking from opposite ends of the table, we talked Cabinet to a standstill. The meeting finally adjourned when we reached agreement on new measures that gave $400 million over five years. It was clearly understood, however, that the Commonwealth funding was not to be a substitute for a commitment to equitable contributions from programs administered by mainstream government departments and agencies. History has shown that it is this commitment which governments at all levels have failed to honour. Over 70 per cent of the additional

Commonwealth funding was to go directly to organisations controlled by the indigenous community.

Many of the responses my office prepared to the recommendations went far beyond what RCIADIC in fact recommended. We did this not only because we wanted to achieve the greatest possible reform but also because a strong Commonwealth response would have the effect of lifting the quality of responses from state and territory governments.

An example is recommendation 315, which stated that the Western Australian government give effect to the recommendations of the 'Millstream Conference'. This proposed involving Aboriginal people in the ownership and management of appropriate national parks and addressing other indigenous aspirations, such as employment opportunities in national parks. Commonwealth support for the recommendation was first obtained and then Commonwealth officials acted to push all state and territory governments to support it for implementation in their state or territory. The result was that indigenous people across Australia can hold governments to their commitments to support the recommendation, which offers magnificent opportunities for indigenous people to play an increasingly important role in the management of the national estate.

The national response of all governments to RCIADIC's recommendations was tabled in federal parliament on 27 March 1992, and the detail of what was to be the first of a two-stage final response by the Commonwealth was also released. The Commonwealth announcements included extensive and creative new programs touching on a wide spectrum of policy.

Resources were provided to develop and enhance Aboriginal employment strategies in police services, custodial and court systems in order to train police in awareness of Aboriginal history, culture and disadvantage, and to help implement the recommendations directed to improving Aboriginal relations with the police. There was now an agreed national agenda for improvement in Aboriginal–police relations based on the unanimous support of all governments for RCIADIC's practical proposals for reform. The Commonwealth announced that it would work with the states, territories and the legal profession to develop a cultural awareness program for judges, magistrates and court officers and staff. It supported and funded a national conference, involving Aboriginal community leaders and police, on Aboriginal–police relations. A commitment was also given to ensure that the Australian Federal Police would introduce new procedures to give effect to RCIADIC's recommendations. Deaths in police custody around Australia have been dramatically reduced since these policies began to be implemented and there is no doubt that the initiatives taken in response to it have contributed to that success. Through

ATSIC the Commonwealth provided additional support to Aboriginal legal services to carry out their responsibilities.

As a part of its first-stage response, the Commonwealth substantially strengthened the capacity of the Human Rights and Equal Opportunity Commission (HREOC) to inform Aboriginal and Torres Strait Islander communities about human rights issues and legislation. HREOC was to work with the National Aboriginal and Islander Legal Services Secretariat to develop an accredited training course for field officers. Further support was to be given to mechanisms for handling complaints by Australians under the First Optional Protocol to the International Covenant on Civil and Political Rights (ICCPR), to better interpreter services for Aboriginal people in Commonwealth courts, to developing options for Commonwealth racial vilification legislation, and to improve cultural awareness training for the Australian Federal Police.

Nearly half the people whose deaths were investigated were separated, as children, from their families through official intervention. Through ATSIC, the Commonwealth was to provide funding to enhance the capacity of link-up services to address unmet demands by Aboriginal and Torres Strait Islander people for help in locating and reuniting with their families. The new funding was to establish link-up services in each of the states and the Northern Territory.

RCIADIC found that alcohol was a factor in the detention of all of the 99 who died in custody. It is also a major factor in family and community breakdown, domestic violence, and the high incarceration rates among Aboriginal and Torres Strait Islander people generally. Through ATSIC, and in cooperation with the states and territories, the Commonwealth provided resources for innovative community-based action to prevent and counter alcohol and substance abuse, especially by young people. Local programs were to be devised by Aboriginal people themselves to strike at the powerlessness that is at the root of the tragedy they are experiencing.

Accurate data is essential for monitoring progress arising from RCIADIC, and funding was provided to enable the Australian Bureau of Statistics to carry out, for the first time, a national survey of Aboriginal people. The survey was to complement information from the Census and from the Aboriginal and Torres Strait Islander Housing Needs and Infrastructure Survey, the first comprehensive national survey of this kind, and was to provide a much-improved basis for policy and program decisions by governments and by Aboriginal organisations themselves. In cooperation with the states and territories, the Commonwealth would also support the continuation of data collection and analysis of deaths in custody by the Australian Institute of Criminology. This commitment was to assume particular importance in the years ahead in keeping up the pressure on state and territory governments to give effect to RCIADIC recommendations affecting their jurisdictions.

On 24 June 1992, Prime Minister Keating announced the second stage of the Commonwealth response and measures that would address the underlying issues in the disproportionate rate of Aboriginal imprisonment:

- funding for a land acquisition and development program that would provide the capital resources and training for better use and sustainable development of Aboriginal and Torres Strait Islander land;
- the establishment of an Aboriginal rural resources program to encourage enterprise, particularly in managing pastoral properties;
- a Community Economic Initiative Scheme, funded over five years, to foster local enterprise;
- the expansion of the Australian National Parks and Wildlife contract employment program for managing natural and cultural resources;
- funding for ATSIC to develop long-term Aboriginal industry strategies in the pastoral, arts and tourism industries;
- significant expansion of the CDEP;
- a Young Peoples' Development Program to encourage planned community action to meet the specific needs of indigenous young people;
- an Aboriginal Youth Sport and Recreation Development Program to provide Aboriginal sports development officers to work in communities;
- an increase of 200 Aboriginal education workers from 1993; and
- 600 more preschool places for Aboriginal children from 1994.

Important as these programs and initiatives were, they could make only a modest contribution to addressing the disadvantage that RCIADIC described as underlying deaths in custody. Nothing less than a total change in the commitment of mainstream government departments and agencies to deliver an equitable allocation of resources is required to ensure a minimal level of services to indigenous communities. There is no evidence yet of either the bureaucratic or the political will to achieve this at any level of government. The House of Representatives Standing Committee on Aboriginal and Torres Strait Islander Affairs subsequently issued a scathing criticism of the government's Access and Equity Strategy. Called *Rhetoric or Reality?*, this unanimous parliamentary report made the point that unless the mainstream agencies began to make it a priority to address the human rights of indigenous people, no real progress would be made.

At the time of writing, rhetoric not action remains the reality for most indigenous people in their dealings with government departments and agencies. RCIADIC clearly set an achievable agenda and all that is needed is the political will to put it into effect. But state and territory governments have allocated next to nothing by way of additional resources in the immediate aftermath of RCIADIC and there is no evidence of a genuine commitment by those governments to an equitable allocation of resources from programs of their mainstream departments and agencies.

It is of course the mainstream state government departments that bear the responsibility for providing roads, health, education, water and housing to all the citizens of the state, including their Aboriginal citizens. It is a responsibility they have failed to carry out in indigenous communities over succeeding decades. But this is insignificant in comparison with the demonstrable failure of those governments to implement the central thrust of RCIADIC's recommendation relating to the criminal justice system, namely that imprisonment should be a last resort.

Across Australia, state and territory governments and political parties have attempted to outbid each other in an unseemly law-and-order policy auction. Policies such as zero tolerance, mandatory sentencing, boot camps for young offenders, increased penalties, failure to decriminalise offences such as drunkenness and a failure to rigorously pursue alternative non-custodial sentencing options has led to an astronomical and shameful increase in the number of both Aboriginal and non-Aboriginal people in custody in direct contravention of RCIADIC's recommendations. Specific examples include the WA juvenile justice legislation and the NT mandatory sentencing legislation.

The Australian Institute of Criminology has confirmed that since RCIADIC began its work the number of Aboriginal prisoners has more than doubled from 1809 in 1988 to 3750 in 1998. The statistics are equally as bleak for juvenile justice sentencing, with continuing massive overrepresentation of Aboriginal youth offenders in juvenile justice detention centres. So how is it that in excess of $30 million of public money (though cheap by royal commission standards) can be spent on a royal commission whose establishment, work and continuing recommendations were endorsed by all state and territory governments, who have then acted in open defiance of its central principle that imprisonment ought to be a last resort? This outcome has not been for want of public accountability measures directed particularly to state governments and put in place by the Commonwealth. Quite deliberately, and in anticipation of what was to come, a strict regime of monitoring and accountability was established in order to keep pressure on all governments to implement the recommendations, as indeed they had promised both indigenous people and the wider community they would do.

The very first RCIADIC recommendation went to the heart of future public accountability by governments for giving effect to their promises and responses. The problem was that it simply did not go far enough. There was no reference to any independent scrutiny of the performance of governments, no reference to parliamentary scrutiny or even the need for comprehensive annual reports by governments on their performance in giving effect to each recommendation. However, the Commonwealth did set up a monitoring and accountability regime, which required:

- detailed annual reports from all jurisdictions, including the Commonwealth, on progress in implementing each of the recommendations, with such reports to be tabled in each parliament;
- independent scrutiny of the performance of governments by the Aboriginal and Torres Strait Islander Social Justice Commissioner;
- reference of the annual reports to the House of Representatives Standing Committee on Aboriginal and Torres Strait Islander Affairs;
- key issues and recommendations to be raised at ministerial forums; and
- a review of the monitoring and accountability process after three years.

The Commonwealth government itself has no general law-making power over the criminal justice system of the states and territories; this is, subject to the Commonwealth's Aboriginal affairs power, seen to be within their exclusive jurisdiction. A federal minister for indigenous affairs has no hope of effectively influencing the decisions of state police and prisons ministers. Hence the importance of listing the implementation of RCIADIC as an agenda item for future ministerial forums of all relevant ministers. Even then the capacity to influence state and territory decision-making is limited. Not only has Commonwealth pressure on the states been ineffective in forcing action on the recommendations, but even the public pressures of well-intentioned community opinion leaders has had a limited effect on state governments.

A welcome development was the establishment in 1994, in Western Australia, of a community-based Deaths in Custody Watch Committee by a coalition of Aboriginal and wider community representatives including churches, trade unions, lawyers and representatives from political parties. This group achieved a high profile in fighting to make the WA government accountable for implementing the RCIADIC recommendations. It is a model for community action and should be encouraged in other parts of Australia. The media, with few exceptions, have shown little interest in holding governments accountable for implementing the recommendations. Such welcome expressions as there have been of community and media opinion have not been able to change the policy direction of state and territory governments.

A further possible strategy of the Commonwealth to push the states and territories to act is by way of the processes of COAG. In 1996 a re-elected Labor government would have been committed by its election policy to take such issues to COAG. Prime Minister Howard should be encouraged to do so and a future Labor government should commit itself to this policy. There is no evidence of such a commitment at this time. Further support for this approach is found in the first report on the performance of governments by the House of Representatives Standing Committee on Aboriginal and Torres Strait Islander Affairs, *Justice under Scrutiny*:

> While the dramatic reduction in the number of Aboriginal deaths in police custody deserves wide acclaim, the reports of the Institute of Criminology show that the number of deaths in prisons is higher than at the conclusion of RCIADIC. The root cause of the disproportionate number of Aboriginal deaths in prison remains as it was at the time of RCIADIC: the disproportionate rate of imprisonment of Aboriginal people. There is no doubt that should the present trends continue, our nation is heading towards a deepening crisis and will deserve international condemnation on the issue of deaths in custody.

After six years in the indigenous affairs portfolio, using almost every available public accountability mechanism far beyond what RCIADIC itself recommended, I have come to the conclusion that serious consideration should be given to the feasibility of overriding Commonwealth legislation to force the states and territories to give effect to the recommendations. There is no question that since the 1967 referendum, the Commonwealth has the constitutional power to make laws on Aboriginal affairs and such laws have the capacity to override inconsistent state and territory laws. That is precisely what happened when the Keating government passed the Native Title Act and set national benchmarks for the recognition and protection of native title. The Native Title Act overrode inconsistent state legislation which sought to take away the rights recognised by the Mabo decision.

The time has come for the Commonwealth to creatively consider the preparation of an 'Aboriginal Deaths in Custody Royal Commission Implementation Act', which would establish minimum benchmarks for state and territory governments to comply with the RCIADIC recommendations. There are of course considerable constitutional and other drafting challenges in such legislation, and limitations on the capacity of Commonwealth legislation to regulate the intricate detail of daily prison administration. However, general principles, in line with key recommendations, can potentially be legislated and enforced by Commonwealth legislation, or at least the threat of it, or by fiscal sanctions directed towards non-conforming states and territories. I do not pretend that there are not serious legal and political obstacles to this approach, but it is one that needs to be seriously explored.

This is not to say that RCIADIC has been wasted. Patrick Dodson, one of the commissioners, has said that if the recommendations were implemented by governments there would be no need for a reconciliation process, so far-reaching and decisive are its recommendations.

Those recommendations are as valid and important as the day they were tabled in federal parliament. They were welcomed by governments at all levels, with ministers representing both sides of politics agreeing on behalf of their governments that the single most important theme to emerge from RCIADIC was 'the need to put behind us a history of dispossession, dependency and efforts of forced assimilation and to move decisively into a new era of Aboriginal and Torres Strait Islander empowerment and self-determination'.

RCIADIC's promise has not yet been fulfilled but as a nation we must act to ensure that these landmark reports are not allowed to gather dust on the shelf. In giving support to the reconciliation process, which the government had already foreshadowed, the national Commissioner, Elliott Johnston QC, penned some magnificent words describing the challenge of the reconciliation process which lay ahead:

> The process may falter at times; appear to get lost; but it can be pulled up again and survive if we are cool and negotiate with open minds and as with equals. And in the end, perhaps together, Aboriginal and non-Aboriginal, the situation can be reached where this ancient, subtly creative Aboriginal culture exists in friendship alongside the non-Aboriginal culture. Such an achievement would be a matter of pride not only for all Australians but for all humankind.

5

MABO: A PEACEFUL BEGINNING

The discredited doctrine of terra nullius, *or 'land belonging to no one', was the legal fiction that provided the justification for the dispossession of Aboriginal and Torres Strait Islander people for over 200 years after the British planted their flag at Botany Bay. The 1992 High Court's Mabo decision changed all that forever. For the first time since 1788 the traditional rights of indigenous people to ownership of their land were recognised by the highest court in the country. These newly recognised but ancient rights of title to land were, however, vulnerable to obliteration by state governments which had mostly, even in the 1970s and 1980s, remained implacably opposed to the recognition of comprehensive Aboriginal land rights.*

Importantly, the Commonwealth's Racial Discrimination Act 1975 *provided a crucial measure of protection of indigenous rights in the aftermath of the Mabo decision, as it had done in the lead-up to that decision. In effect, the RDA prevented Aboriginal people's interests in land being treated less favourably than those of non-Aboriginal people.*

Following the Mabo decision, the Keating government instituted a consultation process in preparation for a formal response from government to the decision. Despite the change in prime ministers from Hawke to Keating, the cross-party cooperation continued and Mabo was not the subject of bitter party-political divisions. On the eve of the 1993 election being called, the government was advised by PM&C to announce that the RDA would be amended as a part of the government's response. Such an announcement would have created anger and division within the ALP and the wider community. In an as yet untold story, a meeting of key ministers, presided over by Paul Keating, rejected the recommendation.

Mabo did not become the election issue that some senior Coalition figures wanted it to be. After its election victory, Labor was on track to deliver what was to become the Native Title Act to protect and enhance the High Court's Mabo decision. From the relatively peaceful beginning, however, the Mabo debate was to develop into a political war.

I never had the privilege of meeting Eddie Mabo, but when I was appointed Minister for Aboriginal Affairs I was conscious of the case that he and the two other continuing plaintiffs, Fr David Passi and James Rice, had pending on behalf of the Meriam people before the High Court of Australia. They were seeking to prove the continuing existence of indigenous title to the remote Murray Islands in the Torres Strait. The action by the Torres Strait Islanders sought to have the Australian legal system overturn the doctrine of *terra nullius*. It was this legal fiction that underpinned and provided legitimacy in the eyes of Australian courts for the ongoing taking of traditional land occupied by indigenous people without consent or compensation since 1788.

An increasing number of Australians were beginning to appreciate that, while this appropriation of Aboriginal land began in 1788, the practice continued well into the 1960s and was based on the legal fiction that indigenous people had no rights of ownership over the land they lived on. The very idea that the ownership of a vast continent, occupied by indigenous people for 50 000 years, could be gained by planting a flag in the ground in one corner of that land is of course absurd, as well as being deeply unjust.

In the United States, Canada and New Zealand the rights of indigenous people had been accorded a degree of respect and recognition never given to Aboriginal and Torres Strait Islander people in Australia. That recognition and respect was reflected in treaties with indigenous peoples which, for all their limitations, at least gave a legal foundation of rights.

In Australia Aboriginal people have had to depend on the fickle, transient and mostly adverse policies of governments for any rights to land. It was only in the 1970s that any Aboriginal rights to land began to be recognised in the most limited way by state governments. Before then, any land designated as Aboriginal reserve land existed only at the whim of governments and was most commonly dealt with according to the practice that what the government could give, the government could take away—and it usually did.

Thus by the early 1980s, considerable frustration and anger had grown in the minds of indigenous people over the lack of progress made by state governments in recognising indigenous rights. Torres Strait Islanders were in a different position from Aboriginal people in that they had never been driven from their lands. They remained in occupation but were not recognised as the owners of their lands under Australian or Queensland law, and they had been subject to oppressive and discriminatory controls by the laws of successive Queensland governments. Indeed, Eddie Mabo had been denied permission to travel to the Murray Islands from his home in Townsville to attend his father's funeral in 1972. It was the Australian historian Henry Reynolds who first told Eddie Mabo that the Torres Strait Islands were regarded as not owned by the Islanders but as crown land. It was this denial of rights that contributed to the undoubted fire in Eddie Mabo's belly and his determination to change Australian law. His ultimate victory would not only secure the recognition of native title rights in the Torres Strait but for Aboriginal people on the mainland as well.

Past attempts to establish native title rights had failed in the Gove land rights case in 1971 before the NT Supreme Court. In that case, Justice Blackburn had ruled against the existence of native title in Australia, but the decision had never been taken on appeal to a higher court. It is important to understand the significance of this history of the continual struggle, including the passage of the RDA in 1975, to appreciate the significance of the Mabo decision and the politics leading to the passage of the Native Title Act.

In 1982 the original five Torres Strait Islander plaintiffs began proceedings in the High Court of Australia in which they asserted traditional rights of ownership over particular plots of land on the Murray Islands and areas of the sea (the claims over the sea were subsequently withdrawn). They further claimed that those traditional rights should be recognised under Australian law. They sought to overcome one of the hurdles raised by the Gove land rights case by asserting that the rights claimed were not communal in nature but an individual private property right over particular garden plots of land, analogous to the rights claimed by non-indigenous Australians. Torres Strait Islander society, where people had gardens and permanent settlement, was organised differently from Aboriginal society where people lived a nomadic life, hunting and gathering in their traditional country.

Both before and after the Mabo decision, the Commonwealth's RDA was to play a pivotal role in the protection of indigenous rights. It is my view, however, as I will explain in later chapters, that the political threats to the RDA became in the minds of some Aboriginal people and their supporters almost the sole focus of their political activism, to the detriment of other issues.

In 1975 the Whitlam government passed the RDA to give effect to Australia's obligations under CERD, which obliges national governments to act within their borders to give effect to the principles of the convention. The effect of the RDA was to prohibit action by governments or any other party that would treat any people less favourably than others on the basis of their race. Its validity was upheld in the High Court decision of *Koowarta vs Bjelke-Petersen*, where the court struck down the discriminatory land transfer policies of the Queensland government.

The existence of the legislation became crucial when the Bjelke-Petersen government passed the *Queensland Coastal Islands Declaratory*

Act 1985, which sought to obliterate any native title rights Torres Strait Islanders may have had when the islands were declared a part of Queensland in 1879. The effect of this law, if upheld, would have defeated the Mabo claim and meant that no native title rights could be recognised by the court, having been effectively expropriated out of existence, without compensation, by the Queensland National Party government.

The validity of the legislation was challenged in what has become known as Mabo No. 1, where in 1988 the High Court, by a bare majority of four to three, struck down the legislation as being in breach of the Commonwealth's RDA. The Mabo case then continued in the Supreme Court of Queensland, which heard detailed evidence on behalf of each of the plaintiffs concerning their particular interests in land. Ultimately it was not Eddie Mabo but the other two remaining plaintiffs, David Passi and James Rice, who were able to prove in evidence their claims of title to the land, but the decision still justly and properly bears the name of Eddie Mabo. Finally the case went before the High Court in Mabo No. 2, the decision commonly referred to as the Mabo decision.

I t was surprising to me that there was so little public debate and discussion of the looming Mabo judgment in the first half of 1992. Eddie Mabo had died on 31 January that year, four months before the High Court brought down its decision on 3 June. The following January he was named Australian of the Year by the *Australian* readers.

I was in the High Court that day, as was my Opposition counterpart Michael Wooldridge, having arranged joint leave from our party Whips. The tension was electric and the courtroom packed with many of the people who were to be in the Senate's public gallery eighteen months later for the historic passage of the Native Title Act. Key Aboriginal and Torres Strait Islander leaders were present, and many non-indigenous supporters of the cause. Unfortunately Mrs Bonita Mabo, wife of Eddie Mabo, was not in the court to hear the judgment—she was driving from Townsville and had only got as far as Sydney when the judgment was delivered.

The decision is one of the most important decisions the High Court of Australia will ever deliver and elevated the process of reconciliation. In the words of Justice Brennan:

> The common law of this country would perpetuate injustice if it were to continue to embrace the enlarged notice of *terra nullius* and to persist in characterising the indigenous inhabitants of the Australian colonies as people too low in the scale of social organisation to be acknowledged as possessing rights and interests in land.

Too many tombstones, too little justice

Highs and lows sometimes came in quick succession in the indigenous affairs portfolio, even on the same issue. On Saturday,
3 June 1995, I flew to Townsville with Annita Keating to participate in the unveiling of the tombstone of the late Eddie Mabo.
Also present were Bonita Mabo, Lois O'Donoghue, many members of the Mabo family and a large crowd of the Torres Strait
Islander community. The unveiling was a powerful and emotional
event, celebrating a life well lived and one that made a real impact
on the nation.

The nextt day I learned that Eddie Mabo's tombstone had been
desecrated, and I phoned Bonita Mabo in Townsville to express my
sympathy and support. The government was determined to right
the wrong, and resources were obtained for the reburial of this
national hero in his homeland on Murray Island. My media release
on the occasion of the tombstone unveiling in Townsville had been
headed 'Too many tombstones, too little justice', and the message
was even more significant the day after.

Justices Deane and Gaudron described the doctrine of *terra nullius*
and the acts and events by which the dispossession was carried out as
'the darkest aspect of the history of this nation. The nation as a whole
must remain diminished unless and until there is an acknowledgement
of, and retreat from, those past injustices'.

From day one of the judgment, I sought to emphasise in the public
debate the just and moral nature of the decision. Non-indigenous
people had nothing to fear from it, but it was also important to
recognise that there was a wider agenda of Aboriginal land aspirations
which would not be met by the terms of the High Court decision alone.
While the judgment was of fundamental importance to all Aboriginal
people, it would not directly benefit the land aspirations of most of
those who had been dispossessed absolutely. The issue of land rights
for such people was primarily one requiring action by parliaments in
line with the RCIADIC recommendations. My objective from the beginning was to push for the establishment of a national land acquisition
fund to address the land aspirations of dispossessed Aboriginal people.

Some key consequences of the decision need to be emphasised.
The Mabo judgment did not challenge any of the legal rights and
interests of non-Aboriginal Australians. Its effect was to recognise that
native title *may* continue to exist in those parts of Australia where
Aboriginal people still occupied or had sufficient continuing association with their traditional lands, *but in no case could the rights of any*

other landholder be eroded. Furthermore, any hope indigenous people had of challenging the sovereignty or supreme law-making power of the parliaments was unambiguously buried for all time by the court.

The court made clear in its judgment that governments acting within their powers could extinguish any native title by granting the land to non-native title holders in a manner that was inconsistent with native title, and that they had done so over much of the continent, for example wherever there had been a grant of freehold interests. The question to be asked in the case of each type of crown grant or crown dealing with the land was whether native title rights could continue to exist over the land after the grant, as it could, for example, in the case of crown land being converted to a national park or following the grant of an exploration licence.

A key question that was left up in the air was whether grant of a leasehold interest, such as a pastoral lease, extinguished native title. This was the issue which the High Court was subsequently to consider in the Wik case when it ruled in favour of Aboriginal people. But it was clear from the Mabo decision itself that whatever interest Aboriginal people might continue to have in such land, it would always be subject to and overridden by any valid interest held by non-indigenous Australians. Thus not one square centimetre of land held by non-indigenous Australians was put at risk by the Mabo decision. Viewed in this context, the Mabo decision is by no means radical, but it did bring Australia to a position of basic recognition of the concept of indigenous title to land, and it had huge symbolic as well as practical consequences.

Another principle flowed from the decision that was crucial to the protection of indigenous rights and to the need for a national response to Mabo. Even after Mabo, Commonwealth, state and territory governments could legislate to take away the native title rights recognised by the High Court, provided they acted within the limits of their law-making power. There is no constitutional constraint that requires a state government to pay fair compensation when acquiring the property of citizens. States and territories are, however, bound by the provisions of the RDA, which requires them to treat indigenous people no less favourably than others in the community.

The Constitution requires that if the Commonwealth is to acquire property it must do so on 'just terms'. The Commonwealth is of course also bound by the RDA, but as this is a law of the Commonwealth parliament it can be overridden by a further act of that parliament to allow discrimination to occur by either Commonwealth or state and territory governments. Much of the public debate over the next eighteen months leading to the passage of the Native Title Act would revolve around this legislation.

Paul Keating was crucial in bringing about the Native Title Act as the government's first-stage response to the Mabo decision. While I strongly disagreed with his actions at particular times during the native title debate, my admiration for his political courage and leadership in bringing about a just outcome is placed unambiguously on the public record. Australia was indeed fortunate to have him as Prime Minister at this turning point in our history. Before becoming Prime Minister he had no personal history of involvement in, or support for, indigenous rights and had seldom spoken about Aboriginal issues during all his time in parliament. I was therefore concerned that the momentum for reform might be lost when he became Prime Minister. As events transpired, he demonstrated, as did all prime ministers between 1972 and 1996, a strong personal interest in advancing indigenous rights. It remains an area of public policy worthy of prime ministerial attention.

As Bob Hawke had said, and as I have always believed, the reconciliation process itself may well be as important as the final outcome. The message is that all of us, indigenous and non-indigenous, learn a great deal about each other as the process evolves and it has the potential to change the way we relate to each other. To paraphrase the RCIADIC final report, at times the government's response to Mabo did falter, and at one stage appeared doomed, but the turning point came when we negotiated as equals with indigenous Australians. It is a lesson Australians should never forget; the reconciliation process itself depends on it.

As the advocate for Aboriginal and Torres Strait Islander people within the ministry, I was always sceptical of the extent to which state and territory governments, including the Queensland Labor government, would be prepared to respect indigenous aspirations in their response to the Mabo decision. My concerns were borne out by events and I was to spend much of the next year locked in bitter conflict with most of those governments as they joined with powerful vested interests in an attempt to force the Commonwealth, at best, to lower its own commitment to protect indigenous rights or, at worst, to abandon its responsibilities altogether.

The predictable early responses to the High Court's decision unfolded. NLC chairperson Galarrwuy Yunupingu called for a national land rights law and a treaty. Queensland Premier Wayne Goss suggested Mabo would have few practical consequences for indigenous claims. He said it might not apply to the mainland and noted that the way in which the Murray Islanders had 'inherited plots of land handed down from generation to generation' was 'very different from the nomadic situation which existed on the mainland. Anybody seeking to initiate a claim has probably got to have a set of facts comparable to the

Islanders' case'. This argument was also raised by John Howard and Ian McLachlan in the coming year, but it was not a view that found favour with the High Court or with Aboriginal Australians.

The day after the High Court's decision Prime Minister Keating moved to soothe the concern of non-indigenous landholders by emphasising that the judgment did not threaten title of either freehold or leasehold land. He recognised that the decision removed 'the great barrier' to reconciliation.

While Michael Wooldridge welcomed the decision, one of the first signs of Coalition opposition came only a month later when a senior WA Liberal, Bill Hassell, considered to be on the Right of his party, moved an amendment at a Liberal Party Federal Council meeting in Sydney seeking to criticise the High Court for being motivated more by politics than law in delivering the Mabo judgment.

Two of the main participants in the forthcoming public debate responded in a considered way to the decision. Patrick Dodson, speaking on behalf of the Council for Aboriginal Reconciliation, said on 10 June 1992 that the council had received the Mabo decision in a spirit of 'joy and celebration' and sought to allay the concerns of pastoralists and miners by describing them as 'understandable but unwarranted'. The Council announced that it would embark on a process of communication and consultation about the issues raised by the decision. Lois O'Donoghue issued a public statement emphasising the importance of the judgment in providing practical benefits to those who could come within its ambit, but she also emphasised that governments have a moral obligation to provide for the land needs of dispossessed indigenous people. The ATSIC Board endorsed the strategy of consultation already announced by the Council for Aboriginal Reconciliation and supported a proposal for a national convention.

The Mabo debate in its most vitriolic form took a considerable time to erupt, and I did everything I could to keep the more extremist critics of Mabo isolated and in their box during that early period. The objective was to work for maximum cross-party cooperation in developing a response to the High Court decision. If the debate were to become a partisan issue it would get ugly—precisely what happened after the 1993 federal election. While such divisions were probably inevitable in the longer term, if the Labor government were to bring forward a principled response that would override the states in the national interest, the longer the tone of the debate could be kept rational and constructive the better the outcome for Aboriginal people.

Because of the pivotal importance of the RDA, it was therefore a matter of great concern when the chief executive of a major mining company and an ultra-conservative social commentator, Hugh Morgan, asserted that the law was in 'disarray' as a result of the High Court decision and that state governments were powerless to act. He characterised the RDA as the impediment to the achievement of his objectives and issued a call to arms for the opponents of the Mabo decision: 'One of the early bills a Coalition government must put to parliament and, if necessary, to a double dissolution election, is either repeal of, or substantial amendment to, the *Racial Discrimination Act 1975*'. Mr Morgan has subsequently been appointed to the Board of the Reserve Bank by the Howard government, which obviously holds his views in high esteem.

I believe that Hugh Morgan's contribution helped the Aboriginal cause because the Opposition, under John Hewson, joined the government in condemning his statement. My continuing dialogue and cooperative working relationship with Michael Wooldridge was important at this time. He understood the importance of the RDA for Aboriginal people. I tried to marginalise Hugh Morgan, asserting that the repeal of that Act would not be supported by any national government. Michael Wooldridge, acting independently, also ruled out overturning the Mabo decision by legislation, saying it would conflict with Liberal principles, respect for the rule of law and property rights: 'The Coalition is not on about taking away freedoms people have won in the courts'. Prime Minister Keating also weighed into the argument when, responding to a question in parliament, he said: 'What we have here is just bigotry. It is the voice of ignorance, the voice of hysteria and the voice of the 19th century'.

Throughout the native title debate, the Australian Mining Industry Council (AMIC) was completely antagonistic to Aboriginal interests. Fortunately they were so hamfisted most of that time that their contribution positively boosted the Aboriginal cause. But on 13 October 1992 AMIC's assistant director, Geoffrey Ewing, expressed concern that Aboriginal groups had started using the High Court's judgment as a basis of claim against mining companies in four places around Australia—the Kimberley, Gove, McArthur River and another unspecified site in Queensland—and in doing so had raised uncertainty for industry.

Seven days later, a more balanced contribution came from Rick Farley, the executive director of the National Farmers' Federation, who called on the federal government to legislate to clarify the High Court decision after consultation with interest groups and the community. Most of the contributions by the NFF leadership during the Mabo debate were thoughtful and constructive. Rick Farley was a member of the Council for Aboriginal Reconciliation and sought to balance his commitment to that process with his responsibility to his rural constituency. By achieving that balance he was able to ensure that in the coming year the NFF was able to remain at the negotiating table.

It was clearly time that the government moved to show some collective leadership. So on 27 October 1992 a joint submission was presented to Cabinet by the Prime Minister, Attorney-General Michael Duffy and myself on options for directions for a government response. A team of Commonwealth officials had prepared an Interdepartmental Committee report for consideration by ministers in which a wide range of options for a response were canvassed. Many options were wide-ranging and visionary and showed that the decision of the court had clearly opened the horizons of at least some Commonwealth public servants to what was possible. Above all, the submission recommended strong Commonwealth leadership and a wide consultative process before a final response was brought down by the government.

The same day Prime Minister Keating announced the government's decision to initiate consultations, directed by the Mabo Ministerial Committee comprised of the Prime Minister and other key ministers. The consultations were to be held with state and territory governments, key indigenous organisations, and the mining and pastoral industries. A discussion paper was to be released by officials. It was of great significance that Paul Keating chose to chair these consultations. His tone was optimistic: 'By rejecting the doctrine of *terra nullius* the court has provided a new basis for relations between indigenous and other Australians and given impetus to the process of reconciliation. It provides both an opportunity and a challenge'.

He reassured non-indigenous Australians that their existing legal rights in property would continue but that there was a 'need for clarity in the definition and application of native title rights, especially in relation to other interests in land'.

Cabinet decided to have PM&C play the leading departmental role in conducting the consultations. This was understandable in the light of the Prime Minister's intended role in chairing consultations, and there were potential advantages in using the prestige and bureaucratic clout of the leading Commonwealth department to conduct direct negotiations with state and territory government officials. It was inevitable, however, that PM&C would seek to advance a much wider bureaucratic and government agenda than the protection and advancement of Aboriginal rights. PM&C was intended by Cabinet to work 'in close cooperation' with the Attorney-General's Department and was to 'consult' with ATSIC. But tensions would inevitably emerge with ATSIC and with Aboriginal organisations across Australia. PM&C had limited history of dealing with indigenous issues and little policy expertise in this area.

It was evident even in those early days of discussions within the government that different objectives would be pursued by various ministers. They varied from the need to ensure justice for indigenous people to the protection and advancement of the interests of the mining and pastoral industries. From the start Paul Keating's objective was to ensure what he saw as a balanced outcome advancing indigenous rights and providing certainty for industry and, ideally, one that was nationally negotiated with the support of state and territory governments. He wanted an outcome that 'would stick', that is, one that commanded the greatest support from those governments.

I was always pessimistic about any outcome that had to win the lowest common denominator support of conservative state governments. It was difficult enough dealing with the Queensland Labor government, but much more difficult dealing with the Court government in Western Australia. I was determined that the government's priority ought to be an outcome that protected and advanced indigenous rights. If that meant non-cooperation by some states and territories, then that was a price I believed should be paid. The Commonwealth had an obligation to use its clear powers to protect indigenous rights and if necessary to override state or territory obstruction with the power conferred on it by the 1967 referendum. After the Cabinet decision I issued a statement welcoming the Prime Minister's leadership role and very deliberately ruled out amending the RDA to override the effect of the Mabo decision.

The public response to the government's announcement was positive, with Shadow Minister Wooldridge describing it as 'not before time' but stressing that the process should 'not be an excuse for inactivity'. Both John Hewson and Michael Wooldridge emphasised the part they saw being played by the Council for Aboriginal Reconciliation.

The government's announcement was welcomed by Lois O'Donoghue, on behalf of ATSIC, who congratulated the Prime Minister on his leadership and welcomed 'the Coalition's support for the consultative process'. This was perhaps putting a generous gloss on the Opposition's response, but it was part of an independently adopted but shared strategy by Lois O'Donoghue, some ATSIC officials and myself to encourage the Opposition to cooperate with the government so as to maximise the outcome for indigenous people.

Events since the 1996 election show how ugly an unprincipled debate on race issues can become. There is no doubt that the climate of the 1992 debate and policy-making on Mabo would have been radically different and deeply disadvantageous to Aboriginal and Torres Strait Islander people had the Labor government not put the reconciliation process in place and striven for cross-party cooperation during the previous two and a half years. Without these initiatives, powerful industry groups and their friends in the Coalition would have hijacked the agenda and Mabo would have become a potentially dominant issue in the 1993 election. As it was, they still did their best to achieve that outcome but were beaten by the strategy that had been put in place.

Even in the lull before the storm I was working flat out to hose down media reports of Aboriginal claims that would inflame wider community sentiments against indigenous people. In the year ahead, the reporting of the native title debate was to be abysmal. It reached its lowest point when the front page of a Sydney Sunday paper seriously reported a Mabo land claim over the Sydney Opera House, which was without legal foundation of any kind. There was, of course, no effective right of appeal in such matters, and never a retraction or a clarification to set the record straight. The only tactic that had any prospect of success was the hard slog of responding to each misrepresentation about Mabo and mounting an ongoing campaign to set the record straight.

On 5 December John Hyde, former Liberal MP and then director of the Institute of Public Affairs, gave an indication of what was to come when he wrote: 'The Justices of the High Court had learnt nothing from the experience of Communism. The particular title that they have "recognised" has all the worst features of property in Russia'. The form of social organisation so condemned by the institute had of course been adopted by indigenous people from time immemorial and had hardly been a creation of the High Court.

Two days later, the NT Chamber of Mines and Petroleum, led by Grant Watt, urged quick Commonwealth action to respond to Mabo and warned that the failure to do so would have serious consequences for Australia. The next day the *Australian* reported a call by mining industry representatives from Queensland, Western Australia and the Northern Territory for an acceleration of the process of public consultation on Mabo to avoid a catastrophic impact on mining investment. The campaign of disinformation and prejudice that was to mar the next two years was hotting up.

In what was to give rise to a landmark speech, and perhaps in hindsight a point of no return for the government, Paul Keating accepted an invitation from ATSIC to speak at the Australian launch of the UN International Year of the World's Indigenous People in Redfern Park on 10 December 1992. I think Paul was largely unaware of the battle that had gone on behind the scenes to ensure a list of speakers acceptable to indigenous people and the concern of many that the often militant Redfern audience would not allow the day to pass without incident. Other speakers included Sol Bellear as the deputy chair of ATSIC; the late and lamented Essie Coffey, a renowned

fighter for the Aboriginal cause and a member of the Council for
Aboriginal Reconciliation; Lyall Munro Jr, who made his usual fiery
contribution; and Dulcie Flower representing Torres Strait Islanders,
who tenaciously forced her way onto the speakers' list at the last minute
as the only Torres Strait Islander speaker, thus avoiding the possibility
of a major confrontation.

I was sitting beside Paul Keating in the hot summer sun as the
launch commenced and surrounding us were dozens of Redfern
schoolchildren who were drinking Coke like it was going out of style.
There was an assorted group of invited guests and a crowd of a few
hundred. The Prime Minister left his seat to speak and received a warm
reception which was to develop into a groundswell of emotion and
admiration as he delivered one of the most important statements ever
made by an Australian Prime Minister. He said, in part:

> Isn't it reasonable to say that if we can build a prosperous and
> remarkably harmonious multicultural society in Australia, surely we can
> find just solutions to the problems which beset the first Australians
> —the people to whom the most injustice has been done . . . The
> starting point might be to recognise that the problem starts with us
> non-Aboriginal Australians. It begins, I think, with that act of
> recognition. Recognition that it was we who did the dispossessing. We
> took the traditional lands and smashed the traditional way of life. We
> brought the diseases. The alcohol. We committed the murders. We took
> the children from their mothers. We practised discrimination and
> exclusion. It was our ignorance and our prejudice. And our failure to
> imagine these things being done to us. With some noble exceptions, we
> failed to make the most basic human response and enter into their
> hearts and minds. We failed to ask—how would I feel if this were done
> to me?

Of greatest significance, however, was what the Prime Minister said
about the Mabo decision and his own commitment and that of the
government to respond to it in a principled way that would meet
Aboriginal aspirations:

> We need these practical building blocks of change. The Mabo judgment
> should be seen as one of these. By doing away with the bizarre conceit
> that this continent had no owners prior to the settlement of Europeans,
> Mabo establishes a fundamental truth and lays the basis for justice. It
> will be much easier to work from that basis than has ever been the
> case in the past. For that reason alone we should ignore the isolated
> outbreaks of hysteria and hostility of the past few months. Mabo is an
> historic decision—we can make it an historic turning point, the basis of
> a new relationship between indigenous and non-Aboriginal Australians.

Paul Keating, despite his commanding parliamentary perfor-
mances, is not an orator in the Gough Whitlam style. In formal
speeches his approach is often much more measured, and at Redfern
Park it took some time for the significance of his words to come home.
When he finished he glanced down to where I sat, and if it was a nod
of approval he was hoping for he certainly got it. I was conscious that
Australian history was being made. When his speech hit the airwaves
and the front pages of the newspapers there was no mistaking its
impact. The Prime Minister's words were heard around the world.
There could have been no greater speech to contribute to the reconciliation process. But most importantly, Paul Keating had greatly raised
expectations about the nature of the government response to Mabo;
he had created a benchmark by which our government's response
would be judged. And still the cross-party cooperation continued and
John Hewson was reported as not significantly dissenting from the
speech.

The pressure from the mining industry, however, continued
unabated, and the day before the Redfern speech Peter Freund,
general manager of the proposed Mount Isa Mines McArthur River
development in the Northern Territory, alleged that the Japanese
Embassy had warned Japanese companies to be 'very cautious' about
resource development in Australia because of the Mabo decision. This
assertion was denied by a spokesman for the Japanese Embassy in
Canberra, Kenji Inaba, who said that the Japanese government had
asked Japanese companies planning to invest in Australia 'not to make
any conflict with local communities'. This was not to be the last time
that Mr Freund and the McArthur River mine-owners were to try to
influence the Mabo debate to the disadvantage of Aboriginal people.

In the week before Christmas 1992, the WA Chamber of Mines
issued a call for governments to guarantee crown ownership of minerals
following the action of the Kimberley Land Council threatening legal
action against a Stockdale-BHP consortium to prevent further drilling
for diamonds at their tenement in the Kimberley. The Federal Minister
for Resources, Alan Griffiths, a person respected by Aboriginal people
for his dealings with them in good faith, was quick to reassure the
chamber that all minerals were vested in the crown.

This account of the Mabo debate and its outcomes is not intended
to be simply a blinkered pro-indigenous view of history. Some of
the tactics of Aboriginal organisations and individuals were in my view
extraordinarily counter-productive and damaging. In particular, the
frustration of dispossessed Aboriginal people who would not benefit
directly from the Mabo decision often flared up and manifested itself

in Mabo 'ambit claims' over vast areas of New South Wales and Queensland. The reality was that any claims over areas of land in private ownership were utterly without legal foundation, as were all claims where indigenous people obviously had no continuing relationship with the land in question. The energies of the proponents of these claims and their legal advisers would have been better spent engaging in more effective tactics in support of Aboriginal rights.

Bogus claims continually provided ammunition to the opponents of Mabo, many of whom knew that they were without foundation but used them to wage an effective campaign against the wider Aboriginal community. On 29 December 1992, the ABC's *AM* program ran a story about a purported land claim over the central business district of Brisbane. It became a national news story which ran for days and was given great prominence in the *Courier Mail*. It was a claim that had no legal foundation whatsoever, but you would never have guessed it from the way some sections of the media ran the story. I did all I could to set the record straight whenever ambit claims were made, and early in the new year launched a media campaign to rebut any suggestion that private land was under threat.

My public opposition to the ambit claims probably caused concern among some Aboriginal groups, but there was no doubt that spurious threats to private lands would evoke a backlash that could sink the government's objective of a just outcome from Mabo. I was not alone in these views. Sol Bellear publicly recorded his disgust at 'outlandish claims' and asserted that 'headline grabbing is going to destroy everything Mabo stood for'.

Late in 1992 conservative critics of Mabo, including ex-National Party senator and former Treasury head John Stone and conservative MP David Kemp, continued the public pressure on the government. John Stone asserted that mining investment was 'now under the growing black cloud of Mabo' and David Kemp predicted that the development of vast mineral resources could grind to a halt unless the government acted to give certainty. They were joined by the chair of Western Mining, Sir Arvi Parbo, who asserted that the Mabo decision was scaring off investors.

On the other side of the debate there were two important initiatives. Early in the new year, the Northern and Central Land Councils, the Kimberley Land Council and the Cape York Land Council released a letter to the Prime Minister calling on him to announce, before the end of the consultation period, legislation that would preserve native title. The letter also sought recognition of native title over specific areas of land, namely national parks, reserves and vacant crown land, immediately after identification of the holders of such title.

The most optimistic and significant development, however, was the agreement reached between the Jawoyn people and the mining company Zappopan NL in relation to a proposed mine adjacent to Tennant Creek. The Jawoyn people had raised the prospect of a native title claim over the proposed Mt Todd Mine site but had agreed not to go ahead because of a comprehensive settlement with the company. Significantly, the normally belligerent NT government was a party to the agreement and had undertaken to ensure Aboriginal ownership of NT freehold title to large areas of land around the mine site and also to the Eva Valley pastoral lease, half of which was to be incorporated into the Nitmiluk (Katherine Gorge) National Park.

The executive officer of the Jawoyn Association, John Ah Kit, confirmed that the three-way agreement 'addresses Aboriginal concerns over land, the environment, jobs and economic development'. Much credit for the achievement of this agreement should go to John Ah Kit, a hard-headed Aboriginal negotiator and a former NLC director. The agreement was significant not only because it showed how native title claims could be the subject of successful negotiations but also because it showed that Aboriginal people were not, as I had continually stressed, anti-mining.

In a disturbing development on 12 January 1993, speaking on Perth talkback radio on the Howard Sattler show, the Leader of the National Party and future Deputy Prime Minister, Tim Fischer, launched a stinging attack on Aboriginal people and their aspirations in a manner that threatened to derail the cross-party cooperation evident in the lead-up to the 1993 election. He attacked what he called the 'guilt industry', asserted that he was 'not going to apologise for 200 years of white progress in this country' and promised to 'take on and fight the guilt industry all the way'. He said that the Aboriginal land claim over the central business district of Brisbane had done the nation 'a service' by jolting Australians into realising the seriousness of the Mabo judgment. He asserted that mining projects could be jeopardised and promised that if a Coalition government was elected it would, if necessary, legislate to provide certainty for the mining industry. On 29 January 1993 he released the Coalition's minerals policy, which again raised the threat to legislate if a satisfactory outcome could not otherwise be achieved. The policy release was welcomed by the NFF and other industry groups. Tim Fischer is a very affable and personally likeable man, but his role in the Mabo debate was that of a warrior for those industry groups and sections of the community who sought to erode the rights recognised by the High Court.

Until now, the leadership of the Coalition had in the main supported a cross-party approach to Mabo, but Tim Fischer's comments made a crack in that stand. I tried to repair the damage and to play down his comments by welcoming 'the fact that both the government [myself] and the Opposition [Michael Wooldridge] have given public commitments not to amend the RDA to override the Mabo decision and I note that Mr Fischer has said nothing in conflict with that commitment'. My aim was to keep the pressure on both sides of politics to respect the sanctity of the RDA.

Not everyone sought to play down the issue. Paul Keating accused Tim Fischer of trying to incite 'fear and resentment' against Aboriginal people. Undoubtedly he was, but I was concerned that the Prime Minister's intervention would raise the stakes and bring Michael Wooldridge into the debate. It was not, in my view, in the interests of either the ALP or the nation for Mabo to become a vitriolic zone of party warfare. Michael said that he would not have used the words Tim Fischer had used but criticised Paul Keating for attempting to drive a 'wedge between the Liberal and National Parties'. He also played down the threat of legislation, saying that this was only one of the options.

Eddie Mabo was voted Australian of the Year by the readership of the *Australian* in 1993. Mrs Mabo attended Kirribilli House on 26 January to receive, on behalf of her husband, a further Australia Day recognition from the Prime Minister.

During late January John Stone stepped up the campaign to destroy the climate of cross-party cooperation. Writing in the *Financial Review*, he described the High Court decision as a landmine which 'cannot be defused without action which Labor's Left will not allow. Labor has worked to divert all political traffic around the mine [Mabo] until after the Federal election'. He went on to attack Michael Wooldridge, asserting that 'extraordinarily, the federal Liberal party seems to be conniving in this Labor-saving device . . . to the point indeed, where its own Aboriginal affairs spokesman, Dr Michael Wooldridge, merely sounds like Little Sir Echo (to Mr Tickner) whenever (rarely) he comments on the issue'.

Later in the month, Hugh Morgan sent me a letter that he also circulated to all members of parliament in which he attacked cross-party cooperation as stifling public debate on some aspects of indigenous policy. He was particularly concerned about claims of Aboriginal sovereignty which, as far as I was aware, were at the fringe of public debate. Contrary to what John Howard and others have falsely suggested, I have never disputed the importance of public debate on indigenous policy issues, including debate between political parties. But I believe that where agreement can be broadly reached between the parties on matters of principle this is a good outcome because it sends an important message to the wider Australian community.

Much of the public debate about the government's response to Mabo over the next twelve months was to centre on its approach to the Racial Discrimination Act, and what I have to say here will not please all Aboriginal participants and their supporters in the debate. The inside story of the first government consideration of the issues associated with that Act has never been told. The outcome of those first deliberations on Mabo and the RDA was not only crucial to the Mabo debate but also important to the re-election of the Labor government in 1993.

My relationship with PM&C, the key bureaucratic adviser to the Prime Minister, during the development of the government's response to Mabo is a sensitive matter. I do not doubt the personal integrity of the public servants in the department, but we found ourselves very much on opposing sides of the debate. I believe they acted in good faith and competently in an attempt to bring about what they believed to be the outcome the government as a whole wanted. This was one which, while respecting indigenous rights, accommodated the states and territories to the greatest extent possible and met the concerns of industry. I fundamentally disagreed with this approach as I knew from the beginning that it was unachievable.

Tensions came to a head in the lead-up to a Mabo Ministerial Committee meeting on 1 February 1993, immediately before the calling of the federal election. AMIC had produced a paper arguing that the legal effect of the combined operation of the RDA and the High Court decision in Mabo No. 1 was to place at risk some existing titles, including mining interests of non-Aboriginal Australians gained after the passage of the RDA in what would otherwise have been native title land.

The argument put forward in AMIC's paper was essentially that after the RDA was passed in 1975, all dealings in land, including native title land, had to be handled in a non-discriminatory way. Because native title holders had not been dealt with by the same processes as other landholders during that period (including rights to be notified of proposed government approvals relating to their land and to compensation for any loss of their land or impediment to their title, for example through the granting of a mining interest), it was argued that they had been treated in a discriminatory manner. Therefore, so this convoluted legal argument ran, native title holders could challenge any grant of interest over their land since 1975 as being contrary to the RDA.

Acceptance of AMIC's view implied that the courts would have been saying that after 1975 and the passage of the RDA, land managers in any part of Australia should have accorded equal rights and processes to native title holders, even though the concept of native title was not recognised within the Australian legal system until 1993. It was argued by the proponents of this view that the failure to give procedural rights to native title holders in these circumstances could only be cured by retrospective legislation to override the RDA.

Underpinning this argument was what I regarded as the absurd view that any defect in title could not be cured by the payment of compensation but required a Commonwealth law to be passed to guarantee title and to overcome the failure to provide proper processes for dealing with native title after the passage of the RDA, that is, to overcome the failure of governments to recognise and respect the interests of native title holders between 1975 and 1993. During this time of course the very existence of their title was unknown to anybody, including governments. How could a failure to give them notice amount to discrimination? My view then, as now, was that the payment of compensation would have been enough to overcome the problem, and that even if it were not, any finding to the contrary by the courts could have been addressed by subsequent Commonwealth legislation. This assurance could easily have been made publicly to confirm that existing titles would never be at risk.

One of my deepest regrets in all the native title debate is that what I regard as a nonsensical legal argument took hold and dominated the agenda of industry groups, politicians and, worst of all, Aboriginal people, even though it was not supported by the government's own legal advice. This legal furphy took hold like a grass fire, with terrible consequences for the progress of the debate.

The issues had been briefly canvassed in October 1992 in the Attorney-General's Department advice to the government before the release of a discussion paper by officials. The department had concluded that the two Mabo decisions raised 'a potential difficulty relating to land which has been the subject of a grant since the RDA was passed. Where the limitation period has not expired, it may be possible for Aboriginal and Torres Strait Islander groups to seek to show that they were the traditional owners of such land and then *possibly* seek compensation on the basis of their property loss'. There was no suggestion by Attorney-General's that any grant of interest in land to non-indigenous people or interests would be invalid in such circumstances. The issue of past grants was not even specifically addressed in the subsequently released discussion and legal issues paper.

On 22 December 1992, Peter Burnett, chairman of AMIC's Aboriginal Affairs Committee, wrote an urgent and confidential letter to a senior PM&C officer, in which he referred to the opinion of two QCs that even freehold grants made after the commencement of the RDA might be invalid. The letter suggested that federal and state governments 'need to take, as a matter of urgency, whatever action they can to ensure that no existing property rights are rendered invalid, or less valuable, by the High Court's decision'. Because of the economic consequences, AMIC 'does not believe that governments can wait until the conclusion of the consultative process'. AMIC urged the Commonwealth to take a lead in resolving this issue, with or without state cooperation.

Contrary to all the nonsense peddled by large sections of the Canberra press gallery and some participants in the Mabo debate, including some within the ALP, it was AMIC that first suggested the validation of titles by means of a special measure under the RDA. Mr Burnett's letter suggested that 'legislation can be framed to represent a *"special measure"* under section 8 of the Racial Discrimination Act'. AMIC enclosed a draft bill entitled 'Confirmation of Titles Act 1992'. Copies of this letter and the bill were sent to the departmental secretaries of all premiers and chief ministers.

Against this background the Mabo Ministerial Committee received papers prepared by PM&C, a wider group of Commonwealth officials, and lawyers from the Attorney-General's Department for its meeting on 1 February 1993. The Attorney-General's Department advice now suggested that the combined effect of the Mabo judgments and the operation of the RDA would result in the invalidity of certain grants of interest in land. The legal advice then posed the question: 'What means are available for retrospectively extinguishing the native titles that would have been extinguished but for the RDA and for validating any post 1975 grants that are wholly and partly invalid because of the RDA?'

The first option canvassed was the Commonwealth amending the RDA to enable state legislation that gave no compensation to Aboriginal people, but this was rejected because it would put Australia in breach of its international obligations under CERD. Option two was for Commonwealth and state legislation with compensation. In relation to the extinguishment of native title, Attorney-General's explored the option of Commonwealth legislation that would retrospectively extinguish such native title as would have been extinguished but for the existence of the RDA and provide for reasonable compensation, either by the Commonwealth or by state and territory governments. The department asserted that Australia would have a 'substantial argument' that legislation to this effect was *not* in breach of Australia's obligations under CERD but conceded that this would be subject to challenge. In relation to the validation of post-1975 land grants, the advice highlighted the need for state legislation. 'It *might* be possible for the Commonwealth legislation to provide that nothing in the RDA is intended to be inconsistent with State legislation confirming the validity of the various land grants.'

Finally, the department explored a third option, regrettably not taken up by the government, with the result that much time and energy in the year ahead was absorbed by the threatened suspension of the RDA. The third option was disarmingly simple:

> for each State to enact legislation extinguishing native title in the State [in the requisite period], providing for the State to pay reasonable compensation to the native title holders, and validating the previous grants. On the view taken above, such legislation would not be racially discriminatory since non-native titles are equally subject to legislation providing for acquisition with compensation. However for good measure, it might be desirable for the Commonwealth to enact legislation to the effect that nothing in the RDA shall be taken to affect State legislation providing for the extinguishment of native title subject to reasonable compensation.

Thus the Commonwealth's clear legal advice was that no Commonwealth action was essential for the validation of titles after 1975. Commonwealth legislation would be enacted 'for good measure'. That was the Attorney-General's Department advice supported by the Acting Solicitor-General, subject to further detailed consideration. This argument about the desirability of Commonwealth legislation became known as the belt and braces argument—one would be sufficient but the other could or should be added as a safeguard.

On the basis of this advice, the officials concluded that 'it *may be desirable* to establish certainty and the States may demand it' for the Commonwealth to pass supporting legislation. The officials did, however, concede that such Commonwealth legislation would be likely to attract criticism 'as an attempt to limit the operation of the RDA'.

Finally, the PM&C advice covering the officials' paper and the legal advice expressly stated that 'the Commonwealth *will need* to legislate to make clear that nothing in the RDA is inconsistent'. It was not clear to me then, and it is not clear to me now, why the Commonwealth needed to legislate in view of legal advice to the contrary.

PM&C proposed that the Commonwealth's legal advice should be provided to state and territory governments. It was also recommended that the Prime Minister issue a media statement acknowledging doubts about the validity of some titles and acknowledging that early legislation (and implicitly including Commonwealth legislation overriding the RDA) was necessary to put 'beyond doubt' the validity of interests in land. This advice, if acted on, would have ignited a multi-megaton bomb of social discord in the Australian community. To adopt these proposals would, in my view, have been wrong in principle and also electorally catastrophic, alienating significant sections of Labor's traditional supporters. This was already to be the election campaign of the true believers, and the whole party was united behind Paul Keating and the central election strategy of opposition to the GST. The last thing I considered we should do was support an announcement of a change to the RDA, which would not only have split the party but also caused great damage to our standing in the community.

The Mabo Ministerial Committee meeting on 1 February was chaired by the Prime Minister. I took up the fight, arguing that even the Opposition was on the record as being opposed to any overriding of the RDA. That very day ATSIC had warned the Prime Minister against any threat to the RDA and the 'principles it enunciates', and its advice to me was that 'Aboriginal groups are likely to object strongly to such amendments, seeing them as legally superfluous and a precedent for further weakening of the RDA'.

At the meeting I appealed to the Prime Minister in particular to postpone any decision on the issue and if necessary return to it in a considered manner in the next term of government in the context of our comprehensive response to Mabo. Paul Keating listened to me that day and my view was adopted by the meeting. This crucial meeting never became public.

The issues were easily publicly put to bed by a form of words spoken by Simon Crean the next day when he addressed the Outlook '93 Conference of the Australian Bureau of Agriculture and Resource Economics, giving an assurance that the rights of existing landholders would be protected. His statement was even welcomed by AMIC's Lauchlan McIntosh.

I was delighted to read a transcript of an interview given by John Hewson on Darwin ABC Radio on 9 February, after the election was called. In reply to a question on Mabo, he said that 'the government had embarked on a negotiation now which runs I think through till about September of this year. It's our view that that process should be allowed to run its course and hopefully it will resolve the problem'. It was, for me, John Hewson's finest hour and I immediately issued a statement headed 'Mabo above party politics': 'There can be no doubt that the Mabo decision is an important one for all Australians. For that reason discussion must remain rational and the interests of all key groups must be taken into consideration . . . It is to the benefit of all Australians that the Mabo decision has not become a party political football'. No doubt Michael Wooldridge strongly influenced those views, but to John Hewson's credit he did not seek to use Mabo and Aboriginal people in a political way during the election campaign.

Five days later Tim Fischer admitted on the Nine Network Sunday program that he was uncomfortable with some aspects of Liberal policies and promised that the Nationals would put a 'twist' on a Coalition government. While he did not name the areas of difference, he reiterated the Coalition's intention to legislate to provide security for industry in the aftermath of Mabo and alluded to the loss of jobs unless this was done. On 20 February 1993, while visiting the Northern Territory, he again publicly referred to the loss of jobs in response to a threatened claim that day by the NLC over the Mount Isa Mines McArthur River lead-zinc-silver project.

On 26 February the *Australian* reported in banner headlines news of a Coalition Mabo split, with Michael Wooldridge asserting that it would be hypocritical for the Opposition to have draft legislation drawn up to protect existing landholders in the aftermath of Mabo. He was unaware of such draft legislation, and the first commitment of the Coalition was to negotiate 'fairly and honestly'. His statement was at odds with Tim Fischer's revelation earlier in the week that the Coalition already had such draft legislation prepared. Tim Fischer had also endorsed the announcement of the NT government that it would legislate to stop some recent Mabo-style claims. When John Hewson criticised the NT government for jumping the gun, Mr Fischer backed off, claiming that the draft legislation was 'unofficial'. I went to great lengths to highlight Dr Hewson's statement and to point out how out of step the NT government was on the issue.

On 4 March 1993 the NT government introduced its so-called 'legislation' into parliament, but the Bill merely amounted to a call on the Commonwealth to legislate. It requested the Commonwealth parliament to enact legislation in the terms of the schedule to the Bill and asked that the Bill not be repealed or amended without the approval of the NT Administrator. Significantly, in the second reading speech it was acknowledged that the post-1975 grants would be invalid if made without compensation or without a right to compensation. There was no question raised of any problem with a lack of past recognition of procedural rights of native title holders that needed to be remedied by legislation.

And so the sun set on the early days of the Mabo debate. The federal election campaign was largely insulated from needless bitter inter-party recriminations and division on the sensitive question of the Commonwealth response to Mabo. The reconciliation process remained on track and it would be for the incoming government to take charge of the response. With all my heart I hoped it would be a Labor government that would take up that challenge.

When I went back to my electorate office at the end of campaigning on election eve on 12 March 1993, there was a fax from Michael Wooldridge on my machine. It read, in part: 'I have found the last three years satisfying because I have done what I think is right. Whether or not the two who occupy our current positions in a week's time will be allowed the same latitude, I am not sure. At least no one can accuse us of not using the opportunity we had'.

6

THE BATTLE BEGINS AND THE LINES ARE DRAWN

Following the 1993 election, as the Keating government continued with its consultation process to formulate the national response to Mabo, the debate became increasingly polarised.

Paul Keating continued to take a principled stand following on from his Redfern Park speech, maintaining Aboriginal hopes and expectations of a just outcome. Representatives of major Aboriginal organisations presented their demands to the government in the form of a Peace Plan that demanded a high price for ensuring the validity of supposedly at-risk non-indigenous titles affected by the passage of the RDA. Within the government, tortuous and ongoing debates proceeded away from the public gaze, with the Mabo Ministerial Committee trying to come to terms with the basis of a response to the High Court decision. State governments and the Northern Territory, with limited exceptions, were hostile and unhelpful from the beginning.

Then Aboriginal trust and confidence in the government was shattered by the unexpected announcement by the Prime Minister and the Special Minister of State that the Commonwealth had secretly agreed with the NT government to pass Commonwealth legislation including, if necessary, an amendment to the RDA in order to ensure the validation of the McArthur River mining project in the Northern Territory.

Aboriginal anger and disillusionment ran deep. The Prime Minister continued with his efforts to achieve a national response to Mabo that could be endorsed by state and territory governments. He went to a COAG meeting prepared to negotiate with other government leaders and if an agreeement had been reached it would have dashed Aboriginal aspirations.

Thankfully, no agreement was reached because of the intransigence of state and territory government leaders, leaving the Prime Minister angry and frustrated with the states and the Northern Territory, and Aboriginal people strategically determined not to be left outside the negotiation process again.

———

The government having been re-elected, I was reappointed Minister for Aboriginal and Torres Strait Islander Affairs. Frank Walker was Special Minister of State with a special responsibility for Mabo. It was always the Prime Minister's objective to ensure that the final government response to Mabo reflected the wider interests of the government, and no doubt he saw Frank's role as a more neutral one than those of other ministerial protagonists, including me. I had some early reservations about his intended role, having been on the other side of major Aboriginal policy debates when he was Aboriginal Affairs minister in New South Wales in the early 1980s, but on the whole I had a reasonable working relationship with him. On the Coalition side, Michael Wooldridge became Deputy Leader of the Liberal Party and was replaced by Peter Nugent as Shadow Minister for Aboriginal and Torres Strait Islander Affairs.

The Mabo Ministerial Committee was re-established, with the Prime Minister again in the chair. Changes to the committee included the addition of Frank Walker and the new Minister for Justice, Duncan Kerr, who was appointed in the absence of the newly appointed Attorney-General, Michael Lavarch, who had been forced to participate in a by-election for his seat after the death of a rival candidate before the federal election. Other members were Simon Crean, Minister for Primary Industries and Energy; Michael Lee, Minister for Resources; Alan Griffiths, Minister for Industry, Technology and Regional Development; John Dawkins, Treasurer; and Ralph Willis, Minister for Finance.

Labor's victory in the 1993 election was unexpected by many commentators. The night before the election Paul Keating spoke at a private dinner with his staff. The speech was not intended to be made public but was recorded and eventually published in the now failed *Independent Monthly* magazine. It gives an extraordinary insight into Paul's thinking at that time and his obvious recognition of the significance of the reconciliation process. Above all else, I think it proves beyond doubt his integrity and *bona fides* in relation to the Mabo response. He said:

> I'm more convinced than ever that we've got to make peace with the Aborigines to get the place right. That's got Australians interested. They think this is a bit different, this is better than economics and social policy; it's something else wrapped around it as well. It's got a binding around it. I think we've been able to do this and of course if we win we will be able to do it in a much bigger way than we've been able to do it . . . I think we've got a tremendous opportunity with the Mabo decision to do something with Aboriginal reconciliation.

The day after the election an editorial in the Sunday *Herald Sun* gave some indication of the coming vitriol when it endorsed Hugh

Morgan's expressed concern that Mabo was affecting investment. 'We are cutting off our economic lifeblood', the editorial thundered, 'because some politicians and their camp-followers have become slaves of the Green movement and others are determined to punish us for crimes by the British against Aboriginals committed before we, our fathers and even our grandfathers were born'.

Immediately after the election, the proposed McArthur River mine project began to again raise its head, soon dominating public debate. Norm Fussell, chief executive of Mount Isa Mines, urged the government to take urgent action to confirm land titles in the wake of the Mabo decision. His concern was given particular focus because of an assertion of native title rights over the MIM McArthur River mine site in the Northern Territory. This $250 million lead-zinc-silver project had been given the go-ahead by the federal government the previous year. None of us knew at that time that this project and what was later to become the Wik claim affecting the Comalco mine at Weipa were to be the two large mining projects that would derail the Commonwealth's Mabo response. In both cases the formidable political clout of the Australian mining industry would see some politicians on both sides urging radical action to extinguish Aboriginal rights.

On the weekend after the election, the Australian business community stepped up the pressure for government action to protect existing property rights. A joint statement was issued by the Australian Chamber of Commerce and Industry, the Australian Chamber of Manufactures, AMIC, the Australian Coal Association, the Business Council of Australia, the National Association of Forest Industries, the NFF, and the National Fishing Industry Council. The statement called for the confirmation of titles Australia-wide, at the same time asserting that 'the call must not be seen as one which was intended to affect the rights adversely of Aboriginal people' and that 'there was no intention to confront the principles in either the Mabo decision or the laudable objectives of the Racial Discrimination Act'.

The statement referred to special measures that might be needed to address Aboriginal needs. It was, by previous industry standards, moderate and constructive. I issued a statement appealing for cooperation and goodwill, referring to 'the most supportive statement ever made by Australian industry in recognition of the need to address the aspirations of Aboriginal people to secure land to meet their social and economic needs'. Australian business is not noted for its championing of Aboriginal social justice issues and it was evident that they wanted something. I particularly welcomed the intention of the industry bodies not to confront the 'laudable objectives' of the RDA, knowing that their words were code for suspension of the Act to allow what they saw as the necessary validation of titles.

Three days later the Prime Minister announced the new portfolio arrangements. Aboriginal and Torres Strait Islander Affairs was shifted from the Department of Employment, Education and Training (DEET) to PM&C. I had no difficulty with this decision and was optimistic that the shift would mean an enhanced focus on government programs to ensure that the interests of indigenous Australians were addressed. This was not to be fulfilled in the way I had hoped. In time I became demoralised by the lack of both will and administrative capacity in PM&C to address the failure of other Commonwealth agencies to apply resources equitably to address indigenous human rights and disadvantage. The economic rationalist ethos that dominated departments such as PM&C, Treasury and Finance meant that there was inadequate or in some cases zero commitment to indigenous social justice, and often there was outright hostility supplemented by disappointing standards of public administration.

My main concern with the new ministerial arrangements was with the establishment of the Office of Indigenous Affairs within PM&C as an alternative source of advice to ATSIC for both the Prime Minister and myself. As stated earlier, I was strongly opposed to the creation of this body, which was Coalition not Labor policy, as it undermined the role of ATSIC as the advisory body to the government on indigenous issues. But the decision was obviously the Prime Minister's and was his prerogative. I never did find out the background to the establishment of the office, but I have no doubt that there had been a bureaucratic proposal in existence for setting up a separate source of policy advice for the government, probably initially prepared for consideration by an incoming Coalition government. Its establishment was met with outrage from ATSIC; such a proposal had been expressly rejected in the parliamentary debates leading to ATSIC's establishment, and it followed that Aboriginal people deeply distrusted PM&C's role in the early part of the Mabo debate.

As the Mabo debate progressed, the hostility to the Office of Indigenous Affairs and to PM&C as a whole by Aboriginal people would become intense, with Lois O'Donoghue openly and constantly referring to it as the 'Office of Insidious Affairs' even in the presence of Paul Keating. For my part, I set out to work as effectively as I could with the public servants in PM&C. As the year progressed, however, relations with the department became strained as we increasingly found ourselves on opposing sides.

On 22 March 1993, Lois O'Donoghue wrote to the Prime Minister, formally alerting him to ATSIC concerns about any attempt to erode the operation of the RDA to validate titles. She enclosed a copy of a pre-election statement of ATSIC's preliminary response to the Commonwealth's consultation, which argued for extensive government action and included:

- proposals to support the RDA;
- revival of native title following the expiration of a finite grant of an interest in land;
- land rights legislation to address the position of dispossessed people;
- the establishment of a specialist tribunal to adjudicate on native title claims;
- the concept of representative bodies for indigenous people that would lodge claims and conduct negotiations;
- royalty payments;
- a public education program to explain the effect and importance of the Mabo decision; and
- a proposal for an international convention on the rights of indigenous people.

In hindsight it is quite remarkable that with one or two exceptions this agenda of indigenous aspirations was to be acted on by the Labor government.

On 29 March the new Minister for Resources, Michael Lee, moved to hose down the concerns of the oil industry by emphasising in a speech to the annual conference of the Australian Petroleum Exploration Association that 'advice to the Government suggests that the offshore petroleum legislation and its administration do not contravene the Racial Discrimination Act' and that 'there is no evidence to suggest that the Mabo decision has major implications in terms of management of petroleum exploration activity in Commonwealth waters'. Tim Fischer, for his part, suggested to the conference that 'Mabo has the potential to threaten the sovereignty of a great deal more land—and sea'.

The next day Patrick Dodson wrote to the Prime Minister raising broader issues that needed to be addressed in any government response and called for national discussions with indigenous people leading to meetings between COAG and representatives of the broader indigenous community. Moves to reform the Canadian Constitution in the early 1980s had led to comparable negotiations between representatives of Canada's indigenous peoples and the leaders of the Canadian national and provincial governments. But Australia, or more specifically its state and territory governments at this time, lacked the maturity and respect for the indigenous people displayed by their Canadian counterparts.

On 6 April the Mabo Ministerial Committee met to receive a report on the progress of consultations and give preliminary consideration to the 148-page report of the Interdepartmental Committee. The report canvassed legal issues and a wide range of possible options for responding to the Mabo decision and set out the views of interested parties. At that meeting the Prime Minister rejected calls for urgent government legislative action, and his office obviously passed on his views to the media.

I had already begun to nail my colours unambiguously to the Mabo mast. The week before I had met privately with land council representatives to discuss the development of the government's Mabo response. I placed great trust and confidence not only in the people in my ministerial office but also in many of the indigenous leaders. I also took into my confidence those opinion leaders in the wider community I judged to be equally prepared to stand and be counted in support of Aboriginal rights, from archbishops to activists, and spoke openly about the ways they could contribute to a just outcome to the Mabo debate.

My greatest source of support came from the ALP Caucus. The most active members of the Caucus Aboriginal and Torres Strait Islander Affairs Committee were Garrie Gibson, Margaret Reynolds, Warren Snowdon, Bryant Burns, Peter Dodd, Chris Evans, Clyde Holding, Jim McKiernan, Daryl Melham and Les Scott. Other Caucus members who were a great support were John Langmore, Bob Brown, and Jeannette McHugh, Minister for Consumer Affairs. There were undoubtedly times when my trust was betrayed. A handful of Caucus colleagues (including people who pretended to be my allies) sought to portray me behind my back as disloyal to the government because of my close relationship with indigenous leaders. This charge could hardly be sustained. I knew that only a Labor government could deliver; the difference for me was that Mabo was a defining issue for the nation and that Labor could not afford to fail.

On 14 April the first meeting of Commonwealth and state officials in the post-election climate was held to discuss the Mabo response. After the meeting, PM&C reported to ministers that state and territory governments wanted Mabo discussed at COAG, which would, in its view, be desirable. I was appalled by the COAG scenario, where the Commonwealth would be potentially outgunned and where the most likely outcome would have been an erosion of its position. It is significant that at this time Commonwealth ministers and departmental officials were still agreeing that the integrity of the RDA was to be maintained and that this was 'non-negotiable'.

State and territory governments clearly had other ideas, and even in progressive Labor states like South Australia the bureaucracy was driving an agenda hostile to Aboriginal interests. A confidential SA Interdepartmental Committee report unanimously recommended in December 1992 that South Australia should request the Commonwealth 'to amend the Racial Discrimination Act to provide that compensation cannot be awarded where native title was extinguished between 1975 and 3 June 1992 which was not carried out with the intention of achieving that result'. It is significant that the SA Department of Aboriginal Affairs was a part of that unanimous recommendation.

Mabo brought out the best of the Labor movement and especially the ALP. An early and consistent participant in the debate was Senator Margaret Reynolds, who had been at my instigation the first government representative on the Council for Aboriginal Reconciliation. Margaret also happened to be married to the eminent historian Henry Reynolds and had been Minister for Local Government in the Hawke government, 1987–90. Both Henry and Margaret had been personal friends and confidants of Eddie Mabo. As a Queensland senator, Margaret was frequently at odds with Premier Wayne Goss and as early as 12 April 1993 was reported in the *Australian* as opposed to his call for early legislation, saying it was 'just too early to talk legislation until we know the terms'.

Early in the Mabo debate the government was on notice that there were likely to be Aboriginal people and groups who would choose to stand outside the mainstream negotiations with it. On 18 April the self-styled Aboriginal Provisional Government (APG) warned the government against thinking it could bind Aboriginal people by negotiating with selected bodies such as the Council for Aboriginal Reconciliation. Although this was never the government's intention, the warning was a timely reminder of the difficulties that lay ahead.

On the same day that the APG was applying pressure on the government from one end of the debate, the WA Pastoralists and Graziers Association vice-president, Tim D'Arcy, attacked the High Court at a meeting of 50 pastoralists at Fitzroy Crossing. One pastoralist told the meeting that the Mabo issue had the potential to turn into a civil war and was reported as claiming that if this civil war resulted in bloodshed it was Aboriginal people who stood to be annihilated.

The first meeting between the Mabo Ministerial Committee and Aboriginal representatives was held in the Cabinet Room at Parliament House on 27 April 1993. The Aboriginal representatives were: Galarrwuy Yunupingu and John Ah Kit representing the NLC; Kunmanara Breadon, chairman and David Ross, director, CLC, and ATSIC Commissioner; Jean George, executive member, and Noel

Pearson representing the Cape York Land Council; Manuel Ritchie, chair, and Danny Chapman representing the NSW Land Council; Rob Riley, executive officer, and Ted Wilks, chair, of the WA Aboriginal Legal Service; Lois O'Donoghue, chair of ATSIC, and Commissioners Gerhardt Pearson and George Mye representing ATSIC; Patrick Dodson and Wenten Rubuntja from the Council for Aboriginal Reconciliation; Mick Dodson, Aboriginal and Torres Strait Islander Social Justice Commissioner; John Watson, chair, and Peter Yu, director, of the Kimberley Land Council; Tauto Sansbury, chair, and Esther Williams, executive member, of the SA Aboriginal Legal Rights Movement; and Getano Lui Jr, chair of the Torres Strait Regional Council and the Island Co-ordinating Council.

The delegation was very well organised and presented a series of proposals to the government called the 'Peace Plan'. This had been put together after a meeting of Aboriginal organisations in Alice Springs which had produced a statement of principles, the Red Centre Statement. The Peace Plan urged the Commonwealth government to take the 'primary role' in the protection of indigenous human rights; to legislate to affirm existing rights; to provide that indigenous rights are not to be extinguished by past or future grants but continue, subject to the interests granted by the crown; to provide that indigenous rights will not be impaired without consent; to vest Aboriginal title in reserves and other defined land; to establish a Commonwealth Tribunal to issue declarations of native (Aboriginal) title on the basis of common law, historical association or need; and to provide for a settlement process that would address a wide range of indigenous aspirations including the establishment of a land fund, new constitutional arrangements, and indigenous self-government.

The plan provided an important basis for future negotiations with the government and put on record a considered agenda by indigenous Australians. In exchange for accepting the indigenous proposals the Commonwealth legislation could provide for the 'validation' of 1975–92 mineral titles that might otherwise be invalid, subject to the Commonwealth and miners entering into an agreement with the relevant Aboriginal land councils or legal services bodies on issues such as compensation and environmental protection. If agreement could not be reached it was proposed that the issues be determined by a tribunal. Finally, indigenous people were to participate as members of the drafting team for all legislation.

The Prime Minister listened intently at that meeting and reaffirmed that he saw the process as 'an historic opportunity to consider a basis for reconciliation that we have never had'. The first meeting with the Mabo Ministerial Committee was notable for another reason—it was the first time that indigenous languages had been spoken at a meeting of Cabinet ministers. Galarrwuy Yunupingu spoke in Gamats, Kunmanara Breaden spoke in Luritja, Jean George in Wik Way, John Watson in Nyikina, and George Mye in his Torres Strait language. This was a subtle assertion of a determination that negotiations should be conducted on indigenous terms.

The late Rob Riley's contribution to that meeting was politically incisive. 'There is a sense of history about this business', he declared, and the capacity for 'the relationship between the indigenous peoples of this country and the Australian nation to take a quantum leap forward'. He then directly addressed the Prime Minister: 'For this to happen requires a political will to do what you know is right. It requires leadership and direction from you as Prime Minister. You can set the agenda in a way that nobody else can'. He concluded with a warning:

> A word of caution Mr Prime Minister, don't exclude us from the process. Don't attempt to do this without our involvement. Please don't dismiss us. If you do so you can forget about reconciliation. If we have to we will wind people up. We will hit the streets. We will go to international forums. The one thing you, your colleagues, the miners, pastoralists and the Australian people have to accept is that the law of the land has changed and we are going to exercise our rights. That is how serious we consider this. The last comment I want to make today is, you don't stop negotiating for justice simply because those around don't like it. We will not stop fighting. Thank you, that is all I have to say.

While from the government perspective the meeting was mainly a listening exercise, the indigenous representatives felt positive about it. Mick Dodson said after the meeting, 'I think what we have achieved today is the beginning of a new future, for not just the indigenous people of this country but the nation as a whole'.

The next day, 28 April, the Mabo Ministerial Committee met with representatives of three industry groups: Dick Wells and Peter Power of the Australian Petroleum Exploration Association; Lauchlan McIntosh and Campbell Anderson of AMIC; and Rick Farley and John McKenzie of the NFF. Paul Keating spoke about the importance of the process for a reconciliation that might otherwise not be possible, but he recognised that it would not be easy. Ministers placed considerable importance on negotiations between industry groups and Aboriginal people. Industry groups, for their part, stressed the need for validation of existing titles, which Campbell Anderson said could be done without running counter to the RDA. Industry representatives were also insistent that any compensation that might be payable should not be paid by industry but by the government. The NFF representatives argued forcefully for their industry position, but at one point during the meeting John McKenzie admitted that some of the Kimberley pastoral representatives were pushing him to take a more 'militaristic' stance and that unless some reasonable assurances were forthcoming from government, some more extreme elements of the constituency would be wanting to take over.

That night the Prime Minister went to the annual dinner of the Evatt Foundation in Sydney. I saw him receive the most effusive acclamation when he spoke of the government's response to Mabo. He said:

> Some of our opponents insist on devaluing the cause of reconciliation by calling it the product of guilt. But it is not guilt which motivates us in this but responsibility . . . The High Court has declared that a native title exists at common law—a declaration which has profound consequences not just for land management but for contemporary issues of social justice and the process of reconciliation. The Mabo judgment constituted recognition of an historic truth and in doing so created the best chance we have ever had for a nationally agreed durable settlement.

The speech was significant as an affirmation to an important Labor institution and to many important Labor identities of the government's commitment to meet indigenous aspirations and of the crucial relationship between its response to Mabo and the reconciliation process. Expectations had thus been raised even higher by the government. On 6 May the Prime Minister publicly confirmed that the Commonwealth would develop a position to take to the forthcoming COAG meeting.

On 14 May Ian McLachlan, Shadow Minister for National Development and Infrastructure and a member of a Coalition Mabo Subcommittee, gave a speech to the right-wing H.R. Nicholls Society in which he denounced the Mabo decision, asserting that 'it had left great tracts of Australia in turmoil as to title and therefore in those areas, risks the stability and future development of the nation'. In deciding to grant a 'new right' the High Court had 'failed to take account of the immense damage it would do to the rights other Australians thought they had'. This was the first manifestation in the federal Liberal Party of the politics of division.

Sharp divisions appeared in the federal Liberal Party in the wake of this speech. The *Australian* reported Peter Nugent, Opposition representative on the Council for Aboriginal Reconciliation (which had unanimously recognised the significance of the Mabo decision to the reconciliation process), as saying that he believed the Opposition needed to treat Mabo 'as a good opportunity for this country once and for all to face up to issues which have been bedevilling it for generations . . . You cannot have 300 000 people in the community significantly disaffected with the broader community and claim to be a harmonious nation'. He would recant some of his views as the Mabo debate got bloodier. Michael Wooldridge tried to hose down the divisions, promising that the Opposition would come to a 'balanced position'.

The genuine liberals in the Liberal Party were trying to rein in the worst excesses of the anti-Aboriginal and states' rights elements in the Coalition, but there was nothing that people like Michael and Peter Nugent could ultimately have done to bring the Coalition to a more moderate and constructive position; so many members of their parties represented the vested interests that lined up in opposition to a principled response on Mabo. The crucial issue was whether there would ultimately be a Senate majority to override Coalition opposition to national legislation on Mabo.

During May there were four meetings of the Mabo Ministerial Committee in which the government agonised over what were to be the core principles of the Mabo response. These deliberations, which did not reach the public domain, were long and tortuous and tested the patience of all involved. Differences had not been resolved when the committee again met with Aboriginal representatives on 18 May.

For their part, Aboriginal representatives made it clear that they were meeting with ministers as a delegation of the large group that had attended the meeting on 27 April. They stipulated that the views put forward in the Peace Plan were to be subject to 'ratification' by indigenous people.

A core Aboriginal demand—consistent with the demands of Aboriginal people since the 1930s—reaffirmed at the meeting of 18 May was the 'assumption of primacy by the Commonwealth for the protection, affirmation and regulation of dealings with Aboriginal title'. The Aboriginal representatives expressly rejected state and territory tribunals; they emphasised that Commonwealth legislative power had been used to extend the Commonwealth's role in protecting the environment, referred to the exercise of Commonwealth power in industrial relations, and claimed that in this area 'the Government has friends to look after', a phrase that raised some hackles on the committee.

The Aboriginal representatives really laid it on the line about the need for a national regime under Commonwealth law and asserted that 'the abrogation of responsibility in this respect will be fatal to any further progress on Mabo'. Furthermore, a document circulated by the delegation rejected the increasingly pervasive view within the government, and one sometimes articulated by the Prime Minister, that land management issues were a matter for the states. It was difficult to maintain such a view after 1983, when the Commonwealth had used its foreign affairs and treaty power to override Tasmanian laws in order to prevent the flooding of the Franklin River. Another focus of the delegation was to argue for Aboriginal rights of veto or consent in land-use decisions affecting Aboriginal land.

The meeting did not go well and the strong line taken by the indigenous representatives did not seem to be appreciated by Paul Keating and several ministers. But it was a timely reminder, in the lead-up to the June COAG meeting, of the consistently expressed core demand of indigenous people that the Commonwealth assert its legislative and political authority over the states.

By this time I was even more convinced that the more the state and territory governments and their officials were able to influence the process, the worse the Mabo outcome would be. Commonwealth officials did not consistently pass copies of state and territory officials' documents to the Mabo Ministerial Committee, but some of those documents were leaked to me.

A document signed by a senior official of the Queensland Premier's Department, one known to have the ear of the Premier and his key minders, opposed any 'naked assertion of Commonwealth power'. When the Commonwealth officials proposed a reference in draft principles to a role for land councils, this was deleted by the Queensland Premier's Department. When Commonwealth officials advanced proposals for land management processes to recognise the rights of indigenous people, the Queensland officials responded with concerns about the 'scope for protracted delays in the business of government in land administration and for a higher level of costs associated with adherence to procedure'. When the Commonwealth proposed that future grants, for example mining leases, should not of themselves extinguish native title, Queensland sought to substantially erode this principle. When the Commonwealth advanced the principle that in the validation of titles the integrity of the RDA should be maintained, Queensland, while stating that post-1975 mining tenures could be validated by 'merely paying compensation', asserted that in relation to validation the Commonwealth needed to 'acknowledge that the act of validation does not itself constitute a racially discriminatory act. It is hard to see how this can be advanced without affecting to some degree the integrity of the RDA'.

Queensland officials were adamant that Aboriginal people should have no rights of consent additional to those exercised by other landholders. This view, of course, ignores the history of dispossession and the special relationship of native title holders to their land. This Queensland Labor view, had it prevailed, would have conferred fewer rights on native title holders than those given to Aboriginal people in relation to Aboriginal reserve areas by the former National Party government. After reading this leaked document I was even more convinced that the forthcoming COAG meeting would never reach agreement on principles that could ever be remotely acceptable to indigenous people, if it reached agreement at all.

On 22 May the *West Australian* published the results of a poll which suggested that 'only 36% of people were aware of Mabo but even the vast majority of those did not know what it meant'. It is polls like this that make all parliamentarians wonder what all the energy expended in public debate is worth. After all the saturation newspaper publicity, television coverage and radio reports there was still such limited awareness of what Mabo meant. I resolved to tackle the issue of public education about the Mabo decision in an even more determined way and a document was prepared, *Rebutting Mabo Myths*, modelled on the earlier *Rebutting the Myths*. It took us until mid-June to complete this document but it was worth it.

In New Zealand on the same day, Paul Keating again emphasised the relationship between the reconciliation process and the Mabo outcome:

> In Australia we are finally coming to a basis of reconciliation with indigenous people . . . Unlike the Maori there was no treaty, no equivalent Treaty of Waitangi . . . Indigenous people since the time of European settlers have rarely had justice and we know that we will never entirely live in peace, or have peace in our hearts, without a true basis of reconciliation.

He was attacked by Tim Fischer, who criticised what he said was the view that the 'land rights legislation is to be driven solely by the agenda of Aboriginal reconciliation'.

On 27 May, while on a ministerial visit to the Torres Strait, I was dumbfounded to learn for the first time that the government had acted in a way that threatened to derail the entire Mabo process. On that day Marshall Perron, Chief Minister of the Northern Territory, issued a statement announcing that legislation had been introduced into the NT parliament to secure the mining leases of the McArthur River mine. He asserted that the legislation had been introduced 'at the request of the Prime Minister, Mr Keating' and that 'the decision to introduce the legislation followed an exchange of letters between the Territory and Commonwealth Governments'.

The legislation had the effect of reissuing the mining leases and producing a right of compensation in respect of any acquisition of native title rights that occurred as a result. It was justified by the Chief Minister on the ground that 'opinions from eminent legal advisers' had suggested that titles issued contrary to the RDA 'may be invalid'.

Mr Perron foreshadowed that the NT Assembly would pass the legislation before 1 July. He said the Prime Minister had given an assurance that the Commonwealth would legislate if necessary should there be unexpected difficulties regarding the validity of the NT legislation. He confirmed that the Commonwealth had also agreed to indemnify the Northern Territory in respect of any challenge to the validity of the legislation and that without such an assurance the NT government would not have acted. He suggested that his government 'would be seeking to reach agreement with Aboriginal groups on an appropriate package of social and economic development'.

The Chief Minister's statement was welcomed by Frank Walker, who said that 'the Commonwealth's role in the matter was consistent with its commitment to the facilitation of major projects announced in the One Nation statement in February last year'. He stressed that the Commonwealth had negotiated with the NLC, Mount Isa Mines and the NT government on how an agreement could be reached that would bring benefits to Aboriginal people. The legislation tabled by the NT government 'is evidence that progress is being made in this cooperative approach' and 'land management is of course the responsibility of State Governments', hence the need for this 'cooperative' approach.

I had not been consulted about this decision and was appalled by what had been done, even more so when the relevant documents were faxed to my hotel on Thursday Island. It was one thing to take the hard political decision that the project would proceed irrespective of Aboriginal wishes, but it was quite another to foreshadow the overriding of the RDA and to work in tandem with avowed opponents of key Aboriginal aspirations.

Aboriginal people were outraged and openly accused the Prime Minister of betrayal. A spokesman for the NLC, Wes Miller, described the legislation as 'a bombshell' and suggested that developments flew in the face of the reconciliation process and were contrary to what 'Keating's been saying publicly about making peace with Aboriginal people'. Lois O'Donoghue was privately very demoralised and said that Aboriginal people were 'extremely concerned' and felt that their position was undermined.

Particular concern was expressed about the content of letters faxed by Frank Walker from the Commonwealth to Marshall Perron. On 26 May Frank Walker had faxed a letter to the Chief Minister in which he said:

> In the event that unexpected difficulties concerning the validity of the legislation were to arise requiring Commonwealth intervention, the Commonwealth Government would take appropriate steps (including the introduction of Commonwealth legislation, if necessary) to rectify

these difficulties. In addition, the Commonwealth agrees to meet
reasonable legal costs and expenses incurred by the Territory in
defence of any challenge to validity based on inconsistency with the
RDA or the NT Self-government Act or any act replacing either of
these acts.

Even this was not enough for Mr Perron, who faxed back a letter the
same day confirming that the proposals were acceptable but that he
was 'looking forward to confirmation from the Prime Minister of your
request to the Territory Government to legislate and the other matters
upon which we have reached agreement'. Later that day, Paul Keating
faxed a brief letter in which he confirmed the 'Commonwealth's
position' as outlined in the letter from Frank Walker.

When I read these letters I remember slumping on the hotel bed
with my head in my hands. The Mabo debate had been derailed, with
a potentially fatal loss of Aboriginal confidence. Within the government
I had been fighting to ensure that the integrity of the RDA was
inviolate. This was a principle of importance, and now at the behest
of Mount Isa Mines and the tiny anti-Labor NT government the
Commonwealth had foreshadowed a commitment to amend or override
the RDA.

My worst fears were confirmed when Ian McLachlan immediately
claimed that the Commonwealth's McArthur River action 'has created
an important precedent on the question of securing title'. A day later
Marshall Perron was publicly advocating that the states adopt the
principles of the legislation introduced into the NT Assembly to secure
mining leases. The Victorian Premier, Jeff Kennett, also endorsed this
approach.

The day after Mr Perron's announcement of special legislation, the
acting director of the NLC, Brett Medina, wrote to Paul Keating
expressing their concerns and making it clear that the legislation was
first presented to the NLC the day before as a *fait accompli*. The letter
expressed concern that the legislation 'was drawn at your direct request
and is so indifferent to the principles presented to you on 27 April
1993 [the Peace Plan] by Aboriginal representatives as providing a
foundation for a broadly constructive Commonwealth response to the
Mabo decision'.

Paul Keating, as was his way, came out fighting, asserting that 'the
people opposed to Aboriginal interests' would have 'banged the drum
. . . loudly if the McArthur River project had been allowed to fail.
You'd have the worst elements of conservative interests in this country
up there blackguarding the Mabo decision and all it stands for'. I had
no doubt that the project would have to proceed given the previous
Commonwealth approval, but I was fundamentally opposed to how it

was done—much to my amazement, no journalist ever sought to put me on the spot. I have never publicly or privately defended this decision and would not in good conscience do so.

On the evening of 29 June the NT government passed its legislation. By that time Commonwealth-brokered negotiations with the NLC had collapsed and the offer that had been made to Aboriginal people by the government and the company had fallen through. Much later, in August 1993, dialogue was revived between the company and the NLC after a chance meeting at Brisbane Airport between the new NLC director, Daryl Pearce, and Mr Freund of Mount Isa Mines. Finally, in March 1994, an agreement was signed which included belated benefits to Aboriginal people such as the purchase by ATSIC of a cattle station, Bauhinia Downs, funding for outstations by the NT government, employment and training opportunities, and a barge contract in which the Borroloola Aboriginal community was to have an interest.

But both the short-term outcome and the processes employed left a very bitter taste in the mouths of indigenous people and their many supporters. At the time of Mr Perron's media release on 27 May, things were very grim indeed. A mining giant and the NT government had pressured the Commonwealth into a commitment to override the RDA. It was a precedent that made it very difficult for the government to regain the confidence of indigenous people.

In the lead-up to the formal release of the government's framework of key principles and discussion paper on Mabo, the debate continued to rage generally and, in particular, over McArthur River. Rob Riley accused Paul Keating of having 'sold out':

> Prior to that time I thought [Mabo] was the culmination, not only of
> the political struggle for Aboriginal people but [of] the ability to bring
> the Australian nation together. But when the deal was done on
> McArthur River, not only did Paul Keating kick Aboriginal people in
> the guts, but he lost the opportunity of being recorded in history as
> the Prime Minister who was able to address social justice issues
> concerning Aboriginal people. It will take a power of persuasion for
> him to be able to convince people like myself and other Aboriginal
> people that we should give him the chance again.

Lois O'Donoghue said the deals apparently done between the Commonwealth and the Northern Territory had effectively undermined the Aboriginal communities' bargaining position. To put it bluntly, if the government was prepared to act at the behest of just one mining company to so readily override Aboriginal rights, what chance did Aboriginal people have of achieving a just outcome in the overall Mabo debate? In all the mire of the Mabo debate I cannot stress how important to the success of the final outcome was the need for genuine dealings with indigenous people. Any government action that under-mined the integrity of the process and shattered Aboriginal confidence subverted the *bona fides* of the government's position. Within the government there was considerable disquiet, with Margaret Reynolds saying, 'this move has jeopardised the hard won patient and positive atmosphere in the Mabo negotiations'.

Before the release of the government's Mabo principles and the forthcoming COAG meeting, not all state governments were bel-ligerent and obstructive. The SA Premier, Lyn Arnold, urged that the complexities of Mabo 'must—and can—be resolved by discussion and consultation, not by scaremongering and confrontation'. He an-nounced that a new petroleum exploration agreement between the state government and Aboriginal people would be signed, illustrating in a very practical way the benefits of cooperation.

On 3 June the government released a discussion paper, prepared by officials, which had deliberately not been considered and cleared by ministers. A framework of 33 principles approved by ministers was also released after an exhaustive process of Mabo Ministerial Commit-tee and Cabinet meetings, but the release was tarnished by the McArthur River issue. The discussion paper, as Paul Keating said in a public statement, was 'not a statement of Government policy nor is it legal advice', but he emphasised that the framework of principles had been 'endorsed by Ministers' to guide the development of a response to the implications and uncertainties arising from the Mabo decision. 'It is not our intention', he said, 'that the principles should be seen as an ultimatum or that they should be set in concrete'. While they were not perfect, they were principles of substance and a good basis for building further rights.

ATSIC focused on the 33 principles (unfortunately presented as a mere appendix) rather than the officials' paper, and its board gave them 'cautious support' but emphasised that 'in key areas they do not go far enough' and that some indigenous interests 'have not been addressed satisfactorily or indeed at all'. Lois O'Donoghue objected to any idea that there could be a validation of titles without simultaneous legislation to recognise indigenous rights.

Following the release of the documents, the NFF recognised the need to validate by legislation land titles issued before 30 June 1993 and for all governments to bear the responsibility for compensation. It took particular exception to the suggestion that legislation might revive native title on the expiry of a pastoral lease. AMIC strenuously objected to the proposal for native title to be revived at the end of a mining lease, in the same way that a freehold or leasehold title, no longer the subject of a mining lease, continues to belong to the owner, thus asserting that native title holders, the oldest continuing owners of land in the country, should have a lesser form of title than other landholders.

Noel Pearson, director of the Cape York Land Council, savagely attacked the 'discussion paper', saying it treated Mabo as an issue relating to land management rather than being one focusing 'on the deeper cultural and spiritual significance of land to Aboriginal people'. The newly appointed Aboriginal and Torres Strait Islander Social Justice Commissioner, Mick Dodson, was also scathing in his criticism, saying that it appeared that the 'rifles and strychnine of the last century had been replaced by bureaucrats' word processors' in defeating Aboriginal ambitions. On the same day, 3 June, Aboriginal representatives formally released the Peace Plan that had been presented to ministers on 27 April. Issues were clouded by a statement issued that day in which the NLC threatened to lodge a native title claim over the McArthur River mine region unless agreement could be reached with Mount Isa Mines in four weeks.

WA Premier Richard Court's response to the government's 33 principles was classic. He predicted that Mabo would deeply divide the Australian community: 'We seem to be subtly heading towards a form of apartheid where we are granting certain lands, certain rights to those lands to a group of people'. The reality was, of course, that governments were not able to 'grant' any native title land to any Aboriginal person as such. Lands belonged to them as a right as a result of the High Court decision. The task of governments was to establish a system to facilitate the determination of where that native title existed as an alternative to simply vacating the field and leaving hundreds of Mabo cases to be dealt with in the courts, a process that would have dragged on over many years.

John Hewson attacked the Prime Minister for raising Aboriginal expectations, while Peter Nugent criticised my call for cross-party support for the 33 principles. There was some substance to his criticism, but the reality was that cross-party cooperation was dead once the Coalition began to launch their attacks, first on the High Court and then increasingly on the government's moves towards national legislation to override the states. The small number of genuine liberals in the federal Liberal Party had no chance of holding the line against the ultra-conservatives in the Coalition or the state and territory governments. In particular, it was the WA government and the influence of the WA Liberals that ensured that the Coalition took a position of total opposition to the government's native title legislation.

A central part of my own strategy was to oppose at every turn the anti-Aboriginal and strident extremist elements within the Coalition. It

The Aboriginal and Torres Strait Islander Social Justice Commissioner

One policy initiative I am very proud of is the creation of the Aboriginal and Torres Strait Islander Social Justice Commissioner. The idea for the position came to me while I was delivering Australia's report to the CERD Committee in Geneva on 6 August 1991. A committee member made a passing reference to the need for monitoring Australia's progress in giving effect to the social justice objective of the reconciliation process.

On returning to Australia on 14 September, I expressed public support for the creation of such a position and was able to persuade my ministerial colleagues of the merit of the idea. Attorney-General Michael Duffy was supportive and the decision was announced in March 1992 in the government's national response to RCIADIC.

The position was created in permanent form by an amendment to the Human Rights and Equal Opportunity Commission Act with Coalition support, and conferred extensive powers over state and territory governments which have yet to be utilised. Mick Dodson was appointed the first commissioner with the active support of Gerry Hand and myself.

The Howard government threatened to abolish the position but subsequently appointed Dr Bill Jonas, who had previously been head of AIATSIS.

was always my view that the government would have to rely on the Democrats and the Greens to secure the passage of any future legislation through the Senate. This view put me at odds with many in the government; it was certainly not the Prime Minister's expressed view for much of the native title debate. However, the best chance indigenous people had for a just outcome were the Prime Minister's strong and unambiguous public statements linking the success of the reconciliation process with the government's response to Mabo.

After the release of the discussion paper and in the aftermath of McArthur River I appealed to Aboriginal leaders not to write off Paul Keating and the Mabo process. I drew a distinction between the discussion paper prepared by officials, which had been so vigorously attacked by Aboriginal people, and the 33 principles, which had been cleared by ministers. The principles admittedly fell short of meeting all indigenous aspirations, but there was much to be commended in them.

A key feature of the first principle was the creation of a tribunal system to establish where native title existed. While there was to be an offer of Commonwealth cooperation with the states and territories to establish tribunals, these would have to be of a standard acceptable to the Commonwealth.

It was made unambiguous in the 33 principles that 'the integrity of the RDA was to be maintained'. They provided that native title should be preserved to the maximum extent possible and where possible native title should revive at the end of a finite grant, recognising that this is more readily applied in future mining leases than in pastoral leases.

They made it clear that while there could be no right of veto over grants of interest in land before June 1993, in respect of future grants in recognition of the special attachment of Aboriginal people to their land, especially protection for sacred sites, there 'could' be additional rights of consent for native title holders in relation to actions affecting their land. Considerable emphasis was placed on negotiation, and the principles foreshadowed a framework that included timetables and arbitration if negotiations failed.

Importantly, the principles ruled out the conversion of common-law native titles to statutory titles, as advocated by Richard Court. An assurance was given that the government was willing to legislate to facilitate the validation of post-1975 grants by the states and territories as long as appropriate compensation was paid and this was done contemporaneously with standard-setting national legislation being put in place.

The principles suggested that legislation should establish parameters for compensation when a grant is made over native title land, but it was made clear that in relation to existing grants governments and not private landholders should bear the burden of compensation. The final principles in the government package raised a wider agenda of social justice and economic development. In this the government made it clear that its Mabo response should go beyond immediate land management issues. Options included a national land fund, a greater stake for Aboriginal people in resource development, the transfer of reserves and other appropriate areas of unalienated crown land to indigenous interest, and improved heritage legislation.

The last principle reaffirmed the commitment to the reconciliation process and made it clear that 'there would be serious consequences for reconciliation if there was an inadequate response to Mabo'. It was acknowledged that there was a need for a program of public discussion about the decision and of the 'broader aspirations seen by Aboriginal and Torres Strait Islander people as arising from it'.

There is no doubt that the core features of what ultimately emerged in the Native Title Act are contained within these 33 principles.

While there were six tortuous months of public and parliamentary debate to come, great progress had already been made, especially on the commitment given to the assertion of Commonwealth constitutional power, gained as a result of the 1967 referendum, to achieve national standards for the recognition, protection and determination of native title.

The question yet to be resolved was what was to be the national standard. Was it to be one acceptable to the indigenous people of Australia or was it to be the lowest common denominator established at the insistence of state and territory governments? In the lead-up to, and during, the COAG meetings it looked as if the states might get their way at the expense of indigenous people. Indeed Patrick Dodson wrote to the Prime Minister on behalf of the Council for Aboriginal Reconciliation, expressing concern that there had been no opportunity for the various industry interest groups to enter into a dialogue with indigenous people. The council suggested a COAG subcommittee do this and offered to facilitate a meeting, but the call went unheeded.

There was another bombshell, this time from Aboriginal people. The day the government released its principles, a 'Mabo' ambit claim by some Wiradjuri people over a third of New South Wales was made public. It was initiated by the NSW Aboriginal Legal Service and received huge media coverage as it purported to cover not only crown land and pastoral properties but freehold property as well. I was appalled by the tactics behind this claim, which had no chance of success and was seriously damaging to the climate of opinion. Richard Court and his state colleagues could not have wished for finer assistance in whipping up a redneck backlash that could erode the Commonwealth position. Numerous similarly baseless claims were to follow. The avalanche of publicity on these claims in the lead-up to COAG was catastrophic. The chief executive of the NSW Farmers' Association, John White, suggested that the Wiradjuri claim was likely to lead to civil unrest, even violence, if upheld: 'The risk of hatred from this is immense . . . hatred leads to violence . . . people are not going to walk off their land without a fight'.

On the Sunday before the COAG meeting, the Prime Minister described the Commonwealth principles as a workable, responsible and decisive response to the challenges posed by the Mabo decision. He had consistently made it clear in Mabo Ministerial Committee meetings that it was a prime objective of the Commonwealth to get the states on board. He was motivated, I believe, by the well-intentioned belief that if the states and territories could be persuaded to come on board then the Mabo outcome would result in a deeper and more substantive shift in the nation's consciousness. Furthermore, in his view, the states were responsible for land management. No doubt these views were seen by PM&C officers as an essential, if not the most essential, element of the government's Mabo strategy.

The Prime Minister played down expectations about the result of the COAG meeting and suggested that a 'good solid discussion would be a valuable contribution to the process'. Finally, the states were warned that, in line with the Commonwealth principles, 30 June 1993 was the cut-off date beyond which the Commonwealth would not be willing to rectify failures to abide by the RDA. This meant that by that date the states had to ensure that native title rights were recognised and respected in their land administration regimes.

Some of the state premiers were reasonably constructive. The premiers of Queensland, New South Wales and South Australia supported a national approach to Mabo and in particular to a national compensation scheme, that is, a scheme funded by the Commonwealth. The NT Chief Minister rejected Richard Court's argument that all Australians should acquire land on the same system and appeared determined to push for the issue to be resolved at the COAG meeting. The Victorian Premier was reported to be prepared to adopt a constructive approach but also as indicating that tribunals would kill new investment. The Tasmanian Premier said he would join with other states to support the proposals but criticised the High Court, suggesting that it had made a politically fashionable decision to appease one group in the community.

Cheryl Kernot, Leader of the Australian Democrats, urged the COAG meeting to set up a subcommittee which could consult with indigenous communities and the mining, pastoral and tourism industries. During my time as minister I found Cheryl Kernot to be a person of great integrity. In the campaign to secure unanimous parliamentary support for legislation to initiate the process of reconciliation she and her party had given me unfailing support without compromising their independence or party views. Likewise, during the Mabo debate the Democrats took a principled and constructive stand.

At a dinner on the Monday night of the COAG meeting, Jeff Kennett announced that he had a circuit-breaker proposal, the essence of which was that most native title claims would be resolved through compensation rather than through the recognition of land titles. This outrageous proposition was explored in the COAG proceedings the next day. Imagine if non-indigenous land title holders were to unilaterally have the title to their land replaced with a right to compensation. Not one Aboriginal person had been consulted about Premier Kennett's plan to unilaterally rip away their rights.

At the COAG meeting the Commonwealth began by presenting a brief working document of core principles that weakened and eroded its 33 principles in a number of key respects. This document had not been considered by Cabinet. At the suggestion of John Fahey, attending officials withdrew, leaving only the Prime Minister, the six premiers and the two chief ministers. At the end of the day's discussion a key sticking point was whether Aboriginal people would have special rights of consent or even negotiation by virtue of their special attachment to the land. The states were reported to be unanimously opposed to the Commonwealth's view that there should be 'qualified consent and negotiation rights' because of this special attachment.

All reports of the meeting suggest that it was a dismal discussion. Jeff Kennett's proposals were entitled 'Mabo—Security, Fairness and Equity for All', but they were slanted almost entirely against Aboriginal interests. On future dealings in land, he suggested that where land was required for mining or other development, the state would provide the necessary title. If 'possessory title' was then sought by Aboriginal people and if title were proven, compensation, not land, would be provided on the basis of a court judgment. The Premier asserted that this approach was consistent with 'the McArthur River solution adopted by the Northern Territory and supported by the Federal Government' and suggested that 'where a claim for possessory title is proved in the court in respect of land which the Victorian Government is satisfied will not be required for the purpose of mining or other development, the grant of an alternative statutory title will be available as an alternative to compensation'. This would have totally undermined the Mabo judgment.

Aboriginal people were being told they could have what would otherwise be their legal entitlements to land if it would 'not be required for the purpose of mining or other development'. As an attempted softener the proposals included a new 'cultural rights title to provide defined access for Aboriginal persons to land for clearly defined traditional purposes'.

Meanwhile, outside, a small group of Aboriginal protesters held a day-long vigil on the steps of the Victorian Parliament where the meeting was being held. The symbolism of Aboriginal people outside while non-Aboriginal politicians decided their future was not new. Geoff Clarke of the APG, speaking as the heads of government decided the future of indigenous Australia, said:

> The fact that we are sitting outside when our interests are being negotiated inside is inappropriate . . . We believe we should be in there negotiating as well with the Premiers on an equal footing. That plea has been rejected by the Prime Minister and we find ourselves back on the streets again.

I was not a supporter of the COAG process for resolving the Mabo debate. I could think of nothing worse than the heads of government stitching up a deal in a closed room to shape the future rights, or lack of them, of indigenous Australians. My fears were justified when in that closed meeting the Prime Minister, under pressure from state leaders, entertained a proposal which, had it been accepted, would have consigned Labor's acclaimed Mabo response to the rubbish bin of history. Proposed changes included deletion of the reference to the role of land councils; a requirement for certainty about the attributes of native title (seen by indigenous people as being an erosion of the role of the courts); the abandoning of any recognition of special indigenous rights to negotiate based on special attachment to the land; and a limitation to consent rights. These proposals would have been a declaration of war to indigenous people had they become public. The problem was not just that the principles were to be amended but that the changes would have occurred in private negotiations with the avowed opponents of indigenous people.

Other Commonwealth proposals were unobjectionable, but that was not really the main issue. In the aftermath of McArthur River, indigenous people would have viewed any deal with the states, especially a bad one, with utter disdain. Thankfully the chances of any agreement being reached were next to non-existent, with Richard Court even refusing to acknowledge the legitimacy of the High Court decision.

At a media conference on 10 June 1993 the Prime Minister summed up the difficulties of achieving a national consensus. Ian McLachlan accused him of 'Mabo failure' and asserted: 'Native title has not yet been proved to exist on the mainland of Australia and it may be some time before the High Court is able to clarify these newly discovered Aboriginal rights which interfere with the long held belief that all Australians are equal under the law.'

7

WIK IGNITES

In the aftermath of the failed COAG meeting, the opponents of a just Mabo response intensified their vitriolic campaign. With the increased pressure on the federal Coalition by conservative state governments, particularly Western Australia, the Leader of the Opposition, John Hewson, was forced to give comfort and support to their demands, thus deepening the division between the Government and Opposition. The political targets of the opponents of Mabo were not limited to Aboriginal people and Labor ministers, but extended to attacks on the integrity and standing of the High Court itself; a referendum was even called for to nullify the decision. These conservative attacks on the High Court led to an unprecedented public defence of the court by the Chief Justice.

Just when the debate appeared to have engulfed the country and to have become exceedingly complex, vitriolic and hateful, a new and dangerous dimension emerged in early July 1993 with the lodgement of the Wik claim. This claim involved the assertion not only of native title rights but breaches of fiduciary duty by government and the potential challenge to titles going back to 1788. This claim was steeped in the long history of Aboriginal mistreatment and injustice in Cape York. Whatever its undeniable merits it also had the effect of derailing the integrity of the Commonwealth's response in Aboriginal eyes.

The claim challenged the interests of CRA, one of the world's most powerful mining companies, which quickly found an ally in the Goss Labor government in Queensland. The opponents of a just Mabo response did not, however, have it all their own way and there were uplifting and principled contributions to the public debate by Aboriginal people and their supporters.

But the pressure on Wik was relentless. The Queensland government and CRA called for a McArthur River solution to override the Aboriginal claimants and to protect the company's economic interests. By the end of July, Aboriginal people were not only fighting back on Wik but also pressuring the government on the content of the crucial drafting instructions for the proposed native title legislation, claiming that government bureaucrats' drafting did not match the Prime Minister's rhetoric.

———

Two days after the collapse of the COAG discussion I wrote to Paul Keating suggesting that it would be possible to neutralise the opposition of the farm sector. I had spoken to Mick Dodson and Peter Shergold about the need for talks with the NFF's Rick Farley. Despite the existence of ALP policy in support of a right of veto by Aboriginal people over mining and other activities on their land, there was zero chance of Cabinet support for such a policy. I therefore argued for modified consent rights, which had been supported by Lois O'Donoghue in a recent public statement. Some weeks earlier I had put to Lois, Peter, and another key ATSIC Mabo participant, Murray Chapman, formerly my trusted senior adviser and now a senior ATSIC officer, that modified consent rights were an achievable goal. Modified rights of consent already existed over the Pitjantjatjara lands in South Australia (put in place by a Liberal government) and had worked effectively.

The weekend after the COAG meeting the NSW ALP Annual Conference was held. ALP conferences can be very staid affairs, but on this occasion there was a sense of overwhelming unity of purpose on Mabo. I wanted the party forums to pass the most progressive and unanimous motions achievable. Michael Lee and I negotiated for the Right and Left factions respectively, with Graham Richardson later joining in the discussion. Paul Keating was phoned at Kirribilli and we discussed the content of the motion to be put to the conference. I was reasonably happy with the draft motion, which supported Common-wealth legislation to establish a 'framework for dealing with native title and to give effect to Aboriginal and Torres Strait Islander aspirations'. The Prime Minister addressed the conference the next day and spoke about the need for a Mabo response that would advance the process of reconciliation. It was, he said, 'a Labor cause and I call on the entire Labor movement in Australia to get behind it'. Other state and terri-tory ALP branches were urged to pass strong resolutions at their conferences in support of a principled response to Mabo, and to the best of my knowledge they all did, without dissent.

The sentiment and sympathies of the party rank and file were overwhelmingly on the side of indigenous people. There would have been outrage if some of the Cabinet protagonists had had their way and eroded the Commonwealth's response in favour of the mining industry or state and territory governments. Paul Keating was clearly conscious of these party sentiments and I have no doubt that the strong manifestation of party support for a principled response to Mabo was a constructive force contributing to the ultimate result. The trade union movement was also a strong source of support for Common-wealth leadership over Mabo. The ACTU Indigenous Affairs Committee met at regular intervals at ACTU headquarters in Melbourne, chaired by president Martin Ferguson, and throughout the union movement there was strong support for a principled stand.

Even before the COAG meeting the Mabo debate was bitter and polarised. In the months ahead it became very ugly as the Coalition and their supporters began to engage in vicious attacks on indigenous people and to appeal to the worst prejudice in the community, as Pauline Hanson would do in 1997. It should be remembered that Pauline Hanson did not pioneer cruel and baseless political attacks on Aboriginal people and organisations: the Coalition developed them into an art-form during the Mabo debate. The director of the SA Aboriginal Legal Rights Movement, Sandra Saunders, at a conference of Aboriginal community leaders in Adelaide on 15 June, warned that Aboriginal people were being harassed in the street and in their homes because of the hateful nature of the debate. She was particularly critical of the beat-up reporting of the so-called ambit claims. Her concerns about threats to Aboriginal people were echoed by other Aboriginal leaders.

Among the politicians, Tim Fischer was first off the starting blocks, saying that the Coalition had been too quiet on Mabo and that it was time to 'take the gloves off' with the Prime Minister. There were also occasional expressions of reason and moderation. The National Party's Deputy Leader and Shadow Minister for Primary Industry, John Anderson, issued a media release on the day Tim Fischer's comments were reported, confirming that 'freehold properties and the vast majority of leasehold properties were safe from [Mabo] claims because native title had been extinguished'. But he did warn of the threat of Mabo claims to forestry and fishing.

Then the WA Chamber of Mines and Energy released a map falsely suggesting that 80 per cent of Western Australia was open to claims for native title. The chief executive of the Chamber, Peter Ellery, though expressing concern that no agreement had been reached at COAG, said this breakdown in negotiations was preferable to acceptance of Commonwealth tribunals.

John Hewson, under increasing internal party pressure, addressed a Queensland State Liberal Party meeting on the Gold Coast at which he accused the Prime Minister of trying to 'ram through' his version of a response to the High Court ruling and of raising Aboriginal expectations and letting 'them down with a thud. Everybody has been left frustrated—miners, farmers, investors, Aboriginals, and not the least the ordinary Australian taxpayers. The intentional uncertainty this has caused has yet to be measured'.

On 17 June the *Australian* published a newspoll that showed a majority of those polled as being against the High Court decision: 46 to 43 per cent. Those polled were also asked whether, if native title was 'given' to Aboriginal people, they should be compensated for mining and farming on their land. A 52 to 39 per cent majority said no, even though non-indigenous landholders would be so compensated. The poll demonstrated that neither Australia's national daily newspaper or its pollsters understood the effect of the High Court decision. The Prime Minister had been criticised by political commentators, including the *Australian*'s Glen Milne, for failing to engage in the Mabo public debate. On the same day as the poll Paul Keating went on the John Laws program on 2UE, where he talked about Mabo and took calls from listeners, most of whom were hostile.

The Prime Minister issued a statement on 18 June announcing that he had written to the premiers and chief ministers informing them that the Commonwealth legislation would provide a framework for certainty in land management and a just and workable approach to native title. He said that the preferred approach was a cooperative one with state and territory governments and that the Commonwealth would pursue bilateral discussions, including discussions between officials, to this end. These were more likely to produce a better outcome for indigenous people than any resumption of the COAG discussions, though he had not ruled that out.

That day the NSW National Party Leader and Acting NSW Premier, Ian Armstrong, gave a public message to farmers from a NSW National Party Conference that he would not allow them to be 'dispossessed' by Aboriginal people through Mabo claims. There was not a credible lawyer in the country who believed that any farmer anywhere was going to be dispossessed, as the High Court had made clear; to make suggestions to the contrary was grossly irresponsible. Speaking at the same conference in Wagga Wagga, Tim Fischer suggested that the Commonwealth government's tough stand on Mabo was likely to give the secessionist movement in Western Australia a 'new breath of life' and that the Commonwealth response could lead to the 'breaking up of Australia'. Tim Fischer made other remarks that caused a public furore, such as that the dispossession of Aboriginal people had been inevitable and was not something to be ashamed of, and that Aboriginal culture had been relatively stationary and had not even produced a 'wheeled cart'. He alleged that the Commonwealth was funding the delivery of alcohol to Aboriginal settlements, an allegation promptly denied by community representatives. The Prime Minister urged Tim Fischer to restrain himself and I accused him of playing on the worst prejudices. Even Peter Nugent suggested that Mr Fischer's comments were unhelpful and appealed for a 'cool' approach.

On 20 June, at a press conference in my Sutherland office I launched the publication *Rebutting Mabo Myths*. The five-page photocopied document was subsequently distributed to churches, local government, business groups, trade unions, government organisations and state and federal MPs throughout the country. It explained in clear and unambiguous terms that Australians had nothing to fear from the Mabo decision. I stressed at the media conference that there was nothing radical about Mabo. It did not mean that Aboriginal people are given any land, only that they may keep land they already have, and where their families have lived uninterrupted for tens of thousands of years.

The document also dealt with the sensitive question of the existence or otherwise of native title on pastoral leases. It sought to dispel the myth that Mabo allows Aboriginal people to 'gain ownership of Australia's farming and grazing land'. Even after the Wik decision, this remains true and it is beyond doubt that any native title rights that do exist cannot in any way limit the pastoralists' rights under their lease. The document received extraordinary and favourable coverage in national and local newspapers.

To give some idea of the intensity of the debate, on the same weekend as Tim Fischer and Ian Armstrong were railing against the government from the Right, and the government was being put on the front foot by the release of *Rebutting Mabo Myths*, Aboriginal community leaders were meeting in Darwin. They had written to the Prime Minister to express concern that they had been left out of COAG talks; there was 'great concern that our communication, consultation and negotiation with you appear to have diminished', and they warned that any Mabo legislation could fail without Aboriginal support.

Richard Court weighed in with his own brand of scaremongering. He had raised the prospect of Mabo-type claims being made over suburban housing blocks. I responded by flying to Perth and at a well-attended media conference said: 'Despite the categorised public assurances of the Prime Minister himself and six federal Cabinet Ministers that not one square centimetre of privately owned land is threatened by the decision, Mr Court continues to peddle the assertion that Perth backyards will be successfully claimed under the Mabo principles'. I assured the people of Western Australia that 'unless Aboriginal people had lived in their backyards without interruption since 1788 . . . they could sleep safely in their beds at night'.

In Perth I did a number of radio interviews, including one with Howard Sattler. Mr Sattler's comments, often openly hostile to Aboriginal aspirations, have on occasion caused great distress to Aboriginal people in Western Australia. In the studio I came face to face with Premier Court for the first time. In an event stage-managed for the TV cameras, he invited me to Parliament House later that day to meet him. At that meeting he showed that he had no idea of the basic principles of the Mabo decision. My senior adviser Peter Schnierer, a senior Aboriginal public servant, and I came out of the meeting and looked at each other and laughed in disbelief. It was a waste of time trying to engage in a meaningful dialogue and I understood the frustrations that Paul Keating must have felt at COAG two weeks before. There was more reason than ever for the Commonwealth to use its legislative power to protect indigenous rights in Western Australia.

From South Korea Prime Minister Keating responded to Tim Fischer's weekend remarks, calling on the Opposition Leader to 'put down' Mr Fischer's 'crude and primitive' comments. He was joined by the Coalition Shadow Treasurer, Alexander Downer, who to his credit dissociated himself from Tim Fischer's remarks, saying it was 'certainly not the sort of language that I would ever use and I don't think it helps much to be patronising about Aboriginal culture'. Tim Fischer was unrepentant, trotting out what was to be the increasingly familiar line that he was going to be realistic and would not be constrained by the 'politically correct speak which had dominated and misled for too long'. In this he was supported by columnist Padraic McGuinness who, in a familiar refrain, accused Mr Fischer's critics of being the 'politically correct elements of the chattering classes . . . whipping themselves into a lather of indignation'.

On Sunday, 27 June, eight significant industry groups launched a campaign focusing on the validation of titles and the confirmation of crown ownership of resources: the Australian Chamber of Commerce and Industry, AMIC, the Australian Petroleum Exploration Association, the Australian Tourism Industry Association, the Business Council of Australia, the NFF, the National Association of Forest Industries and the National Fishing Industry Council. Their statement lamented that 'it is a matter of great concern that the federal government is attempting to finalise legislation without adequate and ongoing consultation with industry'. The statement opposed any right of veto by indigenous groups over development. It advocated the facilitation of continuing grants by the states, opposed revival of native title following a limited grant, for example to a mining company, and advocated a sunset clause for claims of native title. The last demand was, as I have already explained, illogical; as if there could be a sunset clause on anyone else having an entitlement to land they already owned.

The next day, 28 June, the Opposition Leader released the Coalition Mabo issues paper. The first substantive sentence said it all, describing the Mabo decision as 'one of the most important changes to Australia's investment climate for decades'. John Hewson attacked Paul Keating for failing to provide leadership and for raising expectations in all sections of the community of a 'rapid solution'. This assertion was patently untrue; only four months before, Dr Hewson had been publicly expressing approval for the government's 'negotia-tion' timetable on Mabo, which was to 'run through until September'. That night, on the *7.30 Report*, he confirmed that the Coalition paper embodied 'quite a strong pro-development position'.

Frank Walker and I issued a joint statement in response in which we asserted that the statement was 'a superficial fundamentally flawed, inconsistent and poorly thought out document which has a lot to say about development interests and virtually nothing to say about recognising the legal rights of Aboriginal and Torres Strait Islander people'. A central concern was that the Coalition advocated that state and territory governments should be left to determine how native title is to be identified and recorded.

The Coalition paper was in turn criticised by Richard Court as not going far enough, but it gave virtually nothing to indigenous people, not even right of resumption of their native title rights at the expira-tion of a mining lease, which is a property right enjoyed by all other Australians, whether freeholders or pastoralists with a leasehold inter-est. The paper merely adopted an industry and states' rights outcome.

June ended with Hugh Morgan's further contribution to the debate in a speech to the Victorian RSL in which he suggested that 'guilt industry people have great difficulty in accepting or recognising that Aboriginal culture was so much less powerful than the culture of Europeans, there was never any possibility of its surviving', that some cultures will 'wither away', and that Mabo threatens the unity of Australia. Mr Morgan also foreshadowed a referendum to override the High Court decision. On Sydney's 2UE on 2 July, John Hewson refused to distance himself from Hugh Morgan's views, professing instead to endorse the 'centrepiece' of his argument about the 'enormous and growing uncertainty' caused by the Mabo decision.

On the same day the *Canberra Times* reported the largely unprece-dented comments of the Chief Justice, Sir Anthony Mason, in an interview with the journal *Australian Lawyer*. Defending the Mabo judgment, he said:

> The rejection of the doctrine of *terra nullius* is entirely consistent with
> the rejection of that doctrine by the international court in the Western
> Sahara case. So far from being an adventure on the part of the High
> Court, the decision reflects what's happened in the great common law
> jurisdictions of the world and the International Court, except that in
> the case of Australia it's happened later than it's happened elsewhere.
> In New Zealand it happened almost 150 years ago . . . In some
> circumstances Governments and legislatures prefer to leave the
> determination of a controversial question to the courts, rather than
> leave the question to be decided by the political process.

Sir Anthony was correct. No Australian government in the 1990s would have legislated such a sweeping reform as was brought about by the Mabo decision, not because of the inherent weakness of politicians but because of the unchallenged power of industry bodies and the lack of empathy in sections of the Australian community. Fortunately the Mabo decision was brought down at a time when a federal Labor government was in power and there was a climate conducive to government action to protect indigenous rights, brought about in part by the start of the reconciliation process.

Debate during the first two weeks of July 1993 was intense. There were more endorsements of Hugh Morgan's call for a referendum to override Mabo, among them one from Sir Arvi Pabo, the chairman of Western Mining. Both John Hewson and the federal Race Discrimination Commissioner, Irene Moss, also disagreed with the notion of a referendum to resolve the Mabo decision.

On 4 July John Howard, then a Liberal frontbencher, appeared on Channel 10's *Meet the Press* alleging that the Mabo debate had introduced 'cultural McCarthyism' into Australian politics, asserting that anyone opposing the conventional wisdom on matters of race was 'belted over the head with a bit of four-by-two on the basis that they are racist or extremist'. He singled me out as being guilty of this 'McCarthyism' because of my attacks on Hugh Morgan. John Howard's intervention was significant because it was a manifestation of what was to become his ongoing strategy of attempting to marginalise his opponents by describing them as McCarthyist or politically correct or a part of the 'guilt industry'.

John Howard has been practising his craft for a long time now. On 13 July 1993 he wrote an article for the *Canberra Times* in which he again singled me out for special criticism in order to support Richard Court: 'A racist is someone who believes in the inherent superiority of one race over another and who behaves accordingly. He or she is not a person who disagrees with Paul Keating's or Robert Tickner's version of Australian history or for that matter the High Court's decision in the Mabo case'.

Years later, it is difficult to convey the extent to which Mabo engulfed Australia during 1993. For much of the year, hardly a day went past when there was not some new development in the debate. The words were often hateful, and the pressure on key participants was relentless.

The first two weeks of July 1993 were notable also for a further series of ambit claims which provoked ongoing public furore and, most significantly, for the now famous claim by the Wik people of Cape

York, which was anything but an ambit claim. The Wik claim was to derail the Commonwealth's response to Mabo in the same way that the McArthur River issue had done. But this time Aboriginal people were to take on one of the biggest and most influential companies in the Australian mining industry, CRA Ltd, which was very used to getting its own way with governments.

On 3 July the Wik people were reported as submitting a claim under the auspices of the Cape York Land Council over a vast area of the western side of Cape York in Queensland. In the months to come this claim would dominate the Mabo debate. The timing could not have been worse. There is a story yet to be revealed about the influences that led to the bringing of the claim at this time, but it is one others must tell.

The Wik claim was for 35 000 square kilometres, including some CRA bauxite leases, tidal land and coastal waters. The claim sought a share of profits for mining at Weipa, and an injunction to prevent aspects of future mining. Weipa contains 15 per cent of the world's bauxite resources and accounts for 10 per cent of global production. It sought recognition of Aboriginal title including 'sub-surface rights especially ownership of minerals found in, on or below the surface'. The claim included the Archer Bend National Park and also Mapoon, which had been the land forcibly taken from Aboriginal people by the Queensland government for mining by Comalco in the early 1960s. The Wik claim was strenuously opposed by CRA from the beginning.

An unprecedented joint statement by the former five RCIADIC commissioners and the leaders of most Australian churches and faith groups was released on 8 July calling on all Australians 'to speak out for the principles of surviving Aboriginal rights to land, negotiation wherever possible, support for the Racial Discrimination Act, and patient progress towards reconciliation'. It was given very little time and space in the media, but it did have a real impact on the debate as it was widely disseminated within the government, the Caucus and the wider community. It was also read in full at the subsequent UN Working Group on Indigenous Populations (WGIP) held in Geneva at the end of July by my colleague, Garrie Gibson MP, who represented me on this occasion.

Richard Court and Bill Hassell, Liberal Party president in Western Australia, accused church groups of seeking to 'stifle debate' on Mabo issues. Mr Hassell said: 'What they want is for all of us to quietly and meekly accept Mabo but the vigorous debate should go on and the truth about Mabo exposed'. He called for either parliamentary action to override Mabo or a referendum to overturn the decision.

The native title legislation was now firmly on the government's agenda. In the lead-up to the next Mabo Ministerial Committee meeting on 12 July 1993, PM&C officers produced for ministers a new version of the drafting instructions. The advice to ministers made it clear that even the most modest proposals for tribunals to determine native title were unacceptable to the states and territories. It said there was a push by some states and territories for the Commonwealth to define in legislation the connection with the land that would enable Aboriginal people to successfully assert native title, and in particular the physical connection with the land required to prove title. Both these proposals would limit indigenous rights when compared with the scope of the High Court decision. State and territory officials had also made it clear that they wanted a time limit on native title claims. Such a constraint would certainly not be acceptable to indigenous people and it is unlikely that it could be legally enforced. Not surprisingly, both these principles were advocated in 1998 by John Howard in the aftermath of the Wik decision.

A second written briefing was provided by PM&C which suggested that further discussions with some states and territories had revealed 'a growing interest' in advancing a joint response with the Commonwealth as quickly as possible. It was also suggested that opposition to the revival of native title at the expiration of a mining lease was 'hardening' as a result of 'political' concerns.

PM&C advised that the Queensland government and industry interests were concerned about the potential for invalidity of leases 'including those issued before 1975', going back conceivably to 1788, for reasons such as a breach of fiduciary duty, an issue extending well beyond native title. This special legal duty, if it was recognised by the courts, would have limited the capacity of governments to have dealt with Aboriginal people and their lands. Fiduciary duty was an issue in the Wik claim. It was suggested that Commonwealth legislation to address these concerns and implicitly override the claims would be 'consistent with the Government's approach'. It was a forewarning of the pressure soon to be applied to the government.

On the day of the meeting, Aboriginal land councils and other Aboriginal representatives had been in Canberra lobbying ministers and expressing particular concern about a reference in the draft proposals to compensation for loss or use of native title land at the same level as that paid to other landholders, without consideration of Aboriginal special attachment to the land.

For my part, I was satisfied that things were largely proceeding within the Committee according to plan, though there was never a meeting where there was not a fight point after point on issues of principle. Some people who on other occasions have spoken on national television about what happened in past Labor cabinets would suffer considerable embarrassment if their own consistently reactionary contributions to the Mabo deliberations were publicly revealed. There were also things said and language used by some participants in the Committee debate that caused deep offence to the Aboriginal members of my staff and to ATSIC staff.

That night Premier Fahey attacked the Commonwealth's proposals. He had until then been seen as one of the main supporters of a negotiated Commonwealth–state national outcome. Now he took a contrary view, suggesting that if the Commonwealth proposals were not amended 'there will be division in the Australian community the like of which we have never seen before'. The next morning the press reported a further contribution to the public debate by Sir Anthony Mason, who in an address to a law conference at Queen's College Cambridge had again publicly defended the Mabo decision:

> The criticism on the part of interest groups, on behalf of mining and pastoral industries and to a lesser extent politicians, has been the most sustained and abusive that I can recall in my career as a lawyer. More disconcerting has been the concerted campaign run by the mining interests supported by the pastoral interests to discredit our decision in the Aboriginal land rights case.

This was not some partisan voice speaking but none other than the Chief Justice of the High Court of Australia.

On 13 July the Wik claim assumed increased importance, with yet another joint statement issued by the Australian Coal Association, the Australian Chamber of Commerce and Industry, AMIC, the Australian Petroleum Exploration Association, the National Association of Forest Industries, the NFF and the National Fishing Industry Council. The statement warned that the claim reinforced the need for urgent validation of existing property titles and that 'without prompt validation of titles, current and future developments will be placed at considerable risk'.

Because of the complicated modern history of this region, the Wik land claim raised for consideration the impact of a native title claim over various categories of land, such as pastoral lease land, mining leases, a national park, Aboriginal land trust land, and special releases. There were nine defendants to the action, including the Queensland and Commonwealth governments, as well as other parties who held titles or interests pursuant to Queensland legislation: Comalco, the Council of the Shire of Aurukun, the Napranum and Pompuraaw Aboriginal Councils, and an individual, Eddie Holroyd, who had a special lease.

The Wik claimants had done what they could to try and reassure Comalco and the government that they were not intending to shut down the mine. A delegation to Canberra led by Noel Pearson had gained extensive coverage for the Aboriginal position on the claim, with the voice of local community leaders being heard on the national stage. Noel Pearson said that the claim sought recognition of the rights of traditional land owners in coexistence with other interests and sought to distinguish the claim from the ambit claims that had gained so much publicity in recent weeks. He stressed that it was a 'serious' and 'fair dinkum' claim.

The next day, the ALP National President, Barry Jones, entered the debate suggesting that the Prime Minister's first aim should be to get the premiers back inside the tent to work out a national solution with complementary federal legislation. He said that it would be wrong for the Commonwealth to legislate in isolation. Barry Jones is a national treasure, but on this occasion his contribution to the debate was most unwelcome.

In the same week the Anglican Archbishop of Perth, Dr Peter Carnley, was catapulted into the Mabo debate when he said that to deny Aboriginal people freehold title to land they still occupied would be akin to Adolf Hitler's plans to deprive Jews of their property:

> It would be entirely unjust and unequal to dispossess Aborigines occupying their traditional land on the grounds that a particular entitlement does not arise from the land conveyancing law which was introduced from 1829 onwards. Indeed, that idea should send a shudder down every Western Australian spine. It is too reminiscent of Adolf Hitler's strategies to deprive Jews of their property for us to react to it other than with the most grave concern.

His comments prompted anti-Mabo Liberal Party protagonist Wilson 'Iron Bar' Tuckey to threaten to leave the Anglican Church and to call on other members of the Anglican community 'who share my concerns and fears about the Mabo decision to do likewise'. Dr Carnley defended his comments by pointing out that he was not talking about individuals but about 'matters of principle'.

Another welcome contribution to the debate came from a most unlikely quarter. Throughout much of July Richard Court had been suggesting that 80 per cent of Western Australia was subject to successful Mabo claims. That week the WA Deputy Liberal Leader, Colin Barnett, confessed that 'the Mabo decision was very clearly limited to cases where Aboriginal communities could show a continuous occupation and relationship to a particular area of land as was the case with the Murray Islands' and 'there are probably limited areas within Australia, particularly Western Australia, where that continuous occupation was applied'.

And three days later the NFF's Rick Farley went public in the *Age* and elsewhere in banner headlines, 'Mabo law to shield farmers', saying that the Commonwealth proposals thus far 'would largely insulate the farm sector from any direct impact of the Mabo decision'. Frank Walker and I convened a working group of officials and ministerial staff to prepare a wide-ranging paper for preliminary consideration on the necessary wider response to Mabo.

While all this was happening, my Stanwell Park home had been subject to a bomb threat and there was a protective services guard posted out the front. The guard turned out to be no protection at all when on one occasion he actually escorted a TV crew to the front door, which led to a sensationalist account of the bomb threat with pictures of the guarded house and me being very unhappily filmed through the front door on the evening news. In 1992 my electorate office was burnt out in an arson attack and in 1993 a dead rat was posted to my home address but intercepted at the local post office. These events placed intolerable pressures on my family life.

On 21 July there was a further meeting of Commonwealth and state officials in Canberra, the first held since the COAG talks had collapsed. Pressure began to build on the Wik claim, with Premier Goss saying on ABC radio that 'if we can't have some resolution of this by the end of the year then we will be asking for McArthur River type legislation as occurred in the Northern Territory to protect this particular investment in Weipa and Gladstone'. He emphasised that what was at stake was a major Comalco investment in a smelter at Gladstone, but he denied that CRA was holding a gun to the head of the Queensland government on the issue.

The pressure had, however, increased as a result of a television appearance the night before by John Ralph, managing director and chief executive of CRA, in which he set out the company's concerns. Mr Ralph warned that CRA would defer or scrap projects worth $1.75 billion unless the Wik claim issues were resolved. Particularly at risk, he stressed, was CRA's proposal to buy the Gladstone Power Station from the Queensland government and the upgrading of the nearby Boyne Island aluminum smelter.

In an address to the National Press Club on 22 July, Paul Keating gave a very welcome reassurance to indigenous people and their supporters:

> I reiterate what I said to the Premiers and Chief Ministers: in dealing
> with land management issues posed by Mabo, our preferred course is
> complementary legislation cooperatively achieved. But this does not
> mean that we will accept the lowest common denominator or will fail
> to establish appropriate national standards and mechanisms for dealing
> with native title. If Aboriginal and Torres Strait Islander people have

one overriding request of the Government it is that the Commonwealth set the benchmarks. And this we will do.

He promised legislation in the budget sitting that would 'nourish the reconciliation process' and made it very clear that 'the political heat of the issue will not deflect us from that sound, deliberative, consultative course on which we embarked last October'.

The debate, meanwhile, continued on its vitriolic way. On 23 July the former head of the National Companies and Securities Commission, Henry Bosch, was reported in the *Australian* as saying that governments were wasting their time on reconciliation with Aboriginal people, who he described as 'a stone age people . . . the most backward by any objective set of achievements by which I can think'. He described the High Court decision as 'regrettably entirely regrettable'. Such an attitude is not subject to reason or persuasion. It represents very well the depth of what we were up against.

On 26 July representatives of key indigenous organisations sought to redress the imbalance in the public debate in a letter of concern about the progress of the government's Mabo deliberations directed to the Prime Minister and other members of the Mabo Ministerial Committee. The letter, which was released to the media, was signed by representatives of the Victorian Aboriginal Legal Service and the Kimberley and Central Land Councils from Western Australia and the Northern Territory respectively. It supported the Prime Minister's statements on Mabo but expressed concern that his words were not matched by the drafting instructions that had been leaked to them. They sought clarification of the status of the drafting instructions, 'which appears to have been developed jointly between senior Commonwealth and State/Territory public servants' but was being portrayed as having 'senior Ministerial' approval. The letter also expressed concern that the Peace Plan had been ignored.

That weekend, despite the best efforts of Shadow Attorney-General Daryl Williams and Opposition Leader John Hewson, the WA Liberal conference delivered Richard Court a resounding victory. The conference supported a national referendum on Mabo and a proposition that High Court judges be appointed by a two-thirds majority of the Senate. John Hewson to his credit had told the conference he did not agree with a referendum and preferred complementary state and Commonwealth legislation. But the relentless pressure on him from ultra-conservatives in the Liberal Party would drive him to support their opposition to national legislation to protect the Mabo decision.

8

A STRATEGIC WIN AND A BITTER DEFEAT

As the Commonwealth officials themselves conceded, the drafting instructions for the proposed native title legislation was an evolving document. Unfortunately, for Aboriginal people, that evolution was to a large degree initially heavily influenced by the relentless pressure of state and NT governments, almost always against Aboriginal interests. Even PM&C openly advocated the view that there should be no rights accorded to Aboriginal people to control mining on their land.

The understandable close working relationship between Commonwealth, state and Northern Territory officials led to the drafting instructions for the legislation gaining a momentum of its own in the hands of officials. Even the current rights of Aboriginal people under the NT Land Rights Act were threatened with erosion in the course of negotiations as a part of a deal.

Then came a Cabinet meeting at which it was decided that Aboriginal people would have rights to negotiate with miners and others, with unresolved disputes to be determined by the Native Title Tribunal to be created by the proposed legislation. Aboriginal people criticised the decision for not going far enough; miners criticised it for going too far.

Aboriginal people held their mass meeting of Aboriginal leadership at Eva Valley on 3 August 1993, reaching a united position that stressed the need for free and informed consent by them to any legislation, the need for Commonwealth supremacy, and a long list of demands.

By the end of August, the pressure came again from Premier Goss and CRA for the Commonwealth to intervene to override the Wik claimants. The result was a bitter falling out between Wayne Goss and Paul Keating.

Ultimately, the Prime Minister was rolled by his own Cabinet, a fact largely unreported by the media despite the rarity of such an event during the entire period of the Labor government. CRA did not get all it wanted but it got a lot and all at the expense of Aboriginal people.

———

On Tuesday, 27 July 1993, Cabinet held a marathon meeting to discuss the Mabo legislation drafting instructions and received reports on the issues from officials. These reports give an insight into the behind-the-scenes work and into the negotiations with the states. One paper described the drafting instructions as an 'evolving document' in the light of 'consultations with state and territory officials, comments from ministers and representations from interest groups'.

My concern was that PM&C, not ministers, was in control of this evolution. The 'drafting instructions' were principles that would, if agreed by ministers, be passed on to the parliamentary draftspeople for the preparation of the Native Title Bill. Of particular concern was officials' advice that the Bill 'being prepared facilitates validation of existing grants by putting this beyond challenge on Racial Discrimination Act grounds'.

It was recommended that a key principle applying to future dealings was that 'they must proceed on a non-discriminatory basis: that is, grants, crown acts, extinguishment etc. can happen in relation to native title land as they can in relation to other private interests in land'. The fact is that while dealings on a 'non-discriminatory basis' have a superficial appeal, they are a denial of any right of negotiation or control by Aboriginal people over what could happen on their lands, especially in relation to mining. At various times, both Labor and Coalition governments have recognised Aboriginal special attachment to their land and supported the introduction of such rights, the high point being the right of veto contained in the NT Land Rights Act. To propose merely 'non-discrimination' was therefore to argue directly against one of the most important aspirations of indigenous people in the native title debate. PM&C advocated no significant indigenous rights where native title had not yet been proven other than notification rights of a general kind which were not to apply in cases of minor grants with low impact on the land.

The briefing argued against other key indigenous demands and proposed putting a cap on compensation, in apparent flagrant breach of the Australian Constitution, which required 'just terms' to be paid. PM&C's advice reported that negotiations with individual states and territories, while not committing governments, indicated that the Northern Territory, Queensland, South Australia and the Australian Capital Territory were keen to reach agreement on complementary legislation; Victorian and Tasmanian officials would have liked to support a national response 'but at the political level are likely to look with a particularly critical eye at the Commonwealth proposals'. It was doubted that Western Australia would join in the process.

Ninety per cent of the proposals were said to be acceptable to 'most of the States', and it was concluded that, without minimising the significance of the remaining issues, 'it does demonstrate a good deal more common ground, and progress on the substantive issues over the past few months, than would be apparent from the public debate'. It was recommended that the Commonwealth should 'for the time being' at least adhere to the view that a mining lease should not extinguish native title, but even here officials raised concerns about 'mining operations over many years' duration which have major and extensive impacts on land, including in some cases, the creation of townships'. It was proposed that residential, pastoral and tourist leases should extinguish native title.

Turning to the fundamental question of rights of indigenous people to control the activity of others on their land, officials noted that 'the drafting instructions do not provide any consent rights beyond those available to comparable title holders—a position supported by some members of the [Mabo] Ministerial Committee—in comments they have made'.

I found this last comment strange and offensive. Certainly there were members of the Mabo Ministerial Committee who opposed any special rights of consent and who supported the industry line almost without exception, but there were also strong views to the contrary on the record, especially from Frank Walker and myself. If anything told me how tough things were to be, this bureaucratic push against indigenous rights was it. As things stood, the Mabo response was in deep trouble.

The advice from PM&C canvassed but rejected the kind of option I had been advocating in line with the *Pitjantjatjara Land Rights Act 1981* in South Australia. The Prime Minister had already ruled out Aboriginal people having any kind of veto in line with the NT Land Rights Act, and I judged the SA model to be the next best option. However, officials concluded that 'in the final analysis' the proposal 'puts into the hands of a Tribunal rather than a government, whether a grant will proceed. We judge that industry would fight hard against the proposal, and it would in all likelihood preclude agreement with the States'.

The officials were undoubtedly acting in line with what they saw as the government's aim—to achieve a just Mabo outcome but one that was agreed by the states and territories and that accommodated the concerns of the mining and pastoral industries to the greatest possible extent. But the officials' work was gathering a further momentum of its own, and the recommendations to ministers were like a declaration of war to me. What too few people have ever recognised is that the Mabo debate then taking place was at least in part a re-run of the national land rights debate of the mid-1980s, but with the crucial additional intervention of the High Court decision and the launch of the reconciliation process. Ultimately, many of the bureaucratic and industry proposals that were rejected by the Keating government in 1993 were overwhelmingly adopted by John Howard and the Coalition in its legislative response to Wik. This is why it is so important to understand the history of the struggle for Aboriginal rights.

The recommendations also included a number of state requests 'which might be accepted in the "end game" in any negotiation and contingent on a firm commitment from a State or Territory government (not merely its officials) that it accepted the rest of the deal'. These requests included a possible review of the veto provisions of the NT Land Rights Act. The officials recommended that 'we be willing at the end of the day to accept these points on a conditional basis'. In true Sir Humphrey style the officials used the word 'we'. Thus rather than simply providing advice as a basis for decisions by ministers, they were subtly ingratiating themselves into the decision-making process.

Just how far out of touch they were can be seen by the proposal to review the veto provisions in the NT Land Rights Act. This would, if adopted, have destroyed the Labor government's credibility. Like a comparable proposal to weaken the NT Land Rights Act in the 1980s, the land rights debate had resulted in a determined national campaign against the Commonwealth by Aboriginal land councils in the Northern Territory. If such a proposal had been publicly advanced during the Mabo debate there would have been universal condemnation from Aboriginal people and their supporters.

Before the Cabinet meeting I had done my best to encourage Frank Walker to convene meetings of key ministers to advance consideration of the proposals for legislation. Such meetings were necessary to make progress on an extraordinarily difficult drafting job. The necessary progress in the Mabo Ministerial Committee meetings could not be made because of the immensity of the task, the excessively large size of the committee, and the Prime Minister's limited availability. Pressure on the government was growing and I was increasingly frustrated by the slow pace of deliberations. My attempts to advance issues more rapidly failed. While there was a developing consensus on some issues, others could only be resolved through the Cabinet processes.

During the Cabinet meeting tempers frayed and emotions ran high. Some who publicly purported to be the friends of Aboriginal people consistently advocated an industry line in Cabinet. Others who were supporters of the Aboriginal cause (or were assumed to be so by the Left of the party) said little or nothing. I felt like giving some of them a prod with a hot poker to remind them why they were there. Ultimately, however, a strategic victory was won at this meeting through the assistance of some surprising allies.

Lessons in obstruction for Native Title claims from the operation of the NT Land Rights Act

I mean no disrespect to my ministerial predecessors, but I discovered that at least some of them had been furnished with inadequate and erroneous advice about the timing of the exercise of their role and responsibilities under the NT Land Rights Act. As a result there were some land claims which had been outstanding for almost ten years.

The delays arose after the land councils had been able to prove the claim of the traditional owners to the satisfaction of the Land Commissioner, who then made a recommendation to the minister that the claim be granted. The commissioner, quite properly, also highlighted the interests of others who might be adversely affected by the grant. These 'detriment issues' ranged from substantive matters to spurious issues such as the purported concerns of the NT government about whether the area required for roads was wide enough, or bogus claims that the grant of land might affect the water supply of tiny Northern Territory towns.

I found out that, despite the recommendations of the Land Commissioner to the effect that the land should be granted under the Act, subject to the minister considering the issues of potential detriment, the practice of the officers in the former department of Aboriginal Affairs and later ATSIC was not to submit the Land Commissioner's recommendation to the minister until all the detriment issues had been resolved or prolonged attempts to resolve them had been undertaken. This meant that there would be futile and obstructive negotiations with the NT government for years about such issues as the width of a road in the backblocks of the Territory. While such tortuous and futile negotiations occurred, the traditional owners of the land waited for its return. We sought to overcome this problem by requesting ATSIC officers to submit land claim reports and recommendations to me at the first reasonably available opportunity. The detriment issue would then be considered and, if appropriate, as it usually was, the necessary action would be taken to grant the land immediately. Thus within three years we were able to catch up on the backlog of outstanding claims and dramatically reduce the waiting time to finalise subsequent claims.

The expeditious finalisation of land grants under the Act and the 1989 agreement meant driving the bureaucracy, but both they and my office were committed to getting results. The performance of ATSIC officers was first rate. By 1996, 78 areas of land had been returned to the Aboriginal people. With the exception of one, which was returned by the Governor-General at my request, and one which was finalised in Canberra, I personally presented all the title deeds to the traditional owners to accord the event the respect it deserved.

At times the tactics used by the NT government to defeat title claims had reached extremes of absurdity. One tactic involved attempted expansion of the town boundaries of tiny Tennant Creek, with a population of only 3000 people, to a size 30 times as large as the town's present boundaries—a move ultimately struck down by the courts. In fact by the end of my period as minister, the NT government had litigated to frustrate the grant of land in more than 30 land claim cases before the High or Federal Courts and lost virtually every one of them, at great cost to all NT taxpayers and to the sadness of Aboriginal communities since many of their old people did not live to see the return of their lands.

Sadly, most state and territory governments are adopting the same kind of obstructive and delaying tactics towards claims made under the Native Title Act by opposing virtually all native title claims, no matter how soundly based, and refusing to make any meaningful attempt to negotiate settlements. This defeats one of the central purposes of that Act, namely to resolve claims by negotiation. It is not only traditional Aboriginal landowners who will suffer but all taxpayers who will bear the cost of this irresponsible folly.

Cabinet resolved that night that it had 'a disposition to accord to native title holders a right to be consulted on proposed actions affecting their land, with arbitration by the native title tribunal where agreement is not reached, with both consultation and arbitration to be within strict time limits, and for there to be a capacity for a crown (Commonwealth or State) override of a tribunal decision in the national interest'.

Furthermore, it was resolved that before the existence of native title was determined, grants of interest in land should be able to proceed, subject to negotiation with the appropriate Aboriginal authority in the area, with compensation to be paid later if and when native title was established. However, the process would not be applied to proposed uses of the land that would have a 'low impact'. It was made clear that the rights were not to be those of 'veto' but those of 'negotiation' where the existence of native title had been established.

The proposals were to be further developed by the Mabo Ministerial Committee, taking into account relevant provisions under existing land rights laws (i.e. the Pitjantjatjara model).

This was a victory against considerable odds and, while not the ideal outcome for indigenous people, it did establish a core principle of what was to become the Native Title Act. I regarded the achievement of a right to negotiate as not only gaining a substantial human right for Aboriginal people but as vitally important in establishing a framework that would bring the mining industry and Aboriginal organisations and communities into an effective dialogue. This would make a real contribution to changing industry attitudes and advancing the reconciliation process in the years to come, as indeed it has.

This was no doubt a turning point in the Mabo debate. It was light years away from the Commonwealth concessions at COAG. The states and territories that were hired guns for industry groups had missed an opportunity at COAG to reach agreement with the Commonwealth on the best offer they were ever likely to get.

Cabinet also resolved that the Commonwealth Bill be drafted on the basis that states and territories not cooperating with the Commonwealth would not be provided with any protection from the operation of the RDA or assistance with the payment of compensation. Importantly, they would have to meet Commonwealth standards in relation to future dealings on native title land. Ominously, however, Cabinet also agreed that a further memorandum be prepared by officials in relation to the Wik claim. The Minister for Transport and Communications, Senator Bob Collins, and the Minister for Arts and Administrative Services, Senator Bob McMullen, were to be included in the Mabo Ministerial Committee, both having actively participated in the Cabinet debate of the day.

The next day the media reported the previous day's Cabinet meeting as a victory for Aboriginal people, though the government had not yet issued any clear statement. Filling the vacuum, I therefore put out a statement cleared with the Prime Minister's office, seeking to play down the extent of the victory, knowing that there would be massive opposition to it from industry. I emphasised that Aboriginal rights of negotiation

> are not new proposals. They exist already under the 1981 South Australian Liberal Government's Pitjantjatjara land rights legislation and even the 1989 mineral resources legislation enacted by the Queensland National Party Government. These rights have been supported by governments in recognition of the special attachment and relationship of Aboriginal people to their land . . . and have been recognised by both the government and the Opposition in the federal parliament.

I described the decision as 'an important statement in recognition of the human rights of Aboriginal people and their rights in respect of their land', emphasising that 'the Commonwealth will not be conferring a power on State or Territory governments to override a tribunal decision if these governments are not prepared to recognise native title and to deal with that title in accordance with agreed processes and minimum national standards including a tribunal established under Commonwealth guidelines'.

The Cabinet decision was strongly backed by Sol Bellear, who understood what a great battle had been won against some very formidable Cabinet, bureaucratic and industry opposition. Some Aboriginal people expressed their opposition, advocating instead a right of absolute veto. I understood where they were coming from, but such a right had earlier been decisively and irrevocably ruled out by the Prime Minister. We had got the best outcome that could have been achieved.

The mining industry of course attacked the decision. AMIC's Lauchlan McIntosh asserted that 'Australia now faces the situation where the federal government is prepared to replicate the problems of the Northern Territory Australia wide' and pointed out that the national interest clause to override the 'veto' in the NT Land Rights Act had not been used in the eighteen years of the Act's operation. AMIC also attacked the recognition of special attachment and the revival of native title at the conclusion of a mining lease. Of course the Opposition also strongly opposed the government's decision, with Peter Nugent telling us all that the government had failed to answer the concerns of the mining industry.

That night the Prime Minister appeared on SBS's *Dateline* and did an outstanding job of selling the Commonwealth's position, emphasising his belief that Aboriginal people 'understood that a generalised veto was never on' and that 'the job was before the Aboriginal community and Islander community to convince the government that the special attachment they had to the land was such that they deserved a right of consultation and negotiation'. The Prime Minister made it quite clear that if the principles of a state tribunal or its personnel are not up to the Commonwealth standard, then the Commonwealth tribunal would operate in that state. Even if state processes and tribunals were recognised by the Commonwealth, 'once a tribunal does take all the various information into account about the importance of the site to Aboriginal people, the prospects for development . . . and comes to a decision after a period of months . . . then it will not be an easy matter for a government to just come and dismiss all that and to override it'.

On the day of the Cabinet meeting events had been unfolding publicly in a way that gives an important insight into one of the reasons why certain members of the Coalition were taking an increasingly belligerent stand. Richard Court warned John Hewson to toughen his stance in return for continuing crucial support of his leadership. Dr Hewson was needing to maintain the support of a large block of WA votes, led by Noel Crichton-Browne; Mr Court was reminding him that support was a two-way deal. Dr Hewson did not totally adopt the WA hardline position, nor was he likely to be able to do so without alienating other sections of his party, but there can be no doubt that he was influenced to strengthen his opposition and to intensify his attacks on the government and Aboriginal aspirations by pressure from Richard Court.

I regard John Hewson as a decent and well-intentioned man. He is, however, above all else an economist. I honestly believe he did his best to steer the Coalition to a reasonable response to Mabo but he was hopelessly outnumbered by his opponents in the party. None of this is to suggest that I agree with his contribution to the Mabo debate in the latter part of 1993.

The pressures on my staff at this time were considerable as most of the day-to-day Mabo debate responsibilities fell to our office. It was not possible for the Prime Minister to respond every day to the relentless attacks made on the government. Little did I know that the next six months of the debate were to become far more difficult. Conscious that a serious slip could cause real problems for the government, I did my best to clear sensitive issues with the Prime Minister's media staff and to ensure that other key ministers were aware of what was being said. During the Mabo debate I did not enjoy direct and regular personal contact with Paul Keating, as was the case for most non-Cabinet ministers, but for all practical purposes the relationship between our offices was effective; during the whole year I don't recall our statements accidentally clashing once, despite hundreds of opportunities for error or conflict.

In a speech to the Rotary Club of Sydney on 3 August, Tim Fischer made a renewed call for COAG to consider the Mabo issue and attacked his critics with a line by now predictable: 'The politically correct agenda setters have much to answer for in their dictatorial approach to the public debate . . . I have a genuine fear that freedom of speech in this country is threatened'. When I read these comments I was dumbfounded. Mr Fischer of all people had proved by his own unrestrained, repeated denunciations of Aboriginal people, their lifestyle and culture, that under the Labor government you could say just about anything and get away with it. So much for the supposed threats to freedom of speech.

In the campaign against the assault on indigenous rights, 3 August 1993 was a big day. A mass meeting of hundreds of indigenous representatives took place at Eva Valley Station, 100 kilometres by road east of Katherine in the Northern Territory. Patrick Dodson declared that the meeting would be 'free of politicians, free of lawyers and free of the media' to allow wide-ranging indigenous debate. No statement was to be issued until the completion of the talks in three days' time. By all accounts the Eva Valley meeting was a powerful event, with people from all over Australia representing a wide divergence of political viewpoints, from Michael Mansell asserting the viewpoint of the APG to elders representing the views of Aboriginal people from remote parts of the country.

The Eva Valley Statement was issued two days later. The meeting intended that it be presented to the Prime Minister and considered widely by Aboriginal and Torres Strait Islander people. It began by rejecting the government's proposed native title legislation and called for the legislation to advance indigenous rights to land. It emphasised that the government should only 'move on this issue' with the support of Aboriginal and Torres Strait Islander people and that governments need the 'free and informed consent of those people'. It called on the Commonwealth 'to take full control of native title issues to the exclusion of the States and Territories'.

It made clear the wish of Aboriginal people 'for a national standard for our people, not numerous different standards', calling on the Commonwealth to honour its obligations under international law and to agree to a negotiating process to achieve a lasting settlement between government and indigenous people. It went on to call for a legislative response to Mabo which met certain defined important principles: no grant of interest over native title land without the informed consent of indigenous people; no extinguishment of native title by any other interest; Commonwealth declaration of Aboriginal and Torres Strait Islander title in reserves and other defined places; and total security for sacred sites. There was no suggestion in this statement that there was other than a united Aboriginal position to be put to the government.

The meeting nominated a representative body to put forward the views of the participants to government, but after their appointment there was a regrettable loss of momentum. The Eva Valley meeting was nevertheless of great importance in reasserting indigenous rights and in regaining the upper hand in the public debate. Mick Dodson was widely reported as saying, in relation to the proposed native title legislation, 'we don't agree with anything they [the government] have done. They haven't bothered to talk to us about it, they haven't negotiated with us about it and they don't have our consent to do what they want to do'. Galarrwuy Yunupingu accused the Prime Minister of selling out the reconciliation process and alleged that he had 'taken the prerogative to go ahead to undermine the good work we, the Reconciliation Council, have done and overridden the good work that has been done in good faith'.

The convening of the Eva Valley meeting and all statements emanating from it occurred without any consultation or liaison with me. I was with Senator Nick Bolkus at the SBS radio studios speaking to ethnic community reporters when I heard a report of the meeting. Almost at the end of a long session of questioning on Mabo myths, a note was passed asking me to do a live interview for *PM* on the Eva Valley Statement. I did this interview running on instinct and knowing that the statement as outlined to me was militant and aspirational, as it needed to be, but understanding that Aboriginal people wanted to be in the process and were complaining that they were frozen out. There was a need to rebuild the bridges with Aboriginal leadership and to help this objective, I said: 'There is still much talking to do and further negotiations and consultations to be had before the government finalises proposals for legislation and in those processes the government is committed to speaking further with Aboriginal representatives in order to reach a just and practical national outcome from the Mabo decision'. I hoped my response would help continue to engage indigenous representatives and would not alienate the already very angry mainstream of indigenous people.

The Prime Minister, however, was outraged by Mick Dodson's attack and responded by reiterating the extent to which indigenous people had been consulted thus far. He said: 'Despite several meetings held in good faith with the Aboriginal community, the government can secure only private decision and agreement which does not translate into public agreement', and that 'if Aboriginal people seek justice and equity they must provide leaders who accept responsibility of leadership. Some Aboriginal leaders have accepted the responsibility of leadership, others, clearly, have not'.

John Hewson attacked this statement, demanding to know what 'agreements' had been reached, but it was clear to me that the Prime Minister was speaking in general terms about the processes to be adopted by the government; there had been at that stage no agreement on specific principles. Later that day Dr Hewson criticised Paul Keating and called on him to 'close the door Mr Tickner has left open' for further negotiations and responsiveness to indigenous aspirations. These events caused a deeper rift between indigenous people and the government. I did my best behind the scenes with both sides to repair relations, knowing that Mick Dodson himself knew that the Prime Minister was the best hope we had. I knew that if people like Mick were *persona non grata* with the Prime Minister, there was a diminished chance of a just outcome.

The government received some good news in that week in the form of a Saulwick Poll which showed that 88 per cent of voters understood that the principles of the High Court judgment apply only in cases where Aboriginal people can prove that they have maintained a continuous relationship with the land since European settlement.

In the course of the week key ministers continued to meet in the absence of the Prime Minister to hammer out details of the proposed legislation that required participation only by ministers with relevant portfolio interests. Commonwealth officials advising the Mabo Ministerial Committee reported that state and territory officials wanted to water down the Commonwealth position on mining leases, warning that

> by far the most important point on which State and Territory officials took issue with us was the proposal for negotiation and consideration by the tribunal of the proposed grant with a national interest override. They were adamant that the concept was unworkable, given the large number of grants processed. It would lead to an investment boycott. It would unacceptably take the right to manage minerals from the State and put it in the hands of a tribunal. And it would fundamentally change the nature of the tribunal. We explained to the States and Territories our base line set by Cabinet. We invited them to produce—if possible—an alternative proposal in the document which would meet this base line and yet be workable from their point of view. The issue has been held over for further discussion.

At the same time, trouble was brewing in the form of hurricane Wik. On Friday, 6 August, the *Australian* carried a banner headline, 'Goss slates PM's delay on Mabo' and quoted the Queensland Premier as saying that 'unless we get moving and we give the investment community some certainty and some legislation quick smart, then we will start to lose projects'. The same day he called on the Commonwealth to 'clarify as a matter of urgency its stance on the Wik people's claim on Weipa mining leases'. Premier Goss said there were mixed signals coming from the Commonwealth and referred to a statement by Frank Walker doubting that there would be any specific federal action on the Wik claim. 'Not only is there $1.75 billion worth of investment in Gladstone at stake', he said, 'there is also the potential of a new $1 billion refinery in Queensland later this decade. This is not simply some academic argument, it is dollars and cents, it is jobs for Queenslanders'. He made it clear that if the federal legislation did not address his concerns Queensland would prepare its own special legislation, but that legislation would have to have 'the total support of the Federal Government including complementary federal legislation, if we were to avoid any conflict with the Racial Discrimination Act'. Special legislation would be needed 'because the claim related to titles issued in 1958 would not be covered by legislation which only validated title issued after the Racial Discrimination Act was passed in 1975'.

The pressure from the Queensland government had increased as a result of a preliminary hearing of the Wik claim on 1 August before Justice Drummond in the Federal Court in Brisbane. Justice Drummond was confronted by fourteen lawyers and what was described as a potential legal 'disaster' as he sought to reduce what could otherwise be a five to ten-year legal battle. The judge tried to direct the parties joined in the Wik claim to a more manageable arrangement for dealing with the case. No doubt this caused the warning bells to ring within the Queensland government.

On 6 August CRA's John Ralph wrote to the Prime Minister and to other ministers on the Mabo Ministerial Committee, urging them to support the Queensland Premier's request for special legislation and warning that if the Wik claim succeeded 'almost all land titles in Australia would be in similar jeopardy'. He also warned that such special legislation would need to be backed by 'government indemnities in favour of lenders and investors' in case the legislation was challenged in the courts. The letter, of course, restated the threats to investment raised in Premier Goss's letter.

Michael Lavarch attempted reassurance in a public statement: 'The Queensland Government should have no fears about [the] impact of the Wik people's claim for native title on the proposed CRA Ltd Weipa bauxite expansion project . . . A major part of the Wik claim is unrelated to the Mabo decision. It raises issues such as the Queensland Government's fiduciary duty to the Wik people in issuing the original mining leases'. He said the Commonwealth was committed to continuing cooperation with Queensland to ensure that the Wik claim did not jeopardise this major investment project. He warned against unilateral state legislation, which 'runs the risk of conflict' with the RDA and which would create further uncertainty.

That weekend I was interviewed by Laurie Oakes on the Nine Network *Sunday* program. First he interviewed Wayne Goss, who revealed that as CRA had to go to international banks on 20 August, in only twelve days' time, there had to be a clear decision by the federal government 'that they will either back the project or let it fall off the edge'. Premier Goss emphasised that the case was being handled by the same lawyers who were successful in Mabo and referred to my reported comments that there was a 'lot of evidence to support the claim'. I did my best to play down the issue but felt that I performed poorly and remember feeling distinctly ill at ease. I did, however, make it clear that a core issue in the Wik claim, whether there existed a fiduciary duty on governments to act in the interests of indigenous people, was not a principle of law that was recognised by Australian courts.

Thankfully, other comments I made on the land fund were picked up by the *Australian* which, after a further interview, ran a front-page story outlining proposals for the fund and other such initiatives. But the rest of the morning papers were full of Wik, Wik and more Wik, especially with headline accounts of the Prime Minister's attack on Wayne Goss. Paul Keating was obviously furious about Mr Goss's comments and said, 'the idea that the federal government should indemnify companies for leases signed by past Queensland governments was stretching credibility a fair bit'.

At this stage it was obvious from the public statements that the government was all over the place, Frank Walker and I lining up with the Prime Minister and Michael Lavarch, a Queenslander, appearing to line up with Premier Goss. It was also obvious that there was increasing antagonism between Mr Keating and Mr Goss. We were heading for a collision. Wayne Goss hit back on the Monday, issuing a statement again calling for Commonwealth legislation and claiming that Queensland crown law advice was that such legislation was necessary to put the project beyond doubt. He said there was a clear connection between the Wik claim and the High Court's Mabo decision. 'The claim argues that the Mabo decision changed the way in which governments must deal with land potentially affected by native title and it is argued that governments have been defective in the way in which they dealt with native title in the past.' He reminded the Commonwealth of the McArthur River precedent and called for comparable legislation over the Wik claim.

While Wik began to erupt, other developments continued apace. On 1 August Mick Dodson had delivered an angry address to the WGIP in Geneva, describing the Mabo debate as 'intense and acrimonious with extremists in many quarters' and revealing a 'red hot underbelly of racism, bigotry and prejudice' that had diminished the nation.

On 9 August National Party leaders in New South Wales, Victoria, Queensland and South Australia issued a communiqué after a joint meeting in which they accused the federal government of adopting an 'extremist' approach to the Mabo decision and urged all the states to stick together in opposition to the Commonwealth proposals.

The furore over Wik, which the media described as 'Son of Mabo', continued. On 10 August Michael Lavarch told the media that in relation to Comalco's mining leases, including those issued in the 1950s, 'the mining leases which Comalco hold will be validated'. This seemed radically at variance with the Prime Minister's views, a fact not lost on Premier Goss, who immediately asked whether the Attorney-General was speaking for himself or for the federal government:

> I think there are different points of view in the federal Cabinet and that is understandable. Mr Tickner and Mr Walker have taken a very aggressive position in favour of Aboriginal claims and that is fair enough from their point of view, but I want to see Ministers who are concerned about economic growth and jobs for working class people putting their side of the argument.

I found this line of argument reprehensible. It was an attempt to pit the interests of what Mr Goss described as 'working-class people' against those of Aboriginal people, who by any definition would have to be the most 'working-class' people in the country. My position, and I know that of Frank Walker and Paul Keating, was that we should strive to provide economic certainty without undermining Aboriginal interests. Michael Lavarch's comments were not lost on John Hewson, who asserted that he had publicly embarrassed the Prime Minister and called on Paul Keating to move quickly to validate the Comalco leases.

Noel Pearson responded and accused Wayne Goss of 'fundamental personal opposition to the idea of Aboriginal people having traditional rights. When you reject the notion that Aboriginal people have traditional rights you are basically saying that they are animals without rights'. He made the important point that the Gladstone development was not contingent on CRA having security of title over disputed leases south of the Embley River, which were part of the Wik claim, and that 'CRA have reserves north of the Embley River that are going to see them well into the next century. Access to further areas in the future is something that is freely available to CRA by a process of negotiation they can enter into at any time'. Thus CRA had, he suggested, 'contrived uncertainty' as part of an Australia-wide attack on Mabo and Aboriginal land rights. Noel went on to say:

> I think the fact of the matter is that they want to set a precedent for governments outlawing any kind of Aboriginal challenges to mining companies. They know how much power they can wield with politicians. They believe they can deliver an ultimatum and get the politicians running. The Queensland Government gets snapping to attention in

parliament, that's a valuable win for industry, and the more wins they can have, the more times they can have governments jumping to their commands the better.

Things would get much worse before they would get better. On 12 August the Prime Minister, who had been in Nauru, returned home in a feisty mood and gave a media conference at Parliament House. Neither I nor, I am sure, anyone else in the government had any idea what line he was going to take. He was tough and principled, putting on record the history of work within the government to prepare the Mabo response. It was a vintage Keating performance. In recounting this history and the obstacles the government had confronted, he called the issues bluntly as he saw them. He again attacked the Eva Valley press conference and the comments of Mick Dodson in particular. He responded to the criticisms and detailed the consultation that had occurred, including meetings with 'Mr Dodson on three private occasions in my office for over an hour on each occasion'. He greeted with approval the supportive comments of Sol Bellear made on the day the Eva Valley meeting concluded and quoted from the press statement issued by Noel Pearson on the same day that stated: 'Cape York land leader defends Prime Minister's handling of Mabo and urges support from Aboriginal communities'. He referred extensively to Noel Pearson's recognition of his commitment to a just settlement of native title. This defence of the Prime Minister would stand Noel in good stead in their future dealings.

The Prime Minister soon turned his attention to that morning's *Sydney Morning Herald* editorial 'telling us how we ought to be conducting the Mabo debate. As I say, in most other countries this would be a decade process, not a one year process'. And he was right. The immensity of the task confronting the government was not understood by many people in the media, most of whom were prepared to write us off when the going got tough.

He spoke at length about the RDA, making it clear that the very point of the Act is to prevent racial discrimination, and that 'validation' in effect meant suspending the Act. He drew a distinction in the case of 'innocent discrimination' or 'where there was no intended discrimination' with a 'wilful disregard of people's interests'. He made the Commonwealth's position quite clear: it was 'not going to be forced into . . . validating, by suspending the Racial Discrimination Act, discriminatory actions carried out in the past, and in so doing remove from . . . Aboriginal Australians, a right which all other Australians have to litigation in the courts'. The lessons of McArthur River had been learned and this was one of Paul Keating's finest hours.

He was then set upon by the media representatives. I say set upon because it was a feeding frenzy. As far as they were concerned, they had a great story—a federal minister apparently in conflict with other ministers and the Prime Minister, and conflict between the Prime Minister and a state premier and, for good measure, some personal antagonism and hostility between party colleagues. Paul Keating tried to suggest that Michael Lavarch's comments were not inconsistent with his own statements and those of Frank Walker and myself, but 'the rest of the world seems to have missed it', as one media person said.

The Commonwealth did not have to wait long for a response from Wayne Goss, who immediately issued a statement saying, 'I have always sought that such validation be undertaken on a non-discriminatory basis'. Noel Pearson took issue with this, pointing to Premier Goss' press statement of 9 August in which he had said, 'Commonwealth legislation is needed to prevent any challenge to a Queensland law which validated the Weipa leases because of the supremacy of the 1975 Racial Discrimination Act'. He asserted that 'in order to mislead the public, they will not talk about breaching the Racial Discrimination Act, they will instead be suspending the Act—it amounts to the same thing. Suspension of the Racial Discrimination Act is code for breach of Australia's most important human rights instrument, and breaching Australia's obligations under the Convention [CERD]'.

On 13 August, ABC Radio reported that a stony-faced Michael Lavarch had left the Queensland government executive building after a meeting with Premier Goss and officials, making it clear that all he would say about the Queensland government's proposals was that he would communicate them to his federal colleagues. Michael Lavarch's meeting was followed by further meetings of Commonwealth and Queensland officials in which it was made clear that the Queensland government was seeking not only the validation of grants in the 1975–93 period but also grants potentially invalidated because of the existence of native title and by reason of other legal principles such as breach of fiduciary duty, including grants made before 1975. Wayne Goss publicly confirmed that, while he did not believe the Wik claim would be successful, 'we can't leave that doubt, that question mark hanging over all of the deeds and titles in this country'.

Two days later Mick Dodson attacked the Commonwealth's handling of the Mabo issue and the Prime Minister for favouring financial interests. Mick Dodson paid tribute to 'the genuine commitment of the Prime Minister to do what is right for the indigenous people of Australia' but said: 'The problem is he's got different economic and political forces at play which are influencing the people around him . . . The economic imperative has hijacked the human rights and morality issues . . . Robert Tickner is our voice in the government and, in my view, he hasn't been listened to'.

The first I knew of this statement was when I read it in the Sunday *Age*.

By the time Cabinet met on 16 August to discuss the officials' report on Wik, the room was charged with politics, emotion and internecine party intrigue. The lines were drawn between those who shared the Prime Minister's view of the world on this issue and those who were determined to support Premier Goss, even if it meant rolling the Prime Minister. In the entire period of Labor in power between 1983 and 1996 there were few Cabinet meetings at which the views of the Prime Minister as party leader were set to be so brutally overridden.

I was amazed and privately relieved that the parliamentary press gallery failed to give this Cabinet meeting the attention it deserved. The media reported that the Prime Minister's vocal allies were myself, Frank Walker and Nick Bolkus. I can't recall others contributing significantly to the debate. Paul Keating ran the meeting strongly, but the numbers were not there to support him. All those publicly reported as supporters of Wayne Goss were there. I distinctly remember Graham Richardson announcing in a matter-of-fact way that he had just spoken to Wayne Goss and reporting the latest view. Paul Keating deserved better from his ministers that day.

The outcome was that Cabinet indicated a disposition to adopt general principles that would provide for Commonwealth legislation to allow states and territories to validate existing grants of interest in land that could potentially be invalid because of the existence of native title. Cabinet agreed that a working party of officials should hold discussions with Queensland officials to explore the application of this decision to the Comalco Weipa leases and report back to Cabinet in two days' time.

In advice for this extraordinary meeting, Commonwealth officials had reminded Cabinet that

> Premier Goss has publicly said that what Queensland wants to do 'is to validate the mining leases on a non-discriminatory basis and in a manner consistent with the RDA'. On this basis there is an option which would simply allow for Queensland to resolve the problem using only Queensland legislation. It is worth noting that at McArthur River where new leases were issued with procedural requirements and appropriate compensation provided for, the Commonwealth position was that this would satisfy the RDA. Since the Premier says he wants no more than McArthur River, Queensland should be able to validate without Commonwealth involvement.

This clearly vindicated my consistently held view about the effect of the RDA on the invalidity of titles.

These words were followed by a warning: 'It is clear that notwithstanding what he has said about acting in a non-discriminatory fashion, Premier Goss wants a joint legislative response, and there is a risk that if there is no Commonwealth involvement the public perception might be that the Commonwealth was not doing its part'. Cabinet heeded the warning. Wayne Goss welcomed the Commonwealth Cabinet decision and in response to a question on where his relationship with Paul Keating would go from here, replied, 'Up, where else can it go?' The final Cabinet decision on Wik was deferred to allow Commonwealth officials to consult further with their Queensland counterparts.

But in the lead-up to the final Cabinet meeting on Wik none of the parties let up. Noel Pearson asserted that CRA representatives had attended a meeting with a senior PM&C officer, Sandy Hollway, and Kevin Rudd, head of the Queensland Cabinet Office. Wik representatives were not invited to have an input, and Noel was scathingly critical of what he described as the 'conspiracy' against them by officials. During the year of the Mabo debate I had much reason to be sceptical and critical of the role of Commonwealth officials, but I thought Noel's criticisms rather harsh on this occasion and believed his complaint was overwhelmingly with Cabinet rather than with public servants.

CRA too rejoined the fray before the final Wik Cabinet meeting, with a letter from John Ralph to all key ministers in which he advocated the extravagant CRA claims and, to add insult to injury, said: 'You will appreciate that we cannot enter into any consultations with the Wik people until we have an assured position regarding title and absence of liability for any compensation arising out of the invalidity'. This was the bullying behaviour of CRA under its old-style 1950s leadership; it was only when Leon Davis took over the helm after the enactment of the Native Title Act that CRA began to show a sensitivity and a preparedness to negotiate with indigenous interests. This change heralded what I believe to be a very welcome new direction towards social responsibility in the Australian mining industry.

Cabinet met again on 18 August to receive a further submission from PM&C after further consultations with Queensland officials. That day key Aboriginal organisations such as the NSW Aboriginal Land Council and the NT Northern and Central Land Councils had made their views known to the government, strongly opposing legislation that would preclude Aboriginal communities or groups seeking to challenge the validity of interests and tenements granted over Aboriginal traditional lands on the grounds that they constituted a breach of fiduciary obligations. The NSW Land Council challenged the government on whether it 'would legislate to abolish the right of all citizens to seek equitable relief from our courts merely because a giant commercial enterprise says that it is potentially affected in one particular instance'.

Before the Cabinet meeting leading Queensland members of federal Caucus had written both to Wayne Goss and to Comalco, calling on them to negotiate directly with the Wik people. Behind the scenes, in their meetings with Commonwealth and Queensland officials, Comalco made it clear that they were not at all sympathetic to the idea that they be involved in a negotiated settlement since such negotiations to them would 'set an unhelpful precedent'. In negotiations with Commonwealth officials, Queensland officials put forward an extensive list of proposals for Commonwealth action, seeking significantly more from the Commonwealth than was the mining giant Comalco itself, including validation of titles granted before 1993 and invalid for any reason, including fiduciary duty unrelated to native title.

Queensland and Comalco did not get all they wanted, but they got a lot. Paul Keating announced the Cabinet decision the next day: 'Cabinet agreed that Commonwealth and Queensland legislation be introduced to validate all relevant land grants whose validity might be in doubt as a result of the existence of native title and its interaction with other laws. This will be included in the proposed generic Commonwealth Mabo legislation. Such validation of mining leases would not extinguish native title'. He made it clear that Queensland might also legislate to validate leases, on a non-discriminatory basis, against other cases of invalidity unrelated to native title. Claims against the validity of leases would in effect be converted into claims for compensation or damages.

The Wik Cabinet decision had been an awful outcome for the government. Its general Mabo response had again, as it had with the McArthur River issue, been radically derailed at the behest of a mining giant and a state government only too willing to do the mining company's bidding. The Queensland and Victorian premiers welcomed the government's decision, while Mick Dodson described the actions of the federal Cabinet as 'discriminatory and unjust'. Noel Pearson was 'severely disappointed' and said:

> I am sure that the Minister for Aboriginal and Torres Strait Islander Affairs, Mr Tickner, the Special Minister of State, Mr Walker, and the Prime Minister have been unswerving advocates of our position, but the circumstances are such that those with a more squalid sense of this historical occasion, without the same vision, have unfortunately asserted pressure with the federal Cabinet resulting in an unfortunate position.

It was very important that Aboriginal people saw Paul Keating to be on their side on the Wik issue, as he certainly was, and that they understood that the best chance they had was for the Prime Minister to be in there fighting for them. It was the only hope we had to hold at bay the relentless pressure of the mining industry and other powerful Cabinet forces arguing a case less sympathetic to indigenous aspirations.

9

THE COMMONWEALTH DRAWS THE FIRE

After further consultations, on 2 September 1993 the Commonwealth released a detailed outline of the proposed Native Title Bill with the Prime Minister confidently asserting that the government had not been deterred by pressure, misinformation or hysteria from the pursuit of good, durable policy. Predictably, the drafting instructions were assailed from all sides. Aboriginal people were particularly concerned that their wider agenda for a land fund and social justice measures had not been addressed. The mining industry even disputed the revival of native title at the expiration of a mining lease, apparently ignoring the fact that the grant of a mining lease did not amount to the appropriation of the private property rights of other Australians.

The Coalition took an even more hardline position against the Commonwealth legislation and as a result became increasingly marginalised and irrelevant to the final outcome. Aboriginal people began to focus on government proposals to suspend the RDA in order to provide absolute certainty in the validation of titles. These concerns found understandable and ready support with allies in the wider community.

ATSIC thankfully kept much of its political focus on the need for a national land fund and a social justice package. Lois O'Donoghue and others provided the leadership to establish a coalition of Aboriginal organisations to fight for a just Mabo response. Crunch time was coming for final Cabinet deliberations and the direction of the evolving drafting instructions for the final bill was not good news for Aboriginal people.

I knew by now that I could not live with an outcome that failed to deliver justice to Aboriginal people and 'drew a line in the sand' on 4 October. Warning bells should have been ringing for the government in the days leading up to the final Cabinet consideration on 6 October as not one Aboriginal opinion leader was supporting the direction of the government's deliberations. Despite this, Cabinet decided to do a deal with the states and territories at the expense of Aboriginal interests.

My resignation was imminent and the battle appeared lost, but Lois O'Donoghue again provided the leadership to defiantly hold what came to be known as the Black Friday press conference. This united stand achieved saturation national publicity, leaving the government no alternative but to negotiate further with Aboriginal leaders.

———

By late August the deadline for finalising the draft native title legislation was looming. The Mabo Ministerial Committee's drafting instructions were to be publicly released in early September, with the objective of introducing the Bill into parliament by 1 October. Further consultations were to be held with indigenous representatives, with state and territory governments, and with industry.

Mining industry representatives who subsequently met with the Prime Minister included John Prescott from BHP, John Ralph from CRA, and Peter Barnett, president of AMIC. AMIC representatives were roaming around Parliament House promoting something they called a proposed Customary Rights Act, which would have negated Aboriginal rights, denied any right of negotiation based on Aboriginal special attachment to the land, and provided for the extinguishment of native title on the grant of a mining lease.

On the other side, pressure continued unabated from Aboriginal people and their supporters. In a meeting with the Prime Minister on 24 August, the Council for Aboriginal Reconciliation stressed the need to negotiate with, not just consult, Aboriginal people. Michael Mansell, speaking for the Eva Valley delegation, called on the government to slow down its Mabo response, and Mick Dodson said the government processes were 'kneeling and bending to the requirements of vested interests and the States and Territories . . . All this is being done to the exclusion of the people who will be most affected by all this. An issue of such national gravity doesn't really require that sort of haste, because haste can create mistakes'.

Two days later John Fahey released details of the NSW government's proposed Mabo legislation. The proposals were widely criticised, with a representative of the NSW Land Council, Aden Ridgeway (later a Democrat senator) saying that the Bill was 'a blatant discrimination' against Aboriginal people.

Ernie Bridge, former WA Labor minister and now state Opposition Spokesperson on Aboriginal Affairs and a well-known Aboriginal country singer and entertainer, made a number of important interventions in the Mabo debate, one of which was a personal letter to the Prime Minister, dated 27 August, criticising the government's 'cave-in' on McArthur River and Wik: 'As big as billion dollar projects might sound in this fleeting moment of our nation's history, those mercenary considerations will pale into insignificance alongside issues of justice and human rights in the eyes of future generations'. It was refreshing to hear the matter so clearly put.

Lois O'Donoghue argued for a right of negotiation 'through appropriately resourced representative organisations, where a *prima facie* case for native title has been established by the tribunal'. She reinforced the view that an 'appropriately structured and resourced native title tribunal' should be the body that determines whether grants should be made over native title land. This had been the position of the government so far, but there were other ministers within the government advancing the proposition that in relation to mining interests such a determination should be made by mining wardens' courts, an outcome that would have been entirely unacceptable to most Aboriginal people.

The academics weighed in. After speaking at a conference in Townsville on the subject of 'Aboriginal peoples, federalism and self-determination', Professor Henry Reynolds told the *Australian* that most premiers would qualify for the 'Hall of Shame', and branded as 'offensive' the call by Wayne Goss for titles to be validated back to 1788. Another prominent academic, Professor Garth Nettheim, chair of the Aboriginal Law Centre at the University of New South Wales, joined the critics of the states when he branded the New South Wales legislation 'disgraceful and a repudiation of all the principles under-lying the High Court's decision'. Professor Nettheim also raised concerns about possible Commonwealth legislation: 'If the Common-wealth is proposing to roll back its Racial Discrimination Act—the only federal safety net that is available—so as to endorse State legislation of such abysmal quality, then the possibility for a new partnership between indigenous and non-indigenous Australians and reconciliation will be . . . shattered'.

The Mabo Ministerial Committee finally met on 31 August, with torrid debates on key issues. The principles endorsed and submitted to Cabinet the next day were an important advance towards finalising the legislation. On 2 September the Prime Minister issued a statement articulating the core principles of the proposed Commonwealth response to Mabo. He sent a detailed outline of the proposed legisla-tion to state and territory governments, indigenous representatives and relevant industry bodies.

The Prime Minister stressed that 'the Commonwealth's preferred approach is complementary legislation, cooperatively achieved'. Reflecting on the vitriolic Mabo debate, he emphasised that the legis-lation is:

also the product of the extensive process of consultation on which the
Government very deliberately embarked last year. We have not been
deterred in that time by pressure, misinformation or hysteria from the
pursuit of good, durable policy. We have stuck to the timetable
announced at the outset. The outcome will be all the better for the
time that has been taken to hear, understand and reflect upon the
views that have been put.

While I had no doubt about the Prime Minister's *bona fides*, I knew
that without a guarantee on the implementation of a national land
fund and other matters there would be problems convincing indigenous people of the government's commitment. As well, the minority
parties in the Senate were likely to insist on key elements of the
government's social justice response being put forward, either contemporaneously with the Native Title Bill or within a defined time.

The drafting instructions were assailed from all sides. Lois
O'Donoghue, while making it clear that ATSIC would reserve its
detailed response until its board met on 20 September, raised a number
of preliminary concerns. These covered the absence of any announcement of social justice measures including a land acquisition
fund to be implemented at the same time as land management issues
were dealt with. She also expressed concern about the absence of a
right of veto over the use of native title land, as called for by the Eva
Valley meeting, and the potential role of state and territory tribunals
in determining whether mining would occur on native title land.

Michael Mansell was strong in his criticisms:

> The miners have got everything they wanted out of this. They are
> rubbing their hands with glee. The legislation gives the States far more
> powers than the Prime Minister has previously indicated. The States
> can set up their own tribunals and have their own means of defining
> native title, identifying native title owners and deciding what rights they
> have. The States have the powers to allocate leases over native title
> land simply by putting the right sort of people on the right sort of
> tribunals.

The director of the Kimberley Land Council, Peter Yu, accused the
government of completely ignoring the views of Aboriginal people in
favour of miners and attacked the lack of an Aboriginal veto over
mining in the legislation. He said the Prime Minister had ignored 'the
message of the Eva Valley meeting and has produced a document that
appeases miners and pastoralists'. I thought these criticisms excessively
harsh.

Key principles of the Commonwealth Native Title Bill
First, the Bill will remove any doubt which the existence of native title creates about the validity of existing grants of interest in land. Nobody holding any land tenure need have any fear on this score once our Bill is passed.

Second, the Bill will not leave up in the air what implications this validation of past grants has for existing native title. It will make clear that for freehold, and for residential, pastoral and tourist leasehold grants, the validation extinguishes any native title rights inconsistent with those grants. For mining leases, and lesser interests over land such as licences and permits, the validation will not extinguish the native title. But the Bill will confirm that any native title is subject to the lease or licence for as long as it runs. I emphasise that this is totally consistent with existing practice in relation to mining leases over other private interests in land.

Third, the approach to validation will preserve native title to the maximum extent possible. Those who would like to see wholesale extinguishment should be required to answer this question: How can it be just to end an Aboriginal legal right which has, by definition, been preserved for hundreds and perhaps thousands of years in order to validate an invalid grant when there is no need to do so to achieve that objective? Thus: the Bill will permit the reassertion of native title rights at the conclusion of a mining lease or lesser grant; and it will protect any legal rights of native title holders which can co-exist with the rights under the grant.

Fourth, in validating past grants, the rights which people may have to renewals or extensions in the future will also be protected.

Fifth, having cleared up the problems of the past, the Bill goes on to provide a comprehensive framework for future land management by the Commonwealth, State and Territory governments. This will allow dealings in land to go on efficiently, but with native title being properly taken into account. The Bill recognises three basic ways in which future dealings affecting native title land can proceed: it makes provision for conversion of native title to statutory title, should Aboriginal or Torres Strait Islander people wish (in this way they have the flexibility to deal with the land, for example leasing it for tourist development or selling part for a mining project); it makes provision for acquisition of the land by a government (for example for some essential public purpose) and for the extinguishment of native title in this case. The native title holder would be afforded the same protections of fair process which apply to anybody else; and the Bill will provide fair and workable processes of notification, negotiation, arbitration and determination where a government proposes to make a grant of interest over the land. The native title will be subject to the grant for the period of the grant, not extinguished by it forever.

Sixth, the Bill recognises that some grants (for example a major mining lease) will have greater impact on native title holders and their land than other grants (for example most exploration licences). We are therefore providing an expedited process for decisions about grants of the latter kind, a process which still however affords rights to Aboriginal people to be asked and to have their say.

Seventh, the Bill provides processes for managing dealings in land in the inevitable interim period before we know whether native title actually exists in a particular area. There must be no hiatus. Land dealings cannot come to a halt. The key here is appropriate notification of, and consultation with, bona fide claimants and relevant Aboriginal organisations.

Eighth, the Bill gives Aboriginal and Torres Strait Islander people a right to compensation on just terms where native title is extinguished or impaired—whether in relation to validation of past grants or the issue of future ones.

Ninth, the Bill will establish a National Native Title Tribunal, comprising: Judges of the Federal Court who will hear native title claims and determine the existence, boundaries and attributes of native title over particular land; the Tribunal Registrar, who will register claims and decisions about native title, and will need to be satisfied that a claim meets certain standards before it is registered; Tribunal Assessors, who will mediate claims; and Tribunal Members who will assist negotiations between native title holders, governments and people seeking grants, and make decisions if negotiations fail to produce an agreement.

Tenth, the Bill will permit the Commonwealth to accept State and Territory bodies in place of the Commonwealth Tribunal— and State and Territory processes for the handling of grants of interest in land—if they meet the criteria set out. There can be no legitimate complaint that we are putting the States in a straitjacket—they have the option to come up with one of their own which equally well satisfies the objectives.

Finally, the Bill will make certain provisions in the interests of the community as a whole: that laws and regulations of general application apply equally to native title land; that governments are able to confirm existing Crown ownership of resources; and that existing public rights of access to such places such as beaches, waterways, recreation areas and so on can be confirmed.

On this occasion it was AMIC that understood the significance of the government proposals. The director of AMIC, Lauchlan McIntosh, denounced 'the capacity for native title holders to obstruct or prevent mineral exploration and development through the "right of negotiation" set out in the legislation. In fact it would appear that such vetoes will occur at both the exploration and mining stage'. He also attacked the revival of native title at the expiry of mining leases, which would 'serve to devalue existing operations and decrease investment'.

The federal Opposition and John Hewson also attacked the Commonwealth's proposals, as did the states and territories. Wayne Goss, however, publicly adopted a more conciliatory tone, suggesting that the government's principles provided the basis for a 'workable national response' but making it clear there were 'significant issues' still to be addressed.

The hardliners in the Coalition were more scathing. Ian McLachlan said the proposals were 'a blatant attempt to destroy the sovereignty in regard to titles of the Australian States which have administered a settled system of land management for 200 years', and that 'the Prime Minister is proposing to establish a new bureaucratic system to grant a new form of title, based on race, which the States can be part of only if they agree to Mr Keating's bully boy tactics'. The fact was, as I must stress yet again, that the Commonwealth was not 'granting' any titles; it was the High Court that had recognised continuing native title rights, by definition relevant only to Aboriginal and Torres Strait Islander people.

Cabinet had decided to allow a month for further public consultation on the legislation, which it proposed to introduce into the House of Representatives in mid to late October. Ministers were to discuss the proposals with interest groups in their own portfolios.

Peter Reith, the former Shadow Treasurer, returned to the frontbench on 8 September as Shadow Special Minister of State with responsibility for coordinating the Opposition's responses to the Mabo legislation. I was convinced that the legislation was only able to get through parliament with the support of the Greens and Democrats, both of which were seeking changes to advance indigenous interests.

The Greens were, however, far from totally supportive at this stage. On 12 September, the WA Green senators, Christabel Chamarette and Dee Margetts, made public their view that important aspects of the government Mabo proposals were 'unacceptable'. Senator Chamarette raised three issues: the implementation of a social justice package contemporaneous with the native title legislation; federal and not state bodies to hear native title claims; and pastoral and mining leases to revive native title after the expiration of the leases.

While having a lifelong commitment to Green issues, I found Senator Chamarette's politics difficult to comprehend. Too often during the Mabo battle the WA Greens engaged in political posturing, often on superficial issues. They could have provided greater support for Aboriginal aspirations by using what was, at the time, their extraordinary political clout in a more strategic way. But as time went on it seemed that they might vote with the Liberal and National Parties to block the Native Title Bill.

The most damning criticism of the government proposals came on 13 September in a media release by Noel Pearson on behalf of the Cape York Land Council. This substantially boosted the intensity of the public campaign against the government proposals on validation of post-1975 titles. It was, I thought, unfairly critical of Sandy Hollway, the public servant who had been leading the Mabo negotiations with the states and territories. It asserted that the proposals suspended the protection the RDA gave to Aboriginal and Torres Strait Islander people. Noel Pearson stated his belief that 'the Hollway Committee bureaucrats were accountable for the present proposal as they had argued that the validation of titles by a mechanism which would not breach the Racial Discrimination Act would be an "administrative nightmare"'.

Later that day Noel Pearson and Mick Dodson held a press conference to reinforce this line. It was true that PM&C officials had advocated the suspension of the RDA and had, in broad terms, taken up the concerns expressed by AMIC, supported by AMIC's legal opinion. But the proposals for suspension of that Act had also been endorsed by the Mabo Ministerial Committee, despite my strong opposition and that of Frank Walker. The public servants were whipping boys when really responsibility lay with the politicians.

Patrick Dodson, addressing the National Press Club on 15 September, called for further consultations on the Mabo proposals. He made the point that a just outcome 'requires more time, more talk, more cooperation and greater willingness by the nation as a whole to find a generosity of spirit'. There is no doubt that at this stage, despite the huge gains already won, Aboriginal people were clearly not supporting the government proposals. There was both a public perception and a private realisation inside the government that the states and territories had won the day on key issues and that indigenous interests were not seen as the primary focus of the Mabo Ministerial Committee or the Cabinet.

The ATSIC Board met in Canberra between 20 and 23 September and put forward detailed amendments to specific paragraphs of the proposals. Not unexpectedly, they opposed the suspension of the RDA. They also called for the government to limit the hearing of native title claims to a national tribunal and for indigenous control over what happened on native title land, subject only to Commonwealth decisions in the national interest. The board called for the proposals to recognise the special attachment of Aboriginal people to their land in determining compensation payable for diminution of native title rights and expressed concern about the possible use of compulsory land acquisition powers. A further key demand was for a social justice package to be announced contemporaneously with the enactment of the Native Title Act. The social justice package should, in the board's view, include a national land acquisition and land management fund, the development of effective heritage protection legislation, and a scheme for resource revenue equivalents similar to that which operated under the NT Land Rights Act. Finally, ATSIC expressed its ongoing concern that indigenous people were 'not being sufficiently consulted in the government response to the Mabo decision and that complex legislation is being unnecessarily rushed'.

Lois O'Donoghue indicated that ATSIC would be working closely with the Eva Valley group the following week in responding to the government proposals. This was an important development. I had seen how the leaders of land councils and other key national indigenous organisations had treated Lois with great respect and supported her leadership. I was confident that there would be a powerful coalition of indigenous people united in their determination to secure a better deal from the government in the months ahead. I was not to be disappointed.

During the course of that week, Peter Reith wrote in the *Canberra Times* that the 'silence of Ministers Tickner and Walker on the racial discrimination issue has been conspicuous'. Ironically providing support for my own view, he said the lack of ability to provide retrospective procedural fairness to native title holders whose land had been the subject of grants after 1975 would not lead to invalidity; hence the RDA problem was even more of a beat-up:

> There is no 'racial discrimination' in extinguishing title to land, as
> long as it is done on the same grounds as the title belonging to a
> person of any other race would be extinguished. The only complicative
> factor is that the procedural requirements for compulsory acquisition
> (or grant of interest) would not have been met, and it is almost
> impossible to do this retrospectively. However, if land belonging to
> persons of any other race was unwittingly granted to bona fide

purchasers who had no notice of this defect in title, it would seem most logical that the government would grant the previous owner compensation. It would be unreasonable to characterise such a resolution of competitive interests as 'racial discrimination'. The fact that people whose title is extinguished are of one race is merely coincidental.

I thought he was right. It would indeed be bizarre and inconceivable if the rights of the holders of thousands of interests in land were to be struck down by the High Court on the grounds that land managers granting those interests had not taken native title into account at a time when those rights were not known by those land managers to exist, especially when governments were to go out of their way to provide compensation. In my view, the High Court decision in the Mabo case had done nothing to erode the rights of one non-indigenous title holder in the country.

The argument about RDA invalidity was conceived in the mining industry, nurtured by the bureaucracy and then, in a serious tactical error, recognised by some indigenous people and their supporters and given currency as the most serious problem with the government's legislation. Despite my best efforts to persuade otherwise, it derailed the Mabo debate and directed the attention of indigenous people away from more crucial questions concerning the role of the states and territories and other indigenous rights. Because it was an easy and popular issue for supporters of indigenous people to take up, it became the cause célèbre of the native title debate. It never deserved to be such an issue, as Peter Reith recognised.

On 23 September the *Financial Review* carried an exclusive story which provided a graphic insight into the way the bureaucracy was working to achieve an agreement between the Commonwealth and the states and territories. Their success would have meant that Aboriginal people were not part of the agreement; instead their rights would have been determined by governments behind closed doors. The newspaper had got hold of correspondence between Sandy Hollway and the acting deputy director-general of the Queensland Cabinet Office, Jacki Byrne. As a minister on the Mabo Ministerial Committee, I had not been given access to it and the first I knew of it was when I read the details in the *Financial Review*. I believe the same applied to my ministerial colleagues.

The Queensland government had raised numerous issues of concern in this private correspondence. It suggested that key elements of the Commonwealth proposals were 'unworkable' and 'unrealistic'. It was opposed to any right to negotiate for native title claimants; to the Commonwealth's proposals for a right to negotiate for those who were shown to hold native title; to the implicit Commonwealth involvement in state courts; to the involvement of existing land councils only in the land claims process; and to any right to negotiate on exploration. It proposed instead that mining leases that have a major impact on land should extinguish native title, even though this would not occur in the case of land held by other non-title holders; that modified mining wardens' courts be elevated to a 'central principle' of the legislation; the use of existing state compensation regimes for loss or impairment of native title with a cap linked to payments of freehold land compensation; and a sunset clause of twelve or fifteen years over native title claims.

Then came yet another extraordinary outburst from Tim Fischer, speaking in Perth to the Liberal Party's 500 Club. He was reported as suggesting that it was too easy for people to declare themselves Aboriginal and thereby get access to 'taxpayers' money'. He pointed out that Australians of Aboriginal heritage numbered approximately 1.6 per cent of the Australian population and 'Australian taxpayers spent over $1.3 billion on these people, which is approximately $5,000 a head and this does not fully include unemployment benefits'. He asserted that 'many of you would be aware that unemployment benefits are paid out disproportionately to the Aboriginal community who have an unemployment rate over three times that of the rest of the community'. He failed to appreciate that the payment of unemployment benefits in such large numbers was an indication of the extreme disadvantage of Aboriginal people in the community, not a manifestation of some privileged position. He said he was yet to hear representatives of the Aboriginal community acknowledge the enormous income shift from the general community to their community and warned that if the government and Aboriginal people did not 'bring the debate back to a sensible footing, then I fear there will be resentment and it will begin in rural and regional Australia where the issues stare you in the face'. This was a reprehensible speech because he was attacking programs that had long enjoyed cross-party support in parliament.

I think that a fair-minded person reading what senior Liberal and National Party figures said during the Mabo debate, supported by their friends in talkback radio, would conclude that they had been directly responsible for whipping up much of the anti-Aboriginal hysteria that Pauline Hanson later took to a new level. Clearly any charge that a 'pall' of political censorship existed to stifle attacks on so-called political correctness during the time of the Labor government cannot be sustained.

In the last days of September a national meeting of Aboriginal and Torres Strait Islander people was held in Canberra as a follow-up to the Eva Valley meeting. One prominent participant was the fiery Lyall

Munro, who I had worked with ten years previously at the Aboriginal Legal Service. Lyall said that Aboriginal people coming to Sydney for the Olympics should come 'prepared to fight' against legislation that was both racist and unjust:

> We are saying to people all around this country, Aboriginal people in particular—it won't be like 1988 [the bicentenary celebration]. You won't be coming to Sydney to march hand-in-hand with white people. You will be coming to Sydney to demonstrate . . . Our backs are against the wall. We are revolutionary people, and the only way we are going to maintain our rights in this country is through revolution. We have to re-awaken the black power voice of the 1970s.

These comments were opposed by two Aboriginal sportsmen, footballer Gary Ella and boxer Tony Mundine.

At this stage I was frantically urging the ATSIC commissioners and representatives of the Aboriginal land councils to lobby the WA Green and Democrat senators, and doing everything possible to encourage the minority parties to work together. This would increase the likelihood of the government's legislation passing and would result in cohesive and progressive negotiations with the government on the final form of the legislation. These negotiations were crucial because there was still a view in the Mabo Ministerial Committee, on occasions raised by the Prime Minister himself, that the legislation could pass through parliament with the support of the Liberal and National Parties. This, I can only assume, was based on the belief that support from some, or even most, state and territory governments would persuade the federal Coalition to fall into line. I never believed that remotely likely and, if it occurred, the price would be too great to pay.

On 30 September a breakthrough occurred with a meeting held between the Democrats, the WA Greens, and key ATSIC commissioners. They released a joint media statement in which concern was expressed 'at the potential for the current draft to be further weakened as a result of pressure from State and Territory Governments'. Earlier that day ATSIC representatives had met with the Prime Minister. The statement said that 'all participants at the meeting expressed grave concern at the state of the current Government draft legislation'. Three major points emerged from the meeting:

> The legislation must not be weakened any further to accommodate the States; the proposals ATSIC has made to strengthen the legislation in the interests of indigenous people should be accommodated; and the details of the social justice package, particularly with regard to the

government long-term funding commitments, need to be made explicit before the legislation is presented to the Senate.

That morning I had read with concern a story in the *Australian* headed 'States step up Mabo pressure'. The story revealed that the day before, the Queensland, SA, ACT, NT and NSW governments had written to the federal government indicating that there was 'substantial agreement' to the federal proposals as they currently stood but proposing key amendments to meet state and territory concerns. The states were making a further assault on elements of the Commonwealth's proposals that were crucial to indigenous people, including the acceptance by the Commonwealth of more flexible criteria for state tribunals to determine native title restrictions on the right to negotiate. The story summed up the dilemma facing the government: 'If the federal Government accommodates the States it will have to count on opposition support to get the legislation through the Senate because the Australian Democrats and the Greens are seeking changes which move in precisely the opposite direction.' Obviously, acceptance of the state and territory principles would have provoked universal indigenous opposition to the government proposals.

That night, senior officials from the Commonwealth, Queensland, New South Wales, the Northern Territory and the Australian Capital Territory met in Canberra in a meeting that had been foreshadowed at the Mabo Ministerial Committee meeting the night before. Commonwealth officials were doing everything possible to make a deal with the states and territories, which were seeking a wide range of concessions. Such an agreement would have put considerable pressure on the Opposition to support the government proposals, but it was still my view that they would achieve nothing since Richard Court and the Coalition hardliners were unlikely ever to support the government.

On the morning of 1 October, the *Australian* reported that the Prime Minister 'has made significant concessions on his Mabo legislation in order to win a block of support from the States and Territories in a move which risks a serious backlash from his backbench'. I had no idea of the truth or otherwise of the story, but there is no doubt that Paul Keating was angered by it. He issued a media release that day denying that the Commonwealth, through its officials, had made significant concessions to the states and territories and said instead that 'many of their demands had been flatly refused' and that 'the Commonwealth is still involved in discussion with the States but has already informed them that any proposals to water down the principles on which the legislation has been based would be rejected'. He reinforced the message that 'if the States do not accept our principles . . .

then the Commonwealth is prepared itself to operate the system outlined in the legislation'.

My views of the Opposition strategy were confirmed at the end of that week. Peter Reith commented: 'I think a fair political assessment is that you could end up with the Greens opposing it for one set of reasons and us opposing it for another' and confirmed that it was 'not a likely prospect' that the Opposition would support the draft legislation. He confirmed the Coalition view that there was no immediate need for a national legislative response because Mabo was basically a land management issue for the states. How different a place Australia would be if Labor had not been in government in the three years following the Mabo decision. I am utterly convinced that there would have been no national legislation but rather a piecemeal approach state by state, with the lowest common denominator states setting the agenda.

A timely contribution to the debate came on 4 October from Fr Frank Brennan, who was at that time a visiting fellow in law at the Research School of Social Sciences at the Australian National University. Writing in the *Sydney Morning Herald*, Frank made it clear that in his view 'Mr Keating now has a choice. He can bring his legislation up to a standard acceptable to the minority Parties, which will be guided by the Aboriginal groups. Or he can pitch it down to a level acceptable to most States in the hope that the Coalition would pass the legislation through the Senate just to get Mabo off the legislative agenda'. But in view of what Frank saw as a weakening of the Commonwealth's position, beginning with the accommodation on the Wik claim, he also asserted that Aboriginal people had a choice either to support the 'modest legislation' or plead with the government to drop the whole package, preferring to maintain their rights under the Mabo judgment and the RDA.

I had not read this article when I launched a book, *Local Heroes*, that morning in Melbourne that featured indigenous Australians who were heroes to their people. Although I had not confided in anyone, I had decided to resign as minister if the government could not be persuaded to negotiate a more acceptable outcome with indigenous people. I carefully crafted my words that day to make unambiguous my determination to secure a just outcome. It was for me the most important speech I have ever made and explicitly drew a line in the sand:

> It is almost beyond doubt that the hard line and obstructive opposition which Dr Hewson now leads will not pass the Mabo legislation unless there is a dramatic and unconscionable erosion of Aboriginal rights to accommodate Premier Court and the political views of the Liberal and National Parties. The price of conservative support in the Senate for a Labor Government Mabo legislation would be too great to pay. The

Liberal and National Parties would inevitably demand dramatic erosion of the Commonwealth's national principles as the price of their support. Only legislation eroded to meet the approval of conservative governments would suffice, and such an outcome would be an abandonment of the Commonwealth's responsibility and will not be condoned.

But there is another side to this debate which must be addressed and considered by all those in the community who are committed to social justice for Aboriginal people. I urge Aboriginal people and those who support the rights of native title holders recognised by the High Court to consider just how critical it is for this country that Commonwealth legislation be passed. If there is no Commonwealth law to protect native title holders there is little doubt that some State Governments, and in particular, the Western Australian Government, will seek to obliterate the rights of native title holders.

There is a significant body of legal opinion that the High Court's decision in the Mabo case makes it clear that a conservative government such as that in Western Australia would have the right . . . to extinguish native title in a sweeping manner as long as compensation was provided and the proper processes were followed . . . It is becoming increasingly clear that, for the Mabo legislation to pass through the Senate, there will be a need to build a coalition of committed Australians for social justice and Aboriginal rights. Such a coalition is already developing in the parliament and in the community in support of that objective.

Clearly the role of the Australian Democrats, the Western Australian Greens and Senator Harradine will be crucial . . . A sign of great hope and promise of the potential for cross-Party cooperation surfaced when the Australian Democrats, Western Australian Greens and ATSIC released a joint statement last Thursday . . . [which showed] a willingness on the part of them all, to talk together to try and find the largest possible measure of common ground on the proposed legislation . . .

I concluded the speech with an expression of confidence that the Democrats and Greens would be able to find common ground with the Labor government to ensure the passage of the legislation. The closing sentences made it unambiguously clear that I intended to do everything within my power, not only as a minister but as a 'parliamentarian', to ensure the passage of the legislation.

The *Financial Review* epitomised the media reporting of this speech with the headline 'Green, Democrat backing will ensure Mabo success: Tickner' accompanied by a cartoon with the central finger of my right hand directed upwards in a defiant gesture presumably directed at the rest of the government. No one, however, asked me what I meant by 'as a parliamentarian'. Perhaps I was lucky they did not because I was clearly sending a signal that I was not prepared to remain the minister if the Mabo legislation was to be watered down, at the expense of Aboriginal people, so as to be acceptable to the Coalition. My aim was to persuade the Cabinet to avoid a disastrous confrontation with indigenous people should it proceed to agreement with states and territories at the expense of negotiation with them.

October 4 was also a busy day for others. Noel Pearson's comments the previous day on the Ten Network's *Meet the Press* were extensively reported in the morning papers. Noel called for the proposals to be delayed until a better package was crafted, accusing the Keating Cabinet of 'moral scurvy', and he flagged the end of the reconciliation process if the government continued on its present course. Warning bells should have been ringing for the Prime Minister's senior advisers signalling that most of the leadership of national indigenous organisations were already completely offside with the government only two days before a crucial Cabinet meeting to reaffirm the government direction.

The day before, I had received a phone call from another ally, the former Tasmanian Aboriginal Affairs Minister John White, who was then our party's Shadow Minister for Aboriginal Affairs. He and three other Opposition Labor spokesmen for Aboriginal Affairs—Col Markham, Ernie Bridge and Keith Hamilton—wanted me to know that they were issuing a joint statement urging the continuation of consultations with indigenous people and rejecting proposals to suspend the RDA. The four men called on the federal government to ensure that the Commonwealth and not the states had total power in the Mabo response. I was greatly supported by these comrades.

Support also came from a powerful ally the next day. Archbishop Desmond Tutu, who had just arrived in Australia, delivered the message that the Mabo decision was important because of its moral message to Australians:

> Coming out of our own experience in South Africa it is important for everyone who wants to help out to listen to what the victims are saying . . . Nothing has been more galling in South Africa particularly for ourselves than to have people say they know what is good for us. I think that you want to be able to listen to those who are representative of the bulk of that constituency.

But Jeff Kennett announced that day, 5 October, that 'major advances' had been made in addressing the states' concerns about the Commonwealth proposals. After a briefing from his officials following their discussions with their federal counterparts, he proclaimed, 'It appears to me that agreement has been reached'. It was a chilling statement, and confirmed what he'd told the *Australian* on 2 October about wanting to 'make peace' with Paul Keating over Mabo.

I had been doing all I could behind the scenes to arm-twist the Democrats, Greens and Aboriginal leaders to talk to each other. The need for a close dialogue and collaboration between them was essential if the government was to avoid a confrontation with Aboriginal people. The rivalry between the Greens and the Democrats remained a barrier to dialogue. Late that night I was asked to attend a meeting in the Democrat party room with Cheryl Kernot, Christabel Chamarette and numerous key indigenous representatives. The meeting indicated that broad agreement had been reached for the groups to work together to secure the passage of the legislation. It was an uplifting, but short-lived, unity of purpose. I thought it was vitally important for this united front to be presented to Paul Keating and tried to find out if he was still in the building, but he had gone home. Earlier in the day Aboriginal representatives had put a number of key propositions to him, including the non-suspension of the RDA. The director of the NLC, Daryl Pearce, said that the Prime Minister had agreed to explore all options.

The next day, Wednesday, 6 October, the day of the crucial Cabinet meeting, a joint delegation of Senators Kernot and Chamarette, Lois O'Donoghue and Noel Pearson met the Prime Minister to put their joint position, but no detailed public statements were made about it.

The most profound contribution to the public debate that day was that of Patrick Dodson, who said he might resign as chair of the Council for Aboriginal Reconciliation if the Mabo issue was not resolved satisfactorily, and that he would be considering his position at the Council's October meeting. He warned that the reconciliation process would be 'buried if the indigenous people's perception of what governments are doing is simply to leave their interests right outside while the Mabo question is being resolved. Unless a degree of commitment to the reconciliation process is shown beyond what is being shown to date, the federal Government might as well be honest with the Australian people and wind it up'.

But who in the Cabinet was listening? Patrick Dodson has not been one to make outlandish statements or to threaten resignation as a tool of trade. These were expressions of concern by a deeply worried Aboriginal person. But despite all the public statements by indigenous leaders and despite all the threats and the pleading for the government to listen to the voice of indigenous people, it was business as usual in the Cabinet room on the night of Wednesday, 6 October. The room where the Cabinet meets at Parliament House is a room without windows, rather like a bunker. I always had a feeling that decision-making in this windowless room contributed to the isolation of the

Cabinet from the pressures in the community and even the sentiments of the ALP Caucus, let alone those of the wider community. On this occasion those pressures seemed a world away and the isolation of the Cabinet room absolute.

Earlier in the day I had been involved in a very distressing meeting with Left Cabinet ministers, convened to brief them on the latest developments. I became aware that, even at this crucial time when we were fighting such an important issue, my own position was being undermined by some ambitious people outside the ministry. I was so angry and disappointed that I could not speak.

I entered the Cabinet room for this crucial meeting feeling very lonely and deeply pessimistic. Key Cabinet documents to be considered were already in the public domain as a result of leaks from my political opponents, either within the government or within the bureaucracy. I had first seen a key submission when it arrived in my office on 4 October. An appalling part of that submission was a PM&C report that had been reproduced in the press days before most members of the Mabo Ministerial Committee received it. No doubt it was extensively circulated in the bureaucracy. It showed unambiguous departmental advice to ministers:

> . . . It is suggested that Ministers be guided by the following:
>
> (i) the preferable outcome would be satisfactory legislation (even if not our ideal) agreed with a significant number of States/Territories on the basis of which they would give explicit support to the revised Bill and to its passage by the parliament . . .
>
> (ii) Failing such an agreement, the aim should be a Bill which (while criticised by stakeholders) can be confidently defended and promoted to the wider community as fair and workable.
>
> Underlying this approach is our view that there are strong grounds for trying to reach an agreement with at least some of the States, including that: we avoid the administrative and cost problems of setting up a Commonwealth structure across the country; we avoid those Commonwealth institutions becoming a ready made target for blame associated with a slow down in development activity or disruption of land management; the more intransigent States become clearly isolated; more positively State systems are encouraged to make genuine efforts to take account of native title and treat it with justice (rather than the Commonwealth simply coming in over the top).
>
> Obviously, Ministers would need to be satisfied that such an agreement met the requirements of justice for Aboriginal and Torres Strait Islander people, as well as a workable land management system which protected the national economic interest . . .

Let there be no rewriting of history: indisputably, it was Cabinet's priority to reach an accommodation with the states and territories. The strategy was to get the legislation through parliament and an important part of that strategy was securing Coalition support for its passage.

I was by now utterly convinced that the government's Mabo response was unlikely to be supported by the Coalition in any event, but if the government went in this direction it would result in international condemnation and ten times the Aboriginal outrage that greeted the flawed national land rights proposals of the 1980s. The Labor movement would have been deeply split, with hundreds of respected Australian opinion leaders mobilised against the government. In every way it was taking us on a road to nowhere. But still the Cabinet proceeded down this path in that fateful week in 1993.

The outcome of this depressing meeting was Cabinet noting that the position set out in the officials' document 'is close to the terms of a possible agreement with the States and Territories' and authorising the Prime Minister to 'undertake negotiations with a view to reaching a satisfactory agreement with States and Territories, subject to seeking the further views of Aboriginal representatives'. It was proposed that a reformulation of the RDA suspension be put to indigenous representatives for consideration, as well as a proposal for a right for the federal Attorney-General to intervene in proceedings in native title claims lodged with a state and territory body, provided that the Attorney-General was satisfied that the claim raised a matter of national interest. This proposal was put forward as an alternative to allowing indigenous people to have direct access to Commonwealth processes, should they choose to do so. I knew that it was a proposal that would have had some limited value with a Labor government in power in Canberra, but would be worthless under a Coalition government.

Richard Court warned that night that there could be no acceptable legislative solution to Mabo while Western Australia was not accommodated. He maintained that 'Western Australia is the State most affected by the Mabo High Court decision' and that 'the national interest is not served by attempting to enforce an unfair land title system which will be detrimental to a State which is providing more than 25 per cent of the nation's total exports'. No concessions, or even outright capitulation by the Commonwealth, would be enough for the WA Premier, short of the Commonwealth abandoning any role whatsoever in responding to Mabo. This was the very response Peter Reith had recently advocated.

In accordance with the Cabinet discussions of the previous night, Paul Keating spent much of the day in discussions with Aboriginal land council and ATSIC representatives. That night Cabinet met again and heard his report on the progress of negotiations. The Cabinet position was clear: it agreed that the outcome of negotiations was acceptable and 'can form the basis of an agreement with certain States and Territories'. The Prime Minister was to continue discussions with Aboriginal people and officials were to put counter-proposals on the issue of compensation, with the 'Prime Minister having the latitude to adjust upwards if necessary in order to finalise the agreement'. The Attorney-General and the Special Minister of State were to draft the Bill on the basis of the position to be agreed with the states, taking into account the outcome of discussions and negotiations with the 'stakeholders'.

Cabinet suggested an approach to the RDA that deemed the validation process to be consistent with that Act. It did not support access by indigenous people to the federal jurisdiction if there were recognised state and territory bodies for determining native title. It endorsed a proposal put forward by the NSW government that native title holders should be required to demonstrate that they or their ancestors had a physical connection with the land in question in the past. This was of doubtful meaning and was not a concept recognised by the High Court decision.

But in many respects, the issues of detail in the Commonwealth proposals were peripheral to the appalling signals being sent to indigenous people and their supporters about the Commonwealth's priorities. For them Mabo was about the unambiguous recognition of indigenous rights by the High Court of Australia. There was a need for the Commonwealth not only to act but be seen to act in a principled manner through a legislative response that recognised indigenous rights as its guiding priority, rather than to stitch up some deal with a passing parade of state bureaucrats and politicians.

There would never be another opportunity like this. When I trudged back up the stairs to my office I was deeply depressed. I felt I'd done all I could but that nothing I could have said or done in that Cabinet room would have changed the central dynamics of the Cabinet's direction, namely to reach an accommodation with the states and territories in line with advice provided by Commonwealth officials. Yet responsibility for the outcome did not rest with officials. The Cabinet decision was a decision of the elected government and one I simply could not live with.

That night Paul Keating issued a statement:

> Encouraging progress was made—the original 20 or more outstanding issues between the Commonwealth and Aboriginal representatives have now been narrowed to three or four. While there has been progress, I remain concerned that two or three outstanding matters are currently incompatible with elements of the position now emerging in the useful

discussion with the States. On these points the Aboriginal leaders have undertaken to provide a detailed written response as soon as possible . . . Given the progress made over the past 48 hours it is worth exploring every avenue of potential settlement on these outstanding points rather than bring the negotiations to a premature halt . . . The Cabinet also met this evening and agreed to a number of details arising from discussions with Commonwealth and State officials today.

I think that it is important to note that some Aboriginal leaders who have tonight made statements about the Commonwealth's position were not in any of the meetings over the past 48 hours, and have not accurately reflected the constructive approach of the Commonwealth, nor the significant progress made.

Earlier that night, however, as the Cabinet met, Aboriginal leaders had delivered a letter to the Prime Minister's office signed by Lois O'Donoghue, Noel Pearson, Daryl Pearce, David Ross and Daryl Cronin. The signatories, representing some of the most important Aboriginal organisations in the country, put a radically different view of the progress of the negotiations.

Dear Prime Minister

Thank you for the opportunity to hold discussions with you over the last two days concerning the Commonwealth's proposed native title legislation. We appreciate your position and the particular difficulties which you face. We stress that we are not walking away from the process of negotiation. As things presently stand, however, there are major differences between us with regard to the majority of points we have raised with you in discussions over the past two days. In particular, we repeat our advice to you earlier this afternoon that we regard: any measures which have the effect of suspending, impairing, modifying or restricting in any way whatsoever the operation of the Racial Discrimination Act; any restriction of the rights of native title holders or claimants to choose either a State or Commonwealth forum for the determination of interests; any cut off date later than June 1993; any failure to provide a genuine opportunity to negotiate terms and conditions leading to a fair outcome by means of a tribunal arbitration where negotiations fail to yield a result as fundamentally unacceptable. We confirm our intention to provide you at the earliest opportunity with a detailed written response to all the matters we have discussed with you over the past two days. We reiterate that we wish to maintain dialogue with your Government and in so doing, urge you to consider our detailed proposals, bearing in mind the critical nature of these issues to the nation's future. While we will do our utmost to work with you toward a solution, the constituency we represent is extremely vulnerable. To abandon the principled workable and reasonable approach we have advocated would be to betray the responsibility they have entrusted to us.

I did not talk to any of my parliamentary colleagues or anyone else that night after the Cabinet meeting. I just remained, defeated and demoralised, behind my office desk. Then Lois O'Donoghue appeared at the open office door. Sensing my distress, she asked me what was the matter. I told her of my despair and that I could not think of anything else that could be done to retrieve the situation. It was one of dozens of confidential conversations I had with Lois during 1993. I spoke to her that night not in anger against my ministerial colleagues but in very great sadness and regret that my party had failed to deliver the principled response to Mabo I had believed it would. I could foresee long-term damage to the ALP and to Australia if the situation was not retrieved, but there was just nothing more I could do. Only a change of heart by the Prime Minister and a dramatic shift in government direction to meet indigenous aspirations would result in the passing of the legislation with the support of the Democrats and the Greens.

I can remember Lois being joined in my office by other Aboriginal leaders, but I can't remember who they were. I was too devastated to say much. Lois was angrier than I had ever seen her. At first I thought she was angry at me, but it was nothing of the sort. I was witnessing a show of moral and political resolve and strength. That strength was to serve her people well in the next 24 hours and in the months ahead. She did not tell me that night of any strategy she had in mind, if indeed she had one. I do have a stark recollection of her turning on her heels after our talk and striding purposefully out the door and down the corridor of Parliament House.

The morning papers only confirmed to Aboriginal leaders that their understanding of the government intention was right on the mark. There was a reference to 'senior government sources' making it clear 'that if a deal could not be done' with Aboriginal people the legislation would be drafted and introduced into parliament. Leaks to the media supported the line the government was adopting and referred to the views of 'government officials' who had talked to journalists.

Although I was in fundamental disagreement with Cabinet's decisions and approach, leading up to what Noel Pearson would call 'Black Friday', I knew what had to be done and that there was only one person in Australia who could do it, and that was Paul Keating. Although at times I strongly disagreed with some of his actions during the Mabo response, I have abiding admiration for the way he was to seize the

moment during the week ahead to negotiate face-to-face with indigenous leaders. It was not to be a perfect process of negotiation and the
result did not deliver everything Aboriginal people sought, but there
is no doubt that it was a defining point in Australia's history.
Confronted with the choice of going with the states or of negotiating
a historic outcome with indigenous people, the Prime Minister chose
the high road and earned himself a place in history.

On the morning of Friday, 8 October, I was driving to Jervis Bay
to meet with the Wreck Bay Aboriginal Community adjacent to
the national park. The community wanted to speak to me about
proposals to gain title to the park on the model of Kakadu. As I drove
I agonised about what I would do, since I could not live with the
Cabinet decision reached the night before. I distinctly remember
crossing my political Rubicon driving into the small township of Kan-
garoo Valley and decided to tell my staff that I intended to resign from
the ministry.

I telephoned my office in Canberra from a public phone box and
told them that I had no alternative if the government could not be
diverted from its disastrous and unacceptable course. It was the last
thing I wanted to do. All my adult life I had wanted to be a minister
in a federal Labor government. But I had to take a stand. I knew that
whatever the consequences, I was prepared to act. I didn't think for a
minute that I would then be the only Caucus member who was
prepared to speak out and act in opposition to the government. I
believe to this day that there were significant numbers in all the
factions who would take a stand in opposition to the government's
proposals and in support of Aboriginal aspirations.

That day momentous events were unfolding in Canberra. I was
subdued and preoccupied in the meeting at Wreck Bay. As I came out
of Jervis Bay and back onto the highway in the company of Peter Knott,
MP for Gilmore, my mobile phone rang. It was Lois O'Donoghue,
sounding buoyant and confident. She had convened a media conference to speak up for Aboriginal rights and had been joined by other
Aboriginal leaders. She did not go into detail but sounded happy and
in control, making it abundantly clear that she felt she had done the
right thing but that the fight was far from over. I remember her having
a little chuckle about what she had done. I was overwhelmed by her
strength and thought to myself, what a woman, what a fighter.

Lois wrote to her fellow ATSIC commissioners on that 'Black
Friday'. Reflecting the desperation of indigenous leaders, she said she
felt 'pessimistic, and deeply saddened by the likely outcome' of the
government Mabo deliberations. She referred to Paul Keating's

Redfern Park speech and the hope it had given indigenous Australians: 'It looked as if a uniquely Australian cultural identity could be developed in the years leading to the centenary of Federation—an identity built on a foundation of reconciliation between ourselves and non-indigenous Australians. It is now highly unlikely that the vision will be fulfilled'. She emphasised that the coalition of ATSIC commissioners worked on the Mabo response with other Aboriginal organisations to 'secure the best legislation possible' and that strong political encouragement had come from 'some members of the Labour [*sic*] Caucus, the Australian Democrats and the Western Australian Greens. In those talks with government we have sought a reasonable, workable and principled solution. At this moment, it looks as though we have failed'.

The letter stressed the extent of the concessions 'reluctantly agreed' in order to get an 'achievable result'—validation of existing title, no veto, a significant role for states and territories in determining native title and grants on native title land, with the legislation to create a land fund to be introduced not contemporaneously but in the next session of parliament. Lois said she 'remained convinced of the genuineness of the Prime Minister's commitment' but she expressed regret that the concessions made to Aboriginal people 'were not enough' and that 'at this vital juncture in the development of our nation the Prime Minister seems to have decided that "States' rights" are more important than our human rights'. She laid the blame for this situation at least in part on the Office of Indigenous Affairs, which 'has joined with other bureaucrats and advisers in seeking to persuade the Prime Minister that immediate political necessity means sacrificing moral vision to the imperative of striking a deal with the States', and warned that 'it is difficult to see a future for the reconciliation process if this argument prevails'. She explicitly rejected 'suggestions in the press' that most ATSIC demands had now been met, saying 'this is simply not true'. 'Suggestions in the press' was a polite way of referring to Paul Keating's media release of the night before. She continued:

> On the major issues we cannot and will not concede any further. The Racial Discrimination Act must not be suspended simply to satisfy the States and the mining industry. Our people must be able to choose whether they seek the determination of their native title interests through the Commonwealth jurisdiction (in which we retain some faith) or through State/Territory jurisdictions (of which we are deeply suspicious).

The letter ended on an optimistic note, urging commissioners not to despair and saying that 'out of crisis has emerged a new unity and mutual respect between ATSIC and a wide variety of Aboriginal and

Torres Strait Islander organisations. If that unity can be forged we will together be in a stronger position to continue the struggle'. The assertion of the need for the supremacy of Commonwealth tribunals was consistent with the demands of Aboriginal leaders going back to the 1930s.

The media conference in the ATSIC boardroom had gone off with a bang. Media interest was overwhelming. The fight was on. Speakers were Lois, Mick Dodson and Noel Pearson. Other land council representatives stood around, among them Peter Costello, the distinguished chair of the Cape York Land Council, who had already been through a lifetime of struggle for his people.

Aboriginal leaders stressed that they were not walking away from continued talks, but they vigorously attacked the proposed native title legislation, saying it would be essentially racist and would involve 'the largest extinguishment of native title land in Australia's history'. Mick Dodson said the Prime Minister's Redfern Park speech would come back to haunt him. Noel Pearson made it clear that he did not agree with the view that there had been concessions to Aboriginal people and said Aboriginal people would be 'fools' to believe this.

Lois O'Donoghue's letter to the ATSIC commissioners was publicly released and the issues raised at the media conference were given saturation national publicity on television that night and in the morning papers. The publicity was overwhelmingly negative for the government, with the *Australian* headlining the assertion 'PM has failed us on Mabo: Aborigines'. Paul Keating was, of course, very angry that Lois had organised the media conference, and it was obvious from the media release from his office on the Thursday night that his advisers had a very different view of the world. He made it known that he was 'bitterly disappointed' and indicated that the angry views of Aboriginal representatives were 'completely out of the spirit of the agreements we had'. He stressed the 'concessions' made by the states, including acceptance that a mining lease would not extinguish native title, agreement that there would be no sunset clause, and agreement not to cap compensation. He cast doubt on the capacity of Aboriginal people as negotiators.

Sydney Morning Herald journalist Geoff Kitney reported the views of the Prime Minister and his office on Saturday, 9 October, saying that the Prime Minister 'had a clear message for Aboriginal leaders that night: go one more step towards the middle on Mabo or miss an historic opportunity'. Mr Kitney then expressed his own view that, while the government's current proposals were not perfect, 'Aboriginal leaders will be making a mistake if they reject it'. Thankfully, this flawed analysis did not prevail. Mr Kitney also reported that the Prime Minister's office had received two calls from Aboriginal negotiators claiming that they were unaware that the press conference was to be held. Paul Keating said he would continue to argue the case for Aboriginal people with the premiers but warned that 'it would be a tragic mistake for the Aboriginal people to stay outside the process'. He need not have worried; the object of the press conference was not to place indigenous people outside the process but to ensure that the process occurred more on their terms than on those of state and territory governments.

The importance of this press conference cannot be overstated. It was a critical moment in the Mabo debate, after which the government was confronted with a stark choice: either to continue in the same direction with the guarantee that indigenous people and their supporters, inside and outside parliament, would be ranged against it, with the legislation having no chance of passing into law (the Coalition's intention to vote down the legislation was already on the public record); or to negotiate with indigenous leaders and then with the Greens and Democrats to get the legislation through parliament and to make history in the process.

10

GETTING THE NATIVE TITLE ACT OVER THE LINE

In the aftermath of the Black Friday press conference, the Prime Minister entered into direct negotiations with Lois O'Donoghue and the coalition of Aboriginal negotiators. Resolution of one key issue in dispute was assisted by a legally creative way to purportedly avoid suspending the RDA. This was first put forward by AMIC after the 1993 election and again suggested by ALP back-benchers and their legal advisers over the previous weekend. The suspension of the RDA was to be cast as a 'special measure' and therefore consistent with the Act.

A sensitive issue to resolve was the status of native title that affected pastoral leases. This was a very grey area of Mabo policy debate but the bottom line was that no pastoralist was ever going to have any erosion of their existing rights. There were, however, emerging political differences with the NFF which could have developed into deep divisions. The situation was resolved by a deal with Rick Farley. The outcome was that the validation of pastoral leases over which title was in doubt would extinguish native title in those leases but that pastoral leases owned by Aboriginal people could potentially be subject to native title claims. Furthermore, Aboriginal people would still be able to test in the courts (e.g. the Wik case) whether or not the grant of a valid pastoral lease would extinguish native title.

The outcome of the historic face-to-face negotiations with Aboriginal people was triumphantly announced by Paul Keating, to a standing ovation of the Labor Caucus. The hurdle of achieving a Senate majority for the government's proposals remained with the Green senators, who were still expressing strong reservations. They were working with an alliance of Aboriginal people who had a different agenda. They had deliberately stood outside the negotiating process and were described as the 'B Team' to distinguish them from the group led by Lois O'Donoghue, described as the 'A Team'.

The Opposition remained hostile to the entirety of the government's agenda, with the WA government even introducing its own rushed legislation in a ham-fisted attempt to obliterate native title rights. The pressure on the Greens to pass the Commonwealth legislation was intense and came not only from Aboriginal people and their supporters in the wider community but from within the Green Party itself. The Bill was referred to the Senate Legal and Constitutional Affairs Committee, which predictably divided on party lines, and at the same time the Opposition called for a Senate Select Committee inquiry. The longest Senate debate in the history of the parliament at that time then ensued. There were final intense make-or-break discussions between the Aboriginal negotiating teams, the Democrats, the Greens and the government led by Senator Gareth Evans.

The government kept pushing for an outcome, with the Prime Minister threatening to have parliament sit until Christmas Eve, until finally the elation of a Senate majority was achieved and Australia had its Native Title Act unambiguously recognising, protecting and enhancing the High Court's decision in the Mabo case. With all its highs and lows and spilt political blood, it achieved a turning point in Australia's history. As a nation we had taken a huge step down the road to reconciliation.

O
n the morning of Saturday, 9 October 1993, Prime Minister Keating arrived in Perth to fulfil a prior commitment to meet with the Aboriginal community to discuss the government's Mabo response. He had also agreed to meet Premier Richard Court, but even before the meeting Mr Court lashed out in the *Australian*, making it clear that Western Australia would not be supporting the Prime Minister's proposals. The meeting between the two men was totally unproductive. Both subsequently predicted chaos if the other did not give way.

On the same day ATSIC organised a telephone conference to plan tactics for the coming week. There was considerable anger expressed by a number of participants about the Prime Minister's comments on the capacity of Aboriginal negotiators.

On the Monday morning, a letter on behalf of the Combined Aboriginal Organisations Working Group was sent to the Prime Minister. It was signed by Daryl Cronin, Noel Pearson, Daryl Pearce, David Ross and Lois O'Donoghue and set out in detail the 'gulf' between the 'moderate' position of Aboriginal people and that then held by the government. The letter outlined nineteen points on which Aboriginal concerns had not been met or had been only partly met. It proposed a means by which there could be a validation of titles without a suspension of the RDA, in other words that the RDA should specifically apply to the proposed Native Title Act but that a

> special measure would entail a legislative scheme imposing a requirement to negotiate on terms and conditions for coexistence of native title with the validated grant. Terms and conditions may include

site clearance agreements, access for hunting, outstations, etc. In the event of negotiations failing, arbitration by the tribunal would fix the amount and nature of compensation and impose reasonable terms and conditions for coexistence.

This was the approach foreshadowed in the Aboriginal Peace Plan. The difference was that this time the phrase 'special measure' was used. The concept of a special measure was recognised under CERD and also in the RDA, with the latter providing that sections 9 and 10 of the Act prohibiting discrimination do not apply to what CERD describes as 'special measures taken for the sole purpose of securing adequate advancement of certain racial or ethnic groups . . . in order to ensure . . . equal enjoyment or exercise of human rights and fundamental freedoms'.

This concept of a special measure had first been put forward by AMIC in a submission to the government before the 1993 federal election. It had been reportedly raised again by Sydney QCs Greg James and Michael Finnane, who had been consulted by a Caucus Committee member, Daryl Melham, the Member for Banks (who would become the Shadow Minister for Aboriginal and Torres Strait Islander Affairs after the 1996 election). Over the weekend Daryl had been in contact with me, Warren Snowdon, the Member for the Northern Territory, and Nick Bolkus, who was sharing a VIP aircraft back from Perth with the Prime Minister and took the opportunity to raise the proposals with him. They were also discussed with the Aboriginal negotiators and their lawyer, the late Ron Castan QC, who had argued the Mabo case to the High Court. Later it would be questioned whether the totality of the proposals as they were finally enshrined in legislation amounted to a special measure within CERD, as it was not a measure solely to benefit Aboriginal people. My view was that if the proposal could contribute to a negotiated outcome then it was worth supporting.

The problem at this stage was that aspects of the Aboriginal demands, involving as they did a restatement of the essential elements of the Peace Plan, were entirely unacceptable to the government. The Aboriginal negotiators would eventually broker considerable advances, but there were to be no gains on rights to coexistence of title in respect of any validated interests, or rights related to the validation process. Ultimately Aboriginal negotiators were prepared to have the legislation cast as a special measure and, contrary to virtually all media reporting of the native title debate, the Native Title Act in section 7(2) was to disapply the RDA for the purposes of validation.

There were media reports to the effect that Aboriginal negotiators had to be 'persuaded' to go back to the negotiating table with the Prime Minister, but these were without foundation; there was never the slightest suggestion that Aboriginal negotiators were intending to turn their back on negotiations. The main purpose of the Black Friday press conference was to force the government to negotiate with Aboriginal people on their terms.

Paul Keating resumed his negotiations on the Monday and they continued for four days while Commonwealth and state officials continued to liaise. On Tuesday the Caucus Aboriginal and Torres Strait Islander Affairs Committee met and passed a resolution calling on the government to postpone its native title legislation if it could not agree with the views of 'moderate' Aboriginal leaders. That night Paul Keating briefed Cabinet on the progress of negotiations, and the next day a coalition of eight organisations, including the ACTU, the Australian Council of Social Service (ACOSS), the Australian Conservation Foundation (ACF) and FECCA called on the Prime Minister to 'unambiguously recognise' native title and warned that a failure to do so 'could derail the possibilities of reconciliation as a whole' and that a 'suspension of the Racial Discrimination Act opens up grave risks for all ethnic groups subject to discrimination'.

Meanwhile, the Australian Council of Churches wrote to all Caucus members expressing deep concern about the government's proposals, which would 'so interfere with common law native title that it will in fact result in further unjust dispossession'. Bishop Bruce Wilson warned that there was concern that Cabinet was hearing only from 'economic interest groups' and that 'there is a very real risk that if the interests of industry lobbyists carry the day, Australia's human rights standing will be badly damaged overseas'.

In the *Australian* on 14 October, a letter from 32 prominent Australians from all walks of life—Gough Whitlam, former NSW Liberal Attorney-General John Dowd, author David Malouf, actor Ruth Cracknell and many others—expressed opposition to any rolling back of the RDA. They appealed to the government 'not to discriminate against indigenous Australians particularly in the International Year of the World's Indigenous Peoples' but to reflect 'in any legislation the spirit and meaning of the High Court's decision' and to 'promote not jeopardise the process of reconciliation between black and white Australia'.

On Thursday, 15 October, after days of meetings with the Aboriginal negotiators, Paul Keating confidently predicted that a negotiated outcome could be achieved. He believed that existing titles could be secured without overriding the RDA and that Aboriginal people could choose whether state or federal courts could decide their native title claims. He announced that just terms would be paid for the extinguishment of native title, designated Aboriginal organisations would be funded, and a social justice response, including a land fund, would form part of the Commonwealth's package. He also alluded in general terms to the proposal to adopt the special measures approach. In response, Rick Farley made it clear that any proposals that did not see all pastoral leases extinguish native title would be totally unacceptable to the NFF and a recipe for 'confusion and uncertainty'. John Hewson accused the Prime Minister of further confusing the Mabo issue.

A useful insight into the negotiations between the Prime Minister and the Aboriginal negotiators was provided the following Saturday by the political commentator Alan Ramsey, when he revealed the contents of a leaked copy of notes taken at the first negotiating meeting earlier that week. He reported that there were eight people in the Keating group negotiating with seven Aboriginal representatives. The shorthand minutes of the meeting began:

> Keating: Got your letter and note. Not everything in note will be accepted. We want Ab support for the Bill. If we go down route to head States off, and we accept some points, then we want your support. We will not get [Native Title Bill] thru [Senate] without your support. Locking up Greens, Democrats. Don't want unnecessary amendments. Otherwise, we get State support . . .
>
> Lois O'Donoghue: . . . We are warmed by your opening statement and manner. You have come back to negotiation. We [are] talking to Greens, Democrats, Caucus. Can shore up their support . . .
>
> Noel Pearson: . . . My position has been made very clear—just and pragmatic settlement notwithstanding some Ab people have [expectations of] unrealistic outcome. Provided I am satisfied with outcome, we barrack for outcome.

The notes went on to record the Prime Minister as saying:

> We have given option of extinguishing mining titles in favour of native title. Do you object to extinguishing of native title on pastoral leases? Thousands of them not affected. You have common law right to argue inconsistency with native title . . . Will give Farley the shits [but] I will throw on table here and now and try—extinguishment of native title only to the extent of inconsistency with the grant. Gives you the right to argue coexistence in courts. I might not get this past Cabinet. If I don't then you can't hold me to it.

The Prime Minister was referring to the option of coexistence of native title interests on pastoral lands where those titles were being validated, namely those issued since the RDA commenced in 1975. It was always the case that it was open to Aboriginal people to assert that they had coexistence rights over other pastoral lands, though the government's legal advice was that such continuing rights did not exist. This advice was less certain in the case of Western Australia, South

Australia and the Northern Territory, where legislation provided for limited Aboriginal rights of access to pastoral leases for traditional purposes.

It was the government's view, repeated probably hundreds of times by Paul Keating, by me, and by other ministers during the Mabo debate, that although our legal advice was that the grant of a pastoral lease extinguished native title, Aboriginal people, like other Australians, were entitled to test this proposition in the courts. It was not the government's function to legislate unilaterally to extinguish such rights over pastoral land as Aboriginal people might hold. In any event, extinguishment would be likely to contravene the RDA.

As far as I was concerned it was important to keep parroting the government's legal advice incessantly because, though I was aware of a very strong legal argument outside the government to the contrary, to give any currency to such views at this time was to open up a whole new front of attack from the pastoral industry.

Later in the week, when Rick Farley became aware that proposals were being raised that affected the status of pastoral leases and their relationship with native title, he was very angry. The NFF wrote to all Cabinet ministers reminding them that at least seven ministers had given assurances that pastoral leases would extinguish native title and saying that to go back on this would be 'a gross and unforgivable breach of political faith'. Rick Farley's concerns were understandable. He had stuck his neck out to secure some common ground with indigenous people and to moderate the contribution that would otherwise have been made to the debate by some constituent bodies of the NFF. As a member of the Council for Aboriginal Reconciliation he had undoubtedly been a positive force for good in the Mabo debate and now he was in trouble with his own constituency.

The fact was that the government could not, and did not, give an ironclad guarantee that the grant of a pastoral lease would extinguish native title; this was clearly a matter for determination by the courts. It was, however, beyond doubt that Aboriginal people could never claim 'ownership' of that land, and any rights they might be found to have to enter the land for traditional purposes would be subject to the terms of the lease. This, of course, is what the High Court found in the Wik case in December 1996.

On 18 October, in Question Time, the Prime Minister was asked by John Hewson about the coexistence of native title on pastoral leases. He replied by confirming that the government would not legislate to extinguish the rights of Aboriginal people to bring native title claims through the courts. Afterwards Dr Hewson issued a media statement in which he asserted that the Prime Minister had abandoned previous guarantees on the issue of native title and pastoral leases. His claims were supported by John Anderson, who tried to put pressure on Simon Crean to intervene on behalf of the farming community, warning of 'havoc in the bush'.

That day a group of 49 senior Australian corporate executives sent a petition to the Prime Minister warning of 'disastrous effects on investment' if the Commonwealth's legislation did not protect existing title. The petition was reportedly organised by Hugh Morgan and a CRA executive, Mark Rayner, and expressed particular concern that 'existing pastoral and other leases had not extinguished native title'. Both miners and pastoralists were interested in this question as approximately 42 per cent of Australia is covered by such leases and in the past additional areas were subject to pastoral leases which no longer continued to exist but which had arguably also extinguished native title. The mining industry was particularly concerned to avoid any suggestion of 'right to negotiate' processes operating in relation to exploration and mining on such lands. They were substantially to have their way when John Howard responded to the Wik decision in 1998.

Cabinet was scheduled to meet that night to finalise consideration of the government's proposals. Before the meeting news came of an important breakthrough. The previous night, Phillip Toyne, a ministerial consultant to Frank Walker, phoned Rick Farley to convey a proposal that had emerged in discussions with Noel Pearson: that validation of pastoral leases would extinguish native title in return for a concession that pastoral leases under Aboriginal ownership could be the subject of successful native title claims if the requisite connection with the land could be proved. It was also proposed that the government would legislate to ensure that the past creation of a pastoral lease would not in such circumstances be a bar to the claim. This was necessary because the government's legal advice was that such pastoral leases would otherwise have extinguished native title. Rick Farley did not readily agree and made it clear that the rural sector would first want to ensure that there would be an extinguishment of native title, as they had been seeking.

When Cabinet met, there was little substantial resistance to the proposal about converting Aboriginal-owned pastoral land to native title. Announcing the Cabinet decision, the Prime Minister set out the aims and essential features of the proposed legislation and went into considerable detail about its impact on pastoral leases. He pointed out that the legislation would only affect invalid leases:

> There are few pastoral leases which have been issued since 1975 which could conceivably be invalid because the requirements of the Racial Discrimination Act were not met when the leases were issued. There may also have been leases issued before 1975 which may be invalid on

grounds unconnected with the Racial Discrimination Act but connected
to some other rights, as yet unidentified in law, flowing from the
existence of native title.

This latter extension was of course the result of the Wik claim and the
resultant push from the Queensland government and CRA.

The Prime Minister made clear that 'the validation of pastoral
leases will extinguish native title, as provided for in the September 2nd
outline'. He went on to explain the proposal allowing the conversion
of Aboriginal-owned pastoral property to native title. If the requisite
continuing connection with the land could be established, the owners
of this title would get the native title benefits and protection under
the Commonwealth law. To pick up a proposal Rick Farley had advocated, the government would press for codes of conduct where there
are access rights, but this would depend on pastoralists, Aboriginal
people and the states coming together.

The Bill would enhance the right of native title holders to negotiate on proposed actions that affect their land, with time limits to be
extended beyond the period foreshadowed in the outline of 2 September; it would give greater recognition to regional agreements between
governments, Aboriginal people and others with interests and it would
provide for the establishment of a land acquisition fund. Its future
significance was enhanced by the last-minute advancement of indigenous rights in the native title negotiations with the Prime Minister,
which enabled potential native title claims over Aboriginal-owned pastoral land.

The next morning the Prime Minister entered the regular ALP
Caucus meeting to a standing ovation in the presence of a battery of
television cameras. He said that the government's response to the High
Court decision was 'a really historic agreement which will warm the
soul of the Labor Party for two generations. It is the sort of thing our
Party believes in, it's the sort of thing which nourishes our Party'. Later,
at a press conference, he paid tribute to 'the Aboriginal leadership
under Lois O'Donoghue who did the courageous thing, took the step,
seized the moment to negotiate rather than to demand, and to sit
down and work out where Aboriginal interests truly lie and where they
could be offset against the legitimate economic interests of the country'. He said that the government had Aboriginal interests uppermost
in mind but had sought to balance industry interests.

At the press conference, asked about the process for validating
titles, he said it would be the states that legislated to validate titles
since they had issued them, but they would do so with the protection
of the Commonwealth Native Title Act enacted as a special measure
consistent with the RDA. He said that the Commonwealth Bill

'emanates from the RDA and I don't think crosses any of its principles'. He was then asked whether there would be retrospective procedural fairness provisions built into the legislation. (The essential question was whether titles issued after the enactment of the Act in 1975 could be validated by state government legislation and by the simple method of retrospectively paying compensation. If so, there would simply be no need to override the Act.) In his answer, Paul Keating showed how intellectually vacuous the whole RDA argument had been:

> There has always been some very grave legal doubt about whether procedural fairness ever mattered. The preponderance of legal opinion would be that there was not a racially discriminatory thing done by a land manager when that land manager could never have known that native title existed; and that the payment of compensation was sufficient to actually validate a past title.

So what had it all been about?

John Hewson, as expected, was critical of the announcements, arguing that they left 'a huge cloud of uncertainty over thousands and thousands of occupiers of so-called "valid" pastoral leases which are to remain subject to native title claim'. He mentioned Paul Keating's acknowledgement that there were only eleven pastoral leases issued in the period 1975–93 that required validation and hence where native title would be extinguished as a result of the government's legislation. 'All the other leases', he asserted, 'will remain in doubt in respect of potential native title claims. The only "security" offered by the Prime Minister for the huge group in this second category is a "hope" or an "assertion" that native title claims against valid leases will not proceed because Aboriginal people have been offered a more attractive alternative'. He was, of course, correct. There is no way the government could prevent Aboriginal claims on pastoral leases any more than it could properly block legal actions by any other Australians.

During the day the Aboriginal negotiators held a press conference at which Lois O'Donoghue summed up the outcome of the Mabo negotiations:

> Very late last night we secured a negotiated outcome that meets the major interests, not only of our people but of all Australians and by doing so ensures that we start off together down the long path to a genuine reconciliation.
>
> It is an historic decision. The decision is historic not because we have gained from the Prime Minister an agreement to everything we sought. We have been willing to compromise in the interests of a truly national settlement. We have, for example, accepted a greater role for the States than we would have preferred and we have accepted greater

constraints on our right to negotiate developments on our land than
we would have liked.

It is an historic decision for two fundamental reasons. First, we
have managed in the last fortnight to turn around a decision which,
while perhaps satisfying the States, the miners and the farmers, would
have failed to address deep seated Aboriginal concerns.

She went on to talk about the ten major achievements of the negotiations but said that the events and outcome were

historic for another equally profound reason. What you have seen
emerge in the last fortnight, building on Eva Valley and other
meetings, is a powerful new coalition in indigenous affairs . . . A new
political voice has emerged in this country that will have to be listened
to . . . a new generation of Aboriginal leadership, speaking with a
commitment to the past but with the language of today. Strong,
determined, forceful yet able to argue, negotiate and conciliate.

In a not too subtle dig at the Prime Minister, she continued: 'The tired
old arguments that Aboriginal people could not negotiate, that a
united front of indigenous organisations could not be achieved, that
ATSIC could never gain a political voice, independent of Government,
have been laid to rest. Last night those myths were buried. Indigenous
affairs will never again be the same in our nation'.

The NFF supported the government's proposals, with Rick Farley
saying that they would help to create much greater certainty about
land title. He was particularly pleased that the effect of the government's legislation would be to extinguish native title on validated
pastoral leases. On other pastoral leases, he said:

The Commonwealth has given a very clear undertaking and view to the
courts that in the Commonwealth view the grant of a pastoral lease
extinguishes native title. We think that will reduce the scope for further
common law actions to test the relationship of native title to any
pastoral or agricultural lease which has been validly issued. As such it
will provide much greater comfort and security to pastoral leaseholders
than the approach which was flagged initially by the Prime Minister.

The essential outcome of the government's deliberations on pastoral leases was that with the exception of those leases where the title
was arguably invalid and subsequently validated by the government's
action and any native title extinguished, the government did not
otherwise legislate in respect of valid pastoral rights. Some indication
of the difficulty Rick Farley was to face in supporting the Bill was seen
in the public statement issued by John White, chief executive of the
NSW Farmers' Association. Mr White welcomed the Cabinet decision

but suggested that the decision 'removed any suggestion of co-existence of land title between pastoral and agricultural leaseholders and Aborigines'. This was simply not the case.

In essence the government's decision was that Aboriginal people were free to test their rights, if any, to native title over pastoral leases in the courts. This view was not only correct as a matter of principle, it was also pragmatically correct since the RDA was likely to be a barrier to any unilateral action to erode Aboriginal rights. The government's decision on this issue attracted criticism from the Coalition parties, state governments and sections of the pastoral industry. But there was never a suggestion that any farmer would lose their farm, nor even a suggestion that the existing rights of farmers under their pastoral leases would be diminished in any way. The best Aboriginal people could hope for was the High Court to recognise limited rights that would coexist with the rights of a pastoralist, and indeed this was essentially to be the view of the High Court in the Wik case.

The outcome of the Mabo negotiations at first received only a tentative and mildly positive response from state and territory leaders, probably because they did not have the details of the government's decision or understand the significance of the negotiations between the Prime Minister and indigenous leaders. The exception was Richard Court, who foreshadowed a High Court challenge.

Not all Aboriginal people supported the government's announcements at first. In Western Australia they still had a significant association with pastoral land, and inaccurate media reports that native title had been extinguished on all pastoral leases suggested a massive erosion of Aboriginal rights. This was not of course the case, but it prompted critical responses. Rob Riley accused the government of having sold out the rights of Aboriginal people to the pastoralist, mining and tourist industries and foreshadowed that the Aboriginal Legal Service would lobby the Greens and Democrats in the Senate.

The WA Greens foreshadowed a tougher response to the government's proposals. Senator Chamarette said, 'the main concern is that Aboriginal people wanted and deserved far more than this legislation'. There was a clear indication that the Greens did not intend to be rushed into passing the legislation by the end of the year as proposed by the government. Tensions deepened between the WA Greens and the Democrats in the days that followed. Senator Kernot warned the Greens against seeking further substantial concessions from the government at the behest of Aboriginal people in Western Australia, saying there was a possibility that 'they could lose the lot'. There was a real risk that the legislation could fail to pass if the Green senators could not be persuaded to support the Bill. Meanwhile Michael Wooldridge and Peter Nugent indicated that the Coalition could support the government's legislation. I did not believe for a minute that their view would prevail.

A number of informed commentators began to make some interesting objective assessments of the outcome of the negotiations. Garth Nettheim cast doubt on the validity of the 'special measure' device that had been agreed by Aboriginal negotiators and the government. He warned that 'any further erosion of the Aboriginal interests during the legislative process would run the real risk that the legislation would not suffice as a "special measure"'.

Frank Brennan commented in the *Australian* that 'symbols and process have been central to the finalisation of the Mabo Keating package'. In relation to the special measures requirement he said:

> The government argues that if there are more good apples than bad apples in the basket, it is a special measure, [but] some native title holders may later ask the courts to look inside the basket and to remove the occasional bad apple on the grounds that it is removable and is no good in achieving the native titleholders' equal enjoyment of human rights.

Frank took the view, as I had done from the beginning, that 'the debate about validation of titles has been an abstract beat up'. 'The special measure talk', he added, 'has provided a convenient face saver for Government', and he called on Aboriginal people and miners to put it behind them and to return to a consideration of the substantive issues.

On 24 October Tim Fischer, relentlessly hostile as always, called for pastoral lease titles to be 'secured': 'The cloud of uncertainty the government had left over pastoral leases would only increase concerns already held by some leaseholders that Mabo meant a takeover of their properties. The very worst outcome from Mabo would be to force the sale of existing leaseholds, and for them to be converted to native title holdings with public funding'—not a bad piece of work in scaremongering, given that there was no possibility whatsoever of a 'takeover' of rural properties.

On the same day Richard Court indicated there would be a problem for John Hewson if he did not support the Premier's views, and that the WA government could legislate for full extinguishment of native title, replacing it with a proposal for 'the traditional use of the lands by Aboriginal people'. The government was confident that Premier Court's legislation would be in breach of the RDA, a view subsequently upheld by the High Court in a seven to nil judgment. Paul Keating was in Cyprus attending a Commonwealth Heads of

Government meeting, but he issued a statement in which he accused John Hewson 'of failing absolutely' to show any leadership on Mabo because he was 'threatened by his Western Australian Parliamentary supporters'.

To their credit, the true liberals in the Liberal Party were not giving up without at least some attempt to fight the inevitable. On the previous Sunday, Michael Wooldridge had said that in the three years before he became spokesperson on Aboriginal Affairs in 1990, 'all people heard was "we are attacking Aborigines" as numerous examples of "petty maladministration" were pinpointed'. At the next joint party meeting both Dr Wooldridge and Peter Nugent were attacked for taking this stand.

On 27 October in Question Time in the House there was uproar. Frank Walker accused the Opposition of behaving in a racist manner, and Michael Lavarch attacked comments by Peter Reith on the weekend suggesting that the government's Mabo proposals could lead to 'separate homelands for Aborigines into which aspects of our legal system would not reach'.

Four days later, a spokesperson for the Queensland National Party Leader, Rob Borbidge, confirmed that a series of proposed referendum questions on Mabo was being prepared jointly by the Queensland and WA National and Liberal Parties. Rob Borbidge predicted that well over a third of Australia could be in Aboriginal hands by the turn of the century. 'There must be a referendum on the matter, and there must be land justice for all—one set of land laws for all Australians, to be administered, as they always have been to date, by the States.' Tim Fischer supported the idea of a referendum.

On 3 November Richard Court announced that he would introduce his foreshadowed legislation the next day, saying that his proposals would comply with the RDA. One objective of his proposal, he said, was to develop policies to improve Aboriginal standards of living. This is the same political line trotted out by conservative politicians to attack Aboriginal land rights while they do little or nothing effective to pursue their own professed priorities. Whenever Coalition politicians say they have a policy priority in these areas, indigenous people should get worried as to what other rights are about to be attacked, especially their land rights.

On the same day Ian McLachlan tried to put pressure on the Coalition to adopt a more hard-line approach. Speaking at a forum on Mabo in Perth, he said, 'I don't know what anyone else is going to do . . . but I can tell you . . . I could not possibly vote for Keating's legislation if it looks remotely like what he has said he has in mind'. Dr Hewson responded to this by indicating that when the legislation was considered by Shadow Cabinet all members would be bound by its

decision; if Ian McLachlan could not accept the decision he would
have to resign from the shadow ministry. Mr Downer and Dr
Wooldridge distanced themselves from Ian McLachlan's statement.

On 8 November in Adelaide, the outspoken historian Geoffrey
Blainey delivered a speech at a function hosted by Ian McLachlan and
launched a scathing attack on the High Court of Australia, describing
some members of the court as 'noteworthy in their ignorance' and
suggesting that the judgement 'seems to rest on hearsay, prejudice and
misguided research . . .'. He suggested that the decision was not based
on evidence before the court but 'presumably came from the Justices'
own reading, their research assistants and the atmosphere they breathe
and the circles they move in'. Ian McLachlan subsequently supported
the general thrust of Professor Blainey's views. But they were labelled
'utter nonsense' by Sir Ronald Wilson. Michael Wooldridge commented, 'I think it's pretty important we defend the institutions which
are fundamental to this society'.

On 10 November the *Australian* reported that the two WA Greens
were considering delaying the government's Mabo legislation. Senator
Chamarette had been visiting Aboriginal communities in the north of
Western Australia and said there were 'strong views' held by Aboriginal
people that they needed to understand what the negotiators had done.
Both Noel Pearson and the Prime Minister responded with concerns
that without the Commonwealth legislation, Richard Court would move
to extinguish Aboriginal native title rights. Senator Chamarette later
acknowledged the pressure from Aboriginal and church groups seeking
speedy passage of the legislation but said that this should be balanced
by the need for more consultation. She would apply three tests before
making a final decision on the legislation: no Aboriginal group was to
be disadvantaged by it; there would be a focus on what longer-term
gains there would be for Aboriginal people; and the legislation was to
receive proper scrutiny and debate.

Noel Pearson took a prominent role that week, urging support for
the negotiated outcome proposals with feature articles in major newspapers and a speech at the National Press Club. At the Press Club he
acknowledged that 'the High Court has taken the step of reconciliation' but that 'more political steps need to be taken' and 'there can
be no reconciliation without implementation of that decision'. He
made a strident attack on the Coalition and other opponents of a just
Mabo outcome, suggesting that the views of some critics of the Mabo
decision 'go to the question of whether we should be humans that
should be respected as having rights'. In a scathing denunciation of
the Coalition, which caused anger and offence in conservative ranks,
he said the Mabo debate required national maturity to recognise that
Aboriginal people had legitimate land claims and that such a position

could not be reached while 'people are donning hoods and wielding flaming crosses in formulating their policies on Mabo'.

There was heightened tension in Coalition ranks that week in the lead-up to the introduction of the government's Native Title Bill into parliament, with Michael Wooldridge in conflict with Ian McLachlan for remarks made by Mr McLachlan on a Perth radio station. Coalition tensions were on a knife edge. On the other hand, former MP Fred Chaney said the Coalition was 'missing a great opportunity' and that the High Court ruling meant that Aboriginal people had to be treated with some respect 'rather than being treated as some sub-species which has been the position up to this point'. In his WA Liberal Party, Fred Chaney's views were the exception rather than the rule. Fellow WA Liberal Ross Lightfoot asserted that Aboriginal people were 'only the bottom colour of the civilization spectrum' and suggestions that they were civilised 'were about as wrong as you could possibly get'.

Meanwhile dissident Aboriginal interest groups began to put pressure on the minor parties in the Senate and to attack the negotiated outcome reached with the Prime Minister. I considered it inevitable that there would be Aboriginal interests that had not been a part of the face-to-face negotiations that would argue for a stronger line to be taken. Some would do so for personal agendas while others sought tactical and achievable changes. The risk was that the Greens would think that the resulting debate and inevitable divisions made it all too hard and refuse to support the legislation.

On 11 November, however, Paul Coe and Charles Perkins issued a joint media release under the name of the Aboriginal Legal Service in Redfern, which asserted in its opening paragraph that:

> Attempting to legitimise the proposed Commonwealth native title legislation by having the Prime Minister negotiating with five Aboriginals so as to say Aboriginal Australia has been consulted is not acceptable by the majority of Aboriginal people . . . We stress that these Aboriginal negotiators have acted in direct contravention [of] the resolutions passed by two national meetings of Aboriginal people at Eva Valley and Queanbeyan.

In an address to the nation on the evening of 15 November on ABC TV, the Prime Minister asserted for the benefit of industry: 'There is only one way to provide certainty—and that is with a single uniform national approach, a fair and predictable set of rules which everyone can work with . . . This is not just my view, it is the view of seven out of eight States and Territories, all of whom . . . believe this legislation can work'. The reality was, of course, that any state or territory support for the Bill was at best heavily qualified.

Shadow Finance Minister Peter Costello then joined the fray, falsely suggesting that the government had 'entered into' open-ended expenditure commitments as a result of its proposals. The fact was that any exposure to compensation claims arose not because of some free-choice policy decision but because extinguishment of native title would require compensation to be paid to Aboriginal people as a matter of law, just as it would in the case of every Australian whose title right to land had been taken away.

The Prime Minister introduced the native title legislation into the House of Representatives on 16 November 1993, with a number of Aboriginal leaders there to hear his speech. The next day the government received a boost from what would previously have been considered an unlikely source. The NFF Federal Council meeting in Canberra passed a resolution supporting the legislation so far as it affected the farm sector. Graham Blight said that 'the Commonwealth's package satisfied most of the farm sector's concerns' and recognised that 'a national approach to Mabo issues was desirable and this meant that no interest group got exactly what it wanted'.

That day, Hal Wootten QC addressed a Rotary Club luncheon in Sydney and reminded the Rotarians that 'forty per cent of the Northern Territory is held by overseas and interstate interests' and that one person, Kerry Packer, owned a single property as big as Cyprus. By highlighting this ownership of land by non-indigenous and often non-resident owners, Hal Wootten countered concerns raised by Geoffrey Blainey about the extent of Aboriginal land ownership. Referring to the latter's recent speech, he told his audience that 'it was ironic that Professor Blainey was speaking as the guest of Ian McLachlan whose family owns a substantial slice of South Australia'.

The next day the Coalition parties were to meet to determine their final position on Mabo, Richard Court was in Canberra to address the National Press Club and lobby the Coalition. As expected, he predicted the end of Australia as we know it if the government's legislation was passed. He alluded once more to secession: 'if you are going to have a federal government that starts using every possible loophole . . . to continually erode the position of the States, the end result of that is that the federation splits up'. He asserted that his legislation would allow development to proceed while protecting the interests of Aboriginal people.

The position reached in the Shadow Cabinet at its meeting, however, appeared to satisfy both the Liberal wets and the hardliners. The policy unanimously agreed left it to the states to develop their own legislation to deal with native title as long as they complied with the

RDA. During the day the Opposition party room had heard addresses from Daryl Williams, Lois O'Donoghue, Richard Court, AMIC, the NFF and Commonwealth officials. The next day the joint parties met and endorsed the Shadow Cabinet position and that night John Hewson delivered his address to the nation.

The Coalition policy was, of course, no policy at all except for the unanimous affirmation that Mabo should be left to the states, that is, it was essentially a states' rights issue. The cop-out for the genuine liberals in the party was to assert that some of the Mabo opponents had genuine questions and concerns that could legitimately be raised. The Shadow Cabinet plan was to refer the legislation to a Senate Select Committee and to stir up as much dissent as possible in an attempt to derail it.

Effectively the Coalition had dealt itself out of the game. By deciding to oppose the legislation *in toto* rather than consider amendments, it had given the whip hand to Aboriginal people and their supporters in the ALP, the Democrats and the Greens. John Hewson did his best to dress up the Coalition decision, suggesting that it was 'a just and workable alternative'. He foreshadowed the Coalition strategy:

> In view of the fact that there is massive and growing uncertainty in the community about the implications of the High Court's Mabo decision, and given that the Prime Minister has raised expectations unjustifiably and has divided Australia over this issue, the Coalition will seek a full Senate Inquiry into the legislation . . . [to] enable interested groups, who have been excluded from negotiations to date, to express their views.

The outcome was a victory for the hardliners. If a Coalition government had been in power at this time there would have been no national response to Mabo. The outcome would have sunk as low as the most belligerent anti-Aboriginal state government would have taken it. The process of reconciliation would have been destroyed and Australia's international standing would have been in tatters.

The Coalition's decision was compounded by John Hewson's address on television that night in his right of reply to the Prime Minister. He used the opportunity to make his own high-profile contribution to the campaign of fear and loathing, saying that 'in good faith we have bought homes and farms and opened mines and businesses, absolutely confident that we could own them and operate them without legal challenge'—as if the rights of ownership of any other Australians were at risk as a result of the High Court decision or the government's proposals. It was a 'them and us' address, suggesting that 'while Aboriginal people want the land they are entitled to, other Australians want to be sure they do indeed own their own home'.

I responded by accusing John Hewson of reaching an unprecedented moral low in which he tried the 'your backyards are not safe' approach. I said that in view of the Coalition position 'it was now even more imperative that the Western Australian Greens, the Australian Democrats and Brian Harradine give this vital legislation their support'. The Opposition call for a Senate Select Committee inquiry into the government's legislation was a hoax as they 'will never support the government's legislation anyway'. Speaking from Los Angeles, the Prime Minister accused Dr Hewson of a lack of leadership and appealed to the Democrats and the Greens to reject a Senate inquiry.

The Democrats announced that they would not support the Coalition in referring the legislation to a Senate Select Committee but would 'support a review of certain aspects of the Bill by the Senate's Legal and Constitutional Affairs Committee'. Wayne Goss withheld his support for the Bill, telling parliament that it was complex, difficult to understand and poorly drafted and that 'both the Commonwealth and the States may face administrative difficulties in administering it'.

On 19 November, a number of key industry groups placed a large advertisement in the *West Australian* directed to ALP federal members and senators which sought to make out a special case for Western Australia being the state the hardest 'hit' by the 'Commonwealth's Mabo solution'. The advertisement urged MPs to 'keep the administration of Western Australian land and natural resources in Western Australia'. Mining industry pressure intensified, with AMIC and the WA Chamber of Mines and Energy issuing a media release two days later announcing the result of a public opinion poll, apparently conducted at their request, which suggested that 76 per cent of the 1200 people polled around Australia said that 'people should be treated equally in terms of land title', with only 1 per cent supporting different rights for native title holders. The absurdity of asking people whether native title holders should have rights of permanent ownership is beyond comprehension. The High Court had already said these rights existed, and no amount of polling on behalf of incompetent industry organisations would make these rights disappear.

The next day in the *Age*, Henry Reynolds published an article critical of the WA legislation, which would extinguish native title. He surveyed the history of WA colonial governments attacking Aboriginal rights, often against the wishes of the colonial office in London and also out of step with the treatment of indigenous people in comparable legislatures in northern America and New Zealand in the same era:

> Mr Court is the true child of his society. He has read his electorate
> well and there is strong support for his legislation. As on other
> occasions, as in 1850 and 1890, justice for the local Aborigines, if it is

ever to come at all, will have to be imposed from the outside . . . Left to their own devices, Western Australians are incapable of meeting that challenge even though it has confronted them since the first settlement on the Swan 164 years ago.

On 24 November the WA Greens made a bizarre contribution to the public debate, totally unhelpful to the Aboriginal cause and which exposed them to justifiable accusations of naive grandstanding. Senator Chamarette announced: 'The Greens (WA) Senators have delayed a decision on whether the Native Title Bill 1993 will be referred to a Senate Select Committee until 5 December to allow the Government and the Opposition time to consider supporting a piece of "holding legislation"'. This was a five-clause bill, retrospective to 1 July, which states that until the federal parliament provides otherwise, 'No law of the Commonwealth or of a State or Territory enacted after 1 July 1993 was capable of extinguishing or modifying native title'. This ludicrous proposal would retrospectively nullify mining and other interests already granted and effectively bring to a halt land management around Australia. Nothing could have been more calculated to create a public backlash that would completely derail the Commonwealth response.

At the Greens' press conference that day Senator Chamarette made it clear that the Greens 'definitely cannot support [the legislation] in its current form' and indicated that they supported the 'direction' of amendments put forward that morning by a delegation of Aboriginal people led by Michael Mansell (the B Team). The delegation had also met with the Prime Minister. Members of the B Team described themselves as the Aboriginal Alliance and included the self-styled Aboriginal Provisional Government, headed by Michael Mansell, and the NSW Aboriginal Land Council, headed by Aden Ridgeway. Paul Keating had already indicated that the government would not accept some of these proposals, including one that Aboriginal people would have mineral rights and an absolute right of veto. But under questioning from the media, Senator Chamarette still would not indicate in what circumstances the Greens would support the legislation.

Lois O'Donoghue had been present at the media conference at Parliament House and was outraged by Senator Chamarette's comments. After the Greens' media conference she seized the moment to respond. I think it is important to make clear to people who have not met Lois that she is a quietly spoken, gracious, warm and friendly person. She is no political radical and no grandstander. She told the media that 'the Greens have hijacked Aboriginal authority today and I am extremely disappointed . . . I am really devastated'. She defended the representative nature of the negotiators who had dealt with the

Prime Minister and made the point that the level of community awareness of legislation going through parliament was low in both the indigenous and the non-indigenous communities. She asked, 'Do we expect all Australians to understand every detail of every legislation that goes through this House?' She stressed that it was crucial that the legislation was passed before Christmas.

Then one of the other Aboriginal negotiators, Marcia Langton, a very strong woman and chair of AIATSIS, told the assembled media that it was 'naïve in the extreme for Senators Chamarette and Margetts to believe that they are allowing for the expression of Aboriginal views by playing into the hands of mining companies', and hammering home the point that, without federal legislation, 'native title will be extinguished everywhere. The mining companies will do us over'. Rob Riley, who by now understood the advanced and progressive nature of the government's proposals, warned that 'Aboriginal rights would be absolutely slaughtered' unless they passed the Bill.

After the Greens' media conference the Prime Minister issued a statement making the point that 'those trying to turn the screws on the government in relation to the Native Title Act are playing into the hands of the opponents of justice for Aboriginal people and a sound and workable outcome on Mabo'. He did not directly attack the Greens. He said the government was prepared to consider proposals that would improve the Bill but would 'not accept any proposal which is outside the policy parameters to which the government is totally committed'.

Not surprisingly, neither the government nor the Coalition would support the Greens' proposed 'holding' legislation.

On the evening of 25 November, the Native Title Bill passed through the House of Representatives, with the Prime Minister and the Leader of the Opposition trading insults across the dispatch boxes. Meanwhile, in Western Australia the Legislative Council guillotined the WA government's legislation—the first time in 100 years that such an action had been taken. In the House of Representatives, the Prime Minister was particularly scathing in his attack on the WA government and the complicity of the federal Opposition in their actions.

On Saturday, 27 November, the *Canberra Times* reported that the Green senators had strengthened the likelihood that they would eventually oppose the Native Title Bill, with Senator Chamarette declaring to the bewilderment of most Aboriginal people: 'I know that holding high moral principles means that I might make a decision that other people have to wear the cost of, and I'm very painfully aware that it will be the Aboriginal people who suffer'.

It was apparent from the Greens' public statements that they were proposing to side with the worst elements of the Coalition to refer the Bill to a Senate Select Committee that would not report until late February.

The Greens were, however, coming under a lot of pressure and even sections of their own party were speaking out against their actions. The Richmond Clarence Greens from northern New South Wales dissociated themselves and asserted that the two senators 'are not representative of the policies or wishes of Green supporters and are bringing the Green movement into public disrepute'. They supported Lois O'Donoghue's view that the Green senators had 'hijacked Aboriginal authority'.

On 29 November Paul Keating appeared on the ABC program *Lateline* and said in response to a question:

> I think the Greens are standing four square against the best interests of the Aboriginal and Torres Strait Islander community of this country . . . In the end nobody can go hiding. [The Greens] are going to have to sit on the side of the chamber where they believe their interests are, but if they sit on the side of the chamber of the Coalition they will have the result—they will have to live with it for the rest of their days.

The next day Senator Chamarette rejected this criticism, indicating that she and Dee Margetts opposed the Bill being rushed through the parliament and said the 'fundamental question is whether an inadequate Keating Bill is better than no Bill at all' and that 'the major sticking points with the Native Title Bill concern the Racial Discrimination Act, validation of past potentially discriminatory acts, negotiating rights, the reversal of the onus of proof and the proposed social justice package'. Another sticking point for the Greens was that native title should not be extinguished to protect pastoral leases that were potentially invalid but were being validated by the government's legislation. Although only a handful of potential native title interests Australia-wide were affected by this issue, to the Greens it was so important, we are led to believe, that they would have been prepared to vote down the entire Bill. My difference with the Greens was less to do with policy than with the sectarian nature of the tactics they adopted.

The Greens argued that their first test was that the whole of the Native Title Bill needed to be subject to the RDA. Then they argued that there should be a right to negotiate if land was being set aside for 'a town site, State forest or national park' and expressed concern that there were no details on the funding or operation of the proposed land fund in the Native Title Bill. Finally, Senator Chamarette argued that there had been a lack of consultation. Instead of immediately supporting Coalition calls for a special Senate Select Committee, the Greens voted to refer the Bill to the Senate Legal and Constitutional Affairs Committee, chaired by Senator Barney Cooney.

Wayne Goss then introduced Queensland's native title legislation into parliament, and the Prime Minister issued a statement congratulating him, saying that 'Queensland is a case study in how States and Territories can work effectively with the Commonwealth legislation. It is proof that cooperation can work'. The next day Wayne Goss made what the *Australian* described as 'an extraordinary attack' on the Commonwealth's Bill, saying that Queensland held a range of concerns about 'the practical viability of key aspects of the legislation' that needed to be addressed in the Senate debate. He recorded his government's concerns, some of which went to the very essence of the agreement reached between the Prime Minister and Aboriginal negotiators, including concern about the native title claims to land in Aboriginal ownership which, Queensland asserted, 'might have a cumulative effect on the viability of the pastoral industry' in a region.

With the passage of the WA legislation on 2 December, Aboriginal activist Rob Riley said he 'felt numb and ashamed to be a Western Australian' and he urged the quick passage of the Commonwealth Bill. Rob was a gentle, sensitive person who took a front-line position in the struggle for rights of his people because he believed he had to. Like other Aboriginal people in this position, he paid a high price, mentally and physically. In Western Australia especially, Aboriginal leaders face constant attacks from politicians, the mining and pastoral industry, and the media. In 1996, as I was driving across Australia after my defeat at the election, I heard that Rob had died by his own hand in a lonely motel room. I was struck numb with grief and attended the memorial service for him in Perth, sitting quietly by myself at the back of the cathedral, which was packed with mourners from all walks of life. Down in the front of the cathedral sat Richard Court.

Aboriginal people in Western Australia wasted no time in launching a challenge to Premier Court's legislation; the Kimberley Land Council began High Court proceedings less than 24 hours after the law came into force.

Pressure on the WA Greens intensified. Eleven Aboriginal organisations from Western Australia wrote urging them to pass the Native Title Bill, making the point that they 'disagreed with the few individuals who are advising you to delay passage of the federal Bill for several months' and stressing their belief that 'our interests are best served by the immediate passage of the federal Bill. We are very concerned that while the Western Australian Greens procrastinate over the federal Bill, the Western Australian Government will act to extinguish native title and continue to create fear and hysteria towards our families'. The Greens were also urged by both the Australian Council of Churches and Community Aid Abroad to support the legislation. But Senator Chamarette stood firm, saying on 6 December: 'My conscience won't allow me to be a party to rush this most crucial Bill through into law without it being better understood—not just by those debating the Bill in parliament but by those whom it most deeply affects'.

When the Senate Legal and Constitutional Affairs Committee met in Canberra, the result was the inevitable public disagreement between the A and B Teams. Michael Mansell told the committee that the Bill gave fewer rights to Aboriginal people than those recognised in the Murray Islands by the High Court in the Mabo case. The committee reported to the Senate on Thursday, 9 December, and, as expected, divided on party lines. Senator Cooney made the point that while the Bill was not perfect and there would be amendments, it was important that it be passed to avoid the consensus breaking down. The Labor members were joined by Democrat Senator Sid Spindler; the three Coalition members dissented and were critical of the Bill, arguing for a full Senate Select Committee inquiry.

In the lead-up to the Senate vote that would determine whether the Bill was referred to a Senate Select Committee, the government carefully considered the likely numbers. If the Greens voted with the Coalition, the proposal could be defeated if Brian Harradine voted with the government. Behind the scenes, a great deal of attention was paid to Senator Harradine—not for the first or last time. Not many people knew that Lois O'Donoghue had been a school classmate of a much younger Brian Harradine. In any event, a deeply committed Catholic like Senator Harradine was no doubt aware of the strong stand taken in recent years by his church, and particularly during the Mabo debate in support of Aboriginal rights to justice. As it turned out, his vote was not crucial.

In the countdown to that vote the mining industry cranked up the pressure. At AMIC's initiative a letter was sent to government ministers from fifteen chief executives of major mining companies operating in Australia and subsequently published in the *Canberra Times*. It was interesting to see some familiar names emerging in this advertisement: John Quinn of Newcrest, whose company had been involved in the Coronation Hill dispute with Aboriginal people; Norm Fussell, whose company had been in dispute with Aboriginal people at McArthur River, which had so adversely affected the Mabo debate; John Ralph of CRA, which had been so effective in pushing governments around over the Wik claim; and anti-Mabo propagandist Hugh Morgan of Western Mining. The advertisement pushed the now familiar line that the Native Title Bill was 'extraordinarily complex and unworkable' and that the government should get accord with the states and territories before proceeding.

The motion for the Bill to be referred to a Senate Select Committee was moved by Liberal Senator Robert Hill. Brian Harradine, the two Green senators and the Democrats voted with the government to reject it. Senator Chamarette indicated her reasons for 'unhappily' rejecting it as including a concern about racial vilification against Aboriginal people and the time-wasting tactics of the Coalition. This vote in the Senate was a crucial turning point and in some ways diminished the capacity of the Greens to bargain with the government for what could have been constructive amendments on important issues, for example to enhance the role of the Commonwealth in the determination of native title.

The Saturday morning papers on 11 December reported a major initiative by John Hewson to build a public campaign against the Native Title Bill. He had warned the day before that 'now is the time for Australians who are concerned about it, that feel the legislation is against the national interest . . . to speak out'. He said that if the Bill was passed it would be 'one of the greatest debacles to hit this country in decades'.

Debate on the Bill finally began in the Senate late on Tuesday, 14 December, with the Greens originally proposing 83 amendments, the Democrats more than 30 and the government 38 amendments of its own. The Opposition position was extremely negative; Opposition members resolved to oppose every amendment and then to vote against the Bill. In the words of Peter Reith, the Opposition was 'opposed to amending legislation which is rotten to the core'. This decision had been taken by the Shadow Cabinet on the Monday and endorsed by the party room with little or no dissent. The obvious tactic of the Coalition was to engage in filibustering to prevent the Bill being passed by the parliament before it rose for the Christmas recess. In other words, it was a spoiling role. The lines were drawn for what was at that time the Australian parliamentary debate of the century, lasting for 111 hours.

On 15 December the NFF went public, calling for the Opposition to support amendments to the Bill to advance the interests of farmers. Simon Crean tabled a letter from Gordon Blight to John Hewson urging the Coalition to support the NFF's amendments. As Rick Farley pointed out, 'the Opposition's tactics are likely to allow passage of the amendments sought by the Aborigines with support from the Greens and the Democrats, but prevent passage of amendments sought by the NFF, AMIC and the States because the Greens will not support such amendments'. Mr Blight warned that the NFF 'would find it astonishing if the Opposition allowed this scenario to unfold'.

But let it unfold they did. Peter Reith said that the NFF had been 'publicly boasting' that it had done a deal with the government and it was 'no good turning around now and saying to us that suddenly they have found something they don't like'. He confirmed that the Coalition would oppose the Bill and all amendments in their entirety. It was as if they had picked up their bat and ball and gone home. Thus the anti-Labor side of politics marginalised itself in one of the most important debates ever to come before parliament.

On 16 December a special Shadow Cabinet meeting rejected a proposal by Tim Fischer for the Coalition to modify its position of outright opposition to the Bill and amendments. The *Financial Review* reported the next day that this rejection was in part motivated by the threat by 'a number of senior Liberals including Ian McLachlan' to cross the floor if the Coalition changed its position and supported the amendments. Ian McLachlan, however, later denied this threat in a letter to the editor. As a former president of the NFF, he was no doubt outraged by its failure to follow the Coalition line.

That same afternoon Senator Gareth Evans, government Leader in the Senate, supported by Commonwealth officials, began a meeting in the packed conference room of his ministerial office. Alan Ramsey from the *Sydney Morning Herald* described the meeting in his column the following Saturday. Present were the A Team represented by David Ross and Marcia Langton, and the B Team led by Michael Mansell. They were also supported by two legal advisers, Ron Castan QC and Bryan Keon-Cohen, both of whom had been involved in the presenta-tion of the Mabo case to the High Court. Also present was Christabel Chamarette supported by two advisers. The Democrats were repre-sented by Cheryl Kernot and Sid Spindler. The meeting went on for almost seven hours as the parties worked through the provisions of the Bill. At times the debate became acrimonious, with Senator Chamarette threatening to call a late-night press conference, called off at the last minute after some heavy persuasion from Gareth Evans. Despite a great deal of progress being made, the senator was still playing the wild card and the next morning went on *AM* expressing strong criticism of the Bill.

The Greens raised four specific concerns about the Bill as it then stood. First, there was a concern that 'State and Territory laws of general application will not have to take native title into account and they will prevail over native title'. Second, 'renewal of old acts are allowed to proceed with little capacity for a native title holder to assert their native title'. Third was the question of Aboriginal people who have lived on pastoral leases since before they became pastoral leases; Senator Chamarette argued that if native title is not allowed to coexist with pastoral leases there was a 'danger of these people being thrown off their land'. Finally, she expressed concern about extensions of the period of mining leases, 'which were not part of the original negotiated agreement'. Again, there was no reference to the need for a greater role for the Commonwealth in the determination of native title.

Debate resumed in the Senate on Friday afternoon, 17 December, and continued with a special sitting of parliament on Saturday, and still the rest of the country was in the dark about what the Green senators were going to do. There was high drama even over amendments that were peripheral to the crucial principles of the legislation. The Saturday sitting created mayhem for those responsible for organising travel and other arrangements for MPs and senators. By Saturday there were some 250 amendments to be dealt with. At times the debate became very tense.

At 9.30 that night there were near fisticuffs between Liberal Senator Ian Campbell and National Party Senator Julian McGauran, one of the National Party senators to vote in support of amendments to advantage the mining and pastoral industries. During the debate that night, reportedly with the agreement of their own party, Julian McGauran and two other National Party senators, Bill O'Chee and Sandy McDonald, both from Queensland, crossed the floor to vote with the government for these amendments, which failed to pass after the Democrats and the Greens voted with other Opposition senators against them.

This was an unbelievably stupid tactic for the Coalition since their agenda was to stop the legislation by any means possible. Had they voted for the amendments it was highly likely that their passage would have caused the Greens to join them to vote down the Bill as a whole. The first amendment would have provided more certainty for the mining industry, substantially reducing the likelihood, in Bill O'Chee's words, 'of miners having to undergo multiple hearings before an arbitral body before developing a mine when they had already received permission to explore'. The second amendment was 'to have provided certainty for pastoralists by allowing the renewal of existing pastoral leases in the event that native title coexisted with the lease. The National Party Senators', he said, 'had been advised by industry groups that their three votes were all that was needed to assure the passage of these amendments'. The Democrats, to their great credit, failed to support the amendments as expected. They had in fact voted down some amendments they could otherwise live with in order to save the Bill as a whole from being voted down by the Greens.

As a result of the defeat of the amendment to benefit the farming lobby, Rick Farley issued a statement in which he called the Bill 'unacceptable and unworkable' and explained that the failed amendment was to ensure that valid leases could be renewed or regranted without any need to negotiate terms and conditions with native title holders. As things then stood, the only leases that could be renewed automatically were those 'where there was a largely unenforceable right to renew that was created before 1 January 1994, or where no native title existed'. He accused the government of failing to deliver on its commitments 'despite the best efforts of the National Party': 'Personally I feel betrayed, bitter and foolish. It is hard to escape the conclusion that trade-offs occurred at meetings between Gareth Evans, Aboriginal representatives, the Democrats and Greens last Thursday night—meetings from which industry was excluded'. Cheryl Kernot denied any deals and indicated that while she could support a key amendment as it related to pastoralists she could not do so for miners.

The Senate resumed sitting on Monday, 20 December, at 8 p.m. for what would then be the 54th hour of debate on the Bill and its 28th hour in the detailed committee stages. The mood was growing for the Bill to be pushed through the parliament, and the Coalition obstruction voted down. To achieve their purpose of filibuster and delay, the Opposition had organised nine 'tag' teams of senators to oppose each group of amendments.

Earlier in the day the Coalition speakers in the parliament were given support by the Coalition speakers outside parliament with a joint statement of conservative leaders. Parties to the statement were John Hewson, the premiers of Victoria, New South Wales, Western Australia, South Australia and Tasmania, and the Acting Chief Minister of the Northern Territory. The statement called on the Bill to be delayed until the new year. Meanwhile the Prime Minister threatened that the parliament would continue to sit, even on Christmas Eve and Boxing Day, for as long as it took to pass the native title legislation.

The best account of what happened then was written by Margot Kingston of the *Canberra Times*, who was very close to the Greens. Apparently Senator Chamarette and her offsider, Cathcart Weatherly, went back to her office where they met Noel Pearson. Then Ron Castan wandered in and drafted a clause which was intended to meet both the farmers' concerns and protect Aboriginal interests. By some accounts, the idea for the clause came from Richard Court's WA Bill, which included the idea that while native title did not exist, traditional use rights continued. There had been discussions on these kinds of issues within the government for some time.

After drafting the possible new clause, Ron Castan tried to reach Rick Farley to clear it with him, but Rick was uncontactable. Then because of the lateness of the hour (1 a.m., Tuesday morning), Senator Chamarette voted with the Opposition to adjourn the Senate until the next day. The next morning Rick Farley agreed to the clause and the deal was on to move the guillotining. But then Cathcart Weatherly discovered that the government had changed, without consultation, an agreed amendment preserving indigenous hunting and fishing rights, apparently allowing a state government to declare any endangered species, for example a platypus, proscribed and so defeat the intention of the clause.

There was apparently no intention on the part of the drafters to subvert the amendment, nor was there any risk of indigenous people mindlessly wiping out endangered species, but the Greens were sufficiently concerned about possible abuse of power by recalcitrant state governments to seek to totally constrain their powers. Gareth Evans was about to announce the guillotine when Christabel Chamarette told him about the problem and said the deal was off. Gareth hit the roof. An adviser was told to run to the drafters in the room next to the Senate Chamber with the message, 'Gareth says, stuff the platypus'. This hiccup resolved, the deal was on and the native title legislation was on its way.

After the breakthrough a wave of elation, relief and optimism swept over all those hundreds of people who had given so much in 1993 to make the Native Title Bill a reality. Cheryl Kernot let it be known that before the debate concluded she would be moving a technical amendment to ensure validity of all pastoral lease titles, as sought by the NFF. Triumphantly, all of us could rally around the achievement which saw the amendment agreed by the government, the WA Greens and the Aboriginal negotiating teams. The Prime Minister held a media conference which he began by noting that:

> The imminent passage of the Native Title Bill will be a great day for indigenous Australians . . . and I hope a great turning point in their recent history. . .
>
> This has been the longest continuing problem that Australia has faced now for over 200 years recognising that indigenous people, that native people had a right to their own soil. It is the end of the great lie of *terra nullius* and the beginning, we hope, of a new deal, the basis of social justice and reconciliation. A real basis for reconciliation . . .
> In that sense [it is] a turning point for all Australians, something that should raise our self esteem and our pride in this democracy of ours. The important thing is I think it has been a triumph of good will and cooperation between Australians.

John Hewson's press conference on the eve of the passage of the native title legislation could not have stood in starker contrast. 'This is a day of shame for the Australian Parliament', he said. He issued a threat on behalf of the conservative parties which they attempted to carry to fruition: 'Mr Keating has said today that the Mabo debate has ended. Well, I reject that view entirely. Today is not an end to the Mabo debate, but only the beginning of a new stage in that debate. The Opposition will make the Government's unjust, divisive and damaging Mabo legislation a major issue right up until the next election'. He could well have added 'and will seek to use Aboriginal issues ruthlessly as a party-political football until the next election and beyond', for that is exactly what the Coalition did, and ever more so when John Howard ultimately assumed the Liberal Party leadership. Aboriginal people had a great victory with the passage of the native title legislation, but the conservative parties were about to make them pay for it.

John Hewson went on to claim that the Native Title Bill was 'an unprincipled piece of legislation which has lost sight of what Australia is about—a united and democratic country in which all our people are equal before the law'. In other words, he was going out of his way to suggest that Aboriginal people were now in some privileged position before the law, which of course they were not. He further stated:

> This is an excessive piece of legislation because it goes way beyond what the High Court decided and establishes rights in law that the High Court never envisaged . . . It's legislation that typifies the weakness of the Prime Minister and the extent to which he has capitulated to Labor's Left and to the Democrats and the Greens who are even further to the left.

Debate on the legislation continued; then finally the last vote came in the Senate in the early hours of the morning of 22 December. As the vote was taken, and along with hundreds of other people in the packed galleries of the Senate in Parliament House, I stood shoulder to shoulder with other Australians, both indigenous and non-indigenous, and gave a standing ovation for our country. We had won. The legislation had passed through the Senate.

People wept, hugged, clapped and cheered. Down below, the Labor senators, Democrats, Greens and Brian Harradine joined in the celebrations. I remember Gareth Evans going up to Cheryl Kernot and giving her a hug and a kiss on the cheek, while opposite the Coalition senators looked bewildered and disgruntled as the cheers and applause of the packed public galleries and press gallery resounded through the Senate Chamber.

The next day, the legislation passed through the House of Representatives with a commitment of the government to have it operating,
at least in a preliminary way, by 1 January 1994. Its passage was greeted
with overwhelming approval by Aboriginal people, Lois O'Donoghue
saying it was a 'watershed for Australia' and 'the greatest proof yet of
the probability of reconciliation. It transforms reconciliation into a
tangible reality'. Early in the new year, Justice Robert French, a judge
of the Federal Court of Australia, was appointed by Attorney-General
Michael Lavarch as the president of the newly established Native Title
Tribunal after the interim presidency of Justice Jane Mathews, head of
the Administrative Appeals Tribunal.

So the deed was done. We got there with political blood spilt all
over the place, with all the highs and lows imaginable in what many
of us had seen as a defining moment in Australian history. The Native
Title Act would not have been achieved without Paul Keating's courageous leadership. Nor would it have been achieved without the direct
contribution of many other people and, most importantly, without the
courage and integrity of the indigenous people in the front line of the
struggle for justice.

In the aftermath of the 1996 election defeat there were some in
the Labor Party who criticised the emphasis given by Paul Keating and
other ministers to the government's response as a priority issue. Apart
from the issues of high Labor principle at stake, the reality was that
the question of Labor's response was so challenging and so important
for Australia that it demanded a substantial commitment of resources
and time.

There were times when all appeared to be lost, when the government was heading in a direction which appeared to favour state and
territory governments and industry interests. There were other times
when the debate was derailed by decisions on McArthur River and the
Wik claim, when commercial interests seemed to dominate the debate.
But we got there. We got there because there was a political movement
of Australians, led by indigenous people, who were not prepared to
lose. Australia had taken a huge step down the path to reconciliation.

11

LAND FOR THE DISPOSSESSED

An overwhelming majority of Aboriginal people did not gain any rights of ownership of land flowing from the decision of the High Court in the Mabo case. They had been dispossessed of their land absolutely as a result of policies of successive governments which failed to recognise their native title to the land. As a result they did not continue to enjoy the requisite degree of attachment to the land required to satisfy the Mabo principles.

Previous attempts had been made at the national level to address some of the land needs of dispossessed Aboriginal people, but they had not involved a legislated guarantee of long-term funding such as the Indigenous Land Fund the Keating government proposed establishing as its second-stage response to Mabo.

The fight for the passage of this legislation through the Australian parliament was again to see attempts by the Opposition to frustrate its passage at every turn. During the course of events the Leader of the Opposition, Alexander Downer—who had replaced John Hewson in May 1994—was to lose his leadership position, largely because of his failings on Aboriginal policy, and was replaced by John Howard in early 1995.

In a last-minute about-face the Opposition dropped its campaign against the legislation and the Indigenous Land Fund was established with a secure legislated funding base protecting it from what would have been almost certain demolition by the future Howard Coalition government. The Australian government's Mabo response is an unfinished business and will not be complete until the third-stage social justice measures are implemented by a future government.

———

Aboriginal people were determined not to waste the political opportunity presented by the convergence of the Mabo decision and a sympathetic Labor government in Canberra to move the country in the direction of a long-term and durable negotiated resolution of Aboriginal grievances. Paul Keating's justly acclaimed speech

in Redfern Park on 10 December 1992 at the Australian launch of the
UN International Year of the World's Indigenous Peoples was, however,
not the only important political speech made that day.

Commissioner Sol Bellear, ATSIC's elected deputy chair, delivered
a speech in Redfern Park supporting the rights of the overwhelming
majority of Aboriginal people, whose absolute dispossession and loss
of the necessary links with the land meant that the Mabo decision,
while of crucial historical significance, would not deliver ownership of
land without a negotiated political settlement. When calling for the
establishment of a national land fund, he said:

> Too few of our brothers and sisters living in Sydney and Melbourne,
> Brisbane, Perth, Adelaide and Hobart will be able to prove their native
> title to land under the restrictive conditions of the Mabo decision . . .
> A national land acquisition fund would complement the pursuit of land
> rights through legislation and the courts by providing Aboriginal
> people with much greater means to purchase lands and buildings . . .
> and would provide the foundation upon which Aboriginal people,
> Australian Governments and the wider community could build a new
> partnership.

Lois O'Donoghue reinforced the message, speaking on the same day
before the UN General Assembly in New York at the launch of the
International Year of the World's Indigenous Peoples.

In the days following, Commissioner David Ross, one of the
appointed ATSIC commissioners but never any pawn of the Labor
government, kept up the pressure when responding to the Prime
Minister's speech, stressing that the government agenda had 'got to
be more than just a statement' and that the government could 'kiss
goodbye' to reconciliation unless it provided more money to buy land
for dispossessed Aboriginal people.

There had been a roller-coaster history of attempts by federal
governments to make provision for land acquisition by dispossessed
Aboriginal people, beginning with tentative steps by the McMahon
Coalition government in the early 1970s. None of these initiatives,
however, had provided Aboriginal people with a secure ongoing source
of funding.

In May 1975 the Whitlam Labor government had established the
Aboriginal Land Fund Commission. The commission suffered from
continued attacks on its funding by Treasury and Finance. With its
abolition in July 1980, the baton for land acquisition funding was
passed to the Aboriginal Development Commission (ADC). Again, this
organisation did not have a secure legislated funding base.

The ADC became embroiled in numerous parliamentary committees of inquiry and finally erupted in open conflict with the Hawke

government's proposal to establish ATSIC, which was intended to take over most of its functions, including that of land acquisition. The newly established Aboriginal and Torres Strait Islander Commercial Development Corporation was to take over the function of major funding for significant commercial projects.

In 1983 the Wran government, with Frank Walker as Minister for Aboriginal Affairs, passed the *NSW Land Rights Act 1983*, which created a land acquisition fund with a guaranteed funding level based on a designated proportion of land tax collected in the state. While disagreeing with aspects of the NSW government's bill, I strongly endorsed the concept of locking in by legislation the future funding for land acquisition, knowing from my own early experience how important such a fund was to dispossessed Aboriginal people.

Growing up on the north coast of New South Wales and later working with the Aboriginal Legal Service taught me to respect and understand the position of Aboriginal people whose lives were most heavily affected by colonisation. Aboriginal people in the eastern states have been almost completely dispossessed of their traditional lands. Many have lived a marginalised life on the edge of country towns or in the isolation of the city, with dismal prospects of employment and education and limited life opportunities. They are nevertheless a strong people, proud of their identity and heritage and determined to build a future. Essential to that future is an economic base, of which land is a primary component.

Although Labor's national platform had recognised the effects of dispossession and the need for compensation, the Hawke government's proposals for a national Aboriginal land rights initiative were fatally flawed, not only because they proposed a watering down of the NT Land Rights Act and as a result drew opposition from Aboriginal people in the Northern Territory, but because they failed to address the position of dispossessed people who could not sustain a claim of continuing traditional association with the land. For this reason the 1985 national land rights proposals were opposed by most indigenous people across Australia as manifestly inadequate. Any legislative response to the Mabo decision would be equally inadequate and would be rejected by indigenous people unless the rights of the dispossessed were addressed in the government's response, as David Ross had so effectively highlighted.

In 1986, as a backbench member of the government's Aboriginal Affairs Committee, I had prepared and publicly advocated a proposal for a national Aboriginal land fund based on compensation for lost land. A paper prepared with the assistance of the Parliamentary Library and circulated to Caucus colleagues advocated that 'the fund would be established by the Commonwealth government with funds to be set

Aboriginal unemployment

Aboriginal unemployment levels remain four or five times above those in the non-indigenous community. In many communities the unemployment rate is virtually 100 per cent. There are no quick fixes for unemployment, any more than for Aboriginal health or education. Some matters are, however, beyond dispute and the first is that Aboriginal people do want to work. During the time of the Labor government there were over 260 Aboriginal communities across Australia where people work in the CDEP in order to receive money they would otherwise receive as unemployment benefits. In most of these communities, especially those in remote locations, there are no jobs—not even tourism and mining are options—but the people wish to remain in their traditional country. CDEP puts people to work in community improvement projects and has the potential to boost skills and enhance self-esteem and self-reliance, but the scheme is in need of reform to boost training opportunities and income levels.

It is particularly challenging to find private sector jobs for indigenous people in remote communities. The best options appear to be a revitalised and enhanced CDEP scheme, or the generation of jobs in the mining, tourism and arts and craft industries. Comparisons with the record of the mining industry in other countries show that the Australian industry is far behind the international standard. Although the Ok Tedi Mine run by BHP in PNG has been rightly criticised for its environmental record, the level of indigenous employment in that mine is in the order of 90 per cent No mining company operating in Australia comes anywhere near this.

RCIADIC recommended that, while Aboriginal employment remained low in the private sector, indigenous employment in the public sector should be boosted. There have been significant achievements in increasing indigenous employment in the Commonwealth Public Service, and with Commonwealth support, agreements have been reached to improve state government performance under the Commonwealth's Aboriginal Employment Development Policy and to boost Aboriginal employment in local government.

The cuts to programs in the early years of the Howard government made Aboriginal employment prospects even worse. I am, however, encouraged by the apparent reversal in government thinking by Minister Peter Reith in 1999, which appears to show a genuine commitment to consultation and to reversing some of the worst expenditure cuts.

aside for the purchase of land on the open market for Aboriginal groups, both rural and urban . . . A national fund would ensure that [urban Aboriginal people's] need is given national recognition and restitution made'.

An initial allocation was proposed to be supplemented by annual allocations over the succeeding ten years. Future governments would be locked in by legislation, which would require a set schedule of funds to be appropriated. Later, in 1992, in negotiations with ATSIC commissioners on the response to RCIADIC, I had tried unsuccessfully to get support for the establishment of a legislated land fund. Following the Mabo decision I sought to push the idea of a national land acquisition fund in the bureaucracy, at the parliamentary level and among Aboriginal leaders. Three months after the Mabo decision, in September 1992, I had sought formal discussions with Peter Shergold to advance the proposal for such a fund. A month later, on 22 October, I cautioned 'against the mistaken public perception that following the Mabo decision the solution to Aboriginal land ownership was now entirely with the courts' and stressed that the 'Mabo principles' would not help most Aboriginal people, whose dispossession had been absolute. Action by governments was urged to give effect to the RCIADIC recommendations on land, which had stressed the importance of acquiring land for the dispossessed.

During the Mabo debate, in 1993, when dispossessed Aboriginal people made ambit claims over land, with no prospects of success, I continued to argue, both inside the government and publicly, for the establishment of a national land acquisition fund to address their rights. There was no doubt that the leadership of key Aboriginal organisations recognised the importance of such a fund, and it became a consistent demand to government throughout 1993. Ultimately a commitment was given by the government to establish such a fund as the second part of its three-stage response to Mabo, and such a commitment was insisted on by the Aboriginal negotiators. The preamble to the Native Title Act states: 'It is also important to recognise that many Aboriginal peoples and Torres Strait Islanders, because they have been dispossessed of their traditional lands, will be unable to assert native title rights and interests and that a special fund needs to be established to assist them to acquire land'.

There was never any doubt in my mind that the government would support the establishment of a land fund. I cannot remember a single occasion when any opposition to its establishment was raised by a Labor minister during the entire time of the native title debate. The Labor side of politics understood just how crucial the establishment of such a fund was to reconciliation. Regrettably, the Coalition was to take a very different view.

Although there had been discussion on the proposed land fund during the native title negotiations, before introducing a bill into parliament the government consulted all ATSIC regional councils, legal services, land councils, organisations prescribed under the Native Title Act, and peak indigenous organisations to seek views on the structure and method of operation of the proposed fund. It also consulted peak industry, farming, mining, environmental and religious organisations.

On 11 and 18 April 1994, and again on 16 June, Paul Keating, Frank Walker and I met with representatives of major Aboriginal and Torres Strait Islander organisations to discuss the proposed legislation. There was a high degree of consensus about the main features of the legislation, but some changes were made to the government's plans because of concerns raised by indigenous representatives. Paul Keating was in a relaxed mood at the meetings and keen to adapt the land fund to meet indigenous aspirations. I recall that the NSW Aboriginal Land Council representative, Aden Ridgeway, indicated he did not agree with what was proposed but did not go into detail.

The ATSIC Amendment (Indigenous Land Corporation and Land Fund) Bill (Land Fund Bill) was introduced into the House of Representatives on 20 June 1994, with the intention that the debate be resumed in late August, allowing more time for public consideration. The Coalition had already expressed outright opposition. Ian McLachlan, speaking on the ABC's *Country Hour* on 13 May, said, 'I can promise you that Coalition policy is that the land fund will be opposed and that the native title Bill [*sic*] will be repealed'.

On 2 June Tim Fischer said on radio 4CA that

> Aboriginal people have large chunks of Australia [but] they are going on a buying spree additionally. I'm not opposed to Aborigines owning land—I agree they probably manage the land they own—but to descend down this path with a huge buying spree of a $1.5 billion nationwide land fund; I think it's a misplaced priority and I think it will add to the bureaucracy in Canberra.

And Alexander Downer, speaking on 2UE on 16 June in the familiar Coalition refrain, confirmed that the Opposition had 'said that all along that we would oppose the establishment of the fund because purchasing land isn't as big a priority as we see it as dealing with issues of Aboriginal health, education and housing'.

On 2 May I issued a public statement calling on the Coalition to support the land fund, saying that unanimous support 'would make a powerful contribution to the reconciliation process' and reminded them that 'Commonwealth commitment to addressing Aboriginal aspirations to land was a key legislative commitment unanimously given by the parliament in passing the Council for Aboriginal Reconciliation

Act in 1991'. The establishment of the Aboriginal Land Fund Commission during the Whitlam government had at that time received the unanimous support of parliament.

Alexander's Downer's hostility to the land fund was twenty years out of date; even William McMahon in 1972, before the election of the Whitlam government, was prepared to support Commonwealth funding for land acquisition by the states. In mid-March 1994, Fred Chaney had said, 'There has always been a need to show a bit of leadership and to stand up to those interests who would give Aboriginals nothing'. But still the Coalition continued its outright opposition.

During the month ahead, Alexander Downer's leadership was to be fatally weakened as a result of policy blunders in Aboriginal affairs, and the Coalition was left on the back foot on the land fund. My own involvement in the Opposition Leader's demise was bizarre as events unfolded because for much of the time I was on the other side of the world. These events gave me no feeling of triumph or satisfaction. I always found Alexander Downer to be a very reasonable person, but important principles were at stake.

I was aware that Mr Downer had given a commitment to repeal the Native Title Act in a formal interview with the *West Australian* on 9 June 1994. After this provocative statement I took up the issue in the House, emphasising that there had traditionally been a 'large measure of cross-party cooperation' in Aboriginal affairs and saying 'there would be nothing more damaging to the process of reconciliation and more damaging to Australia's international reputation than repealing the Native Title Act'.

I did everything I could that day to encourage the media to report on and follow up the *West Australian* story. All any journalist had to do was pick up the phone to indigenous leaders or any of the leadership of the Australian churches to get strong and principled responses in opposition to the Coalition's plans for the repeal of the Native Title Act. The story would have generated considerable interest in the climate then prevailing. But no one ran the story; it would not be the last time the media failed to pursue a crucial political issue in indigenous affairs. Determined not to let the matter rest, I sent letters to hundreds of leaders from the churches, trade unions and other key areas of public life seeking support for a campaign to urge Alexander Downer and the Coalition to reverse their policy to repeal the Native Title Act.

In a speech at the WA Conference of the Liberal Party on 31 July 1994, Mr Downer attacked the government's Aboriginal affairs policies, and again emphasised his commitment to repeal the Native Title Act:

> I sense at the moment there is a growing unease in some parts of our community about the Labor Government's shift in policy emphasis in

Aboriginal Affairs, particularly under Mr Tickner, who is obviously out of his depth. Mr Tickner, Mr Keating, the federal Government and a few of their strategically placed agitators seem to be trying to shift the concerns of Aboriginal people and the community away from Labor's failure to deal with the health problems, the education problems, the welfare problems, and the housing problems facing indigenous Australians—and they are trying to have everyone focus solely on who controls land.

Mr Downer spoke about his imminent trip to central Australia: 'I want to get information directly from those affected. Free from the lawyers, free from the TV and free from the manipulators'. Then he dropped a bombshell: 'When we win, we'll sit down with the States—especially with Richard Court and his team—and if we have to repeal the Act to achieve our goals, then that is what I will do'.

I was in London at the time, en route to attend the UN Working Group on Indigenous Populations (WGIP) in Geneva, and immediately drafted a comment for the Canberra Press Gallery:

Mr Downer's statement confirms all the worst fears, not only of Aboriginal people but of church and other community leaders. I could not think of a more damaging blow to the reconciliation process and to Australia's standing in the eyes of the world than the repealing of the Native Title Act. The Act is without doubt the most important Aboriginal human rights legislation passed by the Commonwealth using the power given to the parliament by the 1967 Referendum.

Although Mr Downer's comments were less clear than his earlier resolute commitment to repeal the Act, this time they were extensively reported. The issue had begun to gain momentum the week before when my letter to church and community leaders was reported in the *Australian* and elsewhere. Letters of support from the leaders of Australian churches for my campaign to get the Opposition to change its policy had already started to arrive. So when Mr Downer made his comments I was ready to respond. This time my comments were extensively reported in the national print media, and from London I gave several interviews to national radio networks.

It was important that the media accompanying Mr Downer to the Northern Territory kept up their questions on the Native Title Act. Several months earlier he had confused the Native Title Act with the NT Land Rights Act when speaking to ABC Radio in the Northern Territory. He had suggested that the Native Title Act gave a right of absolute veto when it only conferred a right to negotiate. He left for the Northern Territory without being properly briefed on key issues that would inevitably be raised by Aboriginal people and the media during his trip. It is not surprising that he made some blunders.

At Kintore in central Australia, in response to a press question on whether the Coalition intended to remove the veto in the NT Land Rights Act, he said, 'We have no plans to change the Act at all, none'. This was news to me as the federal minister who had endured four years of conservative and mining industry raving against the veto in the existing Act, despite the fact that the legislation had been introduced by the Fraser government in 1976. Four hours later, in Alice Springs, he was reverting to the longstanding Coalition policy: 'Well, we have an existing policy. I had something else on my mind when I was at the press conference. I mean, it was a very emotional time when we had been watching a corroboree and I think all of us felt strongly about that'.

According to media reports, the media contingent covering the tour knew that Mr Downer had first made his comments before the corroboree. That night his office issued a 'clarification statement' which further confused his position.

On *AM* the next morning, Mr Downer confirmed the content of his 'clarification statement'. The 1993 Coalition policy, while opposing a blanket veto, was to acknowledge the need for a one-off veto at the exploration stage to protect Aboriginal rights. This is exactly what the current provisions of the Act provide for and I pointed this out on the same program. Within 24 hours Mr Downer had moved from support for the single veto to apparent opposition to it and then back to explicit support for it. After this Alexander Downer's popularity dropped twenty points in the opinion polls and he was forced to announce a review of his indigenous affairs policy. Later, in parliament, I told members that he had undertaken the most infamous excursion into the inland since Burke and Wills.

Thus by late August 1994, with the Coalition's credibility on indigenous issues destroyed and the debate on the Land Fund Bill expected to be resumed on 31 August, there were signs of some of the more moderate elements in the Coalition attempting to reverse its opposition to the fund. On 24 August the Coalition's Immigration, Ethnic and Aboriginal Affairs Committee agreed to support it.

Lois O'Donoghue also tried to put pressure on the Coalition by issuing a statement on the weekend before the land fund was to be debated, reminding it that it had 'dealt itself out of the native title debate last year through its total opposition and was in danger of doing the same thing in relation to the land fund. Despite Coalition claims to the contrary', she said, 'the issue of land for Aboriginal and Torres Strait Islander people is inextricably tied to better health, housing and employment'.

Then on 29 August the Shadow Cabinet shifted in its attitude to the Bill. The *Canberra Times*, using leaks from the Coalition, reported that the Coalition's intention was to take the focus off their own divisions and turn up the heat on the government: 'Some moderate sources said they believed they [amendments proposed by the Coalition] would be unacceptable to the Government and the Coalition would still be forced to oppose the legislation'. That is exactly what happened when the Bill was debated; as they well knew, there was no way the government was going to accept the Coalition amendments, which had been cobbled together in bad faith.

These amendments were particularly opportunist because they sought to portray the government as excessively preoccupied with indigenous land aspirations to the exclusion of concerns about health and housing, employment and education, which was never the case. This was obviously intended to press the prejudice button in sections of the community. There was, however, no doubt about the priority Aboriginal people gave to their land aspirations.

Debate on the Land Fund Bill resumed in the House of Representatives on 30 August and, without consulting even one indigenous person, the Coalition Aboriginal affairs spokesperson, Christine Gallus, released a document containing what she described as proposed 'major' amendments to the government's Bill. Most Aboriginal people who had been involved in negotiations with the government were outraged both by the Coalition's lack of consultation and by the substance of their amendments.

The government's Bill sought to insert a new Part into the ATSIC Act to establish a fund to be spent not only on land but also to provide support for land management by indigenous people. The focus on management was a recognition that more needed to be done to support existing and future Aboriginal and Islander purchases of pastoral property. There had been examples of Aboriginal organisations buying pastoral properties that were already run down and denuded, without the financial resources necessary to restore the land. The Indigenous Land Corporation (ILC), which was to be created under the Act, was to support the adoption of sound land and environmental management practices and to develop national and local land strategies covering environmental issues as well as acquiring, granting and managing land. Creating the ILC by legislation would lock in the financial commitments to the fund, preventing a future Coalition government from gutting the reform by slashing or withdrawing the funding.

In his second reading speech, introducing the legislation to establish the fund, the Prime Minister set out the government's fundamental objective in creating the land fund:

With the native title legislation Australia took an historic step by firstly acknowledging the truth that Aboriginal people and Torres Strait Islanders were the original owners of the continent. In the legislation before the House today we are giving the spirit of that legislation more tangible expression. We are creating the means by which land may be returned to Aboriginals and Torres Strait Islanders and, with the formulation of their traditions thus partially restored, we trust that they may be able to protect and reutilise their communities, their culture and their heritage.

The Bill proposed to set aside $200 million in the first year with a further $121 million for each of the following nine years, giving a total commitment of federal funds over ten years of almost $1.5 billion. In each financial year some $45 million (indexed) was to be spent by the ILC for land acquisition, land management and running costs. The remainder was to be invested so that when government allocations ceased after 2003–04, the income from the investments would continue to fund the ILC's core activities. The ILC was to be run by a board of directors, most of whom were to be indigenous people, and it was to be otherwise independent of government.

There was to be a transitional period during which both the ILC and ATSIC would receive funds for land acquisition and management, thus allowing ATSIC to continue to acquire land for a further two years; this had been agreed by the government at the request of Aboriginal people. It was based on an attempt by Aboriginal people to respond to an earlier undertaking by the Prime Minister that land acquired by the ILC in the Northern Territory would not be susceptible to a land claim under the NT Land Rights Act which, if successful, would confer a right of veto over mining. This undertaking was given by the Prime Minister to placate the NT government's concerns over the potential for increased Aboriginal land ownership in the Territory, which would carry a right of veto provided for in that Act. Aboriginal people were thus able to get funds from ATSIC sources for that two-year period to acquire land in the Territory; that land could in turn be subject to a claim under the Act and, if successful, the right of veto would apply.

The Coalition's key amendments included a proposal to oblige the ILC to allocate resources to those 'most severely dispossessed', which was opposed by most Aboriginal people as a recipe for divisiveness within the Aboriginal community. ATSIC described it as 'an unsavoury attempt to rank dispossession' which would give rise to administrative difficulties and legal challenges.

Another amendment purported to link land acquisition with health, education and housing. This was a sham, designed for the electoral benefit of the Coalition in the non-indigenous community in an attempt to falsely portray the government as being unconcerned about these issues. Health, housing and education were in any event to be dealt with in the government's third-stage response to Mabo in the form of a social justice package.

The Coalition also sought to allow the ILC to make grants of land to individuals. Such a policy had never existed in any Commonwealth legislation and would be a source of a fertile political campaign in the non-indigenous community. It was presumably motivated by some philosophical objection to the community ownership of land.

A further amendment proposed the disposal of land purchased by the ILC without further reference to it. Unfortunately, as with a number of well-intentioned initiatives in indigenous affairs, the proposal ignored the lessons of history. In the United States, the *Dawes (General Allotment) Act 1883* was enacted in an attempt to integrate native Americans into the wider community. It sought to break up Indian reservations by granting individual title to tribal land and allowing it to be sold off. The result was disastrous, leading to non-indigenous ownership of Indian lands, which weakened the sense of community.

The Coalition then proposed a statutory requirement for consultation with a range of indigenous people with traditional or historical links with the land. The government opposed this, though such consultation was expected and intended to occur in most cases in practice, because a mandatory requirement would inevitably lead to litigation and make impossible quick commercial decisions to buy land to take advantage of market opportunities. In total, the Coalition put forward 37 amendments proposing constraints and prescriptions on the work of the ILC that they would never have sought for any comparable statutory body.

The Coalition stand was unanimously opposed by ATSIC. Charles Perkins, who was certainly not in the pocket of the ALP, stressed that ATSIC supported the 'Indigenous Land Corporation and Land Fund Bill in its current form which was arrived at following consultations with indigenous peoples and which has their support'. Most, but not all, key indigenous organisations were also strongly opposed to the Coalition's proposals. Those who supported the Coalition's approach included the NSW Aboriginal Land Council headed by Aden Ridgeway.

There is no doubt that during the debate on the Land Fund Bill divisions emerged between groups associated with land councils in Western Australia, Queensland and the Northern Territory and with the NSW Aboriginal Land Council. These divisions were unnecessary and regrettable. There was no evidence in the past of serious divisions between organisations associated with remote Aboriginal communities and those representing urban communities. Indeed, there was much evidence of a pan-Aboriginal political movement. The NSW Aboriginal Land Council's concerns about the government's land fund proposals were based on a misconception that the government was biased in favour of the land councils representing Aboriginal people in remote Australia, which was never the case, and my own commitment to push for the establishment of the land fund was motivated by my experience with, and respect for, Aboriginal people I had worked with in New South Wales.

As expected, the Coalition voted against the Bill when the government failed to support the amendments opposed by Aboriginal people. It was pointless to accept Opposition amendments that would arouse Aboriginal hostility when there was not the slightest indication from the Coalition that acceptance of those amendments would lead them to vote for the Bill in the Senate. It was better to pass the Bill through the House of Representatives and then negotiate with other parties in the Senate. There was a sense of *déjà vu* as the Bill went off to its first reading in the Senate after being passed by the House of Representatives on 20 September 1994—the WA Greens proposed to put up 'heaps of amendments' and to make the decision on whether to vote the Bill down on the Senate floor.

The Senate voted to refer the Bill to the Standing Committee on Finance and Public Administration, which reported back on 10 October, splitting on party lines, with the government and Democrat senators voting to support the Bill and oppose the amendments. The main opposition to it in the committee's public hearings came from the NSW Aboriginal Land Council and from Dickie Cox of the Kimberley Aboriginal Association, who was close to the then federal Labor MP for Kalgoorlie, Graeme Campbell, and from Robert Bropho in Perth. The NT government also sought changes to a number of provisions.

The second reading proceeded in the Senate and detailed consideration was given to the provisions of the Bill and to the amendments proposed by the Coalition, the Greens and the Democrats. In all, the Senate, with a Coalition, Green and Brian Harradine majority, supported over 150 amendments to the legislation, a number of which continued to be unacceptable to the government. On 17 November 1994 the Bill was returned to the House with a request for amendment by the Senate relating to a proposal for an extra $3 million per annum for the fund. The request was rejected on the same day.

Also that day, the Council for Aboriginal Reconciliation was to present its first annual report in the presence of the Prime Minister, the Leader of the Opposition, and the Leader of the Australian

Democrats. Speaking to a very large gathering, Lois O'Donoghue launched an unprecedented attack on the Coalition:

> Indigenous people have sadly watched the Opposition Parties attack the two key pieces of legislation introduced by the government to implement the High Court's historic decision—last year's Native Title Act and the current Indigenous Land Corporation Bill . . . The process of reconciliation cannot succeed while the Opposition Parties continue to oppose major legislation to advance indigenous people.

Her speech was like a verbal hand grenade thrown into the proceedings, and Alexander Downer looked decidedly angry at having been put on the spot in such a public forum. But what occurred had nothing to do with the government. It was just Lois speaking out for her people. I was again impressed by the strength of her convictions—a reconciliation process composed of empty rhetoric and not underpinned by social justice was not worth having anyway.

On 24 November there were indications that the Coalition might back away from their amendments because of concern that rejection of the legislation by the Senate could give rise to a double dissolution and an early election. We wanted the Land Fund Bill passed into law, and the Opposition's possible reversal of their position, for whatever reason, would be welcomed.

The proposed legislation was then referred to a Senate Select Committee, established for the purpose, with Ian Campbell (Liberal, WA) as chair and Christabel Chamarette (Green) as deputy chair, plus Barney Cooney (Labor, Vic.), Chris Ellison (Liberal, WA), Meg Lees (Democrat, SA), Margaret Reynolds (Labor, Qld), and Judith Troeth (Liberal, Vic.). About 100 submissions were received and the committee conducted public hearings in Canberra, Launceston, Adelaide, Melbourne, Dubbo, Brisbane, Cairns, Darwin, Broome and Kalgoorlie. This committee was, in my view, an exercise in futility. It ultimately split along party lines, as it would have at the beginning of the inquiry. Senators Reynolds and Lees set out in their minority report:

> Clearly there are obvious double standards in the expectations of the Majority Report's emphasis on consultations and concerns. Should we require unanimity among stockbrokers before changing the securities law? Should we win approval from every farm lobby in the country before legislating for drought assistance? The propositions are absurd, and it is equally absurd to suggest that indigenous organisations should be unanimously behind every detail of the land fund legislation. The process of government would be paralysed if such a position were adopted, yet it is a very similar position which formed the rationale for setting up this Committee.

As a result of the committee's establishment, any hope the government had of having the land fund operational by 1 January 1995 was out of the question.

The government decided that the best approach now was to introduce a bill into the House in a form it considered acceptable, taking up 28 of the 67 amendments proposed by the Senate. The new Bill (Land Fund and Indigenous Land Corporation [ATSIC Amendment] Bill) was introduced into the House on 28 February 1995. The Prime Minister was highly critical of the Opposition's approach, accusing them of 'looking for excuses to sabotage a major legislative achievement. It is no wonder that after one of the longest debates ever held in the Senate, our opponents found it necessary to send a Select Committee off on a whistle stop tour of Australia . . . to find out, after the event, whether the amendments proposed by the Senate were acceptable'.

He appealed to the new Opposition Leader, John Howard, to support the new Bill. The government adopted the tactic of introducing a new bill into the House of Representatives while the original one remained in the Senate in order to force the Coalition and the two Green senators to accept the new legislation by threatening to use Senate rejection of the original Bill as a trigger for a double dissolution. The Opposition responded by reactivating the original Bill in the Senate. Government and Opposition leaders then embarked on a war of words about whether the earlier decision of the Senate to refer the original Bill to a Senate Select Committee amounted to a 'failure to pass the Bill' as required by the Constitution to secure a double dissolution.

On 31 March 1995 the amended 'original' Land Fund Bill was passed by the Senate in a bizarre second attempt in which there was a majority of Brian Harradine and Coalition senators outnumbering the government and the Democrats, with one former Labor, now Independent, senator, John Devereaux, abstaining. True to form, the idiosyncratic Green senators, after having emasculated the Bill with amendments in the course of debate, abstained in the final vote. The high farce was compounded by the earlier failure of a Liberal senator, Baden Teague, to arrive in time for the Senate vote, with the result that the first vote in the Senate was tied and the Bill not passed. It passed only when, with the consent of the government, the vote was recounted to allow the senator to vote.

Two days later, when the amended Senate Bill came on for debate in the House of Representatives, I vividly remember my elation as I sat at the dispatch box on the government side and John Howard rose to announce the Coalition's intention not to vote against the government's redrafted Bill in the House or in the Senate. He did, however, threaten that a future Coalition government would seek to amend the land fund legislation. The Coalition Shadow Ministry meeting at 9 a.m. that day had endorsed the change in tactics, as proposed by John Howard, and the decision was confirmed by a joint Coalition party meeting. The Coalition was prepared to vote for the land fund, even if for the wrong reasons, to avoid a double dissolution, as Tim Fischer acknowledged. The Coalition backflip was welcomed by Lois O'Donoghue on behalf of ATSIC, though she did ask the Coalition to let time judge the merits of the indigenous land fund rather than pre-empt the need for amendments.

The Bill finally passed through parliament on the evening of 21 March 1995, with only the Greens preventing its being passed unanimously. The first chair of the ILC was former ATSIC Commissioner David Ross and the deputy was Peter Yu of the Kimberley Land Council. My attempt to appoint Aden Ridgeway to the board was not accepted within the government.

The divisions between key Aboriginal organisations and individuals arising from the land fund debate regrettably did not stop with the passage of the legislation. ATSIC commissioners decided that most of the funds available through ATSIC for land acquisition should be spent on land in the Northern Territory. This decision was taken to seize the funding window of opportunity they were presented with and was an attempt to circumvent the Commonwealth policy applying to ILC purchases in the territory. Only three commissioners came from the Northern Territory, but the majority of the board was clearly persuaded to take advantage of this strategic opportunity and did so without any input or influence from the government. (As the minister I only found out about the board's decision after it was taken.) The ATSIC decision was subsequently challenged in the courts by the NSW Land Council and the challenge upheld.

The land fund debate was another of the longest and most bitterly fought legislative battles in the history of the Australian parliament. Like the native title debate, the gestation period of the Bill was intertwined with Coalition leadership tensions and divisions and sadly showed that the Coalition parties had an innate incapacity to respond in a principled way to the Mabo decision. However, the battle had all been worth it. An enduring reform had been put in place which no future government could take away at its whim.

12

THE TORRES STRAIT ISLANDERS: AUSTRALIA'S FORGOTTEN INDIGENOUS PEOPLE

The High Court's Mabo decision rocketed the Torres Strait Islands to national prominence when the Islander plaintiffs were successful in overturning for all time the doctrine of terra nullius.

By striking that blow for indigenous rights, Torres Strait Islanders staked a place for themselves in history. But most people on the Australian mainland still know very little of the unique history and culture of the Melanesian people of the Torres Strait.

In the aftermath of Mabo, Torres Strait Islanders did not have to fight in the front line against the pastoral and mining industries to defend their native title rights since their traditional lands were not targets of those industries. Their central objective for the government's Mabo response was to promote recognition of and support for their own considered and moderate political agenda for self-government as part of the Commonwealth of Australia.

There has been incremental progress in the direction of greater autonomy for the Torres Strait, but some dramatic setbacks have resulted in that agenda remaining largely unfulfilled as we move towards the hoped-for date for self-government, 2001. A modern, pluralist, liberal democracy like Australia comfortably embraces the colonial legacy of Norfolk Island self-government within the Australian Constitution. It is hardly a radical demand for the first people of this even more remote part of Australia to ask that they have at least a comparable right to control their own destiny. The spirit of Mabo demands that we listen to their call.

Until the Mabo decision most non-indigenous Australians were probably not even aware that Aboriginal people are not Australia's only indigenous people. Perhaps now more of us know where the Torres Strait Islands are, but most of us probably don't know a lot about them or the indigenous Melanesian people who live there. There are over 100 islands, islets and cays in the remote Torres Strait,

but only fourteen are permanently inhabited. At the time of the 1991
Census, the Torres Strait had a population of 5400 Torres Strait
Islanders, 200 Aboriginal people and 1600 other residents who did not
identify as being of indigenous descent. Half the population lives on
Thursday Island, which is the administrative centre. If most Australians
have been taught little about Aboriginal history and culture, they have
been taught even less about the Torres Strait Islanders and their unique
culture and way of life.

The Islands were named after the Spanish navigator Luis Váez de
Torres, who sailed there as early as 1606. Their history is remarkably
different from that of the mainland. It was not until the late 1800s
that Europeans moved to the Strait in significant numbers. In 1871
the London Missionary Society began its work of converting the Islanders to Christianity, with the Islands being formally annexed to the
crown by Queensland, acting with imperial authority, in 1879. Traditional Island law and title to land was not recognised. Outsiders were
drawn to the Islands by the lure of wealth through the exploitation of
bêche-de-mer (sea cucumbers) and mother-of-pearl shell.

Despite the influx of outsiders, the Islanders were largely unhin-
dered in their efforts to go on living on their traditional lands and
were able to maintain their fishing and gardening practices. They were
even able to gain some superficial control over aspects of their lives,
with elected Island councils beginning to have a local government
function from the 1930s. The reality was, however, that the Chief
Protector of Aborigines in Queensland continued to have sweeping
powers over the Islanders. Journeys between the Islands could only be
undertaken with permission of government authorities and Islanders
could not even marry without permission. It was only really after World
War II that Torres Strait Islanders were allowed to leave to go and
work on the mainland. There are now many more Islanders on the
mainland than on the Islands themselves as people move in search of
employment and education. But links with the Islands remain strong,
as the singer Christine Anu reminds us with her recording 'My Island
Home'.

In the 1990s Torres Strait Islanders adopted their own flag to
signify their identity and culture. Despite the beauty of the Islands and
the strong community and family ties that bind the Islanders, they live
in very poor economic and social circumstances. The infrastructure
deficiencies that bedevil Aboriginal communities are every bit as difficult in the Torres Strait, with all the consequent health problems.
Lifestyle issues also take their toll, exacerbated by the high cost of food
in community stores (as in Aboriginal communities, to be made even
worse by the GST). Despite all this, and with the limitation of a meagre

income largely dependent on work for the dole or CDEP schemes, the people are working hard to resolve their problems.

The social justice issues confronting Islanders are magnified by the fact that the Torres Strait Islands are remote and the costs of transport of people and materials is astronomically high—a trip from Thursday Island to Brisbane, Sydney or Melbourne is higher than many international airfares. Not only are the Islands remote but they have some of the worst and smallest airstrips in Australia, as I was to find out on one of my first trips there as a minister.

During my time as minister I took a special interest in the Torres Strait. In recognition of the separate identity of Torres Strait Islanders, the name of the portfolio was changed from Aboriginal Affairs to Aboriginal and Torres Strait Islander Affairs in 1991 and followed on from the lead provided by the creation of ATSIC. Not long afterwards, on 12 May 1992, the House of Representatives Standing Committee changed its name to reflect this change.

It was impossible not to be deeply conscious of the potential of the Mabo case, initiated by Torres Strait Islanders and then under consideration by the High Court, to change profoundly the position of all indigenous people in this country. When the judgment day arrived it was greeted with jubilation by Torres Strait Islanders, both in the Torres Strait and around Australia.

Even before the Mabo decision in June 1992 Torres Strait Islanders living in the Strait were in a special position, still strongly retaining their culture and in actual possession of their lands but without native title rights, yet formally recognised under Australian law. When a formal process of reconciliation with Australia's indigenous people began, it was important that there were proper consultations and negotiations with the major Islander representative organisations, both in the Strait and on the mainland. I committed the government to ensuring that both would have representation on the Council for Aboriginal Reconciliation. The first appointment from Torres Strait was Allan Mosby, later replaced by Pedro Stephen, while Brisbane-based Bill Lowah was appointed to represent Islanders on the mainland.

A strong push for greater autonomy for the Torres Strait had emerged during 1988, the bicentenary year, when Islanders had publicly demanded sovereignty and independence. There were calls for the UN Special Committee on Decolonisation to visit the Islands. Since then the move by Islanders to have greater control over their own destiny developed and grew more sophisticated. In 1988 calls for sovereignty and independence were received with alarm in conservative circles. The Coalition Shadow Defence Spokesperson, Peter White,

suggested that a successful secession movement would allow the Islanders to establish foreign military bases on their lands. Geoffrey Blainey
spoke out against concessions to minorities.

The calls for sovereign independence had been made at a meeting
on 18–22 January 1988, on Thursday Island, of 400 Torres Strait
Islanders to discuss proposals for the establishment of ATSIC. At first
the main spokesperson for the group was the head of the Island
Coordinating Council (ICC), George Mye, a role later taken over by
his deputy, Getano Lui Jr. The independence call was strongly rejected
by both the Queensland and Commonwealth governments but did
attract a great deal of media attention, as no doubt the Islanders had
hoped.

While the claims of sovereignty were not entertained by the Australian government in 1988, Prime Minister Hawke established an
Interdepartmental Committee to consider Islander grievances. These
centred on some key concerns such as the loss of control of their
future, that governments had ignored them and in particular had not
moved to address issues of disadvantage, and that their social and
cultural identity was not sufficiently recognised by governments.

There was a view then, as there is now, that the Torres Strait is
governed by structures and institutions which duplicate one another,
but none of which ensure that the Islanders have any real self-determination. In 1984 the Queensland National Party government had
created the ICC, which was made up of the chairpersons of the Island
councils, and there had been similar structures in the past. Between
1952 and 1991, although there was a Torres Shire Council covering all
the Islands and extending down Cape York to 11 degrees, there was
no elected council and the shire was controlled by an administrator.
In practice the Shire Council only provided what limited services there
were to Thursday Island and the adjacent Horn Island.

For most of this century Torres Strait Islanders have been accountable to a range of Queensland government departments from the
Department of Native Affairs to the Department of Aboriginal and
Islander Advancement, which later exercised control over 'reserve'
lands in Queensland. Responsibility for providing services was taken
over by the Department of Community Services. With the election of
the Whitlam government in 1972, Commonwealth programs began to
be directed to the Torres Strait through the Department of Aboriginal
Affairs. As with Aboriginal communities, resources are meagre compared with the vast need.

With the establishment of ATSIC in 1990, it was agreed that
separate elections would not be held for the bulk of the Torres Strait
and that the Island chairpersons, who were members of the ICC, would
automatically become members of the ATSIC Regional Council

established for the Torres Strait. However, there were to be separate elections held for Horn and Prince of Wales Islands and for the Port Kennedy area of Thursday Island, which was not represented on the ICC.

There are about 30 state and Commonwealth government departments servicing the Torres Strait, all controlled by politicians in Canberra or Brisbane. Although the Islands are a part of Queensland, Brisbane is 3000 kilometres away and to the people it is as remote as the politicians in Canberra. The Australian Bureau of Statistics conducted a survey in the Islands in 1994 which showed that this morass of government had left the Islands in the same deeply disadvantaged position that Aboriginal people found themselves in on the mainland. Twelve per cent did not have running water connected to their homes; 60 per cent did not have their dwelling situated on a sealed road; and almost 52 per cent of people aged fifteen and over were dependent on government payments. The statistics go on and on.

My own description of the Torres Strait is poverty in paradise. The Islands have some of the most beautiful places in Australia, but on most there is high unemployment or at best a CDEP program and hence a pitifully low per capita income, massive overcrowding in housing, and in several key communities the only access road is impassable, other than by four-wheel drive from the airstrip. The main access road for the whole of the Strait, servicing about 5000 people, is that from the main airstrip on Horn Island to the wharf, where a boat takes people to Thursday Island. This road is about 10 kilometres long and when I last visited in 1995 was unsealed and deeply corrugated.

For Torres Strait Islanders on the mainland there are no elected national representative bodies other than ATSIC, and they are entitled to participate in the election of ATSIC Regional Councils. The ATSIC Act did, however, constitute a Torres Strait Island Advisory Board (TSIAB)—to represent mainland Islanders—chaired by the Torres Strait ATSIC Commissioner with members appointed by the minister. The review of the ATSIC Act in 1993 indicated the strong desire of Torres Strait Islanders, 80 per cent of whom live on the mainland, that TSIAB members be elected. But the ATSIC Board, constituted with only one Torres Strait Islander representative, urged me to abolish TSIAB altogether. I was not prepared to do this, and so maintained the status quo of an appointed advisory board. The other recommendations of the ATSIC Act review as it related to the Torres Strait, however, deserved strong support as they envisaged the creation of a separate statutory authority for the region, which the Islanders saw as a significant step towards self-government, to be called the Torres Strait Regional Authority (TSRA).

There is no doubt that the Mabo decision, changing as it did the relationship between government and indigenous people throughout Australia, was a great source of pride to Torres Strait Islanders, with the *Torres News* proclaiming the significance of the decision in successive editions. It should be stressed, however, that the decision only applied to the Murray Island group and not even to the sea surrounding the islands. There is now no mining in the Torres Strait, the former goldmine on Horn Island having closed down. Therefore Islanders were not under pressure from the Australian mining industry as were Aboriginal people. Nor were they, of course, in conflict with the pastoral industry. For these reasons the epic 1993 Mabo debate did not affect them as harshly.

The central aspiration of Torres Strait Islanders living in the Strait in the aftermath of the Mabo decision was to achieve a form of self-government by the year 2001. They had a modest and reasonable agenda for self-determination, easily able to be accommodated in an advanced liberal democracy like Australia. But it was to be resisted by the Queensland government, by some of my federal parliamentary colleagues, and most of all by PM&C. This demand for self-government did not materialise overnight but was the outcome of decades of being pushed around by parliaments and government departments emanating from Brisbane and Canberra.

In the aftermath of the Mabo decision the Islanders began to get strong support from indigenous people on the mainland for their modest goal, for example in Lois O'Donoghue's speech on 10 December 1992 to the UN General Assembly at the launch of the International Year of the World's Indigenous Peoples. Meanwhile, in Sydney on the same day, I witnessed a flurry of activity behind the scenes as a highly respected Torres Strait Islander woman, Dulcie Flower, told Aboriginal men that Torres Strait Islanders must be represented on the speakers' platform at the national launch of the Year. No Torres Strait Islander was scheduled to speak, but Dulcie Flower had her way and Torres Strait Islanders had a voice.

Eight days later I was on Thursday Island for a meeting with representatives of the ATSIC Regional Council and the ICC. The media release announcing the meeting and visit emphasised that the government had made no decisions on the self-government issue and that 'any changes would have to be subject to exhaustive consultations'. I was aware that there would be opposition to any proposal for self-government from some interest groups in the Strait and from the Queensland government, but I did not anticipate the extent to which the Commonwealth bureaucracy would work to undermine them.

There has never been a serious suggestion that Torres Strait Islanders want to break away from Australia, and indeed some of the tallest flagpoles bearing the Australian flag are on Torres Strait Islander flagpoles adjacent to Papua New Guinea. On those islands there is still a relatively poor standard of living, but there is nothing like the shameful living conditions that exist in the coastal areas of PNG's Eastern Province nearby. The disparity causes pressures on the broader relationship, and PNG citizens often try to cross over to nearby Torres Strait Islands for medical treatment or to buy food.

In his efforts to advance the aspirations for self-government, on 27 April 1993 Getano Lui Jr joined Aboriginal leaders for the first negotiating meeting with Prime Minister Keating and other key ministers on the Mabo Ministerial Committee. A document prepared by the ICC set out the agenda of Torres Strait Islanders in the aftermath of the Mabo judgment, highlighting first the need for Commonwealth legislative leadership to protect native title rights for indigenous people. The ICC called on the government to engage in continuing dialogue and negotiations at the highest levels in determining its response to Mabo. Several issues were on the agenda for negotiation:

- local and regional government powers, structures and revenue sources in the Torres Strait;
- resolution of Islander claims to island marine areas, reefs, etc.;
- implementation of a marine strategy for the Strait;
- the efficiency and adequacy of government programs to tackle disadvantage;
- economic development;
- cultural development;
- reforms to the PNG–Australia Border Treaty; and
- recognition of Torres Strait Islander rights in the Australian Constitution.

The ICC document argued the case with clarity but also subtlety:

> Many Australians do not understand that indigenous autonomy is a recognised world standard for public policy. Indigenous people are not simply another immigrant group to be assimilated. Rather, we are distinct cultures with a will to survive and thrive on our traditional territories. *There is irony in the fact that in order to participate fully in the opportunities and life of Australia, we need more autonomy and self-government.* Today, the countless programs provided by some 35 Government Departments and agencies in Torres Strait result in lack of coordination and concerted impact . . . We find both operating and emerging institutional arrangements abroad [in] many models for consideration. Our purpose is not to import or copy a foreign model but to recognise that practical models exist and that the dangers in

indigenous autonomy and self-government feared by some Australians
have not occurred elsewhere. (Italics original.)

In late May and early June 1993, I was in the Torres Strait for the
Cultural Festival, and Getano Lui and I made major statements in
support of the self-government agenda. But the agenda needed to be
advanced in a practical way, and Mr Lui, as chair of the ICC, wrote to
the Prime Minister on 8 June that the government was not responding
sufficiently to Islanders' concerns and proposing a practical course of
action.

He urged that the government support the creation of the TSRA
(a smaller, autonomous version of ATSIC) as a replacement for ATSIC's
Torres Strait Regional Council, while making it clear that Torres Strait
Islanders had a longer-term aspiration for self-government by the year
2001. It proposed that the government have PM&C's Office of Indigenous Affairs investigate ways in which the programs of other
Commonwealth government departments could be transferred to the
new TSRA. The central point of the letter was, however, to urge the
Prime Minister to enter into a dialogue with Premier Goss on the
devolution of power to the Torres Strait and to convene a high-level
meeting with Island representatives and representatives of the Queensland government, beginning with a meeting of officials. The letter
concluded by reminding the Prime Minister that the concerns of
Torres Strait Islanders had not been addressed in the government's
deliberations on Mabo.

Now the Commonwealth bureaucrats began to exert their influence
to play down, if not stifle, what could have been one of the most
exciting developments in the reform of government structures in
postwar Australia. PM&C wrote me an unsolicited memorandum on
23 June 1993, offering the gratuitous advice that in future discussions
concerning self-government for the Torres Strait it would be important

> for the Government to ensure that Aboriginal and Torres Strait
> Islander expectations in relation to government and self-government
> are not raised unreasonably. In particular, policy decisions which
> specifically canvass greater autonomy for Torres Strait Islanders
> (particularly where they apply to the minority of Torres Strait Islanders
> who live in the Torres Strait) may have implications for the broader
> policy debate on Aboriginal issues and should be considered explicitly
> in that context.

This memorandum, which was copied to the Prime Minister's office,
went on to oppose what ATSIC commissioners and I were advocating:
to provide the TSRA with direct funding from the Commonwealth by
way of a 'single line appropriation' to allow them control over their

own expenditure. The document concluded with the department's own view of what ought to be done. I was shocked by the arrogance of this memorandum, which was completely hostile to the aspirations of Torres Strait Islanders. It confirmed how counterproductive to indigenous aspirations was the creation of PM&C's Office of Indigenous Affairs.

Despite PM&C's view, the Cabinet did agree that month to establish the TSRA. The new authority provided a way of advancing self-government for Torres Strait Islanders, but I sought to play down any concerns that might exist in the non-indigenous community in the Torres Strait and emphasised that no changes towards self-government would occur without a process of negotiation and over time.

Deputy Prime Minister Brian Howe visited the Torres Strait on 20 September 1993 and said publicly that the establishment of a TSRA 'will lay the foundation stone for a progressive negotiated movement toward regional autonomy in the delivery of programs and services for the Torres Strait' and that 'we should not forget that it was a group of Torres Strait Islanders who overturned the principle of *terra nullius* and paved the way for a recognition of native title in Australian common law'.

On 29 September 1993 my office again issued a public statement trying to damp down concerns about the establishment of the TSRA, stressing that 'any further moves towards self-government, including expanding the role of the TSRA, will be done only with the opportunity for affected communities to fully express their concerns'.

In his 30 September reply to Getano Lui's 8 June letter on self-government and related issues, Paul Keating was encouraging and, while indicating support for the establishment of the TSRA, noted that he recognised that the proposals 'for greater autonomy and eventual self-government go beyond arrangements related to ATSIC functions and envisage a devolution of Commonwealth and Queensland government powers to a coordinating body in the Torres Strait. This will of course require careful consideration and discussion between your Council, the Queensland Government and the Commonwealth'. He agreed that a meeting should take place between senior PM&C representatives and, if agreed by Queensland, that government's representatives.

While in the Torres Strait on 4 November 1993, I paid a special visit to remote Darnley Island to meet George Mye, at his request, to hear the concerns of Darnley and Murray Islanders and their aspirations in the aftermath of Mabo. The views put to me that day had a particular focus on indigenous control over reefs and marine resources. The Darnley Islanders emphasised that in the past 'the people of the Eastern Islands exercised effective control over clearly defined areas of sea, marine features and maritime resources' and wanted to do so once again.

It was obvious that the people of Darnley and Murray Islands were less than happy with the TSRA and were working directly with barrister Bryan Keon-Cohen to pursue their own interests. The meeting on Darnley was particularly tense and difficult because there had been an incident in which a licensed mackerel trawler was chased by Murray Island fishermen. The Islanders had purported to place a ban on commercial fishing in waters adjacent to Murray Island as a means of asserting title to their traditional fishing waters. At the meeting on Darnley, David Passi, one of the Mabo plaintiffs from Murray Island, joined in the expression of concern to me about the rights of Torres Strait Islanders to fishing resources and sea rights. It was not difficult to understand their concerns about violation of their fishing areas; apart from fishing there was no other viable employment on the island, and a visit to the commercial centre of the Torres Strait meant an expensive plane flight.

To address these concerns, at my request, a group of officials from PM&C, the Department of Primary Industry and Energy, ATSIC and the Queensland Premier's Department visited Murray Island to listen to the Islanders' complaints and to provide a briefing on the government's Native Title Bill, then before the Senate. The meeting proposed the declaration of an economic zone around the Islands.

After this visit, on the Commonwealth's initiative, an effort was made to have the Commonwealth and Queensland governments, the Queensland Commercial Fishermen's Organisation and the Torres Strait Fishermen's Association work on a committee to resolve the matter. It was intended that a report be prepared for consideration by the Queensland and Commonwealth ministers responsible for fishing; meanwhile self-government considerations were to be put on hold. The result was disappointing. There were some greater opportunities granted to Torres Strait Islanders to participate in fisheries consultations, but little else, though there appeared to be a continuing informal but unenforceable fishermen's agreement that commercial fishing would not occur within 5 kilometres of Murray Island.

On 20 November the *Courier Mail* reported an attack by National Party Senator Ron Boswell, who had asserted that I had wrongly encouraged Torres Strait Islanders to believe that some of their demands for self-government by 2001 were feasible. Senator Boswell urged that 'any Australians who feel that they want to self govern and retain their free association with Australia must carefully consider what they would be giving up in terms of social, economic, political and security support'. Wayne Goss also made it clear in state parliament that the Queensland government had not adopted a policy of support for self-government for the Torres Strait.

Three days later, ABC TV news reported the Queensland Deputy Premier, Tom Burns, as pouring 'cold water' on proposals for self-government in the Torres Strait and suggesting that the modest call was akin to 'splitting up the nation'. This kind of response from the Queensland government was predictable and in line with their attitude to the aspirations of Aboriginal people in the wider Mabo debate. You would think there had been a proposal to establish a Libyan beachhead in the Strait rather than a modest proposal of devolution of power and a democratisation of the institutions of government. The Berlin Wall had fallen, the Soviet Union was no more, but heaven help us all if democratic reforms were to be extended to the Torres Strait.

Some days earlier, on 15 November 1993, Premier Goss replied to Prime Minister Keating's letter of 30 September which had suggested tripartite consultations on the Torres Strait self-government proposals. Premier Goss agreed to meet with Commonwealth representatives but stated, in typical Queensland government form, that 'it would be helpful if a preliminary meeting could be arranged solely between the Commonwealth and State officials' to discuss the issues. Once again, the Queensland Labor government had shown its incapacity to understand the importance of direct negotiations with indigenous people, instead preferring the same kind of backroom bureaucratic political fix that they sought over the native title legislation.

In December 1993 the ICC sent a submission to the Senate Legal and Constitutional Affairs Committee which was considering the Native Title Bill. The submission was based on a paper, 'Torres Strait Self Government and the Australian Nation-State', delivered by Getano Lui to an indigenous conference in Norway. It also quoted from his Boyer Lecture, which Getano had presented on ABC radio in November, in which he argued powerfully for Torres Strait Islander self-government:

> The principles of Torres Strait Islander constitutional renewal are simple. We need to be able to make decisions about social, cultural, economic and environmental matters in our region, not just the right to attend advisory meetings which may or may not pass our ideas up the line. We need a clear, legally enforceable regime of land and sea rights. We need real control of staff and office budgets, not the appearance of control as through ATSIC. We need the means and facilities to secure and develop our culture . . . There are many ways in which such needs may be packaged. We are prepared to sit down and work out the details with Government.

He drew attention to the fact that there was nothing particularly novel about the calls by Torres Strait Islanders for a form of self-government,

that there were already 'special constitutional arrangements in Australia for island regions where the laws and administration have been
designed to accommodate unique historical and cultural values. These
are Norfolk Island, the home of mixed British and Tahitian people
descended from the Bounty mutineers, and Christmas and Cocos-
Keeling Island, each with a significant historical Asian community'. The
submission went on to outline a comprehensive range of detailed
objectives of Torres Strait Islanders.

On 24 March 1994 elections were held for the Island Councils
under the *Community Services (Torres Strait Islander) Act 1984*, and the
chairpersons of the Island Councils automatically became, by virtue of
Commonwealth legislation, members of the newly constituted TSRA
along with the representatives for Port Kennedy (Thursday Island),
Horn and Prince of Wales Islands, who had been elected the week
before. The new authority came into being on 1 July 1994.

There is a close relationship between the northern Torres Strait
Islands and the Western Province of PNG. From the island of
Boigu, PNG can be easily seen across the water, about 5 kilometres
away. The border relationship is regulated by a treaty between PNG
and Australia, necessarily so as the people have so much in common
and border crossings for traditional purposes are frequent.

Long before the 1999 incidents involving illegal immigrants, I had
concerns about the adequacy of customs and policing on this our
closest international border. From the town of Daru in the east of that
Western Province right across to the border with Irian Jaya, there is
not one radio communication device or one government police or
customs official. None of the villages on the PNG side have radio
contact with the outside world, so even if they do see unusual movements of planes or boats there is no capacity to alert the authorities.
Without being alarmist, there is clearly potential for a drugs-for-guns
trade across that remote border. Successive governments have failed to
recognise this. Given the total lack of employment opportunities in the
Torres Strait Islands, there is considerable scope for boosting the
number of people employed in customs and policing.

The Australian government should assist urgently with the upgrading of communications and policing on the PNG side of the border.
Attempts were made to encourage this upgrading by supporting the
construction of a relay device on one of the Torres Strait Islands to
provide the requisite signal to the remote PNG villages. The almost
total openness of the border gives rise to Torres Strait Islander concern
about the transmission of tropical diseases and other plant and animal
diseases through the Strait. There is considerable evidence that the

risk is indisputable and action should be taken. Greater resources need to be deployed in the Australian national interest, and the people of the Torres Strait who experience inordinately high levels of unemployment should be closely involved in that process.

There was, however, another perceived threat from the north, and that was from heavy metal contamination polluting the Torres Strait as a result of discharges of tailings from the Ok Tedi Mine into the Ok Tedi River. The concern was that the pollution would flow from the Ok Tedi into the Fly River and on into the Strait. To address Torres Strait Islanders' concerns, funding was obtained to complete the Torres Strait Baseline Study undertaken by the Great Barrier Reef Marine Park Authority. The pilot stage of this study had reported in 1993 that the 'concentrations of arsenic, cadmium and selenium in the edible portion of foods consumed by Torres Strait Islanders appear at levels close to or above the National Health and Medical Research Council's maximum permitted concentrations for seafoods'. But it also clearly indicated that none of the trace metals are associated with the Fly River discharge to any appreciable degree. The completed study also failed to reveal higher pollution levels in the Torres Strait attributable to the Fly River discharges. It was, however, important that the study be undertaken, given the crucial relationship between Torres Strait Islanders and the sea, which is for them as significant as the land is for Aboriginal Australians.

On 1 July 1994 there was a wonderful and uplifting celebration at the inauguration of the TSRA—as I described it, 'a significant step by the Commonwealth government in recognising the self-determination aspirations of Torres Strait Islanders living in the Torres Strait'. The TSRA was to operate as a 'mini ATSIC' but deal solely with the Torres Strait and have a budget negotiated with ATSIC commissioners. The first budget was $30 million; no longer would decisions on indigenous programs in the Strait be taken in Canberra or Brisbane, but locally.

A further opportunity for the TSRA to push for self-government came on 2 August 1995 when a submission was made on Thursday Island to a visiting Social Justice Taskforce comprising ATSIC officers and others from the Council for Aboriginal Reconciliation serviced by PM&C. They were preparing proposals for consideration in the government's committed third-stage social justice response to the Mabo decision. This document clearly sets out the indisputably reasonable and achievable nature of Torres Strait Islander aspirations to self-government; it rebuts any suggestion that Islanders wish to go it alone and advocates a practical negotiated outcome with continuing close

TSRA proposals for the third-stage social justice response to Mabo

- A formal memorandum of understanding (or framework agreement) between the Commonwealth and Queensland governments, negotiated with the people of the Torres Strait, supporting the long-term aspirational goals of the people of the Torres Strait and setting out a timetable and the steps necessary to achieve self-determination. Such an agreement would provide a basis for discussion and understanding of these aspirations and establish a framework and parameters for future negotiations and relationships.

- Acceptance of the coordinating role of the Authority.

- The registering of native title on a regional basis under the *Native Title Act 1993* and support for claims to rights over our seas and marine resources.

- The transfer of Commonwealth and state funding to the Authority.

- A commitment by government to appropriate monies to the Authority's Land and Natural Resources Fund as a vehicle for economic empowerment and the development of self-sufficiency.

- Acknowledgement of the Torres Strait Development Plan and marine strategy as providing the framework for a comprehensive and integrated approach to development in the Torres Strait area and in particular to promote sustainable economic development to increase the self-sufficiency of the people of the Torres Strait as an essential underpinning of self-determination.

- The accelerated and catch-up provision of essential services commensurate with those provided on the mainland and in accordance with the National Commitment to Improved Outcomes for Aboriginal and Torres Strait Islander Peoples.

- Improvements in health services with access to new programs in Aboriginal and Torres Strait Islander health in cooperation with the Commonwealth and Queensland governments and with the planning and control of culturally appropriate services vested in Torres Strait Islander people.

- The continued provision of housing for people in the Torres Strait at a level commensurate with their needs, with direct funding of the TSRA and in accordance with strategic plans developed with island communities.

- Giving a reference to the Commonwealth Grants Commission to examine the levels of services and standard of living enjoyed by residents in the Torres Strait to establish a benchmark for the provision of community services.

- Access to and Torres Strait participation in the National Aboriginal and Torres Strait Islander land fund.
- Continuing discharge of responsibilities and obligations to the people of the Torres Strait under the Torres Strait Treaty with their full involvement at all levels of decision-making in relation to the Torres Strait Protected Zone.
- A form of indigenous self-government to be negotiated with the people of the Torres Strait, representing an act of indigenous self-determination as the key to change for indigenous peoples.

relations with both the Commonwealth and Queensland governments. The TSRA's submission foreshadowed the achievement of Islander aspirations by a negotiated regional agreement which would define the fundamental aspects of the relationship between the two governments, recognise the rights of Torres Strait Islanders to self-determination and also recognise the rights and interests of all the residents of the Torres Strait.

The document set out the negotiating framework for reaching a regional agreement.

The proposal for self-government put forward in this submission attracted wide and virtually unanimous support, from both ATSIC and the Council for Aboriginal Reconciliation in their submissions to government on the social justice response to Mabo. The ALP Aboriginal and Torres Strait Islander Caucus Committee also gave full support. The Council for Aboriginal Reconciliation's support was particularly significant, not only because the council included representatives of the government, the Opposition and the Democrats but because it also included representatives of a wide range of interest and business groups in the community, none of whom found the proposals to be other than a modest and just aspiration.

The Council recommended the establishment of a negotiating group, comprising representatives of both the Commonwealth and Queensland governments, the TSRA, the Torres Shire Council and Torres Strait Islanders living on the mainland; it also recommended that the negotiating group be required to report annually on progress. The Council made it clear that any form of regional self-government adopted in the Torres Strait should not be seen as a model for regional agreements elsewhere.

An issue that generated some publicity was the question of whether a moratorium that existed on mining exploration and exploitation in the Torres Strait Protected Zone would be extended for a further five years. The issue first arose in the lead-up to the annual PNG–Australian Ministerial Forum held in Melbourne in early December 1994. I supported the continuing prohibition as I knew this was the strongly held view of both Torres Strait Islanders and the villagers on the coast of the Western Province of PNG. There was no pressure on the Commonwealth government to allow mining. I was aware, however, that among elements of the PNG bureaucracy there was support for mining, and I had heard those views expressed at first hand on my previous visit to PNG. There were suggestions that the Queensland government wanted only a three-year extension. Media reports suggested a lack of good faith on the part of the Commonwealth. It was also reported that the TSRA was supporting an indefinite ban, but all these reports were false. The TSRA had formally met and endorsed Gareth Evans' proposal for a five-year extension of the moratorium, which was duly supported by both governments at the Ministerial Forum.

Back in November 1994 I had further first-hand experience of the Commonwealth bureaucracy trying to run the government by advancing an agenda contrary to my views as the minister responsible for Torres Strait Islander issues. PM&C wanted to put forward a Cabinet memorandum advocating a negotiation process for the Commonwealth in discussions with the Queensland government on Islander aspirations. I was far from satisfied with the proposed memorandum and I was even more disturbed by the fact that there had not been proper consultation, let alone negotiation, with the elected members of the TSRA. I wrote to the department seeking to have the memorandum deferred. Again, I stress that in indigenous affairs it is not only what is done by governments but how it is done that is important. I was adamant that there had to be greater efforts to consult and negotiate with the TSRA before the memorandum went forward—it was their future that was being decided.

PM&C pressed on with its agenda, and a very senior officer, who knew nothing about indigenous issues or policy, tried to get round my opposition by going through the Prime Minister's office. After the memorandum was put on the Cabinet agenda, contrary to my wishes, I was able to get it withdrawn. Officials tried to put it on again and it was finally withdrawn only on the decision of the Prime Minister's office after my personal intervention. Getano Lui later wrote to me expressing disquiet about PM&C's actions. He was thus more determined in his resolve to 'ensure that a proper negotiating process should occur before the lodgement of the memorandum and certainly before any discussions are conducted with the Queensland Government'.

I was convinced then, as I am now, that if there is to be a move towards self-government in the Torres Strait it should occur progressively through open negotiations held in good faith, and ideally with a great deal of cross-party support. I was not about to let the self-government movement for Torres Strait Islanders be set back by some transient, self-important bureaucrat. Bureaucratic agendas playing off ministers against one another undermine the process of accountable government.

Over the coming months discussions continued with the TSRA to finalise a Cabinet memorandum on self-government. Getano Lui again wrote to the Prime Minister setting out Islander aspirations for self-government by 2001 and referring to the now redrafted Cabinet memorandum containing suggestions for how the agenda could be advanced. The memorandum had picked up the proposal for a special negotiating group consistent with the views expressed by both ATSIC and the Council for Aboriginal Reconciliation. It would have been very difficult for the Opposition to oppose this, even in the lead-up to the election, as it enjoyed wide support both inside and outside parliament. It had been extensively canvassed among interested Caucus members, and in March Getano Lui had briefed the Caucus Aboriginal and Torres Strait Islander Affairs Committee who had supported it. In his letter, Getano also urged the Prime Minister to announce the creation of such a negotiating group on his forthcoming visit to the Strait on 12 September 1995 en route to PNG.

My staff had sought input into the Prime Minister's visit and an opportunity for me to travel on it, but we were discouraged from doing so by his staff. I could not believe what I heard on the news and read in the newspaper the day after his visit. The Prime Minister, ignoring the contents of the redrafted Cabinet memorandum, effectively killed the proposed negotiating group to advance self-government and instead announced a proposal to fund the TSRA directly from the budget, instead of through ATSIC. I knew that this change was totally symbolic, gave the Torres Strait Islanders no additional resources, and did not significantly advance their self-government agenda. It is an indictment of the media's lack of interest in the Torres Strait that, despite the fact that the Prime Minister's reported statements on Thursday Island were very much in conflict with my own constant public advocacy and numerous other public statements of ministers, including the Deputy Prime Minister, not one journalist even followed up the issue.

Some social and political movements cannot be easily stopped, and in one of the few welcome decisions of the Howard government, the

Minister for Aboriginal and Torres Strait Islander Affairs, John Herron, agreed to a request by the House of Representatives Standing Committee on Aboriginal and Torres Strait Islander Affairs that it conduct an inquiry into greater autonomy for Torres Strait Islanders. I knew where the proposal came from as I had suggested to committee members and staff in 1995 that such an inquiry be conducted. The committee recommendations were modest and fell far short of Torres Strait Islanders' expressed aspirations, but they did propose the establishment of a joint statutory agency (the Torres Strait Regional Assembly) with the Queensland government to represent all residents of the Torres Strait area. This assembly was to replace the ICC, the TSRA and the Torres Shire Council. This recommendation was not supported by the Howard government, let alone the Queensland government, which opposed incorporation of the Torres Shire Council into the new body and failed even to support the amalgamation of the two indigenous bodies, the ICC and TSRA.

I do not pretend that there are not difficult policy issues to be addressed in the move towards self-government, but none I believe that cannot be successfully negotiated to agreement.

Why should Australia move to accommodate the aspirations of Torres Strait Islanders? I would rather phrase the question as, why not? To give a right of greater control, accountability and ownership to Australia's Torres Strait Islanders over at least some of the government structures that influence their lives would be a modest measure of social justice for one of Australia's indigenous peoples who were after all the instigators of the Mabo decision which has so shaped modern Australia.

Such a decision would respect their continuous and ongoing relationship with their traditional lands and their distinctive way of life in this remote and beautiful part of Australia. No harm would be done to non-indigenous Australians in the Torres Strait, whose rights could be protected and accommodated. Certainly no harm would be done to the wider Australian community and, in my view, the quality of our democracy would be enhanced and deepened if we are able to negotiate and put in place a self-government arrangement for the Torres Strait by 2001 or as soon as possible thereafter.

13

HERITAGE, CULTURE AND HINDMARSH ISLAND

Despite the successful passage of the 1967 referendum, no action was taken to enact Commonwealth legislation to protect Aboriginal and Torres Strait Islander heritage and culture until 1984. In that year Clyde Holding introduced legislation which became, after a 1986 amendment deleting the word 'interim' from the title, the Aboriginal and Torres Strait Islander Heritage Protection Act 1986 *(Heritage Protection Act). The Commonwealth legislation was, and remains, far from ideal because the decision whether or not to issue a heritage declaration rests with the minister and not with some independent authority, as in the equivalent NT legislation. The Commonwealth legislation had never been used to maintain a permanent declaration during the time that my predecessors were in office, and its application and operation had been relatively untested in the courts. My decisions under this legislation to protect Aboriginal heritage resulted in a flurry of court challenges and vitriolic political attacks.*

A threshold point that needs to be made is that it was not a matter of electing *to become involved in a heritage application: I was required by law of the Commonwealth parliament to deal with each application through the mechanism of the Heritage Protection Act. In deciding to protect sites that were the subject of claims relating to continuing Aboriginal spiritual beliefs, the issue was never whether I shared the beliefs but whether or not such beliefs were sincerely held by Aboriginal people and ought in all circumstances to be protected under the Act.*

In many ways the recognition and protection of Aboriginal spirituality and heritage is at the cutting edge of relations between Aboriginal people and the wider Australian community. Such issues can give rise to a clash of cultures, as Hindmarsh Island and other heritage claims have so clearly demonstrated.

There is a need to reform indigenous heritage protection legislation at state as well as national level, but without the Commonwealth surrendering its ultimate power and responsibility to protect Aboriginal heritage. The direction of reforms ought to ensure that the responsibility for protecting Aboriginal heritage rests not in the domain of destructive political point-scoring but with some

independent tribunal or authority. The Keating government commissioned
Elizabeth Evatt to conduct a review of the legislation and her report has
recommended this reform and others to the current government.

Only time will tell whether Australia has the maturity to move forward to
a more effective national regime for the proper recognition and protection of
indigenous heritage.

Issues of Aboriginal heritage and culture spring from the nature of Aboriginal spirituality, which is so different from anything the European settlers knew that most of them had difficulty in acknowledging its existence, let alone that it was worthy of respect. It is, in the first place, intertwined with nature and the physical landscape, aspects of the universe for which Western religion has traditionally had scant regard. Second, it is largely a secret, hidden religion passed on by word of mouth, and its practice is divided between men's and women's knowledge and rituals, notions largely alien to Western culture.

I believe that a growing number of non-Aboriginal Australians in the 1990s have a new awareness about the nature and significance of this spirituality. This is the result of the contribution to wider public education by Aboriginal people, the work of anthropologists, a lessening of ethnocentric attitudes concerning spiritual matters, and a developing global commitment to protect and respect the environment. But many Australians still have a considerable mental impasse about this spirituality, and it is this that creates the difficulty of giving legal acknowledgement to what is sacred to Aboriginal people. The clash of industrial and commercial interests with this intangible, spiritual culture has given rise to extraordinary public furores in this land, and they continue.

The Hindmarsh Island case exemplifies this clash in the most extreme manner imaginable, involving as it did spiritual beliefs that were not only secret but were the beliefs of *women,* inaccessible to the eyes of *men.* On top of this, the charge by one group of Aboriginal women that the beliefs had been fabricated by another group brought the whole matter of indigenous beliefs and culture to flashpoint. Hindmarsh Island provoked the greatest backlash from anti-Aboriginal groups of any indigenous issue so far; for the women whose beliefs were at stake, it caused the greatest vilification and intimidation.

Hindmarsh Island was not the only high-profile issue causing a backlash and open disparagement of Aboriginal beliefs. At the time of the Coronation Hill decision, for example, the opponents of Aboriginal heritage protection were to be no less vitriolic and hostile. The Alice

Springs dam declaration also provoked a storm of protest from the NT government and its supporters.

The protection of Aboriginal heritage does not always involve an active spiritual belief associated with a particular site, but that does not mean that sites of ancient rock art, for example, or sites showing past Aboriginal occupation are not worthy of protection. The Commonwealth legislation also allows a declaration to be issued to protect sacred objects as well as sites of significance. On 26 September 1993, responding to an application from the Central Land Council, I issued a declaration to protect and preserve a collection of significant Aboriginal objects, known as the Strehlow collection, then in the custody of the SA government. The objects had been held under South Australian law after their seizure from the widow and son of the late Professor Ted Strehlow, who had collected them during his life's work in central Australia. In 1992 the Strehlows had attempted to sell the collection on the open market for considerable private gain. The traditional owners were concerned that the materials could be injured or desecrated if they left the custody of the South Australian Museum.

The original declaration was for a period of six months and this was extended several times to allow a mediation to be carried out by Professor Elliott Johnston, the former RCIADIC Commissioner. It was not until June 1995 that a settlement was reached leading to a negotiated purchase of what was, beyond doubt, the best known collection of Aboriginal sacred objects in Australia, and these priceless sacred objects were returned to Aboriginal ownership.

Another area that needs continuing government commitment is the return of Aboriginal human remains. There is no doubt that the collection and retention of them by museums and other institutions in Australia and overseas has caused great distress to Aboriginal people. Aboriginal community organisations and individuals have been the driving force for action to address this issue. A major contribution was made by Michael Mansell, who did much to secure the return of the University of Edinburgh's entire collection of Aboriginal human remains—estimated to comprise some 295 skulls and four complete skeletons. Since the 1980s most Australian museums have re-examined their policies on the holding of Aboriginal skeletal remains and, at least publicly, have supported the return of the material where Aboriginal people could establish a claim to it.

In October 1993 state and territory ministers for indigenous affairs joined the Commonwealth in adopting a set of national principles for the return of indigenous cultural property. The adoption of the principles, however, is one thing; implementing them is quite another.

State and territory governments have a direct responsibility for protecting indigenous heritage of all kinds, but in most cases their

The homecoming of Tambo
Many events during those years tugged at the heart. One was the homecoming of Tambo to Palm Island on 23 February 1994. Tambo was a Palm Island (Manbara) man kidnapped and taken to the United States by a circus agent 111 years previously and promoted under the name of Tambo. The return of his body to the island took place in the presence of hundreds of Aboriginal community members and the American Ambassador to Australia, Edward Perkins, an African American who understood the great significance of the event to the community. The body of Tambo arrived at the wharf draped in the Aboriginal flag and was carried along a long line of people to its final resting place in the rainforest cemetery. The return of Tambo was a moving act of reconciliation.

legislation is hopelessly inadequate. I defend the principle that the national government should retain the ultimate power and responsibility for protecting indigenous heritage and culture by virtue of its responsibility under the 1967 referendum, but this protection would also be advanced by the radical overhaul of most of the relevant state and territory legislation.

In 1993 the Council for Aboriginal Reconciliation produced a report, *Exploring for Common Ground*, which recommended sweeping reform of the processes for protecting indigenous heritage, especially in dealings between indigenous people and the mining industry. It proposed a framework of guidelines under which protection of sacred sites would be given priority but which would appropriately balance other interests.

It is notable that this report was publicly welcomed by the government, Opposition, Democrats, mining industry and Aboriginal organisations. However, attempts by Prime Ministers Hawke and Keating to support the Aboriginal affairs portfolio in the reform of state laws were met with a total lack of cooperation from the states and territories. Letters from prime ministers were not even replied to by some state governments—including Labor governments.

It was only after I began to use the power of the federal heritage legislation that an interest in a more coordinated national scheme of heritage protection developed in some state governments, but even then negligible progress was made. It remains to be seen whether or not a national framework to protect indigenous heritage can ever be put in place, given parochial state interests so consistently hostile to that protection.

One of the more difficult applications I considered under the Heritage Protection Act was an application from Robert Bropho in August 1992 for the site of the Swan Brewery in Perth. The proposed redevelopment of the site had been a controversial issue long before I became the minister and I found myself in the hot seat in circumstances over which I had little control because of the long and tawdry history of the matter. The site in question was an old brewery on the banks of the Swan River which an Aboriginal group, led by Robert Bropho, continued to maintain was the sacred place of the Waugal, a powerful serpent-like dreamtime creature. Mr Bropho and his supporters wanted all buildings removed from the area and the land made into a park so that it could be restored to a quiet place in accordance with Aboriginal tradition.

The Swan Brewery had already been the subject of tortuous and ongoing litigation and vitriolic public debate in Western Australia. A 'permanent' declaration had been made over the site by Gerry Hand in 1989 but had subsequently been revoked a month later. I took the view that to commission a heritage report on the application would raise the expectations of Aboriginal people that I could deliver a declaration. I decided that the situation was irretrievable and declined the application on 7 January 1993.

Robert Bropho challenged my decision in the courts, and in a very principled judgment supportive of Aboriginal rights, Justice Wilcox in the Federal Court found that my decision to decline the application was invalid because I had not commissioned an independent report under the legislation before I made my decision. His decision was upheld on appeal. It was to be the last judgment on a heritage issue during my time as minister that was supportive of Aboriginal rights. Of all the issues that crossed my desk, the Swan Brewery was perhaps the most troubling. This affair was the cause of the unpleasant confrontation with Robert Bropho mentioned earlier.

Another issue, already set in train by Gerry Hand, was a report under section 10 of the Act into proposals to mine Coronation Hill, adjacent to Kakadu National Park. The report was to be prepared by Justice Donald Stewart, head of the Resource Assessment Commission, who was also inquiring into environmental consequences of the proposed mine. After receiving Justice Stewart's report, I joined Nick Bolkus and Ros Kelly in a joint Cabinet submission on the effects of mining at Coronation Hill, arguing that mining should not proceed on environmental and indigenous heritage grounds recognised by Justice Stewart, and that Coronation Hill should be protected by its incorporation into Stage 3 of Kakadu National Park. We were supported by an extensive and effective lobbying campaign led by Mick Dodson and John Ah Kit, directors of the NLC and the Jawoyn Association respectively.

On 11 June I had issued a public statement along a similar theme that called for further debate free from ridicule of the spiritual beliefs of Aboriginal people. I pointed out that people had disparaged Aboriginal beliefs in a way they would never dare to do to Christian, Jewish or Islamic beliefs, and that such contempt sprang from notions of racial superiority. I also invoked the Universal Declaration of Human Rights and CERD, which have been supported by successive Australian governments.

Bob Hawke had already made public his opposition to the mine when he told a group of students at St Ursula's College in Kingsgrove on 17 June 1991, the day before the Cabinet meeting, that the Jawoyn people had every right to believe that the mining of Coronation Hill would amount to sacrilege.

The actual Cabinet debate on Coronation Hill was not a particularly heated one, though the proponents of the mine put their views forward at length and in some cases forcefully. Cabinet decided to accept the report of Justice Stewart, which recognised the need for protection of significant Aboriginal areas in the Kakadu conservation zone. There was no need for me to issue a permanent heritage protection declaration, however, because Cabinet decided that the area should be incorporated into Kakadu National Park, thus removing the threat of injury or desecration to the sacred site. Bob Hawke announced: 'The Government accepts the unequivocal and independent evidence that the area in question is fundamental to Jawoyn culture . . . It is extremely presumptuous to question the integrity of Aboriginal beliefs simply because they are outside an intellectual framework with which most of us are comfortable.'

Opponents of Bob Hawke within the ALP attacked both the legitimacy of the decision and his authority. Bob was said to have imposed his will on Cabinet. The decision was portrayed in some quarters as pandering to Aboriginal interests and to the left wing of the party in an attempt to shore up his leadership. But the spiritual beliefs of the Jawoyn had been explored and reported on decisively in the independent report by Justice Stewart.

Although environmental considerations were also relevant, the Coronation Hill decision was a tough one for the government because it involved choosing between protecting an Aboriginal sacred site and a mining industry project—a choice that is in fact the exception rather than the rule. Indigenous people are not inherently anti-mining, as the Jawoyn themselves have subsequently shown with their support for mining and exploration over large areas of their traditional lands. But the Coronation Hill decision was vilified by talkback radio propagandists and by those people in the Labor Caucus who wanted to use the decision to attack Bob Hawke in their contribution to Paul Keating's ongoing leadership challenge. Aboriginal Australians were overwhelmed by the decision and I remember a very emotional Mick Dodson saying that night he was 'proud to be an Aboriginal Australian'.

Two days later, on 20 June 1991, the Cabinet decision not to allow mining at Coronation Hill was confirmed by the Labor Caucus. In an attempt to diminish the inevitable backlash, I issued a statement declaring that Coronation Hill was 'a very special case' and that the decision 'should not be seen as anti-mining or representing a threat to development in Australia'. I was at pains to emphasise the limited nature of the decision because there were currently three major projects then the subject, or likely to be the subject, of heritage applications under the federal legislation and again I did not want to raise the expectations of the applicants. Two of the applications related to mining projects and the third to a proposed dam on the Todd River, adjacent to Alice Springs.

The NT government had described the Todd River project as a flood mitigation dam and at other times as a recreational lake. Applications for protection of the women's site adjacent to the dam had been made by the CLC under sections 9 and 10 of the Heritage Protection Act in February 1991. I wrote to Marshall Perron indicating that there were 'clear and substantial grounds' on which to base an emergency declaration to protect the threatened sites but calling on the government to stop work to allow the issues to be resolved by conciliation and negotiation. The Chief Minister replied that work would not stop, but on 21 March, after a phone call from me, he at least agreed to stop work for two days to allow talks to occur.

At the subsequent meeting held between ATSIC officials and the NT government, including representatives of the NT Aboriginal Areas Protection Authority, it was agreed that work should cease to allow further consultation with Aboriginal people on the dam. Despite the opposition of its own Aboriginal heritage protection body, the government made it clear that it intended to proceed with the dam.

So in the early hours of the morning of 26 March 1991, I signed the papers to allow for the issue of an emergency declaration under section 9 of the Commonwealth legislation, which was duly notified to the assembled bulldozer drivers and Aboriginal opponents of the dam that morning, just in time to avoid a confrontation as work began. The areas protected by the declaration were a cave in the dam site area known as Nyiltye, a women's site known as Tnyere-Akerte in the bed of the Todd River, and a stand of river red gums and white gums in or close to the bed of the river.

After a long delay, a delegation of NT government representatives led by the Minister for Lands, Max Ortmann, came to see me in Canberra on 6 February 1992. Max Ortmann put on his best face and appeared to be rational and sincere in wishing to work with Aboriginal people in relation to the proposed dam. I suggested going to the dam site with him to meet the people who had expressed concerns, which I did on 13 March.

The meeting began in a fairly low-key way and was attended by about 200 Aboriginal people. There were one or two heated speeches by Aboriginal people directed at Max Ortmann, but nothing that should have fazed him. At some point, however, he completely lost it. He started to rant and rave and then stormed through the crowd towards his vehicle, to the amazement of all who were watching. Halfway across the river bed someone called to him and he turned on the crowd and directed his comments to an older Aboriginal woman, telling her to 'get off your fat arse and fix your drinking problem'. The woman was in fact a non-drinker. The gathering broke up and Max Ortmann received a vast amount of adverse national publicity in the days ahead.

After the declaration was issued in March 1991, the NT government had stopped work on the dam and the matter lay more or less dormant for about twelve months. I had done everything possible to bring about a negotiated settlement of the dispute, but in March 1992, after the meeting with Max Ortmann, the government again proposed to send in the bulldozers and I had to issue another emergency declaration on 20 March 1992. I said that the NT government's own Aboriginal Areas Protection Authority had advised it not to proceed with the dam and that I had not met one Aboriginal person from central Australia who supported the dam going ahead.

On 2 April 1992 I announced that Hal Wootten QC had been appointed to prepare a report on whether the site required a longer term of protection and extended the temporary declaration to ensure that the site was protected until he reported. His report was scathing in its criticism of the NT government and he described the proposed 'flood mitigation dam' as 'a very expensive one in terms of money and, as the present conflict shows, in terms of its extremely embittering effect on race relations'.

On Sunday, 17 May 1992, an announcement was made of the historic first use of federal Aboriginal heritage power to issue a permanent declaration. When issuing a public statement in support of this 25-year protection declaration, I referred to Mr Wootten's detailed description of the profound significance of the land in question for Aboriginal people immediately associated with it, and for many others, particularly women. It is land through which passes a major dreaming (the Two Women Track) from its origins in Pitjantjatjara country to its culmination in the Todd River above Alice Springs. Mr Wootten's report concluded that destruction of, or interference with, any of the major sites in the area would cause great anguish and deep affront to many Aboriginal people. In the lead-up to the 1993 federal election, the Coalition in its Fightback documents listed the Alice Springs flood mitigation dam as a project where 'so-called red tape would be untied to allow the project to proceed'.

At this time, before the Mabo decision, the mining industry showed not the slightest willingness to enter into genuine negotiations with Aboriginal people. There were two particular setbacks in dealings with Aboriginal heritage issues and the industry. The first concerned a proposed nickel mine at Yackabindi in Western Australia. This was a very difficult political situation, with some disagreement among Aboriginal people and anthropologists about the significance of the site for which protection was being sought. I declined the heritage application on 10 September 1991 but announced that Alan Griffiths, Minister for Resources, and I would be holding discussions with the WA Labor government, Aboriginal people and the mining industry to address Aboriginal heritage issues in Western Australia.

The second was in February 1992 when I declined an application made by the Karijini Aboriginal Corporation for emergency protection for sites related to the Marandoo iron ore project. The proponent of the development, Hammersley Iron Pty Ltd, was a subsidiary of the mining giant CRA. In my dealings with CRA on Marandoo, I felt as if both I and Aboriginal people had been run over by a bulldozer. It was a crushing defeat for my commitment to direct negotiations between the industry and Aboriginal communities.

Any difficulties experienced with the WA Labor government on Aboriginal heritage issues were to be insignificant beside the disputes subsequently arising with the election of the Court Coalition government. It was that government that led the charge against Aboriginal rights on native title issues. Native title began to be linked with Aboriginal heritage issues.

In January 1994, immediately after the Native Title Act came into force, the Court government issued a lease over a 21-hectare site near Broome to entrepreneur Malcolm Douglas for the extension of a crocodile farm. I received an application for emergency protection from the Yawuru people, represented by the Kimberley Land Council, who were concerned that preliminary ground clearance work had already begun. Patrick Dodson was from this country and was in total support of an emergency declaration. One of the applicants for heritage protection had stated in an affidavit:

> If the ground is dug up, it will disturb the ground and cut the spirit in half. It will hurt the old people—inside their heart, they will cry. They will lose the power. It's like cutting a snake in half. It's the spirit, the power, the songs—it will upset everything and something will go wrong with the old people because they got the power to it that connection of that sing in the tribal way in this land—It's ground for the young men to go through safely.

An emergency 30-day declaration was granted to allow time for the interests of the Yawuru people to be considered. Ten days later I appointed Fred Chaney to prepare a report on the site and try to mediate an outcome to the dispute. The emergency declaration was extended for a further 30 days. Fred Chaney recommended that the whole area be protected and that there be restricted access at times of secret cultural activity. A permanent declaration was subsequently issued on 6 April 1994.

The permanent declaration was successfully challenged in the Federal Court by the WA government and by Malcolm Douglas. The court found against the validity of my decision on grounds of natural justice. The Commonwealth later unsuccessfully challenged this decision in the Full Federal Court. In any event, the developers made it clear that they were not prepared to recommence the project without a significant period of prior notice to the minister and the Aboriginal people. By this time a native title claim had been lodged over the site and, as a result, the immediate pressure went off the Yawuru people.

The year 1994 also brought forward an application for heritage protection in relation to the proposed site of the Hindmarsh Island bridge in South Australia near the mouth of the Murray River. The decision made regarding this application was to develop into a cause célèbre of the shoddiest kind. I have never been involved in a political issue that was to arouse such deep passions, both in support of and in opposition to my actions.

On 12 May 1994, in response to an application, I issued an emergency 30-day declaration under section 9 of the Act after advice from ATSIC to put a hold on the building of the bridge. I stressed that plans for the construction of the bridge had been in existence for some time and the Ngarrindjeri people, as Aboriginal custodians for the area, had brought their concerns about the effects of the proposed bridge on Aboriginal sites to my attention in late 1993 and applied for emergency protection in early 1994, once the SA government confirmed its intention to proceed with the bridge.

In granting the emergency declaration I said that I had also received a very strong letter from the SA State Aboriginal Heritage Committee, which advises the state government on these issues, urging me to protect the interests of Aboriginal people. A state government report revealed that the area in which the bridge construction works were proposed incorporated the remnants of 'a large Aboriginal township incorporating residential areas, shell middens, traditional burial places and specific camping places of the Ngarrindjeri and Ramemdjeri families who have a very deep cultural association with them'.

The proposal to build a bridge to Hindmarsh Island had left both sides of politics in South Australia with a somewhat blemished record. The bridge had been proposed by the Bannon Labor government and was subsequently supported as a pro-development initiative by the Arnold Labor government in the aftermath of the SA State Bank Royal Commission and in the rundown to the 1993 SA election. The SA Liberal Opposition Leader, Dean Brown, was strongly opposed to the bridge and described the contractual arrangements favouring the developer as 'the State Bank revisited' (a government-owned bank which had been involved in a major financial crisis). Alexander Downer, then Leader of the Opposition, and Ian McLachlan, the local federal member for Barker, were also opposed to the bridge at that time. As the alternative premier, Dean Brown was committed to reviewing the contractual arrangements with the developers of the marina and subdivision on Hindmarsh Island, who would have benefited from construction of the bridge.

When Dean Brown and the Liberals were elected to government in South Australia they commissioned a report into the government's contractual liability over the bridge. The report has never been made public, but the SA government has claimed that it was locked into the building of the bridge. The then SA Minister for Aboriginal Affairs, Dr Michael Armitage, issued approval under the SA Aboriginal heritage legislation for its construction.

When the emergency declaration was issued, state government representatives, and in particular Premier Brown, expressed outrage. At that stage the Adelaide *Advertiser* supported my decision, seeing it

as a way out for the state government from what had been a controversial and divisive proposal in South Australia.

I appointed Professor Cheryl Saunders, a lawyer of national standing, to write a report under section 10 of the Act on whether
permanent heritage protection was warranted. Professor Saunders was
the deputy chair of the Constitutional Centenary Foundation and
director of the Centre for Comparative Constitutional Studies in Melbourne and has, since 1989, held a permanent chair in law at
Melbourne University. She was completely independent from me. I had
only met her briefly at a public function and knew only of her standing
as one of Australia's most respected female jurists. She had been
regularly touted as a possible High Court appointee.

What needs to be clearly understood is that at all times during this
unfolding issue I acted with total honesty and in accordance with what
I believed were my responsibilities. Since the decision of the full Federal
Court in the Bropho case, I was required to commission a report when
I received a request for a permanent declaration. In such circumstances
I always sought to remain absolutely neutral and always appointed
respected and independent people to undertake these reports, as shown
by my appointments of Professor Saunders, Hal Wootten and Fred
Chaney. At no time did I ever or would I ever have sought to influence
in any way their independent, arm's-length report to me.

On 10 June 1994 I extended the emergency declaration for a
further 30 days. It was to expire on Monday, 11 July. I received the
final report from Professor Saunders on the preceding Thursday, and
a box of representations also arrived at my office in Canberra the next
day. The time frame was very short; the SA government was now
committed to building the bridge and was ready to send in the
bulldozers, most likely the following Monday.

Professor Saunders' central finding that persuaded me to act to
stop construction was that 'Hindmarsh and Mundoo Islands and the
waters surrounding them have a supreme spiritual and cultural significance for the Ngarrindjeri people, within the knowledge of the
Ngarrindjeri women which concerns the life force itself'. I recognised
that inevitably there would be disappointment as a result of my decision
but I stressed that, as Professor Saunders had highlighted, 'these areas
are important and deserve respect, preservation and sensitive judgement in the interests of all Australians'. There was not the slightest
suggestion in the report that the beliefs were not genuinely held.

I arranged to have the report sent to interested parties, including
the SA government. I had kept the Prime Minister briefed but had
been unable to speak to him that day. The next day, Saturday, I tried
to speak with him at Kirribilli House but he had gone out for the day
so I left a message for him to return my call. I received an extraordi-

nary telephone call from Premier Brown later that Saturday morning. He put his case to me for not issuing a declaration to prevent construction. It was evident that he had no understanding of even the general nature of Aboriginal spiritual beliefs. He kept telling me that the central issue raised in the Saunders report did not relate to an archaeological site; he was apparently totally oblivious to the role of heritage protection legislation in protecting spiritual beliefs.

After this I could no longer delay my decision and decided to issue a long-term declaration. 'If the reconciliation process is to be meaningful', I said later that day, 'it is especially important that the spiritual beliefs of Aboriginal people be accorded no lesser respect than the spiritual beliefs of non-Aboriginal Australians'. I pointed out that the SA government had failed to consult Aboriginal women adequately (as concluded by Professor Saunders) through its own heritage processes. The Saunders report noted an admission by the CEO of the SA Department of Aboriginal Affairs that this omission of women from the consultative process was a problem to be rectified.

The Heritage Protection Act requires the minister's declaration to be tabled in federal parliament. The Coalition moved to disallow the declaration, but their attempt failed even in the Senate because the Democrats and Greens voted with the government to support me. Opposition to the declaration in the House was led by Ian McLachlan, the Opposition spokesperson on the environment and local member for the area where the bridge was to be situated. His criticism of my decision stood in notable contrast to his own former opposition to the bridge.

Ian McLachlan conceded in the parliament on 9 November 1994, four months after the permanent declaration had been made, that in respect of the most high-profile and public advocate of my declaration, 'I am not doubting that she [Doreen Kartinyeri] believes what she says. Nobody seems to doubt that in any way at all'.

Aboriginal people were devastated, as was I, when Justice O'Loughlin of the Federal Court delivered a judgment on 14 February 1995 invalidating the decision to grant the declaration on technical grounds relating to natural justice. The main ground for invalidity was the inadequacy of the content of the notice advertising the proposed report by Professor Saunders, which was an issue outside my responsibility. The judge also concluded that I had failed to consider properly the representations made by interested parties and to read the contents of the Saunders report's confidential annex, which contained details of the women's spiritual beliefs.

The media and political frenzy that subsequently blew up over the Hindmarsh Island bridge was for me the most difficult experience of my term as minister. It also led to the resignation of Ian McLachlan as

a shadow minister. It centred around two confidential appendices to a
report by anthropologist Deane Fergie attached to a supplementary
submission to Professor Saunders by the Aboriginal Legal Rights Movement. The appendices were in an envelope and were referred to in the
Saunders report. They contained information about the women's spiritual beliefs which was not to be read by men. In her report Professor
Saunders twice expressly directed me not to look at the confidential
information. I repeatedly made it clear in my public statements, following the issue of the declaration, that I did not rely on this confidential
information but on Professor Saunders' publicly available report, as
indeed she said I should.

Many people, including sections of the media, were unable to cope
with the idea that Aboriginal women could hold beliefs that were secret
or confidential. Some people appeared to be obsessed by this secret
material. They could not, however, be unaware both of the significance
of the information to the women seeking protection and their deeply
held wish that the material be kept confidential and in no circumstances be read by a man.

The fact that our society accepts that some religious beliefs or
practices are able to be kept secret is not confined to Aboriginal sites
of significance. The Commonwealth Evidence Act of 1995, which had
been unanimously passed by the Australian parliament, recognises that
a member of the clergy is entitled to refuse to divulge that a religious
confession was made or the contents of that confession. I cannot recall
any public criticism of any kind of this legal right of secrecy held by
individuals in the Christian faith. On the wider matter of the desecration of Aboriginal sacred sites, it is also ironic that vandalising a church
is still regarded as criminal sacrilege in South Australia and punishable
by life imprisonment. Very different standards are applied to the
spiritual values of non-indigenous Australians.

On Monday, 6 March 1995, months after both houses of federal
parliament had voted to support my declaration, Ian McLachlan
rose to ask me a question in the House of Representatives. By this time
of my life I knew political deep trouble when I confronted it. Ian
McLachlan, Shadow Minister for the Environment, and Christine
Gallus, Shadow Minister for Aboriginal and Torres Strait Islander
Affairs, alleged by way of a tag team series of questions a serious
impropriety on my part concerning the handling of the confidential
documents, while John Howard, Leader of the Opposition, looked on
approvingly.

The questions came like a bolt out of the blue. Ian McLachlan
asked whether I had read the material in the sealed envelope. I denied

that I had. I had no idea what lay behind the question. Next Christine Gallus asked me whether I could 'assure the House that there are secure arrangements for ensuring their [the documents'] confidentiality at your office or at ATSIC or wherever they are held'. I answered her by confirming that the material had been kept confidential, which to the best of my knowledge it had.

Then Ian McLachlan strode to the dispatch box with a brown envelope in his hand and said:

> Here is a copy of the secret attachments to the Fergie Report, the secret letters, and I am sure you will lock them up in an safe place, otherwise it will be as you say, an abrogation of everything you stand for. Will you explain why you allowed these photocopies of those secret letters to be sent around Australia like flotsam in a wreck, in unregistered parcels, the copies of the letters in an unsealed envelope, addressed to a white Australian male by the name of McLaughlin?

I sat like a stunned mullet, believing that this highly confidential information had, through some fault of my own, been made public. I was already under enormous pressure as the result of my marriage breakup two days earlier. I could barely put one foot in front of the other, but no one outside my office knew of the pressure I was under. At that time I had no idea that my arrogant questioner had sanctioned interference with my mail. I rose to respond, knowing that my colleagues in the ALP and the media had been left with the impression that I had been caught out. I replied that I had no knowledge whatever of the matter he referred to.

I left the House feeling distressed and embarrassed. What could have happened? How could I have allowed myself to be put in this position? I went back to my office with key members of my staff. Not wanting to be set up, I had not taken away the envelope Ian McLachlan had thrown down on the table. We began to draft a letter of reply to him, but I felt sick because we were blindly seeking information about matters outside our control and about which we had no knowledge. Was the information in the envelopes legitimate and, if so, where did Ian McLachlan get it?

Paul Willoughby then took a call from a journalist that left us reeling in disbelief. Ian McLachlan had held a doorstop media conference immediately after Question Time. In response to a question from a journalist, he said, 'The documents came to my office because they were addressed to somebody else'. He went on to say:

> My office only made one copy. I mean, I can tell you what we got was a series of documents that thick. We made one copy of all those documents. I think they were meant for Sean McLaughlin in

[Tickner's] office who is a white Australian male. I mean that is who they were addressed to . . . when it comes to the security of these documents that he thinks are so important he can't even secure them and he can't get his office to secure them.

He went on to admit in response to a further question that the source of the documents was people associated with the court case in Adelaide. 'It was obvious to me', he said, 'that the box of materials had been sent from the Australian Government Solicitor in Adelaide'.

I held a media conference about half an hour after becoming aware of the consequences of Ian McLachlan's confession. I was very angry and determined to fight back. Mr McLachlan sought to destroy me politically and he had done so in circumstances where his and Christine Gallus's conduct—not to speak of John Howard who sanctioned it all—had in my view been totally dishonest and reprehensible. I was cautious with the media, but already sufficiently aware of the detail of what had occurred to start to set the record straight that night.

The next morning I sought to convince my senior ministerial colleagues of the serious and improper nature of Ian McLachlan's conduct. Some really didn't want to know. I found an ally in Michael Lavarch, whose portfolio was caught up in the issue because the parcel had emanated from the Australian Government Solicitor in Adelaide. By mid-morning the facts had become clear and we began to gather documentary evidence to support the case we were to mount against Ian McLachlan in the parliament.

The now indisputable truth was as follows. After the Federal Court case in Adelaide, a representative of the Government Solicitor phoned my office to speak to my Hindmarsh Island adviser, Sue Kee, to arrange for the return of the documents that had been used in the case. In Sue's absence on leave my senior adviser, Sean McLaughlin, took the call and, as he was well acquainted with the sensitive nature of the documents, asked the Government Solicitor's office in Adelaide to forward them to him for safe keeping until Ms Kee returned. My staff confirmed that when the box arrived in our office some time later it was apparently unopened, sealed and in proper form. No one in the office could have known that our private mail had been tampered with and copied with the authority of another member of parliament who was later to become Minister for Defence in the Howard government.

Through no fault of my own and through no fault of my staff or my solicitors, mail properly addressed to my senior adviser by the Australian Government Solicitor had, through a simple mistake over the names by Parliament House attendants, been inadvertently delivered to the office of Ian McLachlan. Mr McLachlan, at that time in South Africa, sanctioned by telephone the multiple copying of virtually all of the 8 kilos of confidential documents, among them those relating to the secret beliefs of the Aboriginal women. Copies of a vast quantity of sensitive material, including the Commonwealth's confidential legal documents, were sent to journalists and others, including the solicitors for the developers Tom and Wendy Chapman, who were at the time opposing the Commonwealth in the Federal Court case challenging my decision on the Hindmarsh Island bridge site. Then, after all this, Ian McLachlan, with the approval of John Howard, had stood up in the parliament alleging improper conduct by me, knowing that he had improperly sanctioned the copying and dissemination of private mail. Incredibly, Christine Gallus had collaborated in exploiting the Coalition's possession of the confidential information and caused great distress to the Aboriginal women concerned.

A government tactics meeting held at midday decided that the matter was so serious that a censure motion should be moved against Ian McLachlan. I was not rostered to be in Question Time that day and it was agreed that Michael Lavarch would move the motion and I would then stride into the parliament to second it. Michael's job that day was to be the politician and my job was to put the facts clearly on the public record. The motion was carried on party lines.

Within the government it was difficult to keep the issue alive, let alone convince anyone of its potential to force the resignation of Mr McLachlan or Ms Gallus. The next day I decided to use debate on the Bill to create the Indigenous Land Fund to respond to attacks made on me by Christine Gallus in debate earlier that week. I mounted a strong case against her conduct in the McLachlan affair and backed this up with a media statement. But there was little media coverage of my remarks, even though my call for her resignation was strongly backed by Ngarrindjeri women. She was later able to escape ultimate accountability for her actions as a result of some support given to her by Tracker Tilmouth from the Central Land Council.

Despite my best efforts to convince senior ministerial colleagues that there was clear evidence that Ian McLachlan had misled both the parliament and the public, the issue was in danger of fading. But the next day I was able to take another question in the House from Les Scott, the Member for Oxley, who asked what the reaction of Aboriginal women had been to the McLachlan affair. In hindsight, my answer was too long and diminished the effectiveness of my tactic, which was to take into the chamber the actual envelope sent from the Government Solicitor in Adelaide which had previously contained the confidential information. Sue Kee confirmed that the envelope was sealed when she opened the box of documents on her return from holidays. The Government Solicitor's office in Adelaide had confirmed by statutory declaration that the envelope was sealed when it was dispatched from

Adelaide. Ian McLachlan had consistently maintained that the document was not in a sealed envelope when it was copied by his staff member.

It was Sue Kee's suggestion that I take the actual envelope into the Chamber. I must say at the time I felt a little bit uncomfortable with it, even though the document had already been removed and handed back to a representative of the Ngarrindjeri women, who had come from Adelaide to collect it. In parliament I quoted what Ian McLachlan had said in a media release the day before: 'The secret letters arrived in an unsealed envelope without any markings on the outside'. I held up the original envelope on which were the words 'CONFIDENTIAL—FOR WOMEN'S EYES ONLY'. I asked, 'If the letters were in an unmarked and unsealed envelope and were not read, how were they identified?'

Ian McLachlan rose and, through the Speaker, asked that I table the envelope. His demand was reinforced by John Howard. I tabled the envelope and directly asked John Howard when he had learned of Ian McLachlan's conduct. Mr Howard did not reply.

The next day there was no media coverage of my parliamentary question, despite my best efforts after Question Time to highlight the seriousness of the revelations and that, in my view, Mr McLachlan had misled the parliament and the public. The media, who constantly lament the decline in the importance of parliament, had failed to report an important development which would lead the next day to the momentous news that Ian McLachlan had resigned.

But there was more work to be done. On the following Saturday morning I had a sixth sense that Bruce Jones, a *Sun Herald* Canberra journalist, would call me, as I had always found him to be very astute in following up key stories of the week. Sure enough he did, and he told me that he had interviewed John Howard the previous Wednesday night and had been told by Mr Howard that he had known about Ian McLachlan's sanctioning the copying and disseminating of my mail some three weeks before and that he, John Howard, had sanctioned the questions being asked in parliament. Mr Howard had accepted Mr McLachlan's resignation from the frontbench only grudgingly and had written to him after that resignation saying 'My personal esteem for you remains undiminished'.

That night and the next morning I did as much radio work as I could in raising public awareness of the role John Howard had played in the McLachlan affair. It was agreed by the Prime Minister's office the next day that it would be useful for the Attorney-General to push the issue for television that night, and the Prime Minister subsequently issued a statement from Europe putting further pressure on John

Howard and calling on him to answer specific detailed questions about his role in the affair.

On the following Monday the Attorney-General wrote to the Leader of the Opposition seeking the return of the documents still held by Ian McLachlan. The return of the documents was also pursued by solicitors for the Commonwealth, with letters to Mr McLachlan, Ms Gallus, and solicitors for the Chapman family, who had received the 8 kilos of documents courtesy of Ian McLachlan's office and had subsequently sought to use those documents in the court challenge to my declaration. On Tuesday SA Liberal Aboriginal Affairs Minister, Michael Armitage, appealed to 'everyone who has copies [of the documents] to return them forthwith to the Federal Minister'.

Paul Keating had been in Europe throughout this miserable business. When he returned he held a media conference in which he continued the attack on the Coalition for its actions in the Hindmarsh Island affair. On John Howard, in particular, he made a number of telling points about the role of the Coalition in passing documents to the solicitors in the court case. He increased the pressure on the Coalition to return the documents. The next day Ian McLachlan returned what he claimed were the documents in his possession, but I was not satisfied; a check revealed that key documents which Mr McLachlan said had been originally copied were not returned. One can only assume that there were so many documents being photocopied and handed around that ultimately they had no idea of what they had and what they distributed.

The Coalition were clearly damaged by the affair and one senior Coalition member had lost his job as a result of it. Despite all this, John Howard continued to endorse the conduct of Ian McLachlan. His deputy, Peter Costello, soon foreshadowed the return of Ian McLachlan to the Coalition frontbench. The fall of Ian McLachlan followed Alexander Downer's resignation as Leader of the Opposition after his disastrous tour to Aboriginal communities in central Australia. Within nine months two of the most damaging blows to the Coalition's credibility had come as a result of its leaders' incompetence in Aboriginal and Torres Strait Islander affairs.

If I ever had any doubts about my own role in the Hindmarsh Island heritage declaration they were put to rest when I visited Adelaide a short time later. I have never had the privilege of such a warm and supportive welcome, from a meeting with senior members of the Adelaide Christian community, a major function at the Adelaide Town Hall, and a well-attended and strongly supportive public meeting representing a wide cross-section of the South Australian community.

As matters stood on 18 May 1995, the declaration on the Hindmarsh Island bridge remained in place pending the hearing of an appeal against Justice O'Loughlin's decision to quash the original declaration. Ian McLachlan had been forced to resign and the Liberal Party establishment was not happy. On Friday, 19 May, Adelaide journalist Chris Kenny ran a story on Channel Ten news suggesting for the first time that the women's beliefs were fabricated because other Ngarrindjeri women had stated that they either did not know or did not believe in the claims about the women's business. This story was also carried in the Adelaide *Advertiser* the next day. For those out to attack Aboriginal people the story was a perfect opportunity to climb on the bandwagon of prejudice—here was a story which not only involved Aboriginal spiritual beliefs but women's beliefs and private ones at that.

After these stories, based on the media reports, I issued a media release accusing the Liberal Party of orchestrating the latest attacks on the spiritual beliefs of Ngarrindjeri women. I said that the attacks 'have the fingerprints of Mr McLachlan and the Liberal Party all over them'. I recorded the fact that the Channel Ten report on Friday night suggested that one of the dissident women, Dorothy Wilson, had 'been encouraged to speak out by a Liberal Party activist . . . who's received support from . . . Ian McLachlan'. It was also significant to me that the Monday editions of the *Daily Telegraph* and the Melbourne *Sun* carried stories which sought to undermine the veracity of the Ngarrindjeri women's spiritual beliefs and stated:

> Both newspapers quote from a document which was one of those
> improperly taken from my mail and copied by Mr McLachlan's office
> . . . Mr Howard and the Liberal Party should be aware that Aboriginal
> people were like other Australians when it came to adherence to
> spiritual beliefs. Some were believers and some were not. The only
> difference is that the Liberal Party would not dare to play politics with
> the spiritual beliefs of non-Aboriginal Australians as they continue to
> do with those of Aboriginal people.

Mr Howard had already called for an inquiry into the Hindmarsh Island issue.

I made it clear that, should the Full Federal Court support the decision of Justice O'Loughlin, I would be obliged by law to commission a further report since the Commonwealth legislation, as interpreted by the courts, required that 'I would again appoint an independent person of unquestioned ability and integrity to prepare that report'. Four days after the Channel Ten story it was revealed in the *Australian* that Sue Lawrie, an employee of right-wing Liberal

Victorian MP Ken Aldred, was the catalyst for the five so-called 'dissident' women speaking out.

For the record, I have never attacked the so-called 'dissident women', in public or in private. I have no doubt that they do not share the beliefs of the applicants for heritage protection. The case which has never been established, however, is that there was ever any 'fabrication'. Because other people hold beliefs different from your own does not mean that these beliefs are not sincerely held, as Professor Saunders had unambiguously reported to me.

The Opposition then began a new campaign in parliament on the Hindmarsh Island issue, and started throwing smearing allegations at me already raised in the Federal Court case before Justice O'Loughlin and decisively rejected by him. Christine Gallus and John Howard asked me in parliament on 28 May whether my staff had cut the tops off facsimiles to destroy documentary evidence of the timing of the Hindmarsh Island heritage declaration. In response I pointed out that these allegations had been 'trotted out' by some of the litigants in the court case and rejected as being without foundation (as they were) by a judge of the Federal Court.

Next came questions from Ian McLachlan and Christine Gallus on the timing of my decision to ban the bridge, in an attempt to undermine me. Ms Gallus did not let up and on Thursday, 1 June, asked me another question in the House suggesting that I had made this decision on the Friday, and not the Saturday morning as I had constantly stated as being the truth. In response to a question, I had said that I had not made a decision on whether to grant a declaration at the time I had been telephoned at my home on the morning of Saturday, 9 July, by Dean Brown.

When I was next in Question Time, Ian McLachlan rose to ask me a Question Without Notice in which he revealed he had obtained Premier Brown's telephone records and said: 'Optus records show that Premier Dean Brown's telephone call to you finished between 11.07 and 11.08 am Eastern Standard Time, that morning. Your Senior Adviser stated in the Federal Court that you had made your decision at 11.15 am Eastern Standard Time, that morning'. He asked whether I had misled Premier Brown or whether I had made the decision to issue the declaration 'within seven minutes after I put down the phone to the Premier'.

I replied with conviction, knowing that I had behaved honestly, and confirmed that 'there is absolutely nothing raised in the Honourable Member's question which in any way contradicts my public statements in the matter, including my statements in the Parliament'. The Premier's telephone records confirmed that I had made my decision after his phone call, as I had continually stressed. The truth was that the Premier's call was the catalyst for taking my decision that I could postpone no longer. I was, however, astounded by the lengths that the Coalition was prepared to go in attempting to undermine my stand. It also shows without doubt the extraordinary degree of complicity between the SA government and the federal Opposition.

The pressure continued relentlessly, with Ms Gallus debating the Hindmarsh Island issue in the House of Representatives on 6 June, and again raising the smears already decisively rejected by the Federal Court of Australia.

That night Chris Kenny ran a further story on Channel Ten in which it was alleged that Doug Milera, a former chairman of the Lower Murray Aboriginal Heritage Committee, had claimed that the women's business was a fabrication. This was followed on the morning of 7 June by a story by Colin James in the Adelaide *Advertiser* headed 'The great lie of Hindmarsh Island', which reported that an Aboriginal woman, Sarah Milera, had also claimed that the women's business was fabricated. Not knowing at that time of the credibility or otherwise of these media reports, I issued a brief four-paragraph statement that day saying that I was considering 'what course of action I should take'.

On 2 June Dean Brown had written a letter to the Prime Minister where he referred to the 'latest developments', which 'raise serious questions about the conclusions of the report presented to the Minister by Professor Cheryl Saunders'. Despite subsequent suggestions to the contrary, the Premier did not call for a further Commonwealth inquiry but concluded his letter by saying, 'In the event that you are not prepared to revoke the ban within the next 24 hours, I must advise that the South Australian Government will consider other options to prevent further damage being done to Aboriginal interests and communities'.

By this time it had become clear that whatever the result of the Federal Court appeal, the political campaign against the women's beliefs and against me would continue, and I decided that there had to be a further inquiry and report to end the matter. I had already been considering who to appoint to undertake the task. I was searching for another woman of high integrity as the applicants for heritage protection had repeatedly made clear they would only talk of their beliefs to another woman. After consulting with the Attorney-General and his department, it was agreed that Justice Jane Mathews would be an ideal person. I was advised that her appointment was to be cleared with the Chief Justice of the Federal Court of Australia, Justice Michael Black. I spoke to Justice Mathews, who agreed to the appointment, and I prepared a media release announcing it.

One hour later, I heard on the ABC news that the SA government proposed a state royal commission into the Hindmarsh Island issue.

The announcement by Premier Brown had been made before the expiration of the purported deadline given in his letter to the Prime Minister. The Premier later said that he had acted on the basis of a media report, suggesting that the Prime Minister had rebuffed his letter. But the Prime Minister's office strenuously denied issuing any such statement.

I rushed down to the Prime Minister's office and told his senior adviser, John Bowen, what had happened. He suggested I speak to the Prime Minister urgently and got him on the phone at the Lodge. He sounded as angry and astonished as I was and suggested I call Premier Brown urgently and find out if the Royal Commission was a *fait accompli*. The Premier confirmed that it would be going ahead. I terminated the conversation with more civility than Dean Brown deserved and returned to my office to issue my own media release announcing the Mathews reporting procedure that I already had in place. I said that the reporting process by Justice Mathews would begin once the Full Federal Court had handed down its decision on my appeal against Justice O'Loughlin's invalidation of my declaration on the bridge site.

In later debates before the SA Estimates Committee on 29 June, Michael Armitage said: 'The South Australian Government's position was quite clear in that it was, we believed, a role for the Federal Minister to have an inquiry. We are on record for a number of days asking the Federal Minister to have that. The Premier wrote to the Prime Minister and almost immediately the Prime Minister turned down that request'. This was simply not true. The Premier did not ask the Commonwealth to hold a fresh inquiry, and in any event there was no response from the Prime Minister to Premier Brown before the calling of the SA Royal Commission.

In Question Time that afternoon Ian McLachlan asked me why I took so long to announce an inquiry, 'which you seem to have done some hours after the Premier of South Australia wrote to you by facsimile telling you that he had decided to announce his own inquiry'. Again, that assertion was simply not true and I can only assume Ian McLachlan was notified of the SA government's decision before I was.

The first the Commonwealth government heard about the South Australian Royal Commission was on ABC radio. In answer to a question by Ian McLachlan, I asked those who adhere to other religious faiths and beliefs how they would feel if a royal commission was held into their spiritual beliefs. I then tabled copies of transcripts of separate radio interviews of Doug and Sarah Milera in which Mr Milera said 'No I don't believe it's a fabrication', and Sarah Milera expressly denied the accuracy of the *Advertiser*'s story. Christine Gallus then moved a censure motion against me which was lost on party lines.

The SA Royal Commission was always going to be an exercise in futility. The decision of the Full Federal Court in *Bropho v. Tickner* made it clear that whenever the federal minister received an application for heritage protection under the Act, there was an obligation on that minister to commission a report under section 10. Clearly, as the Howard government later acknowledged, a royal commission established under state law could not be relied on by the Commonwealth minister.

Speaking to the media, Premier Brown made it clear that he had called the Royal Commission on the basis of media reports alleging fabrication, 'and it could well be that there was no fabrication'. It was subsequently revealed that the Kenny report on Channel Ten on which the Premier relied had only run selected statements from Doug Milera, while other statements not shown did not lend weight to allegations of fabrication. Furthermore, it was revealed that Mr Milera had been drinking before the interview and was given \$200, allegedly for accommodation by Channel Ten. When I heard Dean Brown's admission about the flimsy reason for calling the Royal Commission, I issued a statement noting that it was 'remarkable for a Premier to apply the heavy hand of government at vast public expense through a Royal Commission without having sought and considered direct evidence on the issue at the centre of the inquiry' and concluded that 'Premier Brown's admission indicates that the motivation behind the Royal Commission is purely political'.

The role of some sections of the media in reporting claims, or alleged claims, by the Chapmans and their supporters, was truly reprehensible. Story after story was run without even the most basic attempts to check the facts, or to seek comment from me.

The Chapmans made 150-odd allegations against me and Professor Saunders in the original court case challenging my decision. Justice O'Loughlin said of them, 'the litigation was unnecessarily prolonged as a result of their fixation that they have been the victims of a conspiracy to ignore their rights'. Notably, Justice O'Loughlin, who was to invalidate my original decision to issue a declaration on other legal grounds, expressly rejected attacks on the independence and professionalism of Professor Saunders:

> I accept without qualification Professor Saunders as a witness of truth.
> She performed her tasks professionally, dispassionately and with
> competence. I reject the aspersions which have been cast on her and
> on the manner in which she performed her duties. There are areas in
> which I find myself unable to agree with her but they are matters of
> law. Such disagreement does not reflect in any way on her integrity.

And so the media furore raged on as the Royal Commission was set up, and then throughout the rest of the year. Article after article, smear after smear, not only of me but especially of the claims of spiritual beliefs by the Ngarrindjeri women. The worst elements of talkback radio were busy disparaging Aboriginal beliefs and there was little I could do to respond effectively. It was a small-scale version of what was to come with Pauline Hanson. There is a ready market out there in radio land for prejudice and hostility to Aboriginal people and their beliefs.

The Hindmarsh Island Royal Commission began in Adelaide on 19 July 1995 with a retired District Court Judge, Mrs Iris Stephens, appointed as the Commissioner. The Commonwealth Solicitor-General, Gavin Griffiths QC, made the Commonwealth's opposition to the Royal Commission clear at the start and presented legal argument on issues of concern about the Royal Commission. The Commonwealth was not otherwise represented during proceedings as it was not a royal commission inquiring into my conduct and could not replace the responsibility of the Commonwealth minister under the Commonwealth legislation to commission a further report.

Nor did the Aboriginal women who had sought heritage protection appear before the Royal Commission, making their views on the Commission clear through their legal representative. Their submission reads in part:

> We are deeply offended that a government in this day and age has the audacity to order an inquiry into our secret sacred spiritual beliefs. Never before have any group of people had their spiritual beliefs scrutinised in this way. It is our responsibility as custodians of this knowledge to protect it. Not only from men, but also from those not entitled to this knowledge. We have a duty to keep Aboriginal law in this country. Women's business does exist, has existed from time immemorial and will continue to exist where there are Aboriginal women who are able to continue to practice their culture.

There were attempts by Ngarrindjeri women to have the Royal Commission stopped as being in breach of the Racial Discrimination Act, but these claims were rejected by the SA Supreme Court, and the Royal Commission continued. But opposition to it grew. Even before it began hearings, a national meeting of representative Aboriginal bodies and land councils issued a strong statement of concern on 22 June in which they claimed that the Royal Commission 'is a corruption of the concept of democracy under the Westminster system of government and represents a gross misuse of public funds for political purposes' and 'a concerted, orchestrated attack by the SA Government upon the rights of Aboriginal peoples of Australia to maintain and exercise their cultural identity and religious obligations'. They also condemned the Australian media for its overall racial bias in reporting on the Hindmarsh Bridge affair. The Royal Commission was condemned by the leaders of virtually all the churches in South Australia as well as by the Democrats, the Greens, the SA Trades and Labour Council and unanimously by the SA ALP.

On 27 July, soon after the Royal Commission started, Doug Milera, the person named by the Premier as the very foundation for the inquiry, issued a statement through his solicitors in which he denied any fabrication and, among other things, apologised to me for the 'inconvenience and upset' that had been caused. The statement was tendered to the Royal Commission by his solicitors but was not accepted. Mr Milera's statement reads in part: 'I do not believe that the Women's Business was fabricated. I do not dispute the validity of the beliefs held by those women who have those beliefs. I do not believe it is for me—as a man—to be involved in a Royal Commission into whether the women's business is true or not'.

Doug Milera admitted he was drunk when interviewed by Chris Kenny, on camera, on 5 June: 'I said a number of things in the interview which I did not believe. I spoke in anger. My anger arose out of aspects of the Hindmarsh Island Bridge issue which are outside the terms of reference of this Commission'. He declined to be further involved in the Royal Commission and instructed his counsel to withdraw.

There was no end to the skullduggery of the campaign against the Aboriginal women. On 16 August a number of media organisations were sent a letter, purportedly written to me by Patrick Dodson, in which he supposedly confirmed that the Ngarrindjeri women's business was fabricated. The letter was, of course, itself a fabrication. The perpetrators of this hoax were never found.

Opponents of the Royal Commission were, however, successful in having the SA Supreme Court declare that SA Aboriginal Affairs Minister, Michael Armitage, had unlawfully authorised the release of Aboriginal heritage documents to the Royal Commission. The effect of this decision was that the SA minister had to consult the Aboriginal community of South Australia again before the information could be validly released to the Royal Commission. Despite the fact that the overwhelming majority of Aboriginal people subsequently consulted by Michael Armitage objected to the passing of the information to the Commission, their views were ignored and he passed it on anyway.

On 7 December the Full Federal Court had brought down its decision upholding the decision of Justice O'Loughlin against the validity of my declaration on natural justice grounds, and, among other things, made it clear that the determining minister was legally required to look at all material provided to him, even if it was confidential spiritual beliefs of Aboriginal women. Once this was known to be the law it was not difficult to comply with it by the temporary appointment of a female minister.

The day before the Royal Commission reported I issued a pre-emptive media release in which I again emphasised that it was 'legally untenable' for me to rely on the SA Royal Commission report as a basis for decision-making under the federal legislation. I placed on record key issues of fact that had consistently been misrepresented in the media. I emphasised that there had been a further application for heritage protection lodged by the Ngarrindjeri women and that the women maintained their view that their private spiritual beliefs should not be revealed to men and for 'this reason only' had requested that the application be considered by a female minister. Late in December 1995 the Prime Minister designated Senator Rosemary Crowley to act in assessing the application submitted by the Ngarrindjeri women, and in January she formally appointed Justice Jane Mathews to produce a further report under section 10 of the Heritage Protection Act.

When the Royal Commission report was released with a finding that beliefs had been fabricated, there was a predictable media frenzy. Premier Brown jubilantly proclaimed that the conclusions of the Royal Commission on fabrication 'could not be clearer' and that, as a result, work on the bridge 'must be allowed to proceed as soon as possible'. I gave a press conference and accused Premier Brown of 'blowing $2 million of public money on a witch hunt. The extraordinary find-ings of retired District Court Judge Stephens simply fly in the face of evidence which was before the Commission.' I stressed that Premier Brown was 'backing off at a million miles an hour from any possibility that any individuals would be charged with committing offences flow-ing from the Royal Commission'.

As far as I was concerned, if there was evidence of any fabrication of spiritual beliefs, the people responsible should be charged with any available offence under either state or Commonwealth law, including perjury charges arising from the Royal Commission itself. But of course none would be charged because there was no evidence of fabrication. The key event where fabrication was said to occur was at a meeting also attended by Aboriginal Legal Rights Movement solicitor Tim Woolley, who had acted for the applicants for heritage protection. Mr Woolley gave evidence on oath that directly contradicted the evi-dence given by the person who alleged fabrication. He said at page 4357 of the Royal Commission transcript, 'If I had been aware that there was a fabrication I would not have continued to act. It was quite clear to me that there was no fabrication'. Yet the Royal Commission accepted the allegation of fabrication but no action was taken to charge anyone with perjury or any other offence.

My media release said:

> The indisputable fact is that if Commissioner Stephens' findings were to be relied on by the Premier the inescapable conclusion is that individuals giving express evidence disputing allegations of fabrication and the occurrence or non-occurrence of certain specific events would in the normal course of events be subject to a serious criminal charge of giving false evidence to the Royal Commission. But of course no one will be charged because Premier Brown knows full well that any such charge would be bounced out of a court of law. The Royal Commission is now, and always was, pure politics.

I do not propose to make a detailed analysis of the findings of the Royal Commission here. This has already been done by Adelaide lawyer Greg Mead in *A Royal Omission*, published before the release of the Commission's report. Mr Mead concludes that the evidence given by women opposing the claim of secret spiritual beliefs held by other women falls 'far short of proving that any fabrication took place . . . The highest point of evidence was that if there were any women's business then some or all of the dissident women should have known about it, [but] there are ample anthropological reasons why knowledge in Aboriginal societies is selectively handed down and restrictively disseminated'.

The allegations of fabrication and the campaign against my declaration to prevent construction of the bridge were led by a small band of journalists and commentators, most of whom are acknowledged political conservatives. Others have approached the reporting of issues associated with the Royal Commission not as reporters but as public advocates for a particular position.

The Aboriginal women seeking heritage protection had boycotted the Royal Commission with the exception of one woman who had given limited evidence consistent with her beliefs. I asked: 'How can one take seriously findings of this kind when only one side of the story was presented? The Royal Commission had no credibility when it was established and it has none on its conclusion'. Most journalists were not remotely interested in any serious analysis, and junior journalists who knew nothing of the issues wrote with mindless authority about the fabrication of the spiritual beliefs.

Perhaps the most damning criticism of that Royal Commission came from Mick Dodson in a statement read to a public meeting in Adelaide on 26 August 1995:

It is hard to find the right words to convey the mixture of outrage, distress and shame that I feel about what is happening in South Australia . . .

The right to religious freedom and respect for spiritual beliefs lies at the heart of human rights. It is a right which all Australians are obliged to respect, and all Australians entitled to enjoy. And that principle holds irrespective of whose beliefs are at issue, or on what basis those beliefs are held. What we have in this Royal Commission is the abuse of the human rights of Aboriginal people masquerading as a lofty legal procedure.

For the record, let me add this. In the year 2000 nothing I have heard, read or seen since my first contact with heritage claims concerned with Hindmarsh Island would provide even the flimsiest foundation of evidence that such claims were fabricated. I have never attacked those Aboriginal women who do not share those beliefs, but nothing they have ever said has convinced me that claimants for heritage protection do not genuinely hold those beliefs. If there was evidence to the contrary I would be prepared to change my views and make judgments accordingly. Until that day I will rely upon the report of Cheryl Saunders, whose competency and integrity in that regard has been upheld by the Federal Court.

As I had predicted, the Royal Commission did not resolve the Hindmarsh Island matter. The Chapmans kept up the pressure on me, announcing during the federal election campaign that a legal action was to be commenced against me and the Commonwealth government seeking substantial damages. In a public statement I restated the position I had consistently taken: 'The Federal Government's legal advice is that it is not liable to pay compensation in the circumstances of this case'.

The Mathews report was completed on 27 June 1996, and delivered to John Herron, the first Minister for Aboriginal and Torres Strait Islander Affairs in the Howard government. The report was not released to the public at that time, pursuant to an undertaking given by the minister after a legal challenge to the appointment of Justice Mathews lodged by the dissident women. That challenge was upheld by the High Court on the basis of the separation of powers doctrine in an unexpected landmark decision that has significant ramifications for the Commonwealth for its dealings with Commonwealth judges, far beyond the indigenous affairs portfolio. In essence the decision has the effect that a Commonwealth-appointed judge cannot be allocated a non-judicial function or position by the Commonwealth. This means that, contrary to long-established practice, Commonwealth-appointed judges can never be appointed to conduct reviews or inquiries outside their strict legal functions as judges. The decision by the High Court must be respected, but it was a fatal blow to the Ngarrindjeri women seeking heritage protection.

When the Mathews report was publicly released, virtually all media reports suggested that it supported the allegation of fabrication. Hearing and seeing those reports, I felt very depressed, believing that if the reports were true both Cheryl Saunders and I had been misled by the Ngarrindjeri women claiming heritage protection. But I thought I had better look at the Mathews report myself rather than rely on what the media said about it, and when I did my opinion of the competency of the Australian media fell even lower. I only had to look to page 2 of Justice Mathews' report, where I read that it was

> anticipated that restricted women's knowledge would also be the focus of this report, an expectation which was supported by a request in the application that a female Minister be appointed to consider the matter. That request was originally granted (by the Keating Government) but a male Minister was later appointed. For this and other reasons . . . the applicant women have not been prepared to reveal the contents of any restricted women's knowledge. Accordingly, it has been unnecessary in this report to embark upon the vexed issue of whether 'women's business' or restricted women's knowledge exists in Ngarrindjeri culture.

In all the circumstances and in the absence of evidence of the private spiritual beliefs of the women, Justice Mathews concluded that, while the other evidence put forward 'may well make the [Hindmarsh Island] area a "significant Aboriginal area", there is insufficient material from which the Minister could be satisfied that the building of the Hindmarsh Island Bridge would desecrate this area according to these traditions. This assessment of course does not involve any consideration of the confidential women's spiritual beliefs'.

This, of course, was the very essence of the application. One simple fact is indisputable. The women claiming private spiritual beliefs did not reveal those beliefs to the Royal Commission or to what was to be the subsequent reporting process of Justice Jane Mathews. Only Professor Saunders' inquiry had the opportunity to hear of these beliefs and her report was unequivocal in recognising the veracity of their existence. The Howard government deserves to be condemned for the waste of public money caused by the conduct of the Mathews inquiry and the failure to appoint a female minister in circumstances where it was already known that the women would not disclose their secret religious beliefs to a male.

In September 1996 John Herron foreshadowed special legislation to exempt the Hindmarsh Island site from a further inquiry under the Commonwealth heritage legislation. His proposal was initially objected to by the federal Opposition, but the ALP leader, Kim Beazley, and the shadow minister, Daryl Melham, subsequently issued a joint statement in which they said that 'the Opposition believes that the Hindmarsh Island Bridge can now proceed' and that special legislation was not necessary 'according to legal advice obtained by Mr Melham'. They went on to say: 'If the Minister for Aboriginal and Torres Strait Islander Affairs, John Herron, were to decide on the basis of all the material now on the public record, including the Mathews report, that further pursuit of the claim was vexatious, the Opposition would not contest that decision'. I can only assume that the legal advice, which was not made public, was based on the wording of the decision of the Full Federal Court in the Bropho case, where the court indicated that a section 10 heritage reporting process was not necessary when the claim was 'vexatious'.

It is impossible to argue reasonably that the Ngarrindjeri claim was vexatious. The women provided their confidential information in good faith to Professor Saunders but then had refused to participate in the SA Royal Commission into their spiritual beliefs, which had put those beliefs on public trial in their absence. They were subject to ridicule and vilification by large sections of the print and electronic media in a manner that no other religious or spiritual group in the Australian community would have to endure. The very idea of 'secret women's business' became the subject of facile, snide disparagement among right-wing commentators and others who were prepared to thoughtlessly parrot their views. That so-called Royal Commission had found a fabrication despite any substantive evidence to support such a finding. The women had subsequently been prepared to tell their story to a female minister but this had been refused by the Howard government and Minister Herron.

For the Ngarrindjeri women whose beliefs had been trampled on, the pain must have been very great, and deepened by the subsequent decision of the federal Opposition to support the Howard government's legislation, which dispensed with the need for any further inquiry when the Hindmarsh Island Bridge Act passed through parliament in May 1997. To their credit, the Democrats and the Greens opposed the Bill.

The validity of the Act was upheld by the High Court in *Kartinyeri v. Commonwealth*, where it was argued by the Ngarrindjeri women that the power granted to the Commonwealth by the 1967 referendum could only be used for the benefit of Aboriginal people. Only Justice Kirby dissented, concluding that the Constitution 'permits special laws for people on the ground of their race. But not so as to adversely and detrimentally discriminate against such people on that ground'.

I knew that the moment I acted to call for an independent report of the initial application by the Ngarrindjeri women for heritage protection, as I was obliged by law to do, the issue would be extraordinarily difficult to deal with. I saw it involving a clash of cultures and resulting in political point-scoring, but I could not have anticipated the extraordinary forces which the decision to grant a declaration unleashed.

14

ABORIGINAL HEALTH: A FIXABLE PROBLEM

When ATSIC was established it was never intended that it would be immediately responsible for anything other than its very limited health expenditure to supplement the vast health programs of the Commonwealth, state and territory health departments directed to all Australians. Five years after the establishment of ATSIC it was clear that limited progress had been made in addressing poor indigenous health. Expenditure levels in indigenous communities remained woefully inadequate and health departments had failed to apply principles of equity in allocating resources to indigenous health.

This book was never intended to be a whitewash of the failings of the Labor government. This chapter tells the inside story of the wasted last opportunity this century for the Australian Labor Party in government to mount a serious program to tackle what has wrongly been seen as intractable problems of Aboriginal health. It is unarguable that the appalling health of indigenous Australians and the related third world living conditions in Aboriginal communities is a blight on Australia's international identity. What is not recognised by most non-indigenous Australians, including politicians, is that these are fixable problems. They should not be put in the policy too-hard basket.

While it is undeniably important that indigenous people play their part in improving health through personal responsibility and community-driven programs to tackle such issues as bad diet and substance abuse, they cannot make the necessary changes alone. Without the strategic intervention of the national government, driven if necessary by a campaign of public opinion, no lasting change will be possible. Indigenous people living in isolated communities are among the poorest Australians and do not have any hope of addressing the $2 billion plus infrastructure backlog in those communities, which has a direct relationship to poor health standards.

In the last year of the twentieth century, Australia, one of the most affluent nations on earth, cannot stand by while large sections of its indigenous population does not enjoy the most basic housing, water, infrastructure, roads, water and sewerage facilities. This is a precondition to improved indigenous health across Australia.

Diverse Australians from Fred Hollows to Malcolm Fraser, RCIADIC, and every independent view of Aboriginal health have concluded not that governments are 'throwing too much money at the problems but that so much more needs to be done'. There is already a strategy in existence to bring about the necessary dramatic change to indigenous health ready to be embraced by a Commonwealth government with the political will to act.

———

The period of the Hawke and Keating governments was a time of genuine progress in addressing indigenous aspirations and social justice. It gives me no joy to record that there was, at the same time, a major failing on an issue that amounted to a blow to progress in addressing the social justice agenda of the reconciliation process. That failure was the decision not to tackle Aboriginal and Torres Strait Islander health issues effectively, especially in the 1995/96 budget. Those people reading this account of these events should not construe it as an attack on Paul Keating, who did more than any other Australian prime minister to advance indigenous rights. The government's failure to act was, in my view, a reflection of a much wider failure of the nation as a whole to understand and to care sufficiently about the issues.

Everything possible had been done to prepare the climate for a favourable decision by the government in that budget. Indigenous people were badly let down by our government, which had failed to support the sweeping reform initiatives being proposed. I believed then, and still believe, that the 1995/96 budget presented the last real opportunity to put initiatives in place to tackle indigenous health and infrastructure issues in the remaining years to the centenary of Federation.

From the beginning, ATSIC had only a subsidiary role and limited resources compared to the vast power and resources of the health departments of the Commonwealth and the states. The challenge was to get those departments to allocate an equitable share of resources to Aboriginal health. While Gerry Hand was minister, considerable work had been done by government officials and representatives of indigenous health services on a National Strategy on Aboriginal and Torres Strait Islander Health (NAHS). The work had yet to be endorsed by governments when I was appointed minister in April 1990.

Having been informed there was to be a national meeting of Commonwealth, state and territory health ministers in Brisbane on 10 June 1990, Aboriginal affairs ministers convened an urgent meeting with health ministers to seek ministerial endorsement of NAHS. The proposal taken to the meeting was unanimously endorsed in less than twenty minutes. But endorsement by ministers was one thing; action by governments to give effect to that strategy was another. At the conclusion of the ministers' meeting a joint Commonwealth–state decision to establish NAHS was announced.

The central thrust of NAHS was that public (or environmental) health issues had to be addressed as a precondition of good health for the people in those hundreds of communities around the country living in third world conditions. It was a strategy based on cooperative action between the Commonwealth and the state and territory governments. 'Health hardware', as Fred Hollows used to call it, is the major health issue requiring government's capital funding; indigenous communities with their meagre resources cannot be expected to fund it. My immediate challenge was to try and secure Commonwealth, state and territory dollars to give effect to the adopted strategy. I did not know then, but am convinced now, that no strategy can be successful without the Commonwealth using its constitutional power over state and territory governments to force the pace and direction of change.

On 25 September 1990, at a conference on OTITIS Media in Darwin, I gave a speech reviewing the latest figures on Aboriginal health, stating that to be born Aboriginal in Australia in 1990 means being 'statistically doomed' and that a massive financial commitment of $2.5 billion was required to address environmental health problems afflicting Aboriginal communities. As a new minister I was seeking to build what public support I could for the allocation of funds by governments to the problem.

Cabinet considered a joint submission from myself and the Minister for Health, Brian Howe, in December 1990 and committed an additional, but meagre, $232 million over five years, with the bulk of funds to be directed to ATSIC's housing, water, sewerage and community infrastructure programs. This amount was a drop in the ocean compared with the vast need. After the Cabinet meeting Brian Howe and I issued a joint statement expressing high hopes for the health strategy. But its goals are as far from achievement in 2000 as they were a decade ago.

The provision of infrastructure to all citizens has been seen historically as a direct constitutional responsibility of state and territory governments. It is a responsibility they have abjectly failed to fulfil in Aboriginal and Torres Strait Islander communities, and this failure has, then and now, bedevilled policy development in indigenous health. Cabinet's decision to make Commonwealth expenditure on the health strategy conditional on comparable expenditure by state and territory governments was well intentioned, both to maximise the total government expenditure and to lock in the states and territories to a national commitment. But it was tortuously difficult to get commitments from the states and territories. So while securing additional Commonwealth funding was a step forward, the outcome fell woefully short of what was needed to address the infrastructure backlog.

Negotiations with state and territory governments were overseen by Peter Shergold. Extracting enhanced expenditure commitments from those governments was, however, like pulling teeth. In many cases it became very difficult to verify commitments as new expenditure. This time-consuming exercise impeded the progress of implementing the NAHS.

The cause of indigenous health was assisted by the RCIADIC recommendations, about twenty of which were related to Aboriginal health. The recommendations had a particular focus on access and equity in the provision of mainstream health services but also covered a wide ambit of health policy, including cross-cultural training of health workers, adequate representation of indigenous people in all aspects of the health care industry, adequate resources of indigenous health services, indigenous mental health, and continuing indigenous involvement in all health care programs.

The Commonwealth's financial commitments in response to RCIADIC boosted key aspects of indigenous health and funded a national survey of indigenous people which was to include health-related issues. Funding was also to be provided over five years for the establishment of additional drug and alcohol services designed, controlled and staffed by Aboriginal people, which were to have a particular focus on the needs of youth. No state or territory government made any substantial financial commitment to Aboriginal health in response to RCIADIC, even though they had followed the Commonwealth in giving unanimous support to its recommendations.

RCIADIC had emphasised the need for governments to apply principles of access and equity, especially in recommendation no. 198, which was supported by all governments. But subsequent deeds again did not match words, and failure of all governments to give effect to it is a bedrock issue in Aboriginal and Torres Strait Islander affairs.

To give an example, despite the fact that Aboriginal and Torres Strait Islander people are beyond doubt the most afflicted Australians, they use mainstream health services and benefits less than non-indigenous Australians. The Aboriginal and Torres Strait Islander Social Justice Commissioner reported in 1995 that in 1993–94 the sum of mainstream and specific health expenditure on indigenous people was 1.26 per cent of total Commonwealth health expenditure even though indigenous people constituted 1.6 per cent of the population at that time.

Increasingly, I came to the view that either the Commonwealth should take over the entire responsibility which the states and territories had refused to fulfil, or those jurisdictions must be compelled by the exercise of Commonwealth power to fulfil them. In either case, policies should be implemented in the context of self-determination, with indigenous people having the maximum direct control over programs. In turn, the Commonwealth could only fulfil its proper role in addressing indigenous human rights and disadvantage if, within its own jurisdiction, principles of access and equity were applied. I fought a losing battle on this front during all my time as minister, and was convinced that real changes would only occur with prime ministerial intervention and leadership across the whole of government.

After the 1993 election, indigenous affairs, as mentioned earlier, was transferred from Employment, Education and Training to the Prime Minister's portfolio. Supervising the implementation of the government's Access and Equity Strategy, as it related to indigenous people, became an additional portfolio responsibility. This strategy was intended to ensure that disadvantaged groups in the community gained access to and a fair share of government programs. I approached this task with enthusiasm and considerable optimism and promptly sought a briefing on current initiatives from PM&C's Office of Multicultural Affairs, which was responsible for the strategy.

There was a naive belief in the ALP Caucus that there was a high-powered bureaucracy with PM&C riding shotgun over other federal departments to ensure compliance with the strategy, or at least effectively monitoring their non-compliance. Nothing could be further from the truth. The briefing showed that there was little more than one fairly junior person dedicated to work on the task and that the strategy as it related to indigenous people was a sham. An ensuing meeting with key departmental officials convinced me that an independent review of the government's performance was needed. The effectiveness of the strategy's implementation was subsequently referred to the House of Representatives Standing Committee on Aboriginal and Torres Strait Islander Affairs for inquiry.

The committee, comprising Liberal and National MPs as well as Labor members, reported unanimously in December 1993, finding in their report, *Rhetoric or Reality?*, that there was still a large proportion of Aboriginal and Torres Strait Islander people not getting appropriate access to, or a fair share of, the government services available to all other Australians and ATSIC's limited budget cannot overcome this failure. A blunt comparison proves the point—the Commonwealth's diesel fuel rebate scheme costs as much as all ATSIC activities put together.

The then Minister for Health, Graham Richardson, began to take a strong public stand in support of a more concentrated effort on Aboriginal health. Senator Richardson's manifestation of interest was to boost the hopes of Aboriginal and Torres Strait Islander people that government support for a change in policy would be forthcoming, but those hopes were dashed only a few months later. The early signs were again optimistic. Soon after the Christmas break, on 20 January 1994, Senator Richardson visited remote Aboriginal communities in the Northern Territory, described the conditions faced by many of them as a national scandal, and said that not enough money was being spent on Aboriginal health.

As environment minister, Graham Richardson to his great credit had done much to advance Labor's cause and on the way protect the environment in the lead-up to the 1990 election. In a strategic political operation he had formed alliances with key elements of the environment movement, to the mutual benefit of both the environment movement and the party. Now he was presenting himself as the champion of Aboriginal health. He appeared on *60 Minutes* and huge expectations began to grow in the Aboriginal community about what he might deliver on Aboriginal health. The broad thrust of his proposals were leaked to the media by sources that appeared to be very closely connected to him, to put it in its politest form. I had no great problem with this as it was obviously done with the intention of building public support for government action.

In essence, he was proposing $1.3 billion in new funding, with responsibility for indigenous health to shift from ATSIC to the federal health department. ATSIC would keep all its existing health funds and, though they were fairly modest, would at least be able to apply them to the infrastructure backlog. Graham Richardson showed a commendable willingness to negotiate the funding package and other proposals with the ATSIC Board. The board in turn was willing to, or at least had an open mind on, the idea of shifting ATSIC's limited responsibility for indigenous health to the Commonwealth health department, on the condition that ATSIC receive a substantial boost in funding for infrastructure.

I saw Graham Richardson's intervention as a potential opportunity, if it could be modified, to make the radical changes necessary to make a difference. The support being shown for reform in indigenous health by the AMA's president, Brendan Nelson, was also welcome—the AMA had historically been an enemy of the ALP.

On 10 March 1994, in an address to a health summit meeting in Canberra, convened by the AMA and chaired by Brendan Nelson, I again pushed the agenda for change, saying that Graham Richardson's proposals would be welcome but that they were 'really more crumbs from the table in terms of the inexcusable backlog [in infrastructure] that exists and the need that has got to be addressed'. In other words, there needed to be a much sharper focus on infrastructure in the proposals. In an off-the-cuff but recorded address to the AMA I warned that even 'the proposal by Senator Richardson to leave ATSIC with the money would invariably be resisted by the Department of Finance and Treasury and, Dr Nelson, they don't leave their guns at the door, let me tell you. They come in going for blood at every opportunity'. How right I was.

As a way of driving home the need for greater accountability by the Commonwealth for its own health expenditure, the record of the Royal Flying Doctor Service was highlighted. The organisation received, even then, some $13 million per annum in public funding; half of its clients were Aboriginal people, but not one Aboriginal person had a position on its numerous boards.

There were high hopes that Graham Richardson had convinced Paul Keating of the need to move on a broad agenda of indigenous health reform. But the reality was, as I was to find out, that it was never the case. Within a matter of months Graham Richardson had retired from public life and his place at the Cabinet table was taken by the newly elected Member for Fremantle, former Western Australian Premier, Dr Carmen Lawrence. Virtually all the national media believed that Senator Richardson had done a deal with Paul Keating which the new minister would be able to guide easily through Cabinet. What the media did not report and what I subsequently found out was that his $1.3 billion proposals were supported by one and a quarter pages of Cabinet submission. On inspection, when I finally saw them, the proposals revealed a cobbled-together, half-baked scheme which had never been discussed with the people it was designed to help.

Media reports have confirmed that when the proposals were taken to the inner coterie of the Cabinet's Expenditure Review Committee (ERC), they never stood a chance—if they ever had one. The level of debate, some of it driven by other political agendas, was abysmal, with only Carmen Lawrence and myself strongly arguing any substantial case for increased expenditure.

When the budget was announced, Carmen Lawrence and I issued a media release that tried to put the best face on what had been an absolute drubbing. There had apparently been no deal between Graham Richardson and Paul Keating, and the outcome for indigenous people was deeply disappointing. The only ray of light was that there was to be an evaluation of the NAHS during the year, with the issues to be considered further in a year's time in the 1995/96 budget.

The next opportunity to strike a blow for change was the release of the NAHS evaluation results on 23 December 1994, which was the

first day it could be made public. At a media conference I spoke
strongly in support of the government action but was shocked at the
degree of media ignorance. Margot Kingston, who certainly gives the
impression of being sympathetic to Aboriginal causes, attended as a
representative of the *Sydney Morning Herald*. I was dumbfounded when
she asked me why Aboriginal people living in poor conditions in
remote communities did not move to the city, ignoring both their
connection with their traditional lands and the failure of assimilation
policies of the past.

Nevertheless, my strong comments that day effectively endorsing
the crucial findings of the evaluation were extensively reported, as were
the terms of the joint media release with Carmen Lawrence, which we
titled 'Indigenous Health Report—A Call to the Nation'. (In hindsight,
I am struck by the extent to which the government, the media, and
indeed the nation as a whole, was on notice as to what had to be
done.) In our joint statement Carmen and I said that the report had
confirmed our strongly held view that the most important factor in
improving indigenous health was to meet infrastructure needs as the
NAHS and all governments of all political persuasions had agreed five
years previously. What could be clearer and less unambiguous than
these definitive public statements? But it was not to be. Despite the
continuing campaign over the months ahead, when the issue was
considered again in the inner sanctum of the federal Labor government, the political will was not there.

Working closely with Lois O'Donoghue and Caucus backbench
colleagues, we used every opportunity to highlight the extent of the
backlog in vital health infrastructure in indigenous communities in the
lead-up to the Cabinet meeting. On 10 February 1995 I joined with
Lois and Brian Howe in the launch of two major reports on infrastructure in Aboriginal communities. My media statement said that the
housing and infrastructure needs of Aboriginal and Torres Strait
Islander people were 'bigger than Mabo, but fixable', and that 'these
issues must be addressed and to do so will require only one thing—
political commitment'.

The infrastructure backlog was starkly revealed by the two surveys
released that day. The first stage of the infrastructure survey was
carried out by Australian Construction Services and the results were,
in my view, an irrefutable indictment of Australia's human rights
record. It showed that:

- $1088.4 million was required to provide additional housing for the
  40 764 people living in inappropriate and overcrowded conditions.
- Aboriginal and Torres Strait Islander organisations owned or

administered almost 12 000 dwellings (excluding shelters) in rural and remote areas.

- Around 4700 (38%) of these dwellings required major repair or replacement. The total cost of repairs required was estimated at $245.3 million.
- 34% of discrete communities had a water supply which was below the standard set by the NHMRC as being safe for human consumption.
- 13% of discrete communities (2760 people) did not have water supplies maintained to an acceptable standard.
- 15 835 people did not have access to an appropriate sewerage system.
- 64% of discrete communities had less than 50% of their internal roads sealed.
- 72% of discrete communities had less than 50% of their access roads sealed or had no road access.
- $347 million is required for the upgrading of remote communities' internal and access roads.
- 8438 people do not have access to an appropriate electricity supply.
- 5465 people do not have access to an airfield.

The second stage, *Housing Need Analysis*, gave an assessment of indigenous housing using information derived from the 1986 and 1991 Census. The analysis measured two components of housing dis-advantage:

> housing adequacy, which was assessed by the amount of overcrowding and the extent of other forms of inadequate housing; and financial housing stress, measured by the level of after-housing poverty (where the remaining income after meeting housing costs is insufficient to maintain a reasonable standard of living).

According to the 1991 Census, almost 30 per cent of Aboriginal and Torres Strait Islander people were living in the major urban centres, 42 per cent in smaller urban centres, and the remaining 28 per cent in rural areas. The results of the analysis emphasised the severity of the housing disadvantage of indigenous people living in the north-ern and central areas of Australia and the relative advantage of those living in the state capital cities and the south-eastern and eastern areas of Australia. There is no doubt that the position has become even more critical during the time of the Howard government.

By the time these damning surveys were released, I was even more convinced that this time Cabinet could be persuaded to act to address this well-documented social need. The time had come to develop a proposal to address the backlog of infrastructure. This would involve other key Commonwealth departments and agencies working in partnership with ATSIC in order to win the Prime Minister's support. Arrangements were devised that would secure the resources but that would not require additional budget outlays by means of securing a commitment to redistribute existing resources to the most needy. A Cabinet submission was prepared to establish a framework to mount the necessary massive construction effort over a realistic five-year time frame to 2001 to address the backlog in water, sewerage, housing and other key infrastructure.

Key ministers and officers from their departments were pulled together to tackle the issues in a comprehensive way, including the vast financial resources of DEET (supported by Minister Simon Crean), which had the capacity to direct money to training indigenous people in the construction and maintenance of community infrastructure and housing. The Department of Administrative Services and its minister, Frank Walker, strongly supported the proposal. From the beginning, a core part of the proposal was to encourage and promote community self-reliance and self-sufficiency in accordance with indigenous wishes.

The Cabinet submission on infrastructure was to dovetail with a separate submission from Carmen Lawrence which would seek greatly expanded funding for Aboriginal medical services; it would also assert Commonwealth constitutional power to require states and territories to implement the NAHS and allocate an equitable share of resources to indigenous communities.

Much of the debate before the Cabinet meeting became side-tracked by the preoccupation of some Aboriginal Medical Service representatives, whose sole objective was to achieve a shift in responsibility for funding Aboriginal medical services from ATSIC to the federal Department of Health. To advance their limited agenda they attacked ATSIC, but the real cause of their complaint was the inadequacy of resources. Their campaign received considerable support from prominent talkback radio hosts because it involved attacks on ATSIC, and it was extensively reported by the media. While their demand was easily understood and reported, it was far more difficult to campaign for a major national initiative to tackle the lack of infrastructure in remote communities.

The Cabinet submission on infrastructure proposed two national priorities. First, it proposed what the NAHS evaluation had described as a 'bold and comprehensive national initiative which would step over the shambles of unconsolidated and trivial programs and undertake the necessary public infrastructure which can ensure the supply of water, sewerage, housing and roads to all Aboriginal communities by 2001'. The program to give effect to this initiative was the Aboriginal and Torres Strait Islander Centenary of Federation Infrastructure Project.

It was emphasised that an increase in total Commonwealth outlays might not be needed if a clear examination of priorities attached to existing Commonwealth resources was undertaken with a view to reallocation, for example earmarking a fixed part of the 1995/96 $844 million Commonwealth Specific Purpose Payment allocation for national roads to indigenous communities for access and internal roads for the rest of the decade. There had been, and continues to be, no requirement that even one dollar of the $1000 million Commonwealth expenditure on roads be spent to directly benefit remote Aboriginal or Torres Strait Islander communities. Another important principle of equity was to allocate a higher proportion of the annual $1 billion of Commonwealth housing funds to Aboriginal housing. ATSIC had confirmed the cost of meeting the housing backlog in remote communities as $2244.3 million.

The second priority was seen to be the assertion of Commonwealth power to drive better outcomes in indigenous health. The question of which agency is to control funding of Aboriginal and Torres Strait Islander medical services was a second-order issue. The following were also needed:

- a significant boost to resources for establishing more realistic levels of core funding for different types of Aboriginal Community Medical Services;
- improving levels of specialist and other medical services for remote communities;
- community health education;
- employment opportunities in Aboriginal and Torres Strait Islander health;
- research and development and project funding; and
- addressing communicable diseases.

As well as this, effective action was required by the Commonwealth to enforce accountability for state and territory implementation of the NAHS through provisions in Medicare agreements; Commonwealth monitoring of access and equity outcomes and benchmarking in relation to services provided to indigenous people; and direct funding of indigenous organisations wherever possible. It was also necessary to ensure a proper decision-making role for indigenous people, including the participation of the ATSIC Board.

These priorities and objectives are as valid in 2000 as they were in 1995. They were intended to address infrastructure but also lifestyle issues and substance abuse, which were always an essential part of the equation for improved health outcomes; there was never a suggestion that the infrastructure program on its own would be enough.

Communities themselves had their own responsibilities for tackling substance abuse and lifestyle issues.

No Australian government has yet taken up the challenge these issues present. Whether or not action is taken by a future government is a question of political will and the determination of the national government to tackle the states and territories and hold them accountable for indigenous health. If the federal government can elevate issues of competition policy, electricity reform and gun control to national priorities, then surely indigenous health should receive no lesser priority in the public policy forums of the nation.

During the subsequent budget discussions on the possible use of Commonwealth power to address indigenous health, I took great delight in reminding ministerial colleagues and reluctant bureaucrats that the Commonwealth was not averse to dictating to the states on the most trivial issues if political imperatives required it. For example, in 1988 the Commonwealth was prepared to insist on the states acknowledging its financial contribution to the bicentenary roads program by a mandatory requirement that acknowledgement signs be erected by the roadside, and even the size of the lettering, the type of paint to be used, and its degree of reflectivity was prescribed. How then could any government possibly justify the refusal to use Commonwealth power over the states to bring about improvements in indigenous health?

The push for government action on indigenous health appeared unstoppable after Paul Keating's visit with Noel Pearson to the Hopevale community on Cape York on 24 February 1995. What he said there was inspirational and unambiguous, and filled me with confidence that he would support the initiatives I was developing in close liaison with his staff. He devoted much of his speech to the very issues that were the priorities of Aboriginal people.

> Now, health is a problem. It is a problem because of . . . inadequacy of
> resources, and we know crowded accommodation in communities,
> former mission stations . . . produces all sorts of health problems. And
> we have not seen the public facilities there in the environmental
> health: like the roads, the sewerage systems, the hospitals, the
> immunisations, the various things that the non-Aboriginal community
> has . . .
>   That there is no point in trying to protect yourselves from things
> like scabies, or from diseases of the kidneys, or nephritis, if in fact
> there is a run-over of sewerage [sic]. So the sewerage system has to
> work—it has to be adequate. It's not good for Aboriginal women to be

leaving their communities to have their children—none of our women do that. Why should you? Because you have the nurturing and you have the support that you need—but you don't have the midwives, you don't have the facilities, and you don't have the doctors when you need them, because you don't have the facilities to get the doctors here, and they don't work here. All this implies to me that there is a reasonably comprehensive strategy to take this on . . .

Some of them are location specific—and they can be done. And you have got to wonder why they haven't been done—whether it is the road through from here that should have been tarred. I mean dust is a problem—dust is a problem for respiratory complaints, of which Aboriginal people have many. Access through strips and things like that—through airports—these are simply a matter of funds and the doing of it.

These things can be done—but what has to be done is to put the strategy together, and not be territorial about it. So for my part, I said in Redfern in 1992, we—this community of Australia—want a new relationship with the Aboriginal community. We understand the history, we understand the sins, and we want to make reparations, and we want a reconciliation. Of these we have now sought step-by-step to do. Mabo, the Land Fund, now health. And with health will be the environmental issues—housing, sewerage etc. We should be able to do it together but together is the only way to do it. And I think that is the message of this visit. Thank you very much for having me, and for the welcome.

This magnificent speech went virtually unreported, mostly because the rest of the media was miffed because the Prime Minister had invited Ray Martin exclusively to cover his Hopevale visit. Not even *A Current Affair* reported its significance.

In a buoyant mood, the proposals for the major national initiative were taken to the Cabinet ERC and I believed that, given the wide community, indigenous and Caucus support, and with the Prime Minister's own public statements, the case for Commonwealth action was unstoppable. But on the day of reckoning, 24 April 1995, immediately after the Canberra by-election, I was left virtually on my own in the ERC process. The outcome was that there was a minuscule increase in expenditure to address the infrastructure backlog and no decision was taken in the ERC processes to use Commonwealth power to overrule the states.

When the government's decisions were announced in the budget, I refused to make public comments welcoming the decision on indigenous health. There were others who were prepared to leap into the breach. The Coalition, the AMA and even a number of Aboriginal medical services welcomed it because they had achieved what they

wanted, namely the transfer of Aboriginal medical service funding from
ATSIC to the Health Department. To achieve this, however, ATSIC was
financially gutted and a miserable $20 million extra annually allocated
to the infrastructure backlog. This endorsement of the government's
announcements showed that the proponents of these views either did
not understand the issues or were prepared to act against their con-
sciences. I was sick to my stomach.

I had done my best to have aspects of the proposal incorporated
in the ERC decision as a rearguard action when I had lost the battle
for a significant shift in policy. The government did at least decide to
take up aspects of indigenous health policy with the states and territories, and there was a limited commitment to use Commonwealth
power to push them to act by such means as provisions in Medicare
agreements for reporting access and equity outcomes in mainstream
health programs.

Significantly, the government also decided that the Prime Minister
should ask COAG to establish a high-level task force on indigenous
health to include ATSIC representation, which would, among other
things, recommend initiatives to achieve equitable access to health
services for indigenous people.

Another reform was the related decision that Aboriginal Rental
Housing Program funds supplied to the states and territories under
the Commonwealth State Housing Agreement should be targeted to
remote and rural areas. In remote communities the housing crisis was
greater and there is no alternative to public housing. Principles of
access and equity ought to apply to the housing needs of Aboriginal
and Torres Strait Islander people in cities and towns, and they ought
to be able to obtain an equitable share of such housing.

Overwhelmingly, the government decisions on indigenous health
in the 1995/96 budget were a devastating blow to indigenous aspirations. Australia still awaits a national government with the will to tackle
indigenous health. There is no indication yet that John Howard will
rise to this challenge or that he has any interest in doing so, despite
his rhetoric to the contrary and the best intentions of Minister
Wooldridge. If Mr Howard were to do so he would be acclaimed for
his contribution to indigenous rights, as Paul Keating has been for the
native title legislation. Governments in the comparable countries of
the United States, Canada and New Zealand have been able to work
with indigenous people to dramatically reduce life expectancy gaps
between the indigenous and non-indigenous communities. We should
be able to do the same.

Creative policy responses are to be encouraged, and while I believe
that the army can play a useful part in building infrastructure in
remote communities, as it did during the period of the Labor govern-

ment, it must be done in such a way that local communities control the work and have a sense of ownership and responsibility for it. But despite media perceptions to the contrary, the size of the program is minuscule, in the order of $40 million over four years compared to the backlog of infrastructure in the order of $2 billion.

Sir Gustav Nossal, deputy chair of the Council for Aboriginal Reconciliation and noted medical scientist, in an article in the *Age* in September 1998 confirmed that the health of Australia's indigenous people was 'worse than many third world countries'. It is inevitable now that Australia will be celebrating the centenary of Federation with many thousands of indigenous people still living in third world conditions. Unless these issues are addressed as a national priority by at least a locked-in government commitment, together with other indigenous social justice issues, the opportunity presented by the reconciliation process will be wasted.

The status quo is unsustainable morally and politically. Ultimately global opinion will force Australia to act. There is a likelihood that if we do not act we will face a determination by a United Nations human rights complaints tribunal ruling against Australia for the undoubted systemic discrimination that still occurs against Aboriginal and Torres Strait Islander people in the provision of basic services. The world is watching and will judge us harshly.

15

THE WORLD IS WATCHING: INTERNATIONAL ACTION TO PROTECT INDIGENOUS RIGHTS

During the Hawke and Keating governments, Australia was increasingly recognised at international forums as a 'world champion' in promoting respect for the human rights of indigenous people. The government's focus was twofold: to use the existing structures of the UN, such as the Working Group on Indigenous Populations and the reporting mechanisms of international conventions, to set a benchmark of honesty, openness and accountability in Australia's reports; and to elevate Australia's commitment to international treaty obligations such as ICCPR and CERD by providing a right of individual complaint to the international forums established by the treaties wherever Australian governments were alleged to be in breach of their international obligations. This right of access to international complaint forums is particularly important as Australia remains out of step with comparable democracies in not having a Bill of Rights.

Australia now stands at a major crossroads between heeding or ignoring the moral imperatives of dealing justly with its original inhabitants. And we do not stand here in isolation. There is an international context for this imperative which all Australians would do well to recognise. No country can continue to stand in open defiance of legitimate international human rights concerns and flagrantly violate accepted international human rights standards.

The WGIP was established in 1982, set up by the UN Commission on Human Rights. It had two primary mandates. One was called 'review of developments'. Under this agenda it listens to reports on the position of indigenous peoples from many countries. It does not, however, function as a 'chamber of complaints'. Rather, it uses the information provided primarily to inform itself for the purpose of its other primary mandate, 'evolution of standards'. Its major achievement under this agenda has been the preparation of the Draft Declaration of the Rights of Indigenous Peoples which is now under consideration by the UN Commission for Human Rights. It is composed of five appointed human rights experts chaired by Professor Erica-Irene Daes, a Greek academic.

The drafting process for the Declaration and the WGIP forum are very informal and are designed for maximum participation by indigenous people, many of whom attend the occasion in their traditional dress and speak their own indigenous language. Regrettably, in the early days very few governments took an active interest in WGIP's preparation of the Draft Declaration and instead reserved their position for UN forums further up the hierarchy, where indigenous voices were not expected to be heard with such strength and determination and where governments had in the past dictated the agenda free of non-government organisation (NGO) interference.

I attended WGIP for four of the six years I was minister. Australia's leadership role on the Draft Declaration meant lobbying sympathetic countries such as New Zealand, Canada and the Scandinavian nations to get support for a progressive draft. The United States took a very conservative approach before the election of the Clinton administration but then became more progressive.

In its review of developments, WGIP hears reports from governments and from the indigenous representatives. The Australian delegation sought to drive the group's processes and set a standard of openness and accountability for our human rights record and our treatment of indigenous Australians. I was also determined to set out a formal agenda for action by Australia on indigenous issues and to try to meet the expectations of that agenda set during the subsequent year. Public statements made in Geneva were thus used as a tool to advance the policy implementation within Australia.

Thus at the WGIP meeting on 30 July 1990, the Australian government delegation foreshadowed the reconciliation process when it stated that 'a process of education and reconciliation must be established within Australia which will assist non-Aboriginal people to have a greater level of understanding of Aboriginal history, culture, dispossession and continuing disadvantage and what is needed to address those issues adequately from an Aboriginal perspective'.

This is almost exactly the phraseology subsequently included in the 1991 legislation to establish the Council for Aboriginal Reconciliation. Our statement went on to say:

> We believe that there is a consensus on the need for such a process to
> be established within Australia and that Aboriginal people will join with
> the government and the Opposition to support such a process . . . A
> precondition for any reconciliation must be the adoption of a national
> goal for all levels of government to work with Aboriginal and Torres

> Strait Islander people to address cooperatively issues of land, housing, health, infrastructure, education, employment and economic development of Aboriginal Australia in the lead up to the centenary of Federation in 2001.

A year later, the Australian parliament unanimously adopted this agenda.

From time to time Australia was complimented by WGIP's chairperson and members for our open, honest and accountable approach and our strong stand on indigenous rights. I was, however, appalled by what I learned of the treatment of indigenous people in other parts of the world, which in many cases paralleled Aboriginal experience in Australia. There are so many shared histories of theft of lands, loss of language, discrimination, human rights neglect and conflict with mining and other commercial interests.

Soon after my appointment as minister, I began to lobby my ministerial colleagues to win agreement to Australia taking the necessary steps to allow its people to have the right of individual complaint to the forums established by key UN Conventions. I first wrote to the Minister for Foreign Affairs, Gareth Evans, on 30 November 1990, urging that Australia become a party to ICCPR, and subsequently proposed that Australia lift its reservation to CERD, which denied a right to individual complaint under that convention.

By the time the WGIP met in 1991 I had been able to convince my ministerial colleagues that our government would agree to accession to the First Optional Protocol of the ICCPR, and it did so in September of that year. For the first time, the accession enables approaches by individual Australian citizens, including Aboriginal and Torres Strait Islander people, to the UN Human Rights Committee established under that covenant. When it reported in 1991, RCIADIC had also recommended acceding and had rightly emphasised that, by doing so, Australia could demonstrate before the international community that it is confident it is complying with ICCPR and that its domestic laws provide adequate opportunities for citizens to get relief for any act that is inconsistent with the Covenant.

Despite the Covenant and the existence of the Optional Protocol, Australian parliaments retain their sovereignty, and any suggestion that they have surrendered that sovereignty to some 'foreign body', is without foundation. But by being a party to international human rights complaints processes, Australia is becoming a better global citizen. All political parties have supported Australia being a party to ICCPR and CERD. We can have no credibility if we endorse international standards and then allow state or territory governments, or the national government itself, to flout them.

I have always believed that the UN is, with all its failings and limitations, the best hope the world has for a peaceful and just future. The limitations are, however, considerable. During the time I was minister, the Centre for Human Rights in Geneva had only four full-time positions responsible for administering six international human rights treaties, and staffing levels are still woefully inadequate. Indigenous people and their supporters in Australia should be under no illusions about the limitations of the UN processes. Nevertheless, if used properly they do provide an opportunity for individuals to seek a degree of justice and recognition at a UN forum. Covenants such as ICCPR provide a practical opportunity for a case to be heard, unlike the International Court of Justice which, despite repeated inaccurate media reports to the contrary, is not accessible to NGOs and individuals.

Whenever reporting to WGIP, the Australian government was frank about its views on indigenous issues and placed on record its concerns about the performance of state or territory governments wherever necessary. In 1991 our report took up the concerns of Aboriginal people in Queensland, who were outraged about the failure of the Goss government to consult them adequately on that government's land rights legislation. The report expressed hope that the Queensland government would use its recently passed legislation as the basis for further legislation to set up a land acquisition fund for dispossessed Aboriginal people.

In indigenous affairs it is not only a matter of what governments do, it is also, crucially, a matter of how they do them. It is seldom possible to get unanimous agreement from Aboriginal people for policy initiatives, any more than it is from other groups in the community, but it is certainly possible for governments to seek the widest possible consensus and to negotiate openly and in good faith. This principle was applied to the approach Australia took to preparations for WGIP. Preceding each meeting, a two-day consultative meeting was held involving key indigenous organisations from around the country and Commonwealth public servants from all relevant agencies.

At the July 1992 Working Group meeting, the government responded to concerns expressed by some indigenous representatives about whether the reconciliation process had led to the abandonment of any possible agreement or treaty with indigenous people. The exchange between the Australian government and the indigenous NGO, the National Aboriginal and Islander Legal Services Secretariat represented by Paul Coe, remains a rare example of serious dialogue between governments and NGOs before a UN forum, and it was welcomed by WGIP members.

At this same meeting I announced that the federal Attorney-General, Michael Duffy, was taking steps towards Australia acting under the UN Convention Against Torture and Other Cruel, Inhuman, Degrading Treatment or Punishment and CERD to allow individuals access to other international complaint forums established under those conventions, namely to the Convention Against Torture and CERD respectively. These initiatives were potentially extremely important to Aboriginal and Torres Strait Islander people. Our report was also critical of the repressive juvenile justice legislation promoted by the WA Labor government, which had been swept up in a public frenzy of antagonism towards young offenders, particularly Aboriginal offenders. According to advice provided by HREOC to the federal and WA governments, this legislation was in breach of the Convention on the Rights of the Child and ICCPR.

Australia took a strong stand in support of an expanded and important role for WGIP in the future drafting of the declaration after it left the group and proceeded through the UN hierarchy at the meeting. The strategy of the Australian government was to ensure that any newly established Commission on Human Rights Working Group, which would consider the Draft Declaration, be open-ended to allow for the participation of non-government indigenous organisations and individuals. The Australian government advocated the widest possible NGO participation.

There is no doubt that, as the Draft Declaration moves through the UN machinery, a core issue will be the extent to which the nations of the world, who must ultimately adopt it, are prepared to embrace the concept of self-determination. Indigenous people consider the principle of self-determination to be the very essence of the Draft Declaration. At the 1992 meeting the Australian delegation made an important contribution to the debate.

Self-determination was not at that time controversial in Australia, having been endorsed by governments of all political persuasions in their response to RCIADIC. In the international arena, however, the concept of self-determination is far more difficult to advance because of the unnecessary and alarmist perception of some governments that it will lead to the breaking up of nations. The 1992 Australian contribution to the international debate on self-determination was positive and creative, adopting in part a formulation of self-determination advanced by the late Dr Peter Wilenski when Australian Permanent Representative to the UN:

> Realisation of the right of self-determination is not limited in time to the process of decolonisation nor is it accomplished solely by a single act or exercise. Rather it entails the continuing right of all peoples and

individuals within each state to participate fully in the political process by which they are governed. Clearly, enhancing popular participation in this decision making is an important factor in realising the right to self-determination. It is evident that, even in some countries which are formally fully democratic, structural, attitudinal and procedural barriers exist which inhibit the full democratic participation of particular groups.

The Australian government delegation to this meeting considers that indigenous peoples are among those groups which may have to overcome barriers inhibiting their full democratic participation in the political process by which they are governed so that the full range of human rights are theirs to enjoy. Specific recognition of the right of self-determination for indigenous peoples, as separate and distinct peoples, will assist them to overcome the barriers to full democratic participation.

But the concerns of indigenous peoples clearly do not stop here. Given the variety of circumstances in which indigenous peoples find themselves, we would not want to be prescriptive as to the exact form self-determination should take for indigenous peoples. Obviously, it should encompass a range of possibilities. In our view a system which guarantees full and genuine participation and fundamental human rights as well as recognising the special position of indigenous peoples could provide an adequate and real realisation of self-determination.

Regrettably, despite the fact that even in opposition the Coalition had not opposed the advancement of self-determination at the UN forum, Foreign Minister Downer, and Senator Herron have now opposed the use of the term, instead advocating terms such as 'self management' or 'self empowerment', which have no political standing in Australia and no basis in international law. The change has been motivated by expressed concerns about 'separate countries' being created for indigenous people. The reality is, as Mick Dodson has stressed, that not one significant indigenous organisation, including the APG backed by Michael Mansell and others, has supported independent statehood.

At the CERD Committee's 1994 meeting I delivered Australia's report under the convention. For this meeting it was accepted that Mick Dodson, as Aboriginal and Torres Strait Islander Social Justice Commissioner, would also represent Australia. Government officials envisaged that he would attend as an observer, but I thought that Australian democracy was sufficiently robust and confident to allow Commissioner Dodson to appear in his own right with full freedom to express his own views independently and to be questioned by members of the committee.

And that is what happened. It was a world first. No nation had ever allowed such an independent expression of opinion by a national human rights body in the reporting processes under any UN human rights treaty or, I believe, under a UN treaty of any kind. Our appearance took the CERD Committee by surprise, and its members found it difficult to comprehend the openness and accountability of the government's approach. In its concluding observations the committee recorded that 'members of the committee highly commend the composition of the delegation', describing it as an example to be followed by other reporting nations. The committee further stated that 'appreciation is also expressed for the opportunity to engage in frank, serious and extremely constructive dialogue with a delegation led by the responsible Minister'.

The message to indigenous people from John Howard's government is very clear. There appears to be no hope that his government will move seriously to address their human rights and disadvantage in health, housing, education, employment and the provision of infrastructure in the year before the centenary of Federation in 2001. Despite the commitment to do so as an essential part of the reconciliation process, the current government has shown open hostility to Aboriginal aspirations and has cut back funding in crucial social justice and human rights programs. Nor can Aboriginal people expect that there will be the necessary leadership from the Commonwealth on Aboriginal deaths in custody. The Prime Minister's ten-point plan in response to the Wik decision and the subsequent legislation passed by the parliament represents a new attack on indigenous human rights.

In each of the instances I have referred to above, there is arguably a breach of Australia's international human rights obligations under CERD, ICCPR, the Convention Against Torture, or the Convention on the Rights of the Child. In the case of the first three of these, there is a right for individuals, or in some cases groups of individuals, to complain to an international body provided for in those conventions. I raise these violations of indigenous human rights in Australia and the feeling of despair felt by indigenous people to point out the likelihood of continuing international action to fight for indigenous rights. Indigenous people have few other options in the face of federal government hostility to their aspirations.

When Australia became a party to these international complaints processes it did so with cross-party support. There is very little on the public record of the Coalition parties objecting to Australia becoming a party to these processes. Australia had been a party to ICCPR and CERD for many years. In the case of CERD, Australia became a party in 1975 during the Whitlam government, and to ICCPR in 1980 during the Fraser government.

In my opinion, the Australian government remains particularly vulnerable to being found to be in breach of CERD in the high-profile area of Aboriginal health, as indeed were the previous governments. Chapter 14 rebuts the myth that adequate amounts of funding have ever been applied to the massive backlog in housing, roads and community infrastructure, a core issue in tackling appalling standards of indigenous health. The current rate of expenditure on tackling this backlog is barely enough to keep pace with population growth and routine maintenance. In his second report in 1994, focusing on health, the Social Justice Commissioner, Mick Dodson, also identified a failure to comply with Articles 3 and 5 of the Universal Declaration of Human Rights, Article 6(1) of ICCPR, Articles 11(1), 12(1) and (2) of the International Covenant on Economic, Social and Cultural Rights, and Article 24 of the Convention on the Rights of the Child.

It is my view that the living conditions in hundreds of remote communities also place Australia in breach of its obligations under CERD and that successive Australian governments of all political per-suasions have been guilty of systemic discrimination against indigenous people. Article 5 of CERD requires the Australian government and all other governments that are a party to it to guarantee the right of everyone, without distinction as to race, the enjoyment of economic, social and cultural rights and, in particular, protection against unem-ployment, the right to housing, public health, medical care, education and training and the right to equal participation in cultural activities. Australia is clearly in breach of Article 5 and it is surprising that no indigenous people have at the time of writing pursued the issue by way of a formal communication to the CERD Committee.

It is no defence for the federal government to assert that the failure to ensure, for example, an adequate standard of housing in Aboriginal communities is somehow a state or territory government responsibility. It is quite remarkable that Australian national governments of all political hues think that in the year 2000 in an affluent country like Australia they can avoid responsibility for government inaction on such discrimination.

This discrimination is particularly easy to prove in the case of those hundreds of remote communities where, except for CDEP, there is virtually 100 per cent unemployment, appalling overcrowding in hous-ing, little infrastructure, negligible public health facilities, inadequate school facilities with little or no training opportunities, and perhaps limited opportunity to participate in recreational activities. Australians who have not visited Aboriginal communities need to understand that the basic acceptable standard of community facilities, infrastructure and quality of life has never existed in those communities. They are unacceptable, in violation of international law, and the most stark embarrassment to Australia.

In my view, Australia is also in breach of Article 2 of the convention, which provides in part that governments which are a party to the convention shall, 'when the circumstances so warrant, take in the social, economic, cultural and other fields, special and concrete measures to ensure the adequate development and protection of certain racial groups for individuals belonging to them, for the purpose of guaranteeing them the full and equal enjoyment of human rights and fundamental freedoms'.

Should indigenous people make a complaint to the CERD Committee concerning an alleged violation of the convention or complain about a breach of ICCPR and should such complaints be upheld by the committee, then the Australian government will be under extraordinary political pressure to act on the finding.

In response to one complaint unrelated to the Aboriginal affairs portfolio—the Toonen case—resulting in a finding that the Australian government was in breach of its international obligations, the Australian parliament, by an overwhelming majority, supported legislation to override the laws of the Tasmanian government, which were found to be in breach of the ICCPR, discriminating against homosexuals. John Howard voted in support of that legislation.

There has, of course, been a subsequent finding of Australia being in breach of ICCPR for its treatment of refugees by the former Labor government; this finding was not accepted by the Howard government. Australia has also been found to be in breach of CERD. In August 1998 the CERD Committee requested information from Australia on three areas of concern, namely, changes to the Native Title Act (following the Wik decision), changes to policy on Aboriginal land rights and proposed changes (ultimately not proceeded with) to the position and function of the Aboriginal and Torres Strait Islander Social Justice Commissioner. The committee gave its decision on 18 March 1999 after considering the response of the Australian government to its concerns: 'While the original Native Title Act recognises and seeks to protect indigenous title, provisions that extinguish or impair the exercise of indigenous title rights and interests pervade the amended Act'. It noted, in particular, four specific provisions that discriminate against indigenous title holders in the amended legislation: 'The Act's "validation" provisions; the "confirmation of extinguishment" provisions; the primary production upgrade provisions; and restrictions concerning the right of indigenous titleholders to negotiate non-indigenous land uses'.

The committee went on to express the view that the amendments raised concerns about Australia's compliance with Articles 2 and 5 of the convention. Furthermore, it concluded that the 'lack of effective participation' by indigenous communities in the formulation of the amendment raised further concerns about Australia's compliance with Article 5(c) of the convention.

The committee called on the Australian government to address these concerns as a 'matter of utmost urgency' and to 'suspend implementation of the 1998 amendments and reopen discussion with representatives of Aboriginal and Torres Strait Islander peoples with a view to finding solutions acceptable to them and which would comply with Australia's obligations under the convention'. Finally, the committee stressed that because of the 'urgency and fundamental importance of these matters', the issues would be kept on the agenda of its early warning and urgent action procedures to be reviewed at its next session.

Back in Australia, the Howard government dismissed the committee's finding and attacked its procedures in an attempt to further discredit the decision, despite the government's own legal advice confirming the discriminatory nature of the Wik amendments.

However, if the CERD Committee were to uphold a complaint, or communication as it is more formally called, concerning a breach of the convention relating to the allegation of systemic discrimination in basic living conditions, such a finding could not be so readily dismissed. It would, in my view, leave even the Howard government, or a future Labor government, with no political alternative but to use the power given to the Commonwealth by the 1967 referendum to address Aboriginal and Torres Strait Islander living conditions in remote communities, as indeed they ought to have done long ago. John Howard or his successor could not credibly respond with any lesser commitment to respecting and addressing the human rights of Australia's indigenous people than was done in respect of the human rights of gay rights activists in Tasmania.

On 28 May 1997, the *Sydney Morning Herald* reported that at the Reconciliation Convention in Melbourne the day before, just over a year after the election of the Howard government, visiting North American indigenous leaders lamented the fact that 'Australia had tumbled from its position as world champion of indigenous rights, leaving 300 million people with no nations to represent them in the international arena'. Dr Ted Moses, Grand Chief of the Grand Council of Crees of Canada, recognised that Australia's leadership had been a breath of fresh air, bringing 'encouragement and hope' to many but that 'with the change of government that leadership role has been abandoned and . . . indigenous people around the world must find another nation that is willing to make the first move, to take the lead to fight internationally for the recognition of the rights of indigenous peoples'.

The abandonment of that leadership role has been compounded by government attacks on the UN treaty monitoring committees over the course of 2000.

In the face of the Howard government's about-turn on Australia's principled stand on indigenous human rights issues, it will be Australia's indigenous people themselves who will be increasingly asserting their human rights using the international legal remedies put in place by the Hawke and Keating governments.

16

DOES RECONCILIATION STAND A CHANCE?

The reconciliation process between indigenous and non-indigenous Australians, launched in 1991 with the unanimous support of the Australian parliament, has received potentially fatal setbacks as a result of policies of the Howard government.

In its efforts to silence its critics by labelling them as the purported architects of 'political correctness', the Howard government began soon after its election to launch a series of calculated policy assaults on Aboriginal people, their organisations and aspirations in an attempt to win the approval of Pauline Hanson's supporters on indigenous issues. Sadly, in doing so it gave succour and comfort to One Nation's extremist and anti-Aboriginal views.

The cross-party cooperation which was the hallmark of indigenous policy between 1990 and 1993 had been sacrificed to states' rights during the native title debate. From that point on, Coalition policies on indigenous issues had moved to an even more belligerent position.

The Council for Aboriginal Reconciliation Act 1991 *remains the key to a fresh start for the Howard government in indigenous affairs. If the Coalition were to take up positive proposals for action it could breathe new life into the reconciliation process. If it fails to act it will be left to a future government to take the initiative.*

The jury is still out on whether the ALP is committed to policies and programs that will deliver on the social justice agenda of the reconciliation process.

In any event, it is now beyond doubt that the process needs more time. Australia is not yet ready to reach a negotiated settlement with the indigenous people of the land, at least until there is a binding commitment to address seriously the non-negotiable social justice agenda.

313

It is now the year 2000, and the reconciliation process, born in a spirit of hope and optimism in 1991 with the unanimous support of the parliament, is in serious trouble. It will take real national leadership and goodwill from non-indigenous Australians across the political spectrum and from all walks of life to retrieve the process—if that is now possible. Indigenous people could be forgiven for feeling that their legitimate and modest aspirations had been subject to an ongoing assault by the Coalition government.

For most of its time in office, the Coalition government has appeared hell-bent on using indigenous people as some kind of party-political football, the consequence of which is that public opinion in the wider Australian community has become heavily polarised.

It is such an indictment of the Coalition government that, even after only eight months in office, a Herald AGB McNair Poll showed that 55 per cent of people polled agreed that the federal government treats Aboriginal people over-generously. A few months before, after the federal budget, a similar poll revealed that 77 per cent of Coalition voters supported the drastic cuts inflicted in the indigenous affairs budget. These cuts were worn like a badge of honour by the government. This climate of public opinion has been in large part orchestrated by the government itself, and the direction was set long before the Hanson One Nation bandwagon hit the road.

In one of their first actions in government, Mr Howard and Senator Herron held a special media conference to denounce public accountability in Aboriginal and Torres Strait Islander affairs. It is of course common practice of new governments, of either complexion, to denounce the previous government. There is no doubt that one of the results of this media stunt was to paint a false public picture of accountability in the indigenous affairs portfolio in preparation for a deep funding cut in the forthcoming budget. It has been reported that Minister Herron was not the orchestrator of the Cabinet decision leading to the media conference; the charge was apparently led by others in the Cabinet. But the general smearing of the indigenous portfolio was a poisonous contribution to public debate, deliberately calculated to inflame public opinion. The stunt rebounded when the government's move to appoint a special auditor with a price tag of about $1 million was declared illegal by the Federal Court of Australia. But the mud stuck; it was little wonder that the public climate was so ripe for Pauline Hanson's agenda.

Coalition attacks on Aboriginal people and organisations after the 1996 election were consistent with their code words used during that election campaign about governing for 'all of us', their continuous attacks on so-called 'political correctness' since the Mabo debate, and their unrelenting criticisms of Labor government support for the human rights of minority groups. The problem for indigenous Australians is that the Coalition saw these issues as an opportunity to press the prejudice button in the community for the direct benefit of the Liberal and National Parties.

Then there is the Hanson factor. Pauline Hanson was the endorsed Liberal Party candidate for the safe Labor seat of Oxley in the 1996 election, but by a strange twist of fate she was disendorsed because of her letter to a paper attacking me in regard to RCIADIC and critical of the alleged privileged position of Aboriginal people, though she retained her Liberal Party description on the ballot paper. In a huge 22 per cent swing she won the Ipswich-based seat of Oxley from sitting member Les Scott. His successor has had more column centimetres of newspaper coverage than any other backbench MP in the history of the Australian parliament and I don't intend to add one more. But it was the response, or rather the lack of it, from the new Prime Minister that gave her views a degree of legitimacy and contributed to John Howard's legacy of division and discord in Aboriginal affairs. In essence, my charge is that in relation to Aboriginal issues the Prime Minister went chasing the One Nation voters instead of exercising moral and political leadership.

Instead of immediately rejecting the Hanson views on Aboriginal people and the extent of their disadvantage, Mr Howard provided comfort for them. For months after the election, he trumpeted the virtues of the alleged new era of freedom of speech in which people could say what they thought, and it was seen almost as a moral virtue to speak out against 'political correctness'. Simple statements in support of Aboriginal rights were, of course, 'politically correct' in John Howard's view of the world. Unrelentingly, he asserted that people who disagreed with the Keating government policies on indigenous affairs were called 'racists'.

This assertion, often made against me, was utterly without foundation but has been repeated *ad nauseam* by conservative commentators. I simply did not believe in the violence of the language directed towards an individual and thought the label was a poor communications tool and had made my views clear to my staff on this issue since 1990.

When questioned by his close ally, Alan Jones, on 2UE as to whether he, as prime minister, believed in anything that Pauline Hanson said, his first response was, 'I certainly believe in her right to say what she said. I thought that some of the things she said were an accurate reflection of what people feel. I think she said, as I have said, that there were many times under the previous government where people felt intimidated out of saying what they really believed'. This statement was clearly intended to politically profit from anti-Aboriginal sentiment in the community.

In the light of all I have written about Coalition attacks on Aboriginal people and their rights during and since the Mabo debate, Mr Howard's reply to Alan Jones is untrue. You only have to look at the outpourings of John Howard's associates, referred to in this book, to know that John Hewson, John Howard himself, Tim Fischer, Hugh Morgan, Richard Court, Geoffrey Blainey, Ian McLachlan and other Coalition frontbenchers, with their mining and pastoral industry supporters, had hurled everything they could in their campaign against Commonwealth legislation to protect and enhance native title rights. It was the content of their public statements that was the subject of opposition, not their right to speak.

In response to Pauline Hanson's attacks on modest government programs, previously supported by the Coalition itself, and designed to tackle the horrendous state of indigenous disadvantage, John Howard was seen by commentators as merely recognising that her views 'reflected' those held in sections of the community. It was as if he had become some moral neuter or remote social commentator instead of a leader displaying the leadership necessary to rebut such views.

When the Howard government did eventually join with the Opposition in a joint resolution of both Houses opposing discrimination and supporting the process of reconciliation, it was too late. In any event, the motion was a watered-down version of that proposed by the Labor Opposition and its content seems to have been driven by concern about loss of trade and business opportunities with Asia rather than by any moral imperative, and certainly not by any concern with the process of reconciliation with Australia's indigenous people.

Then John Howard attacked the efforts being made in schools throughout Australia to teach students about Australia's history, including the mistreatment of Aboriginal people, which he labelled the 'black armband' view of history. The Prime Minister was immediately condemned by leading historians and in newspaper editorials, some likening his approach to Japan's unwillingness to teach students what happened during World War II.

Next came his belligerent outburst at the Reconciliation Convention in Melbourne in May 1997, the subsequent refusal of his government to apologise in response to HREOC's report on the stolen generations and the erosion of Aboriginal rights in the aftermath of the Wik decision.

There is an objective truth about how this dreadful turn of events came to pass, about how the principled and pragmatic idealism of the reconciliation process is in danger of being irredeemably wrecked by the Howard government.

In my first three years as federal minister in this controversial portfolio, I initiated a dialogue with the Opposition and campaigned in the community for cross-party cooperation in indigenous affairs. The move for cooperation was greatly assisted by my Liberal counter-part, Michael Wooldridge. It is indisputable that at the end of those three years, the bitter point-scoring and divisiveness that had accom-panied the establishment of ATSIC in the previous parliament had disappeared. By March 1993 and the time of the federal election, there existed unanimous parliamentary support for legislation to establish the Council for Aboriginal Reconciliation and the reconciliation process, and even unanimous support for the Commonwealth's far-reaching response to RCIADIC's recommendations.

It was not as if that period was a time of political calm. It was nothing of the sort, and many controversial and difficult issues had to be addressed within the portfolio during those three years, including the RCIADIC response itself, the start of policy formulation in the aftermath of the Mabo decision, and the heritage declaration to prevent construction of the Alice Springs Dam. But none of the many high-profile and volatile issues derailed the reconciliation process or the commitment to cross-party cooperation.

Most commentators forget that there was even cross-party support for the government's negotiating process and a timetable for respond-ing to Mabo, articulated by John Hewson and publicly welcomed by me even during the 1993 election campaign. Cross-party cooperation thus clearly survived the transition from Prime Minister Hawke to Prime Minister Keating. Its achievement was no accident; I knew how crucial it was for the national parliament to show leadership in edu-cating the wider community about the need for the nation to address indigenous issues.

It is important that all Australians remember that the Council for Aboriginal Reconciliation Act was negotiated word for word with the ATSIC Board, key indigenous organisations, the Australian Democrats and, most significantly in this context, with the Liberal and National Parties themselves. The Act set out a three-pronged agenda for the nation and was endorsed by the Coalition in 1991.

First, it recognised the need to educate non-indigenous Australians about the 'history, culture, dispossession and disadvantage continued to be experienced by Aboriginal and Torres Strait Islander people and the need to address that disadvantage'. In the words of award-winning historian and author Roger Milliss, at the launch of his work on the Waterloo Creek massacre: 'Unless we face up to the brutal reality of the past and how we came to acquire the continent, then we cannot understand the present and chart the course for a better future. Once we succeed in doing that, then perhaps we will have begun to come to terms with our own Australianness . . . living in this land together'.

The Coalition not only supported the commitment contained in the Act to educate the community about indigenous issues, they also supported two other key commitments.

Second, the Act provides that:

> As a part of the reconciliation process, the Commonwealth will seek an ongoing national commitment from governments at all levels to cooperate and coordinate with the Aboriginal and Torres Strait Islander Commission, as appropriate, to address progressively Aboriginal disadvantage and aspirations in relation to land, housing, law and justice, cultural heritage, education, employment, health, infrastructure, economic development and any other relevant matters in the decade leading to the centenary of federation, 2001.

Third, the Coalition also voted to support a role for the Council in consulting the community on whether or not the reconciliation process would be advanced by a document of reconciliation. All the members of the Council since its inception had been appointed with the express approval of the Coalition leadership.

It was a deliberate strategic decision to initiate the reconciliation process by legislation so that there could be no doubt about the agreed national agenda. So what went wrong? Anyone who reads the history of the Mabo debate will know how cross-party cooperation and Coalition support for indigenous aspirations sank without trace.

After the 1993 election the Coalition was confronted with a stark choice: to support Commonwealth legislation in some form to protect the native title rights recognised by the High Court or to oppose such legislation outright. It chose the latter course, and the outcome of the Mabo debate was shaped by their decision to accord a higher priority to states' rights than to the human rights of Aboriginal and Torres Strait Islander people.

The Howard government subsequently walked away from the agreed agenda of the reconciliation process. Sadly, there has been an appalling lack of media scrutiny of the failure of the government even in areas of 'practical reconciliation' in their own professed priority areas such as education, employment, housing and living conditions which impact on health.

I sometimes wonder whether John Howard realises how seriously out of step he is with leaders in the United States, Canada and New Zealand. Governments of each of these countries respect and negotiate with their indigenous peoples. While indigenous people in these countries still struggle to have their rights recognised, they are not the subject of the open vilification and disparagement that Aboriginal and Torres Strait Islander people still experience in Australia. There are numerous easily readable source materials for people wishing to learn about the indigenous policy of governments in comparable democracies.

It is also inevitable that Australia's indigenous people will lodge further complaints or communications under CERD alleging breaches of the Convention. Such complaints may well focus on allegations of systemic discrimination in the provision of government programs to indigenous communities in education, health, housing, the provision of infrastructure and employment programs, which are the expressed priority areas of policy of Mr Howard's own government. An alternative may be to complain about government policies that amount to a breach of ICCPR. Further findings by an international treaty committee against Australia's treatment of its indigenous people is, in my view, inevitable.

Some Australians may not give a damn about such a finding and some will decry the role of international treaty bodies or the UN and alleged interference in Australia's domestic affairs. But Australia will be forced to respond. With the demise of apartheid in South Africa and the fall of repressive regimes in Eastern Europe, indigenous issues are going to be much more in the international human rights spotlight.

Within Australia itself there are strong signs of the depths of community support for indigenous social justice. The most powerful public statement in support of indigenous rights in the aftermath of the 1996 election came not from the politicians but from the Governor-General, Sir William Deane, in the August 1996 inaugural Vincent Lingiari Lecture organised by the Council for Aboriginal Reconciliation. In this erudite and principled contribution to the public debate, Sir William left no doubt about where he stood, stressing that 'genuine reconciliation between the Aboriginal and Torres Strait Islander peoples and our nation as a whole should be in the forefront of our national aspirations between now and 2001'. He traced the history of the demise of the now discredited policy of assimilation, quoting Liberal Prime Minister William McMahon, who said: 'The Government recognises the rights of individual Aborigines to effective choice about the degree to which and the pace at which they come to identifying themselves with [Australian] society'. Prime Minister Howard would do well to commit to memory another part of the Governor-General's speech:

> It should, I think, be apparent to all well meaning people that true reconciliation between the Australian nation and its indigenous peoples is not achievable in the absence of acknowledgement by the nation of

the wrong of the past dispossession, oppression and degradation of the indigenous peoples. That is not to say that individual Australians who had no part in what was done in the past should feel or acknowledge personal guilt. It is simply to assert our identity as a nation and the basic fact that national shame, as well as national pride, can and should exist in relation to past acts or omission, at least when done or made in the name of the community or with their authority. Where there is no room for national pride or national shame about the past, there can be no national soul.

The present plight, in terms of health, employment and education, living conditions and self-esteem, of so many Aborigines must be acknowledged as largely flowing from what happened in the past. The dispossession, the destruction of hunting fields and the destitution of lives were all related. The new diseases, the alcohol and the new pressures of living were all introduced. True acknowledgement cannot stop short of recognition of the extent to which present disadvantage flows from past injustice and oppression.

Sir William went on to highlight what is effectively enshrined in the Council for Aboriginal Reconciliation Act: 'it is apparent that recognition of the need for appropriate redress for present disadvantage flowing from past injustice and oppression is a prerequisite for reconciliation'.

If there is one central objective I have in writing this book, it is to highlight and encourage renewal of the commitment which the Australian parliament unanimously gave in 1991, committing successive Commonwealth governments to address those issues of indigenous disadvantage and human rights as a non-negotiable element of the reconciliation process. Indeed, the Council for Aboriginal Reconciliation Act is the key to a fresh start in indigenous affairs by the Coalition should they wish to pursue it.

In his 1996 speech, the Governor-General hammered home the message, pointing out how much remains to be done to overcome or alleviate the terrible problems which are the present consequences of past oppression and injustice. Those problems include:

The inadequacies of much Aboriginal education; the vastly higher than average levels of Aboriginal unemployment, particularly youth unemployment; the deficiencies of Aboriginal housing; and the problems of water supply and infrastructure in many Aboriginal communities. It is true that, with the abolition of the notion of *terra nullius* and the enactment of the various Aboriginal and native title statutes, we have made great progress towards addressing the immediate issue raised by the dispossession. Nonetheless, few would assert that the problems of Aboriginal land rights have now been fully and finally resolved. And, above all, there are the appalling problems relating to Aboriginal health . . . which can be traced to the past dispossession, oppression and injustice.

Providing moral leadership to the nation, the Governor-General then made it unambiguously clear that there will be no true reconciliation until it can be seen that we are making real progress towards the position where the future prospects of an Aboriginal baby in terms of health, education, life expectancy, living conditions and self-esteem are comparable to those of a non-Aboriginal baby. He posed the question, 'How can we hope to go forward as friends and equals while our children's hands cannot touch?'

So how can this be done and what can the Coalition or a future Labor government do to breathe life back into the reconciliation process?

First, the Australian government needs a circuit-breaker to re-establish dialogue with indigenous leaders. This could be achieved by several means, but one viable option would be to invite a wide range of indigenous leaders to the Cabinet room for a discussion and to hear their views about how a relationship of trust can be restored. Mr Howard would certainly be told that indigenous people have no wish to be in a state of conflict with his government, that their aspirations are overwhelmingly modest and achievable, but that they have a right as the first people of this land to respect from the prime minister of this nation and his government.

Despite Mr Howard's assertions to the contrary, indigenous leaders were never the captives of the Hawke or Keating governments, as the record of the Mabo debate shows. However, as the representatives of their people they did receive from the ALP in government a clear acknowledgement that without respect, dialogue and negotiation, no progress would be made in reconciliation.

Second, the government must put back on the nation's policy agenda a commitment to a third-stage response to the Mabo decision in the form of a social justice package. The Prime Minister should be aware that there is before him a unanimous report of the second Council for Aboriginal Reconciliation supporting a 78-point social justice package agenda. The Coalition representative on that Council agreed to its being proposed for consideration by government. Also represented on that Council were leading representatives of the Australian Chamber of Commerce and Industry, the NFF, and the mining industry.

There were more far-reaching proposals for a social justice package put forward by ATSIC and the Aboriginal and Torres Strait Islander Social Justice Commissioner. These reports are no less worthy of consideration by government and should contribute to the ongoing community debate as future Commonwealth action on the social justice agenda as a third-stage response to Mabo. It is also imperative that the Labor Opposition and the ALP national platform be committed to implementing the unfinished response to Mabo. This, in my view, is the essential but missing component to the lasting and durable settlement we should be seeking.

Not every proposal of ATSIC, or perhaps even the very modest but unanimous recommendations of the Council for Aboriginal Reconciliation, will be universally supported. What is required is an acceptance that they embody key indigenous aspirations that deserve to be treated seriously and be the subject of informed debate and consideration by both the indigenous and non-indigenous community, by government and by the parliament itself.

A further important contribution to debate on the unfinished social justice agenda was made by the publication of the Council's strategies at Corroboree 2000 in May.

An option that would further the social justice proposals and have the potential to restore a degree of cross-party cooperation in the indigenous affairs portfolio would be to refer these reports, together with the Council's final report, to a high-calibre joint select parliamentary committee to conduct public hearings and particularly consultations with the indigenous community on the form of the social justice package over a period extending into the next parliament.

It may be that indigenous people themselves, through their nationally elected representative body, ATSIC, and their community organisations, will wish to undertake their own revision of the social justice proposals. However, in one form or another such proposals provide a blueprint to address indigenous disadvantage which all fair-minded Australians would see as a national priority.

Fundamentally, what indigenous people are seeking as a national government social justice response to Mabo is not some new addition to Commonwealth outlays but a shift from a welfare-based attitude to an acknowledgement of the inherent human rights of indigenous people. Aboriginal leaders have not advocated a welfare-based dependency but one based on self-determination and self-reliance. Such a shift in government policy will require a policy review across the whole of the government and the assertion of Commonwealth government power over the states wherever necessary. In many areas this acknowledgement and the commitment to do something about it should not be difficult for a national government in an affluent country like Australia in the twenty-first century.

Third, if the reconciliation process is to have any hope of success, the government must take priority action to address what, I believe, is Australia's most pressing human rights issue. The national embarrassment of the living conditions in remote communities highlighted time and time again, domestically and internationally, is the starkest reminder of the failure of all our governments to allocate the nation's resources equitably to the poorest and sickest Australians.

In this book I have told the history of efforts to have this agenda addressed by the former Labor government, and how Cabinet support was not there to achieve change. The NAHS review said that 'the difficulty lies in the . . . lack of political will to make the financial investment necessary to achieve environmental equity'. There is no evidence as yet of that political will on either side of politics.

The evidence is undeniable. John Howard, who displayed real political leadership on the issue of gun control and East Timor, has the power in his hands to bring about change. The history of both Labor and Coalition governments has shown that, by listing other national policy proposals for discussion at COAG, it was possible to use the power of the prime minister and the national government to drive a reform process. Labor went into the 1996 election with a policy commitment to remove the backlog in indigenous housing and infrastructure by 2001, and to take this commitment to COAG to secure resources and intergovernmental cooperation. At the 1998 election, this commitment had been dropped by the Beazley Labor Opposition.

If Mr Howard is sincere in his rhetoric about giving priority to Aboriginal health, education and employment and really wants to make a difference, he should refer these issues for consideration and national priority action by the heads of government. After six years in the portfolio I am utterly convinced that the necessary changes to improve Aboriginal and Torres Strait Islander health, education and employment will never occur if they have to be driven by even well-intentioned ministers for indigenous affairs or by employment, health or education ministers alone. The indigenous affairs portfolio has never been allocated a Cabinet position and even if it was, this alone would be insufficient to achieve the necessary reforms. Prime ministerial leadership is required, and if that leadership comes from the Coalition I would be the first to applaud it. If it fails to come from the ALP it will stand condemned.

Fourth, there is a need to take a stand against open and increasingly hostile disparagement of indigenous people and their aspirations. The Prime Minister could begin by ceasing to refer to people working in their communities on low salaries for the common good as 'the

Aboriginal industry'. He has also yet to take a stand against those talkback radio elements who peddle incessant propaganda against indigenous people and organisations and are totally unaccountable for the truth of their public pronouncements. No politician, lawyer, real estate agent, banker, doctor, plumber, electrician or local council can escape public liability and accountability for misrepresentation or negligence as can talkback radio hosts and journalists. Even the national parliament, which has been described as a 'coward's castle', confers a right of reply to aggrieved citizens. A right of reply is more than any citizen will ever get from talkback radio propagandists. Addressing junk journalism requires political leadership and at least an industry code of conduct with teeth which has as a number one requirement to tell the truth. Surely this is the least we should expect from our media.

Fifth, I would urge John Howard to open his heart to HREOC's report into the stolen generations. Even before the report was delivered, on at least three occasions the Prime Minister pre-empted the government's response and disparaged the report and its authors. This was despite the fact that he had reportedly not taken up the offer of HREOC's president, Sir Ronald Wilson, to be provided with a briefing on the work of the inquiry. Action taken in response to the report, including responding to the call for a formal apology, remains another litmus test of the government's commitment to the reconciliation process. Proposals for creating a specialist tribunal to settle legal claims as an alternative to expensive confrontationist court cases deserves government endorsement.

Finally, I would urge the Coalition government or a future Labor government to have a serious dialogue with indigenous leaders and others in the community about a document or documents of reconciliation foreshadowed in the Council for Aboriginal Reconciliation Act. A document has already been released by the Council. Debate needs to remain focused on not merely the name of a possible document, whether called a Treaty or something else, but also on the even more challenging question of the content of the document and who might negotiate it. These are weighty questions for debate by the whole Australian community and I would caution against any rushed process and outcome that did not enjoy wide-ranging indigenous support. It is better to have no document of reconciliation than one which does not enjoy that support. I would also warn indigenous people not to have any faith in any government's promise to commit to a 'strategy' to address indigenous disadvantage at some time in the future. Such documents are not worth the paper they are written on. What is required at the very least are legislated binding commitments, the outcomes of which could be measured and reported on by the Aboriginal and Torres Strait Islander Social Justice Commissioner.

A further agenda for reform is the constitutional recognition of the special place of indigenous people. This latter possibility is not far-fetched; the Coalition, when in Opposition, supported the Constitutional Centenary Foundation headed by Sir Ninian Stephen, a former governor-general. Exploring in a cross-party way the possibility of just such a constitutional amendment was one of the foundation's primary areas of work. John Howard himself proposed constitutional change to the preamble, but his proposal was not subject to any hint of negotiation with indigenous people outside parliament and was bound to fail.

If the Howard government fails to respond to the desperate need to breathe life back into the reconciliation process, it will be left to a future Labor government to take up this agenda and especially the promised third-stage social justice package in response to the Mabo decision. Only time will tell whether Labor will rise to meet this challenge. Going into the 1998 federal election, there was no commitment that a Labor government would act to give effect to the unfinished business of the social justice measures promised by the Keating Cabinet. Nor was there any financial commitment of any kind to reallocate resources to address the living conditions in remote communities. Indigenous people and supporters of the reconciliation process need to continually scrutinise the policies of all political parties and hold them accountable.

Whatever government is in power, I have come to the view that more time is required for the reconciliation process. Much more work has to be done by the social and political movement of Australians seeking a just reconciliation before a permanent and lasting negotiated settlement can be reached. Sadly, it seems that as a nation we have lost the opportunity to celebrate the centenary of our Federation with acceptable progress towards a genuine reconciliation. But there is too much goodwill and optimism for the momentum of reconciliation to be lost.

The legislation establishing the Council and the objectives of the process should be extended another decade by the Australian parliament with the support of all state and territory governments, and the Prime Minister should provide the leadership to enable this to happen. When I proposed 1 January 2001 as the end date to the process, I was criticised for legislating for an excessively long period. It is now clear that our country needs a significantly longer time to get it right.

Of critical importance is that there remains in place a legislative framework for the reconciliation process which the reconciliation Act provides. Without a continuation of this Act—or its reenactment once it ceases to exist—with minor amendments or an alternative embraced with unanimous parliamentary support, the government of the day can turn its back on the process.

Reconciliation is at the crossroads. My message to the wider Australian community is that it is time to become involved and work for the achievement of a just reconciliation with Australia's indigenous people.

During the course of the native title debate in 1993, the forces of the Coalition were openly advocating opposition to any Commonwealth legislation to protect native title. They were pitted against a coalition of progressive Australians who supported the rights of indigenous people ahead of states' rights. At that time, and during the later Wik debate, many people of goodwill were prepared to take a stand and I believe this time has come again.

I ask every reader of this book: which side are you on? This is not a time for Australians who care about a process of reconciliation to sit on the fence. Unless we as a nation acknowledge the equal human worth of Aboriginal and Torres Strait Islander people and address their basic rights and aspirations, there is no hope for reconciliation and Australia will remain a diminished and discordant nation.

In the lead-up to the centenary of Federation, should the opportunity be lost and this outcome come to pass, the fight for indigenous rights will not stop, nor will the quest for an enduring and just settlement with the first Australians. I am confident, however, that there are enough people who care and who are prepared to take up the fight for justice and work towards that settlement. The sea of humanity walking across Sydney Harbour Bridge in May 2000, and later in Melbourne and other parts of the country, confirm my belief in the importance of the reconciliation process to this country.

Above all else, people of goodwill, both indigenous and non-indigenous, must take a stand to ensure there is no turning back.

PRIMARY WRITTEN SOURCES

In addition to the author's direct experience, the principal sources for material in this book include personal papers, diaries, ministerial media releases and press clippings held by the Commonwealth Parliamentary Library. The sources listed below are those that are not otherwise expressly referred to in the text.

The principal source of materials for the Mabo chapters were the author's personal notes and records compiled during the course of the Mabo debate, both within the government and publicly.

Reference has also been made to Cabinet debates and Cabinet advice, but in a manner that attempts to give the reader some insight into the political and institutional forces at work in shaping the outcome of the Native Title Act. Deliberately, the personal role of neither individual ministers nor individual public servants has been revealed. The collective advice of the public service to the Cabinet during the course of the Mabo deliberations has, however, been quoted verbatim as necessary throughout these chapters in order to reveal the institutional forces at work favouring a states-based outcome. In view of the passage of time since these events, it is considered that the publication of this material is in the public interest to demonstrate the operation of the Cabinet processes.

This material has been supplemented by reference to what was occurring within the public debate which raged throughout 1993. Sources for this material included ministerial, Opposition and interest group media releases together with newspaper, television and radio reporting of these public statements.

1   THE HISTORICAL CONTEXT:
D. Horton (ed.) *Encyclopaedia of Aboriginal Australia*, AIATSIS, 1994.

2   THE RECONCILIATION PROCESS
C. D. Rowley, *Recovery: The Politics of Aboriginal Reform*, Penguin, 1986.

Council for Aboriginal Reconciliation Act 1991.
The assistance of Lew Griffiths in providing a tape of Woompi Keppel's speech at Meripah is appreciated.

3   ATSIC

Foundations for the Future, Policy Statement by Gerry Hand MP, Minister for Aboriginal Affairs, AGPS, December 1987.
Bringing Them Home, a report by the Human Rights and Equal Opportunity Commission, 1987.
Social Justice for Indigenous Australians, AGPS, first published 1991–92.
ATSIC Annual Report 1994–1995, ATSIC.
Rebutting the Myths, AGPS, 1992.

4   ABORIGINAL DEATHS IN CUSTODY

Encyclopaedia of Aboriginal Australia (see chapter 1).
Reports of the Royal Commission into Aboriginal Deaths in Custody.
National Government Response to the Royal Commission into Aboriginal Deaths in Custody.
Vicki Dalton, 'Aboriginal Prison Deaths in Prison 1980 to 1988: National Overview', *Trends & Issues,* no. 131, Australian Institute of Criminology, 1999.
Justice Under Scrutiny, House of Representatives Standing Committee on Aboriginal and Torres Strait Islander Affairs, AGPS, November 1994.

5   MABO

Mabo: The Life of an Island Man, film by Trevor Graham.
Mabo v. Queensland (No 2), 175, CLR.
'High Court decisions condemned' by Karen Middleton, *Age,* 4 July 1992.
Hugh Morgan, 'Mabo Reconsidered' the Joe and Enid Lyons Memorial Lecture 1992, ANU, 12 October 1992.
'Parties firm on land rights' by Margot Kingston, *Age,* 13 October 1992.
'Blacks launch four native land title claims' by Paul Chamberlin and Peter Hartcher, *SMH,* 14 October 1992.
'Farmers seek to block land claims' by Tim Stevens and Deanie Carbon, *Australian,* 20 October 1992.
'Government response to High Court decision on native title', statement by Prime Minister Paul Keating, 27 October 1992.
'Court decision creates development crisis' by David Kemp, *Canberra Times,* 3 December 1992.
'Second-rate land title robs us all' by John Hyde, Executive Director, Institute of Public Affairs, *Australian,* 5 December 1992.
'Resolve Mabo concerns, Canberra urged' by Margaret Easterbrook, *Age,* 8 December 1992.

'Executive investors warned on Mabo impact', *Canberra Times*, 10 December 1992.

'Miners ask for support over Mabo' by Graham Lloyd, *Australian*, 23 December 1992.

'No future in looking back' by John Stone, *Financial Review*, 31 December 1992.

'Parbo warns of investment loss', *Age*, 9 January 1993.

'Fischer in land rights outburst' by Paul Chamberlin, *SMH*, 13 January 1993.

'Mabo fall-out continues' by John Stone, *Financial Review*, 21 January 1993.

Transcript of ABC Radio interview with John Hewson, 9 January 1993.

'Fischer admits unease with Liberal stance' by Nicholas Johnston, *Age*, 15 February 1993.

'Coalition's Mabo split widens' by Tim Stevens and David Nason, *Australian*, 26 February 1993.

6   THE BATTLE BEGINS AND THE LINES ARE DRAWN

'Authentic Keating', transcript of address to staff by Prime Minister Keating, Imperial Peking Restaurant, Sydney, 12 March 1993, *Independent Monthly*, April 1993.

'Put nation's future first', editorial, *Sunday Herald Sun*, 14 March 1993.

'Rights—Right or Wrong?', speech notes for address by Ian McLachlan MP, Shadow Minister for National Development and Infrastructure, H. R. Nicholls Society, Canberra, 14 May 1993.

'Top Libs split on approach to Mabo' by Lenore Taylor, *Australian*, 17 May 1993.

'Ignorance on Mabo a "concern"' by Liz Tickner, *West Australian*, 22 May 1993.

'Mabo: equity, not guilt', media release by Tim Fischer, Leader of the National Party, 24 May 1993.

'Blacks accuse PM of betrayal' by Gay Alcorn and Paul Chamberlin, *SHM*, 28 May 1993.

'Mabo indecision puts new investment at risk', media release by Ian McLachlan, 28 May 1993.

'PM: why we backed McArthur River mine' by Geoffrey Barker, *Age*, 1 June 1993.

'Chance meeting may have set-up McArthur deal' by David Nason, *Australian*, 14 Aug 1993.

'Mining bill "threatens reconciliation"' by Paul Chamberlin and Gay Alcorn, *SMH*, 29 May 1993.

'SA to adopt balanced approach on Mabo', media release by Lynn Arnold, SA Premier, 30 May 1993.

'Mabo: nightmare from dreamtime' by Liz Tickner, Malcolm Quekett and Amanda Hurley, *West Australian*, 3 June 1993.

'Mabo paper a "slimy" document' by Paul Chamberlin, *SMH*, 4 June 1993.

'Goss, Court warn of threat to investment' by Jamie Walker, Madonna King and APP, *Australian*, 4 June 1993.

'Kennett pushes state compo plan' by Lyn Dunlevy, *Age*, 8 June 1993.

'Premiers ready to say no' by Geoffrey Barker and Margaret Easterbrook, *Age*, 8 June 1993.

'Heads of government meeting "somewhat curious"', *Canberra Times*, 9 June 1993.

'PM's Mabo failure has created political disorder', media release by Ian McLachlan MP, 10 June 1993.

7   WIK IGNITES

'Blacks report post-Mabo racism' by John Kerin, *Australian*, 16 June 1993.

'Fischer promises fight with PM' by Jamie Walker and Madonna King, *Australian*, 11 June 1993.

'Mabo—farmers safe, but concerns for forestry and fishing: Aboriginal leaders should rein in silly claims', media release by John Anderson MP, 11 June 1993.

'Miners fear losing 80pc of WA to Mabo claims' by John McIlwraitt, *Australian*, 14 June 1993.

'Community divided on native title but most oppose compensation', Newspoll, *Australian*, 17 June 1993.

'Libs attack Keating on handling of Mabo', Geoff Kitney and Michael Millett, *SMH*, 15 June 1993.

'Armstrong contradicts Fahey on compo for Aborigines' by Natasha Bita, *Australian*, 19 June 1993.

'Fischer's Mabo outburst' by Mark Coultan and Mike Seccombe, *SMH*, 21 June 1993.

Media release by the Kowanyama Aboriginal Community Council, 21 June 1993.

'Keating calls for Hewson to act over Fischer's remarks' by Tom Burton and Tim Dodd, *Financial Review*, 22 June 1993.

'Downer attacks Fischer outburst' by Jamie Walker and Ann-Maree Moodie, *Australian*, 22 June 1993.

'Mabo opponents must be heard' by P. P. McGuinness, *Australian*, 23 June 1993.

'Judge rejects Mabo critics' by Rod Campbell, *Canberra Times*, 2 July 1993.

Meet the Press, Channel Ten, appearance by J. W. Howard, 4 July 1993.

'Parbo backs Morgan' by Peter Gill, *Financial Review*, 6 July 1993.

'Top Liberals reject churches on Mabo' by Malcolm Quekett and Amanda Hurley, *West Australian*, 10 July 1993.

'Fahey splits from PM on Mabo' by Mark Coultan and Paul Chamberlin, *SMH*, 13 July 1993.

'Judge hits at Mabo critics' by Paul Chamberlin and Anne Davies, *SMH*, 14 July 1993.

'Archbishop brings Hitler into Mabo debate', *SMH*, 16 July 1993.

'Tuckey threat to quit church', *Canberra Times*, 16 July 1993.

'ALP chief questions PM's Mabo tactics' by Rachel Hawes, *Australian*, 17 July 1993.

'Mabo law to shield farmers, says chief' by Innes Willox and Tom Ormonde, *Age*, 17 July 1993.

Transcript of ABC Radio interview between Rod Henshaw and Wayne Goss, 21 July 1993.

'$1.7b CRA projects face axe over Mabo' by Jamie Walker and Ewin Hannan, *Australian*, 21 July 1993.

'Bosch blasts "backward 1pc"', *Australian*, 23 July 1993.

'Delegates vote for Mabo plebiscite' by David Humphries, *Australian*, 26 July 1993.

8   A STRATEGIC WIN AND A BITTER DEFEAT

'Decision exacerbates uncertainty', AMIC media release, 28 July 1993.

Transcript of television interview between Paul Murphy and Prime Minister Keating, *Dateline*, SBS, 28 July 1993.

'Hewson gets a Court warning' by Malcolm Quekett and Randal Markey, *West Australian*, 28 July 1993.

'Blacks meet to map the future' by Chips Mackinolty, *Age*, 3 August 1993.

'Fischer calls for conference on Mabo' by Gerard Ryle, *Age*, 4 August 1993.

Eva Valley Statement, reproduced in the *Australian*, 6 August 1993.

'Tough black stand on Mabo policy' by Chips Mackinolty and Paul Chamberlin, *SMH*, 6 August 1993.

'Mabo—the truth about consultation', statement by Prime Minister Keating, 6 August 1993.

'Time for the Prime Minister to act on Mabo', media release by John Hewson MP, 6 August 1993.

'Goss slates PM's delay on Mabo', *Australian*, 6 August 1993.

Age and *SMH* Saulwick Poll, 4 August 1993.

Letter from John Ralph, MD and chief executive, CRA, to Commonwealth ministers, 6 August 1993.

'New fund to help Aborigines buy land' by Robert Garran and David Nason, *Australian*, 9 Aug 1993.

'PM rejects Goss's plea on mining' by Ross Peake, *Canberra Times*, 9 August 1993.

'NP leaders tackle Canberra on Mabo' by Brad Collis, *Age*, 10 August 1993.

Transcript of ABC Radio interview between Ellen Fanning and Michael Lavarch, *PM*, 10 August 1993.

'Aborigines "seen as animals without rights"' by Philip Cornford, *Financial Review*, 11 August 1993.

Transcript of ABC Radio interview between Ellen Fanning and Wayne Goss, *Early PM*, 13 August 1993.

'Blacks sacrificed to mining, claims leader' by Peter Fray, *Sunday Age*, 15 August 1993.

9   THE COMMONWEALTH DRAWS THE FIRE

'PM told: slow down Mabo or face second-best result' by Peter Gill, *Financial Review*, 26 August 1993.

'Blacks angered by rushed laws' by Jodie Brough, *Canberra Times*, 26 August 1993.

'Aborigines slam Fahey title Bill' by Natasha Bita, Mark Irving, Madonna King and AAP, *Australian*, 28 August 1993.

'"Hall of shame" for anti-Mabo premiers' by Fiona Kennedy, *Australian*, 31 August 1993.

'Mabo approach not practical', AMIC media release, 2 September 1993.

'Keating reveals his plan to bulldoze State sovereignty', media release by Ian McLachlan MP, 2 September 1993.

'It fails on three fronts, says ATSIC' by Jennifer Sexton, David Nason and Fiona Kennedy, *Australian*, 3 September 1993.

'Greens target Mabo, IR plan' by Jodie Brough, *Canberra Times*, 13 September 1993.

'Hollway plan for Mabo certainty suspends (i.e. denies and breaches) protection of RDA to Aboriginal and Islander People', press statement by Cape York Land Council, 13 September 1993.

'Mabo debate drifts as Caucus divides' by Peter Reith, *Canberra Times*, 20 September 1993.

'States unite on "unworkable" Mabo' by Peter Gill, *Financial Review*, 23 September 1993.

'Fischer brands Aboriginal people as ungrateful lot' by Tom Connors, *Canberra Times*, 24 September 1993.

'Aborigines told: be ready to fight' by Adam Harvey, *SMH*, 27 September 1993.

'Mabo statement', joint media release by ATSIC, the Australian Democrats and Greens (WA), 30 September 1993.

'States step up Mabo pressure' by Lenore Taylor and David Nason, *Australian*, 30 September 1993.

'Keating yields to States on Mabo' by Lenore Taylor and David Nason, *Australian*, 1 October 1993.

Newspoll, *Australian*, 1 October 1993.

'Stall on native title Bill likely' by Keith Scott, *Canberra Times*, 2 October 1993.

'Tutu praises morality of title ruling' by Duncan Graham, *SMH*, 5 October 1993.

'Aboriginal leader threatens to quit over discord' by Cameron Forbes, *Australian*, 6 October 1993.

'PM fights to save Mabo deal in marathon talks' by Peter Gill and Nigel Wilson, *Financial Review*, 7 October 1993.

'Govt to bulldoze Mabo legislation', *SMH*, 8 October 1993.

'PM has failed us on Mabo: Aborigines' by Laura Tingle, *Australian*, 9 October 1993.

'PM's Mabo plea: go one more step' by Geoff Kitney, *SMH*, 9 October 1993.

10   GETTING THE NATIVE TITLE ACT OVER THE LINE

'Keating goes west to face his foes' by Mark Irving, *Australian*, 9 October 1993.

Letter from the Combined Aboriginal Organisations to the Prime Minister, 11 October 1993.

'Groups press Keating on native title' by Innes Willox and Martin Daly, *Age*, 14 October 1993.

'Government moves on Mabo worrying', letter to editor by Phillip Adams et al, *Australian*, 14 October 1993.

'Preparation for the Essfight of the century' by Alan Ramsey, *SMH*, 16 October 1993.

'The Making of Mabo' by Innes Willox and Brad Collis, *Age*, 26 November 1993.

'11th hour offer clinched Farley' by Laura Tingle, *Australian*, 20 October 1993.

'Mabo', media release by John Hewson MP, 19 October 1993.

'Mabo measure must be made to fit the Bill' by Garth Nettheim, *Financial Review*, 20 October 1993.

'Ticking Points' by Frank Brennan, *Australian*, 23 October 1993.

'WA warns Hewson of trouble on Mabo split' by Innes Willox, *Age*, 25 October 1993.

'Miners reject government's Mabo approach', AMIC media release, 25 October 1993.

'Mabo debate divides Opposition' by Paul Chamberlin, *SMH*, 27 October 1993.

'Conservatives break ranks on Mabo ballot' by Mike Seccombe, *SMH*, 1 November 1993.

'Blainey lashes "ignorant" Mabo judges' by Jenny Brinkworth, *Australian*, 9 November 1993.

'Wootten rallies to blacks' defence' by Jonathan Porter, *Australian*, 17 November 1993.

'Green threat to delay Mabo' by Lenore Taylor, *Australian*, 10 November 1993.

'Koori leader attacks Libs over Mabo' by Innes Willox, *Age*, 11 November 1993.

Joint Press Release by Paul Coe and Charles Perkins, Aboriginal Legal Service, 11 November 1993.

'Court poised for Mabo challenge' by Lenore Taylor, Scott Henry and Mark Irving, *Australian*, 18 November 1993.

'Hewson defuses Mabo threat' by Geoff Kitney and Paul Chamberlin, *SMH*, 18 November 1993.

'Hewson finds path out of Mabo maze' by Lenore Taylor, *Australian*, 15 November 1993.

'Coalition's policy on Mabo', media release by John Hewson MP, 18 November 1993.

'Use rights are not land rights' by Henry Reynolds, *Age*, 22 November 1993.

'Greens move to put Mabo legislation on hold', media release by Christabel Chamarette, 24 November 1993.

'Blacks slam Greens for threat to Mabo Bill' by Lenore Taylor, *Australian*, 25 November 1993.

'Greens stronger on "no" to Bill' by Ross Peake, *Canberra Times*, 27 November 1993.

'Chamarette rejects PM's claim that the Greens are unwilling to deliver justice for Aboriginal people', media release by Christabel Chamarette, 30 November 1993.

'Chamarette details problems with proposed native title legislation', media release by Christabel Chamarette, 30 November 1993.

'Mabo Bill threatens growth, says Goss' by Madonna King and David Nason, *Australian*, 3 December 1993.

'WA native title in danger, PM warns' by Paul Chamberlin, *SMH*, 3 December 1993.

'Green hardens against Mabo Bill' by Lenore Taylor and Ewin Hannan, *Australian*, 7 December 1993.

'Mabo a national disaster: Hewson' by Innes Willox, *Age*, 11 December 1993.

'Farmers attack Opposition on Mabo' by Tom Burton, *Financial Review*, 16 December 1993.

'Coalition splits over Mabo bill' by Tom Burton, *Financial Review*, 17 December 1993.

'Even at Christmas there was mud' by Alan Ramsey, *SMH*, 18 December 1993.

'Tempers fray as debate marathon wears thin' by Keith Scott, *Canberra Times*, 20 December 1993.

'Current native title bill unacceptable', news release by NFF, 19 December 1993.

'Of platypuses, pollies and a clever QC' by Margo Kingston, *Canberra Times*, 22 December 1993.

11 LAND FOR THE DISPOSSESSED

Hansard reports of debate on the ATSIC Amendment (Indigenous Land Corporation and Land Fund) Bills during 1984 and 1985.

Speech by Sol Bellear, Redfern Park, 10 December 1992.

'Lib switch on land fund Bill' by Keith Scott and Ross Peake, *Canberra Times*, 30 August 1994.

Report of the Senate Select Committee on the Land Fund Bill, Parliament of the Commonwealth of Australia, February 1995.

12 THE TORRES STRAIT ISLANDERS

Departmental advice provided by PM&C.

Encyclopaedia of Aboriginal Australia (see Chapter 1).

Report of the Interdepartmental Committee on the Torres Strait Islands, August 1988.

National Aboriginal and Torres Strait Islander Survey: Torres Strait Area, Australian Bureau of Statistics, 1984.

'Items for discussion by Torres Strait Islanders with the Prime Minister and Cabinet on 27 April 1993', prepared by the ICC, 17 April 1993.

'Islanders "misled over self-rule"' by Wallace Brown, *Courier Mail*, 20 November 1993.

Transcript of item concerning Queensland government opposition to self rule, ABC TV, *7pm News*, 23 November 1993.

Submission by the ICC to the Senate Legal and Constitutional Affairs Committee re the Native Title Bill 1993, 6 December 1993.

'Torres Strait Regional Authority: An Act of Self-Determination for the People of the Torres Strait—A Framework for Achieving the Aspirations of the People of the Torres Strait', a response by the TSRA to the Mabo Social Justice Task Force.

Going Forward: Social Justice for the First Australians, Council for Aboriginal Reconciliation, AGPS, August 1996.

'Torres Strait Islanders: A New Deal—A Report on Greater Autonomy for Torres Strait Islanders', House of Representatives Standing Committee on Aboriginal Affairs, August 1997.

Government Response to 'Torres Strait Islanders: A New Deal', June 1998.

13 HERITAGE, CULTURE AND HINDMARSH ISLAND

Exploring for Common Ground, Council for Aboriginal Reconciliation, 1993.

Reports prepared for the Minister pursuant to Section 10 of the *Aboriginal and Torres Strait Islander Heritage Protection Act 1984*.

Hansard reports of debate and questions in both the House of Representatives and the Senate concerning Hindmarsh Island during 1994 and 1995.

Channel Ten news reports beginning 19 May 1995 concerning alleged fabrication of Hindmarsh Island heritage claims.

Advertiser reports during 1994, 1995 and 1996 concerning Hindmarsh Island.

Daily Telegraph and Melbourne *Sun* reports in 1995 concerning the veracity of the Ngarrindjeri heritage claims.

Report of the Hindmarsh Island Bridge Royal Commission, State Print Adelaide, 1995.

Greg Mead, *A Royal Omission: A Critical Survey of Evidence Given to the Hindmarsh Island Royal Commission with an Alternative Report*, PO Box 6042, Halifax St, SA 5000, 1995.

Review of the Aboriginal and Torres Strait Islander Heritage Protection Act, Report by the Hon. Elizabeth Evatt, AC, August 1996.

14 ABORIGINAL HEALTH

Recommendations on Aboriginal health made by the Royal Commission into Aboriginal Deaths in Custody.

Rhetoric or Reality?, Report of the Inquiry into the Implementation of the Access and Equity Strategy, AGPS, 1993.

Selected Cabinet documents referred to in the public interest after a considerable lapse of time.

The National Aboriginal Health Strategy: An Evaluation, December 1994.

Transcript of Prime Minister Keating's comments to *A Current Affair*, 24 February 1995.

15 THE WORLD IS WATCHING

UN Draft Declaration of the Rights of Indigenous Peoples.

Australian government statements to the UN Working Group on Indigenous Peoples, 1990–95.

Australian government reports to the CERD Committee 1994, including oral presentations by the author and the Aboriginal and Torres Strait Islander Social Justice Commissioner.

16 DOES RECONCILIATION STAND A CHANCE?

Letter to the *Queensland Times* by Pauline Hanson, 6 Jan 1996, attacking the author and leading to her expulsion from the Liberal Party.

2UE broadcasts of Prime Minister Howard on the Alan Jones program following the 1996 election.

Council for Aboriginal Reconciliation Act 1991.

Indigenous Affairs in Australia, New Zealand, Canada, USA, Norway and Sweden, Dept of Parliamentary Library Background Paper, No. 15, 1997–98.

INDEX

A Team, 191, 213, 215
ABC *Four Corners*, 37
Aboriginal Advancement Leagues, 5
Aboriginal and Torres Strait
    Islander Commercial
    Development Corporation, 223
Aboriginal and Torres Strait
    Islander Social Justice
    Commissioner, 80, 123, 124, 290,
    307, 309
Aboriginal children
    removal from parents, 2, 54–7
Aboriginal Councils and
    Associations Act, 18
Aboriginal culture
    derogatory comments on, 133,
        136, 143
Aboriginal deaths in custody, 67–73,
    77; *see also* Royal Commission into
    Aboriginal Deaths in Custody
    of Malcolm Charles Smith, 69–72
    reductions in, 76
Aboriginal Development
    Commission, 19, 51, 222
Aboriginal disadvantage, 65, 73, 78,
    320–1
    programs to address, 75–7, 78–80
Aboriginal flag, 12
Aboriginal health
    expenditure on, 289, 290
    infrastructure needs for, 294
    Keating government's failings,
        288–301 *passim*
    RCIADIC recommendations, 290

Aboriginal heritage *see* heritage
    protection; Heritage Protection
    Act
Aboriginal Hostels, 14, 51
Aboriginal human remains, return
    of, 257–8
Aboriginal Land Fund Commission,
    15, 19, 222, 227
Aboriginal Loans Commission, 14–15
Aboriginal organisations, 18; *see also*
    names of specific organisations
Aboriginal people
    community cohesion among, 12
    need for constitutional
        recognition, 325
    political attacks on, 132, 175
Aboriginal Protection Boards, 5, 6
Aboriginal Provisional Government,
    112, 209
Aboriginal self-reliance, 14
Aboriginal spirituality, 256, 268; *see
    also* sacred sites
    disparagement of, 260, 274, 285
    respect for, 267, 283
Aboriginal treaty; *see also* treaty
    Aboriginal Treaty Committee, 20,
        27
Aboriginal unemployment, 224
Aboriginal vote, 12
Aborigines Progressive Association,
    5, 7
Access and Equity Strategy, 78, 291
ACTU, 36, 131–2
Ah Kit, John, 98, 112, 260
alcohol abuse, 72, 77
ALP *see* Australian Labor Party

Anderson, John, 132
Anglican Church, 3
anti-Aboriginal attitudes, 132, 133,
   136, 145, 175, 315–16
anti-welfare rhetoric, 64–5
apology to stolen generations, 56–7,
   98
appropriation of Aboriginal land, 84
Armitage, Michael, 280
Armstrong, Ian, 133
assimilation policy, 6
ATSIC (Aboriginal and Torres Strait
   Islander Commission),
   48–65 *passim; see also* O'Donogue,
   Lois
   accountability, 25, 50–3, 58–9,
      62–3
   administration and
      decision-making, 49, 57–8,
      60–1, 64, 75
   Black Friday press conference,
      187, 189–90
   commitment to a treaty, 38
   creation, 27, 49–51
   distrust of Office of Indigenous
      Affairs, 109
   elections for, 53–4, 60, 61–2
   funding, 52, 58, 78
   and government's Mabo
      response, 90, 93, 109–10, 122,
      168, 172–3, 176, 181, 187–9,
      192–3
   health and medical
      responsibilities, 292, 300
   land acquisition, 236
   ministerial authority over, 52, 59
   Office of Evaluation and Audit,
      59
   opposes erosion of Racial
      Discrimination Act, 109–10
   powers, 49–51
   *Social Justice for Indigenous
      Australians,* 58
   Torres Strait Islander
      representation, 240–1
Attorney-General's Department,
   101–3
Aurukun, 18
Aurukun Shire, 140
Australian Aborigines League, 5, 7
Australian Council of Churches,
   194, 213

Australian Institute of Aboriginal
   and Torres Strait Islander Studies
   (AIATSIS), 7, 51
Australian Labor Party
   Caucus Aboriginal and Torres
      Strait Islander Affairs
      Committee, 111, 194, 253
   conferences support principled
      Mabo response, 131
   no Aboriginal parliamentary
      candidates, 11
   supports Hindmarsh Island
      Bridge Act, 285
Australian Mining Industry Council
   (AMIC), 91, 100–2, 114, 122–3,
   140, 171, 193, 208, 213
Australian Petroleum Exploration
   Association, 110, 114, 140
Ayers Rock *see* Uluru

B Team, 191, 209, 213, 215
Bamblett, Alf, 54, 62–3
bark petition, 7, 11
Barnett, Colin, 141
Barunga Statement, 25, 40–2
Baume, Peter, 20
Beazley, Kim, 46, 285
Beazley, Kim (senior), 8, 9
Bellear, Sol, 39, 60, 94, 97
BHP, 96, 166
Bicentenary protests, 25, 33
Bjelke-Petersen government, 15, 16,
   18, 20
Black Friday, 187
Blackburn, Justice Sir Richard,
   10–11, 85
Blainey, Geoffrey, 204
Bolkus, Nick, 161, 193
Boney, Lloyd, 68
Bonner, Neville, 11
Bosch, Henry, 143
Breaden, Kunmanara, 112, 114
Brennan, Fr Frank, 33, 178, 202
Brennan, Justice Sir Gerard, 86
Bridge, Ernie, 166–7
Bringing Them Home, 55
Broome crocodile farm, 263–4
Bropho, Robert, 39, 259
Brown, Dean, 265, 266–7, 275–8, 281
Bryant, Gordon, 8, 14
Burke government, 22, 23

Burnett, Peter, 101–2
business groups, 108, 114

Cabinet; *see also* Mabo Ministerial
    Committee
    Aboriginal infrastructure
        expenditure, 299
    Coronation Hill decision, 259–61
    endorses reconciliation process,
        35
    Keating defeated in, 161
    leaked documents, 182
    Lois O'Donoghue addresses, 54,
        75
    overrides Wik claimants, 157,
        161–3
    rejects recommendation to
        amend RDA, 104
    response to RCIADIC, 74–5
    Wik decisions, 161–3
Canada, 12, 38, 84, 110
Cape York Land Council, 138, 172
Carnley, Archbishop Peter, 141
Castan, Ron, 193, 215, 217
Caucus Aboriginal and Torres Strait
    Islander Affairs Committee, 111,
    194, 253
Cavanagh, Jim, 14–15
CDEP *see* Community Development
    Employment Project
Centenary of Federation
    Infrastructure Project, 45,
    296–301
Central Land Council, 13, 36–7, 97,
    257
CERD (International Convention on
    the Elimination of All Forms of
    Racial Discrimination), 16, 40,
    85, 102, 124, 193, 304, 306,
    307–11, 310–11, 319
Chamarette, Christabel, 171–2, 181,
    209–12 *passim*, 215
Chaney, Fred, 18–19, 264
Chapman, Tom and Wendy, 271,
    278, 285
children *see* Aboriginal children;
    stolen generations
Christian missions, 3–4
churches, 31, 33, 35–6, 138, 194, 213
Clarke, Geoff, 34, 128

COAG (Council of Australian
    Governments), 81, 110–11, 115,
    126–9
Coalition parties
    denunciation by Aboriginal
        leaders of, 204–5, 234
    involvement in Hindmarsh Island
        dispute, 268–73, 275–7
    and Land Fund Bill, 226–7, 229,
        231–4
    in the Mabo debate, 90, 93,
        98–9, 115–16, 123, 132, 133,
        135–6, 141, 143, 152, 157–8,
        171, 173–4, 175, 177–8, 183,
        199, 202–5, 318
    and Native Title Bill, 206–7,
        214–17, 219
Coe, Paul, 205, 305
Coe v. the Commonwealth, 19–20
Coffey, Essie, 39, 94
Comalco, 158, 161
Committee to Defend Black Rights,
    67
Commonwealth of Australia *see*
    Constitution (Australia)
Community Development
    Employment Project (CDEP), 18,
    78, 224
compensation, 56, 101–3, 125, 127,
    173
Coniston massacre, 2
consent rights, 113, 117, 125, 128–9,
    131, 146
Constitution (Australia)
    Aboriginal affairs power, 7, 8
    recognition of indigenous people
        in, 325
    referendums, 7, 8–9, 28, 43
    section 127 repeal, 8
Coombs, H.C. (Nugget), 10, 20
Coronation Hill, 259–61
Council for Aboriginal Affairs, 10
Council for Aboriginal
    Reconciliation, 34–5, 38–9, 43–4,
    90, 239, 251, 258, 317
Council for Aboriginal
    Reconciliation Act, 317
Court, Richard, 123, 134–5, 136,
    138, 141, 152, 183, 192, 201, 202,
    206
CRA Ltd, 19, 138, 142, 156, 158,
    162–3, 263

Crawford, James, 33
cross-party cooperation
on Mabo response, 90, 98–9,
104–5
on reconciliation, 30–1, 35, 37–8,
42, 45, 317
Crowley, Rosemary, 281
culture *see* Aboriginal culture
Cummeragunja reserve, 6
custody; *see also* Aboriginal deaths in
custody
Aboriginal people in, 67, 73, 79

Davis, Leon, 162
Day of Mourning, 5
Deane, Sir William, 30, 45, 319–20
Deaths in Custody Watch
Committee, 67; *see also*
Aboriginal deaths in custody
Democrats, 171, 176, 179, 180–1,
190, 208, 216; *see also* Kernot,
Cheryl
Department of Aboriginal Affairs,
13, 50
Department of the Prime Minister
and Cabinet (PM&C)
Aboriginal peoples' distrust of,
109, 172
lack of expertise in Aboriginal
policy, 92, 252, 291
Mabo advice rejected, 103–4
Office of Indigenous Affairs, 60,
109, 188, 245
role in Mabo response, 83, 92,
100, 102–4, 139, 146
seeks accommodation with states
and territories, 146, 174, 188
Tickner's clashes with, 60, 61, 109
and Torres Strait Islands
self-government, 244
urges suspension of RDA, 103,
172
in Wik negotiations with states,
162
Dexter, Barrie, 10, 13
disadvantage *see* Aboriginal
disadvantage
Djerrkura, Gatjil, 63, 64
Dodson, Mick, 55, 123–4, 153–4,
157, 160–1, 260, 307
Dodson, Patrick, 39, 43, 44, 68, 90,
110, 112, 153, 172, 181, 264

'dog licences', 6
Douglas, Malcolm, 263–4
Downer, Alexander, 226–9, 307
Draft Declaration of the Rights of
Indigenous Peoples, 302–3, 306
Duffy, Michael, 92, 124, 306

economic rationalists, 23
education, 40, 44, 76, 78
employment programs, 18, 78, 121,
224
equal pay, 10
Eva Valley Statement, 153–4
Evans, Gareth, 215, 218, 219
Evatt, Elizabeth, 256
Exploring for Common Ground, 258

Fahey, John, 140
Farley, Rick
on Council for Aboriginal
Reconciliation, 39, 44
in Mabo negotiations, 91, 195,
196, 200
and Native Title Bill, 214–15,
217–18
FCAATSI *see* Federal Council for the
Advancement of Aborigines and
Torres Strait Islanders
Federal Council for Aboriginal
Affairs (FCAA) *see* Federal
Council for the Advancement of
Aborigines and Torres Strait
Islanders
Federal Council for the
Advancement of Aborigines and
Torres Strait Islanders
(FCAATSI), 8–9
Federation of Land Councils, 34
Fergie, Deane, 268
Ferguson, William, 5
fiduciary duty, 139, 156–7, 162
Fischer, Tim, 98–9, 104–5, 110, 118,
132, 133, 135, 152, 175, 202, 215,
226
Flower, Dulcie, 95, 242
Forrest River massacres, 2
Fraser, Malcolm, 17, 57
Fraser government, 13–14, 17–21
freedom ride, 7–8
French, Robert, 220
Freund, Peter, 96
Fussell, Norm, 108, 213

Gallus, Christine, 268–70, 271, 275, 277
genocide, 56
George, Jean, 112, 114
Gibson, Garrie, 67, 138
Glenn, Howard, 44
Gordon, Steve, 54
Goss, Wayne, 89–90, 138, 140, 142, 155–7, 171, 208, 212, 246–7
Gove Land Rights Case, 11, 85
Gray, Bill, 53, 57
Green senators, 171–2, 176, 179, 180–1, 190, 204
Gurindgi people, 8

Hand, Gerry, 25–6, 27, 50–1, 75
Hanson, Pauline, 132, 175, 314–16
Harradine, Brian, 179, 213
Hasluck, Paul, 7
Hassell, Bill, 138
Hawke, Bob, 19, 21, 25–6, 41–2
Hawke, Stephen, 19
Hawke government, 223
    proposed national land rights scheme, 21–5, 223
    reconciliation policy, 34–42 *passim*
health *see* Aboriginal health
heritage protection
    applications, 257, 259, 261, 263, 264
    declarations, 257, 261–3, 264–5, 267
    legal challenges, 259, 264, 267, 271, 280–1
    reform proposals, 257–8
Heritage Protection Act, 23, 255
Herron, John, 46, 63, 285, 307, 314
Hewson, Dr John
    opposition to Native Title Bill, 196, 199, 203–4, 207–8, 214, 219
    in Mabo debate, 62, 91, 104–5, 123, 132, 135–6, 143, 152, 154
    support for reconciliation process, 30–1, 35, 93
High Court
    attacks on, 112, 136
    Chief Justice defends, 136, 140
    Coe v. the Commonwealth, 19–20
    invalidates Judge Mathews' report, 283–4
    Kartinyeri v. Commonwealth, 285–6

Koowarta v. Bjelke-Petersen, 20, 85
    Mabo No. 1 Case, 85–6
    Mabo No. 2 Case, 2, 86
    Wik case, 88, 140, 196, 201
Hindmarsh Island Bridge Act, 285–6
Hindmarsh Island heritage dispute, 264–86 *passim*
    heritage application, 264, 285
    heritage declarations, 265, 267
    invalidation of declaration, 267, 271, 280–1
    Mathews report, 276, 283–5
    Opposition parties' involvement in, 268–73, 275–7
    proposals for bridge, 265–7
    Royal Commission into, 276–83
    Saunders report, 265–6, 268, 276
    secret women's beliefs, 279, 281, 285
        alleged fabrication of, 274–5, 281–2, 285
    South Australian government and, 265
Holding, Clyde, 21, 22–4, 50
Hollway, Sandy, 162, 174
Holroyd, Eddie, 140
Holt government, 10–11
Horton, David, 1
House of Representatives Standing Committee on Aboriginal and Torres Strait Islander Affairs, 15–16, 78, 80, 81, 239, 254, 291
housing, 294–7, 300
Howard, John
    alleges 'cultural McCarthyism', 137
    failure to rebut Pauline Hanson, 315–16
    involvement in Hindmarsh Island dispute, 268, 272–3, 275
    opposes treaty, 28
Howard government, 14
    anti-welfare rhetoric, 64–5
    and indigenous human rights, 308–12
    and reconciliation process, 46–7, 314, 316, 318
    response to stolen generation inquiry, 56–7
    response to Wik decision, 308
    and Torres Strait Islands

self-government, 46–7, 253–4,
314, 316, 318
Howe, Brian, 289
Howson, Peter, 10
human remains, return of, 40, 257–8
human rights
Australia's violations of
indigenous, 308–11
Barunga Statement of
indigenous, 40–1
international forums for,
302–12 *passim*
Human Rights and Equal
Opportunity Commission
(HREOC) *see* stolen generations:
inquiry into
Hyde, John, 94

ICC *see* Island Coordinating Council
ICCPR (International Covenant on
Civil and Political Rights), 40,
304–5, 308–11, 319
Indigenous Land Corporation,
230–2, 236
industry groups, 108, 114, 135
infrastructure backlog, 294–7
International Covenant on Civil and
Political Rights *see* ICCPR
Island Coordinating Council (ICC),
240, 243, 247

Jawoyn people, 98, 260
Jervis Bay, 24
Johnson, Les, 15
Jonas, Bill, 124
Johnston, Elliott, 68, 82, 257
Jones, Alan, 60, 315
Jones, Barry, 141
Jones, Bruce, 272
juvenile justice, 79, 202, 212

Kakadu National Park, 260
Karinji Aboriginal Corporation, 263
Kartinyeri, Doreen, 267
Kata Tjuta, 24
Keating, Annita, 87
Keating, Paul
angered by Eva Valley criticism,
154, 159
commitment to Mabo and
reconciliation, 89–96 *passim*,
107, 115, 118

conflict with Goss, 157
critical of Aboriginal negotiators,
189, 192
defeated in Cabinet, 161
Hopevale visit, 298–9
indigenous leaders' criticism of,
121, 154
media conference on Mabo
negotiations, 159
negotiates Mabo settlement, 193–8
opposes suspension of Racial
Discrimination Act, 159
Redfern Park speech, 94–5, 187,
189
seeks accommodation with states
on Mabo, 121, 133, 142
supports NT's McArthur River
mine deal, 118–21
Keating government; *see also* Land
Fund Bill; Mabo: legislative
response; Native Title Bill
reconciliation policy, 42
Kee, Sue, 270, 271, 272
Kemp, Dr David, 97
Kennett, Jeff, 127–8, 180
Keppell, Woompi, 32–3
Kernot, Cheryl, 39, 44, 127, 181,
201, 215, 217–18, 219
Kimberley Land Council, 96, 97,
212, 264
Kingston, Margot, 217, 294
Koowarta, John, 20, 32
Koowarta case, 20, 85

land acquisition, by dispossessed
Aboriginal people, 15, 21, 78,
222–3, 225; *see also* Land Fund
Bill
Land Fund Bill, 226, 229–36
land rights; *see also* native title
campaign by the Gurindji for, 8
national system of, 21, 40
Woodward Commission, 13
land rights legislation
Northern Territory *see* Northern
Territory Land Rights Act
proposal for uniform national,
22–3
states, 21–3, 166, 223
land titles (non-indigenous)
effect of Mabo decision on,
100–4, 108, 113

effect of Racial Discrimination
    Act on, 100–4, 113
indigenous consent rights, 113,
    117, 125, 128–9, 131, 146
right of Aboriginal veto, 131,
    145, 146, 147
validation of 1975–92 titles,
    100–4, 113, 140, 159–62, 173–4
Langton, Marcia, 44, 210
Lavarch, Michael, 156, 158, 160, 270
law-and-order rhetoric, 79
Lawrence, Carmen, 293–4
Lee, Michael, 110
Lingiari, Vincent, 8
Long, David, 36–7
Lui, Getano, 243, 245, 252–3

Mabo, Bonita, 86, 87, 99
Mabo, Eddie, 84–5, 87, 99
Mabo: High Court decision, 2, 11,
    16, 83–105 *passim*; *see also* Mabo:
    the debate; Mabo: legislative
    response; native title
ambit and bogus claims
    following, 94, 96–7, 126
call for referendum on, 136–7,
    138, 143, 203
Chief Justice defends, 136, 140
Coalition parties' response to,
    90, 93, 98–9
combined effect of Racial
    Discrimination Act and, 90–1,
    100–4
cross-party cooperation, 90, 98–9,
    104–5, 123
early responses, 89–102 *passim*,
    108–10
effect on Torres Strait Islanders,
    242
end of cross-party cooperation,
    123
implications and uncertainties,
    87–8, 110
the judgment, 86–7
Keating government's response
    see Mabo: Mabo legislative
    response; Mabo Ministerial
    Committee; Native Title Bill
Keating's commitment to,
    89–96 *passim*, 115, 118
Liberal Party attacks on, 115,
    123, 129, 134, 143

Liberal Party divisions, 115–16,
    143, 152
mining industry opposition to,
    90–1, 94, 96, 108
public opinion on, 118, 132, 155
as threat to mining investment,
    94, 96–7, 107–8
Mabo: the debate, 89–104 *passim*,
    108–29 *passim*, 132–7 *passim*,
    141–3, 157–60; *see also* Mabo:
    legislative response; native title;
    Native Title Bill
Coalition parties in, 115–16, 123,
    132, 133, 135–6, 141, 143,
    152, 157–8, 175
polarisation of, 132, 134–5,
    141–3, 157, 175, 207, 314
Mabo: legislative response, 46, 111;
    see also COAG; Department of
    the Prime Minister and Cabinet;
    Native Title Bill
accommodation with states and
    territories, 177, 182–4
Cabinet decisions on, 147,
    149–51, 161–3, 182–5; *see also*
    Cabinet; Native Title Bill
Cabinet's key principles for, 116,
    122, 124–5, 127–8, 167, 169–71
Coalition parties' opposition to,
    152, 157–8, 171, 173–4, 175,
    177–8, 183, 199, 202–5, 318
community support for, 194
consultative process for, 92–3,
    110, 126, 170
deal with NT government, 118–21
Democrat senators and, 171, 176,
    179, 180–1, 190
discussion paper, 122–3
drafting instructions, 145–7,
    167–8, 170
government's options and
    dilemmas, 111, 183, 187, 190
indigenous demands, 109–10,
    112–13, 116–17, 123, 139, 143,
    153–4, 166–8, 170, 172–3, 176,
    180, 181, 185, 188–9, 192–3,
    209
industry demands, 108, 114–15,
    122–3, 132, 135, 139, 140,
    142, 151, 166, 197, 213–14
ministerial conflict on, 157, 160–1
ministerial consideration of, 92,

100, 104–5, 107, 111, 112–15, 116–17, 122, 139–40, 147, 155, 167
negotiated settlement reached, 198, 199–200
reactions to, 201–10, 212
negotiations with indigenous representatives, 89, 112–14, 116–17, 121–2, 139, 153–4, 166–7, 168, 172–3, 181, 183–5, 185, 187–90, 193–5, 197–8, 199–200, 201, 243
objections of dissident Aboriginal groups to, 201, 205
negotiations with industry, 114–15, 166
negotiations with states and territories, 111–12, 127–9, 139, 142, 145–7, 155
officials' role in, 100–3, 122, 145–7, 172, 174, 177, 182
social justice agenda, 249–51
state and territory demands, 139, 140, 142, 155–7, 160–3, 174–5, 177, 180, 181, 185, 187–90
WA Green senators and, 171–2, 176, 179, 180–1, 190, 204
Mabo Ministerial Committee, 92, 100, 104–5, 107, 111, 112–15, 116–17, 122, 139–40, 147, 155, 167
'Makarrata', 20
mandatory sentencing, 79
Mansell, Michael, 34, 170, 209, 213, 257, 307
Marandoo iron ore project, 263
Mason, Sir Anthony, 136, 140
massacres, 3–4
Mathews report, 276–81, 283–4
McArthur River mine project, 96, 108, 118–21
McGuinness, Padraic, 135
McLachlan, Ian, 115, 129, 171, 203–4, 215, 226
role in Hindmarsh Island dispute, 265, 267, 268–73, 275–7
McLaughlin, Sean, 269
McMahon government, 10, 11, 12–13, 319
Mead, Greg, 282
media, 94, 107–8

Melham, Daryl, 193, 285
Menzies government, 7–8
Meriam people, 84
Meripah Station, 32
Milera, Doug, 277, 280
Millirrpum and Others vs Nabalco Pty Ltd and the Commonwealth of Australia, 11, 85
mining
Aboriginal veto rights over, 17, 131, 135
on Torres Strait Islands, 252
mining industry; *see also* names of specific mining companies
Mabo demands, 108, 122–3, 132, 151, 166, 197
opposition to Native Title Bill, 213
political influence of, 22–3, 120–1, 163
reaction to Mabo decision, 90–1, 94, 96, 108
mining leases, 118–23, 158
missions *see* reserves
Moree, 7–8
Morgan, Hugh, 90–1, 99, 108, 136–7, 197, 214
Mornington Island, 18
Moss, Irene, 137
Mt Isa Mines, 96, 108, 119–21
Mt Todd mine project, 98
Muirhead, Justice James, 68
Munro, Lyall, 95
Murray Islands, 84, 246
Mye, George, 113, 114, 240, 245

Nabalco; *see* Gove Land Rights Case
Napranum Aboriginal Council, 140
National Aboriginal and Islander Legal Services Secretariat, 305
National Aboriginal Conference (NAC), 18, 27
National Aboriginal Consultative Committee, 14, 18
National Farmers' Federation (NFF), 36, 91, 114, 122, 140, 196, 200, 214, 218
National Land Fund, 46
national parks, 76, 78
National Strategy on Aboriginal and Torres Strait Islander Health, 288–9

native police, 3
native title; *see also* Gove land rights
    case; land titles
    (non-indigenous); Mabo: High
    Court decision; Mabo: legislative
    response; Native Title Act; Native
    Title Bill; Wik land claim
    compensation for loss of, 101–3,
        125, 127, 173
    consent rights, 113, 117, 125,
        128–9, 131, 146
    extinguishment of, 88, 89, 102,
        108, 146, 169–70, 195–8
    High Court's recognition of, 86–8
    limited scope for claiming, 23
    national standards for, 126
    over pastoral leases, 134,
        195–202, 214–18 *passim*
    tribunal to hear claims for, 113,
        170
Native Title Act, 46, 150
    in breach of CERD, 310–11
    Coalition to repeal, 227
    High Court challenge, 201
    sets national benchmarks, 81
Native Title Bill, 149–50, 169–71,
    206–20 *passim*
    native title holders' right to be
        consulted, 149–50
    passage, 219–20
    Senate's consideration of, 210–19
    as special measure under RDA,
        192–3, 198–9
    WA Greens and, 201, 209–12,
        212–13
native title legislation; *see* land
    rights legislation; Mabo:
    legislative response; Native Title
    Act; Native Title Bill
Native Title Tribunal, 220
Nettheim, Garth, 65, 167, 202
New South Wales government
    land acquisition fund, 223
    land rights legislation, 21–2, 166,
        223
    re Mabo, 140
New Zealand, 57, 84
NFF *see* National Farmers'
    Federation
Ngarrindjeri people, 264–5, 266,
    274, 279, 285; *see also* Hindmarsh
    Island heritage dispute

Noonkanbah dispute, 19, 22
Northern Land Council, 13, 97,
    120–1, 260
Northern Territory
    Mt Todd mine project, 98
    Todd River dam project, 261–3
    Woodward Commission, 13
Northern Territory Chamber of
    Mines and Petroleum, 94
Northern Territory government
    ensures Jawoyn land ownership,
        98
    secures McArthur River mining
        leases, 118–21
Northern Territory Land Rights Act,
    14, 17, 23, 145–7, 148–9, 228–9
    right of Aboriginal veto in, 22–3
Northern Territory Supreme Court
    see Gove Land Rights Case
Nossal, Gustav, 301
NSW Aboriginal Land Council, 209,
    232–3
NSW Aboriginal Legal Service, 19,
    205
Nugent, Peter, 39, 44, 107, 115–16,
    123, 133, 202, 203

O'Dea, D.J., 68
O'Donoghue, Lois, 18, 32, 39, 44, 54
    addresses Cabinet, 54, 75
    as ATSIC chairperson, 32, 90, 52,
        60, 63, 64, 113, 167–8, 172–3,
        181, 185, 187–9, 192
    Black Friday press conference,
        187, 189–90
    criticises coalition, 234
    on reconciliation process, 234
    role in Mabo negotiations, 90,
        113, 167–8, 172–3, 181, 185,
        187–9, 192, 198, 199–200,
        209–10
Office of Evaluation and Audit, 59
Office of Indigenous Affairs, 60,
    109, 188, 245
Olgas *see* Kata Tjuta
O'Loughlin, Justice Maurice, 274,
    277
Olympic Games protests, 175–6
One Nation Party *see* Hanson,
    Pauline
Ortmann, Max, 262

Parbo, Sir Arvi, 97, 137
Passi, Fr David, 84, 246
pastoral leases
    conversion of Aboriginal-owned
        to native title, 197–8
    native title over, 134, 195–202,
        214–18 *passim*
Patten, Jack, 5
Peace Plan, 113, 143, 193
Peacock, Andrew, 28
Pearson, Noel, 113, 123, 141, 159,
    172, 180, 181, 197, 204, 217
    denounces Coalition parties,
        204–5
Pemulwuy, 3
performance monitoring, 80
Perkins, Charles, 7–8, 15, 19, 22,
    44, 50, 51, 62, 205, 232
    conflict with ministers, 15, 21, 25
Perron, Marshall, 118–21
petroleum exploration, 110
Pitjantjatjara Land Rights Act, 21,
    146
PM&C *see* Department of the Prime
    Minister and Cabinet
police
    enforce CRA's oil-drilling, 19
    involvement in massacres, 2–3
    relations with Aboriginal people,
        76
political correctness, 135, 152, 315
Pompuraaw Aboriginal Council, 140
Prescott, John, 166
prisons, 67, 73, 79
protection policies, 4
    Aboriginal resistance to, 4–5, 6
public accountability
    of ATSIC, 25, 50–3, 58–9, 62–3
    of talk-back radio hosts, 324
public opinion polls, 57, 118, 132,
    155, 208, 314

*Queensland Coastal Islands Declaratory
    Act 1985*, 85–6
Queensland government; *see also*
    Bjelke-Petersen government;
    Goss, Wayne
    attitude to Mabo decision, 117,
        139, 155–7
    controls over Torres Strait
        Islanders, 84

demands special Wik legislation,
    155–7, 160–3
discriminatory land transfer
    policies, 20, 85–6
land rights legislation, 22
legislation to deny native title,
    85–6, 212
opposes Torres Strait
    self-government, 246–7, 254
Quinn, John, 213

racial discrimination, 15, 16; *see also*
    CERD
Racial Discrimination Act, 16, 85
    Cabinet endorses overriding of,
        118–22
    calls for suspension of, 91,
        102–4, 108, 112, 117, 159, 172
    opposition to, 159, 181, 188, 194
    inapplicable to Native Title Act,
        192–3
    Keating's support for, 159
    special measures under, 192–3
    validity of non-indigenous land
        titles under, 100–4, 173–4,
        192–3
    validity upheld, 20, 85
Ralph, John, 156, 162, 166, 213–14
Ramsay, Alan, 195, 215
Rayner, Mark, 197
RCIADIC *see* Royal Commission into
    Aboriginal Deaths in Custody
RDA *see* Racial Discrimination Act
Rebutting Mabo Myths, 118, 133–4
Rebutting the Myths, 60, 118
Reconciliation and Schooling
    Strategy, 44
Reconciliation Convention, 46, 316
reconciliation process, 27–47 *passim*,
    82, 89, 303–4, 317–21; *see also*
    Council for Aboriginal
    Reconciliation; treaty
    churches' support for, 31, 33,
        35–6, 138
    community support for, 36, 319
    cross-party support for, 30–1, 35,
        37–8, 42, 45, 317
    fundamental principles, 29–30
    future agenda for, 314, 321–6
    Howard government and, 46–7,
        314, 316, 318
    legislation for, 38, 45–6

linked to Mabo response, 125
need for prime ministerial
    leadership, 47, 323
public awareness strategy, 29, 35
search for bipartisanship, 30–1
social justice and, 29–30, 34–5,
    45, 47, 319–20, 321–2, 349–51
referendum(s)
on Commonwealth's Aboriginal
    affairs power, 7, 8–9, 28, 43
to repeal section 127, 8
sought on Mabo decision, 136–7,
    138, 143
Reith, Peter, 171, 173, 177–8
reserves, 6–7, 9, 18, 84
Reynolds, Henry, 84, 167, 208
Reynolds, Margaret, 39, 44, 112,
    122, 234
Rhetoric or Reality?, 78–9, 291
Rice, James, 84
Richardson, Graham, 292–3
Ridgeway, Aden, 11, 166, 209, 226,
    232, 236
Riley, Rob, 113, 114, 121, 201, 212
Ross, David, 37, 236
Rowley, Charles, 15, 28
Royal Commission into Aboriginal
    Deaths in Custody, 66–82 *passim*
    ATSIC response to, 54
    findings, 66, 69, 72–4, 224, 290,
        304
    implementation of
        recommendations, 54, 66, 74–82
    outcomes, 66, 290
Royal Commission into Hindmarsh
    Island, 276–83
Rubuntja, Wenten, 39, 41, 44
Rudd, Kevin, 162
Ruddock, Phillip, 46

sacred sites, 19, 40, 259, 260, 261,
    264
Saunders report, 265–6, 267, 278
    confidential appendices to, 267–8
schooling, 44
Scott, Evelyn, 44
secret women's beliefs, 267–8, 279,
    281, 285
self-determination, 40, 63–4, 73,
    306–7
    for Torres Strait Islanders,
        242–54, 306–7

self-management, 40
self-reliance, 14, 63, 296
Senate
    Aboriginal members, 11
    committees, 16, 20
Shergold, Dr Peter, 57–8, 225, 290
Smith, Malcolm Charles, 69–72
social justice for indigenous
    Australians, 28, 29–30, 34, 45, 47,
    249–51, 319–20, 321–2
South Australian government
    attitude to Mabo legislation,
        111–12, 122
    land rights legislation, 21
'special measure' (under RDA)
    Native Title Bill, 102, 192–3,
        198–9, 202
spirituality, 257; *see also* Aboriginal
    spirituality
Stanner, W.E.H., 10
states and territories
    bound by Racial Discrimination
        Act, 80–1
    need for Commonwealth
        pressure on, 80–1
stolen generations, 2, 54–7
    inquiry into, 55–6, 324
Stone, John, 97, 99
Strehlow collection, 257
Swan Brewery site, 259

Tambo, 257
Taperell, Kathleen, 75
Tasmania, 22
Tatz, Colin, 56–7, 67
tent embassy (Canberra), 11, 13
terra nullius doctrine, 2, 19–20, 84
Thomas, Harold, 12
Tickner, Robert
    admiration for Keating, 89, 95,
        107, 168, 186
    advocates reconciliation,
        28–45 *passim*
    Caucus supporters, 111
    and Charles Perkins, 62
    clashes with PM&C, 60–1,
        103–104, 252–3
    commitment to public
        accountability, 52–3, 62
    contemplates resignation, 178–80,
        187

devastation at Cabinet decision, 184, 186
lacks regular contact with Prime Minister, 152
loses budget battle, 298–300
main goal as minister, 28–9
not consulted on Eva Valley Statement, 154
not consulted on NT deal, 119
opposes ambit land claims, 96–7
proposes land acquisition fund, 223, 225
sceptical of COAG involvement, 111, 117–18, 128–9
threats against, 142
Tiwi Land Council, 64
Todd River dam, 261–3
Torres Strait Islanders
fishing rights, 246
impact of Mabo decision on, 242
Mabo demands, 243–4
native title rights, 84–6
relations with Papua New Guinea, 248–9
representation on ATSIC, 241
self-determination for, 242–8, 251–3, 306–7
Torres Strait Islands, 237–41
administration of, 84, 238, 240–1
autonomy for, 26, 239–40
mining moratorium, 252
Torres Strait Regional Authority, 50, 63, 244, 249, 254
Toyne, Phillip, 197
treaty (between indigenous people and the government); see also reconciliation process
Aboriginal calls for, 41
ATSIC commitment to, 38
Coalition opposition to, 25, 28, 38
as outcome of reconciliation process, 29, 35, 324
proposals for, 25, 27–8, 30
Treaty of Waitangi, 57
tribunal (for land rights claims), 113, 124–5
TSRA see Torres Strait Regional Authority
Tuckey, Wilson, 141
Turner, Pat, 58
Tutu, Archbishop Desmond, 180

Uluru, 10, 24–5
UN Commission on Human Rights, 302–3
UN Convention Against Torture, 306, 308
UN Convention on the Rights of the Child, 306, 308
UN Human Rights Committee, 304
UN Working Group on Indigenous Populations see Working Group on Indigenous Populations
unemployment, 224
Universal Declaration of Human Rights, 40
US Bureau of Indian Affairs, 12

validation
of existing non-indigenous land titles, 100–3, 113, 117, 125, 140, 158–63, 169, 173–4, 192, 198–9
of McArthur River mining lease, 118–19
of pastoral leases, 195–9
veto, right of, 17, 22–3, 125, 131, 135, 145–6
Victorian government
land rights legislation, 22
Mabo proposals, 127–8
Viner, Ian, 17–18, 43, 62

WA Chamber of Mines and Energy, 132, 208
WA Green senators, 171–2, 176, 179, 180–1, 190, 204
Walker, Frank, 107, 119–20, 136, 142, 146, 147, 161
Watson, John, 113, 114
welfare dependency, 63–4, 175
Wentworth, W.C., 8, 10, 12
Western Australia
land rights legislation, 23, 202
native title legislation, 202, 212
Noonkanbah protest, 19, 22
Western Australian Chamber of Mines, 96
Western Australian government; see also Court, Richard
attitude to Mabo decision, 123
capitulates to mining companies, 22

enforces mining companies'
    rights, 19
opposition to draft native title
    bill, 183
rejects Seaman report, 22
WGIP *see* Working Group on
    Indigenous Populations
Whitlam, Gough, 8, 9, 10, 19
Whitlam government, 13–17
Wik case, 88, 140, 157, 196, 201
Wik land claim, 137–8, 140–1
    Cabinet's decision on, 157, 161–3
    Queensland government's
        demands, 155–8, 160–3
Wilcox, Justice Murray, 259
Wilenski, Peter, 306–7
Williams, Gus, 37, 44, 48–9, 52
Willoughby, Paul, 36, 41, 269
Wilson, Ian, 20–1
Wilson, Sir Ronald, 20, 39, 43, 324
    heads inquiry into stolen
        children, 55
Wiradjuri land claim, 126

'women's business' *see* secret
    women's beliefs
Woodward reports, 13
Wooldridge, Michael, 31, 37–8, 90,
    99, 105, 107, 202, 203, 317
Wootten, Hal, 68, 69, 262
Working Group on Indigenous
    Populations, 302–6
Wreck Bay, 24, 187
Wright, Judith, 20
Wyvill, Lew, 68

Yackabindi nickel mine, 263
Yangngara people, 19
Yawuru people, 264
YBE, 64
Yirrkala mining project, 7
Yirrkala people, 10–11
Yu, Peter, 170, 236
Yunupingu, Galarrwuy, 34, 39, 41,
    44, 54, 89, 112, 114, 154

Zappopan NL, 98

Printed in Great Britain
by Amazon